The Management of Quality and its Control

The Management of Quality and its Control

Charles S. Tapiero

Ecole Supérieure des Sciences
Economiques et Commerciales
Paris
France

CHAPMAN & HALL

London · Glasgow · Weinheim · New York · Tokyo · Melbourne · Madras

Published by Chapman & Hall, 2–6 Boundary Row, London, SE1 8HN, UK

Chapman & Hall 2–6 Boundary Row, London SE1 8HN, UK

Blackie Academic & Professional, Wester Cleddens Road, Bishopbriggs, Glasgow G64 2NZ, UK

Chapman & Hall GmbH, Pappelallee 3, 69469 Weinheim, Germany

Chapman & Hall USA, 115 Fifth Avenue, New York, NY 10003, USA

Chapman & Hall Japan, ITP-Japan, Kyowa Building, 3F, 2-2-1 Hirakawacho, Chiyoda-ku, Tokyo 102, Japan

Chapman & Hall Australia, 102 Dodds Street, South Melbourne, Victoria 3205, Australia

Chapman & Hall India, R. Seshadri, 32 Second Main Road, CIT East, Madras 600 035, India

First edition 1996

Printed in Great Britain by St Edmundsbury Press, Bury St Edmunds, Suffolk

ISBN 0 412 55720 7

A catalogue record for this book is available from the British Library

∞ Printed on permanent acid-free text paper, manufactured in accordance with ANSI/NISO Z39.48-1992 and ANSI/NISO Z39.48-1984 (Permanence of Paper).

Contents

Introduction

Throughout the management literature, as elegantly trumpeted by management consultants and gurus, there seems to be a common message: *for a firm to be competitive it must produce quality goods or services.* This means that firms, to remain competitive, must at the same time produce at the least cost possible to be price competitive and deliver high quality products and services. As a result, quality has become strategic overnight, involving *all*, both in and out of the firm, in the management of its interfaces with clients and the environment. To give quality, suppliers, buyers, operations and marketing managers, as well as corporate management must become aware of the mutual relationships and inter-dependencies to which they are subjected, so that they will be able to function as a coherent whole. This involves human relations and people problems, organizational design issues, engineering design options, monitoring and control approaches and, most of all, a managerial philosophy that can integrate, monitor and control the multiple elements which render the firm a viable quality producing and profitable whole.

To realize the benefits of quality it is imperative that we design products to be compatible with market needs, market structure, competition and, of course, that we are constantly aware and abreast of consumers' tastes and the manufacturing technologies that are continuously emerging. It is also imperative that we design our manufacturing environment and tools by integrating the management of quality and that of quantity, both in the factory floor and in managing the manufacturing interfaces with consumers, suppliers, technology, government and all the myriad of business functions to which manufacturing relates. It is also necessary to integrate the process of product design and manufacture with that of post-sales management and services, so that greater profitability is achieved. As a result, the management of quality becomes pluri-disciplinary, involving simultaneously the many facets of management, men, machines and materials. The emerging broad framework underlying the management of quality, much more in tune with consumer desires, provides intellectual, managerial and operational challenges which require that far greater attention be given to the study and modelling of quality-related management processes and how they affect an organizations' performance.

The purpose of this book is to deal with the management of quality and its control. Unlike the important contributions of 'Quality management and control theorists' such as Deming, Juran, Duncan, Leavenworth, Wetherhill, Montgomery, John and many others, this book adopts managerial and modelling points of view, seeking to integrate quality and its control in the basic managerial functions of the firm and, as a result, to reach a better design and appreciation of quality management-related functions. The recent growth of books in quality control, total quality management, experimental and robust design have spearheaded a new sensitivity to the management of quality, and a spirit of managerial integration. Nevertheless, the development of models which allow a commensurate understanding of inspection, assurance and control processes have been lacking. For these reasons, a modelling approach, illustrated by many examples and exercises dealing with problems often discussed in quality management books, but rarely integrated explicitly in models, is emphasized. For example, models for the assessment, management and control of services are developed, and models for integrating quality-related issues in an industrial strategy are presented and discussed. Attention is devoted to the control of quality in technology-intensive manufacturing systems. New ideas for the control of quality incentive contracts (based on game theory) are introduced. Through such ideas, we develop a greater understanding for the application of quality control tools in a conflictual environment (as exists in some producer supplier contracts). We also construct a framework for the control of quality in an organizational framework by introducing and elaborating on the effects of information, and the asymmetry of information, in organizations on the management of quality. Applications such as the control of quality in franchises and producer supplier management are then highlighted. To properly apply methods of statistical control, experimental and robust design and the economic evaluation of quality programs and control schemes, we devote particular attention to the foundations in statistics and decision making under uncertainty. The study of these tools is illustrated through quality management examples. Of course, much further knowledge in probability and statistical theory would be useful, but the current availability of software packages in quality control and in experimental design simplifies these quantitative requirements. There are many issues, both in planning experiments and in analysing data, which require expert statistical advice. While this book does not give a complete treatment of these topics, it provides a basic and working knowledge which is necessary to communicate with statisticians. Some topics are not covered at all in this text, but can be found elsewhere. For example, problems of statistical data analysis, linear and multiple linear regression, analysis of variance and non parametric statistics, although important in statistical quality control and experimental design, are barely covered. It is, therefore, essential that such topics are studied as well, prior to or following this book. The book has a planned 'unevenness', assuming for the most part little quantitative background, while in certain places it deals with certain problems quantitatively. These topics can be skipped by the quantitatively unmotivated reader without losing the book's continuity. These topics are, nevertheless, important, as they clearly point out to the mutual relevance and importance of basic management science and quality tools.

The book is divided into three parts. The first part introduces the basic concepts, definitions and the management of total quality (or TQM Total Quality Management). Concepts are defined and expanded. In addition, learning, quality improvement and other factors of importance in applying a program of TQM are briefly discussed, with further study in subsequent chapters. We review a number of applications and approaches to quality management, such as Deming, Juran, Crosby, and the Japanese and European approaches. At the same time, we develop the underlying foundations of TQM embedded in data collection, measurement and communication. A number of applications by some leading firms are also used as case studies.

The second part of the book is oriented towards techniques. We first provide a brief overview of a managerial tool-kit applied in the management of quality, including Pareto charts, Fish bone or cause effect diagrams. In addition, methods such as FMECA, quality circles, and so on, are presented, linking these tools with the underlying industrial and managerial strategies upon which they are based. After a review of statistical and decision theory principles, motivated through a large number of quality management and control examples, we consider the basic SQC/SPC tools. The managerial and quantitative approach to acceptance sampling, to control charts, to experimental and robust design, to Taguchi's techniques and, finally, to RSM-Response Surface Methodology are outlined.

In part three, we consider application areas of particular importance in quality management. The applications and themes considered include among others, the control of quality in producer supplier contractual agreements, quality in franchises and in various organizational structures, strategic issues and approaches to quality management and reengineering, and quality in a technology-intensive manufacturing environment. Finally, we consider intertemporal issues in the control of quality. This last chapter is of an advanced nature, however, and provides further study for some of the topics covered in the book. Through such application areas, the book opens up a broader perspective to both the study of quality management and its control and application.

The book is intended as a textbook in 'Quality management and its control' for courses given in business and industrial engineering schools. It is also intended for advanced students and academics who, on the one hand, find the technical texts of quality control limited and the broad managerial texts on TQM not specific enough. The technical level of the book is intermediate but will be accessible to second year MBA students, industrial engineers and students, and professionals and managers with a year's background in statistics and probability theory. Many sections of the book do not require any previous such background however and provide an introduction to management models for quality control. Other sections, however, may require some prior technical background. These can, of course, be bypassed by the unprepared reader without loss of continuity.

It is impossible to thank all those who have helped and encouraged me to write this book. Throughout this project, I have been helped by my students at ESSEC (Ecole Superieure des Sciences Economiques et Commerciales), at the Universite Louis Pasteur (Strasbourg), Case Western Reserve University in Cleveland, Ohio, where my interest in the management of quality began, Ecole des Mines Nantes, the University of Washington in Seattle and the University of Texas in Austin. Many colleagues have made many suggestions which I have included in the book. Some of these include Pillar Arroyo at Monterey Tech (Mexico), who shared her practical experience of experimental design, Leon Lasdon, Peter John and Jim Dyer at the University of Texas, Frank van der Duyn Schouten at Tilburg University, Diane Reyniers at the London School of Economics, Vincent Giard at the University of Paris I, Menahem Berg at Haifa University, Morton Posner at the University of Toronto, Elizabeth Murf at the University of Texas, and so many others who have made useful suggestions in the professional meetings where I had the opportunity to present some of the ideas in this book. The Economic Union Human Mobility grant given to ESSEC and other European universities, for the study of quality, maintenance and reliability, has also been a major source of encouragement and support, providing the oppportunity to exchange ideas in these important fields at a European level. My greatest debt, however, is to my children, Daniel, Dafna and Oren, who give me satisfaction and happiness, and to whom I dedicate this book.

Charles S. Tapiero
Paris, November 1994

CHAPTER 1

The concept and the definition of quality

1.1 Introduction

Quality is neither a topic of recent interest nor a fashion. It is, and has always been a problem of interest, essential for a firm's and to a nation's competitiveness. Colbert, the famed Minister of Louis the XIV, already in 1664 stated:

> If our factories will impose through repeated efforts, the superior quality of their products, foreigners will find it advantageous to supplying themselves in France and their wealth will flow to the Kingdom of France.
>
> August 3, 1664

This is one example of many. The 'American Industrial Way' has traditionally been based on excellence in manufacturing, product innovation and a sensitivity to consumers. The test of the market, which brings some firms to profitability and others to oblivion, is also a pervasive part of the American scene. It is these same market tests, expanded by a globalization of business, manufacturing technology and competition, that have raised the priority of quality in industrial business strategies.

In this chapter we shall be concerned with the definition of the concept of quality. Such definitions are important, for it may mean different things to different people in various circumstances. The industrial notions of quality, although clear and well stated, need not be the true measures of quality. Although they are important and serve many purposes, they are only part of a larger picture.

1.2 The concept of quality

Quality can be several things at the same time and may have various meanings, according to the person, the measures applied and the context within which it is considered. Below, we shall consider below, several dimensions and approaches along which quality could be defined. These are based on both objective and subjective notions of quality, with both tangible and intangible characteristics.

'Quality is the search for excellence'

'*Citius, Altius, Fortius*' meaning 'Faster, Higher, Stronger', engraved on Olympic medals, symbolizes the spirit of competition, seeking an ever greater excellence in man's achievements. The 'search for excellence' is not new, however; it is inbred in a Darwinian philosophy for the survival of the fittest. Quality is thus an expression of this excellence, which leads one firm's product to dominate another, and to guarantee its survival by establishing a new standard of quality. Over time, excellence creates an image of quality. This is how English clothes, German cameras, French wines and cheeses, and so on, have become marks of excellence. In this context, quality is a perpetual challenge which results both from a process of perpetual improvement and a domination over other, similar products. Of course, new technology can alter such domination. American cars, once an image of excellence, have been gradually been replaced by Japanese cars; for some in the US, French wine is gradually being replaced by Californian wine, etc. In this sense, quality is a mark of excellence, persistent and maintained over long periods of time. Such excellence is, of course, a function of habits, culture and values, and may thus vary from person to person and from time to time.

'Anything you can do, I can do better'

Are Japanese cars better than American? Do blades produced by Gillette last longer than Wilkinson's? Such questions, although hard to answer, may in some cases be dealt with an apparent sense of objectivity. In other words, quality is defined by implication in terms of attributes and some scales used to measure and combine these attributes. In some cases, these attributes may be observed and measured precisely, but they can also be difficult to observe directly and impossible to measure with precision. These situations are some of the ingredients that make quality the intangible variable that firms have difficulties dealing with. Nevertheless, a combination of such attributes, in 'various proportions' can lead to the definition of a concept of quality. In this sense, quality is defined relative to available alternatives, and can be measured and valued by some imputation associated with these alternatives.

'Quality is in the eye of the beholder'

Do French perfumes have a better smell than American? Is French Chablis of a better quality than California Chablis? Is French cheese tastier than comparable cheeses produced in the US? Of course, this is a matter of smell and taste! Quality is then in the eye of the beholden, established over long periods of time by habits, culture and customs which have created 'standards of quality'. In this case, quality is not what we think it is, but what the customer says it is. J.F.A Sloet, President of KLM, while addressing the European Council for Quality stated that the essentials of quality is to do what you promised ..... It is not relevant what we think quality is. The only quality that matters ... is what our clients think. Peter Drucker, put it in the same terms by stating that it is not what the 'supplier' puts in, but what the consumer takes out and is willing to pay for. This 'downstream' view of quality, emphasizing a sensitivity to consumers is in sharp contrast with the traditional 'upstream' conception of quality. In the early 1980*s*, for example, American car manufacturers were satisfied that they were producing quality cars, only to see consumers turn towards Japanese made cars. Similarly, at Renault, great efforts were put into developing more efficient engines, while consumers were valuing attributes to which Renault designers were oblivious. Of course, American and European car manufacturers have since learned that in an open world, with global competition, quality cannot be poor long.

'Quality is the "Proof of the pudding" '

Quality is what the market says it is. In this sense, quality is only a term that we can define *aposteriori*, once consumer choices have been expressed relative to a range of potential and competing products. Of course, there may be many reasons for these choices, including each and all of the reasons stated above. Nevertheless, the underlying fact is that we cannot *apriori* say what quality is. The best of intentions to produce quality products or deliver quality services can falter. In this sense, quality is a variable which can at best be guessed *apriori* and, perhaps, through successive experimentation, learning and adaptation, it can be refined and improved.

'Quality is Value Added'

Business preoccupation to measure and value its product and services leads to another view of quality. This view defines quality as value added. It is both what the consumer wants and *is willing to pay for.* Such views are, of course, motivated by the need to value quality so that sensible decisions regarding a firm's quality supply can be reached. For example, how much is a firm willing to pay for shorter and more reliable supply delays of materials it uses in its manufacturing processes? This is, of course, measured by what value added the buyer gets by such a supply quality. Although difficult to assess, it might be possible to do so in some cases. Inventory stocks, reduced administration costs and smoother production flows may be only a few of the many facets the buyer may consider to value shorter and more reliable delays. The value added in consuming well known label goods compared to unlabelled ones, although much more difficult to measure and define, do exist, since there is clearly a market for 'overpriced' goods whose essential characteristic is their label. How else could we explain a Chevignon Jacket or Hermes scarf costing three times the price of the same jacket and scarf without the label!

As a result, quality is not a term that can be defined simply. Rather, it is a *composite term, expressed in terms of attributes which define quality by implication.* These attributes express:

- The relative desirability of products, items, services
- The potential for substitution and product differentiation, both objective and subjective.

In this sense, the concept of quality is both objective and subjective, and is based on product and service differentiation, on substitution, as well as on buyer perception and heterogeneity.

Substitution combined with subjective (or objective) differentiation thus provides some means that we can use in appreciating and valuing quality if it can be measured or estimated directly or indirectly in terms of other variables. If products are not substitutes (meaning that they are not comparable), then quality as a variable used to compare these products is not relevant. Differentiation of products can be subjective, perceived differently by consumers. Beauty, taste, smell are perceived differently by buyers. In this sense, quality is a concept expressed by a consumer population's heterogeneity, as we pointed out earlier. Thus, heterogeneity induces an unequal assessment of what is quality. If consumers 'are the same' in terms of how they value and assess characteristics associated with a product, then they may be considered homogeneous, and the concept of quality would be well defined in terms of 'agreed on' properties. For example, the number of shaves one can have with a Gillette sensor blade compared to a standard one, the temperature tolerance of Titanium (needed to fabricate jet engines) compared to some other materials, the hardness of graphite steel compared to other types of steel, are all objective dimensions along which quality is measured.

1.3 Quality and uncertainty

Uncertainty has several and simultaneous effects on quality, as will be studied later. Obviously, if value added is quality, and if it is well defined, the measure of that value is what makes it possible to distinguish between various qualities. When value added is uncertain or intangible, its measurement is more difficult, and therefore quality is harder to express. In this sense, uncertainty has an important effect on the definition, measurement and management of quality.

How does uncertainty affect quality? First, a consumer may not be able to observe directly and clearly the attributes of a product. And, if and when he does so, this information is not always fully known, nor true. Misinformation through false advertising, the unfortunate acquisition of faulty products, and poor experience in product consumption are some of the problems that may beset an uninformed consumer. Similarly, some manufacturers, although well informed of their products' attributes, may not always fully control the production of their products. Some items may be faulty, the outcome of a manufacturing process' complexity and the inherent difficulties in controls. As a result, uncertainty regarding a product's qualities induces a risk which is imposed on both the firm-producer and the buyer-consumer. This risk has a direct effect on the valued added of quality, and is, of course, a function of the presumed attitude towards risk. The approaches used to manage these risks, both for the firm-producer and the consumer-buyer, and how to share these risks, is particularly important. Warranty contracts, service contracts, liability laws and the statistical control of quality in a factory are some of the means available to manage these risks, as we shall see throughout this book.

Perceived risk has been envisioned as consisting of two essential components: consequences and uncertainty. For a consumer, uncertainty can be viewed as the 'subjectively measured probability of adverse consequences' (Ingenes and Hughes, 1985). As such, we can postulate that the quality of a product is inversely related to its risk. A non-risky product, meaning a product having desirable consequences with large subjective probabilities, is a quality product. For example, if we buy a part from some supplier, what would we consider quality? It may be several things, but generally it will be defined in terms of an attribute of a part with desirable consequences, and little variation (i.e. high probability). Why were Japanese and European cars at one time considered quality products? Buyers had the subjective estimation that these cars would not fail and require repairs, and with a high probability! In this sense, quality is consistent with an inductive reasoning which is reinforced once consumption experience of the product is registered. For example, Jacoby and Kaplan (1972, p.383), attempted to measure quality by asking 'What is the likelihood that there will be something wrong with an unfamiliar brand of XXXX or that it will not work properly?' Quality was meant then to be a perceptive attribute which can, of course, be influenced by the marketing mix, good management of the factory, post sales attention and services. Ingene and Hughes (1985) claim that a brand is perceived as being risky (and thereby of lower quality) by a consumer if and only if that consumer is uncertain as to what level (of at least one attribute about which he/she is concerned) will be obtained if the product is purchased.

Uncertainty regarding product quality has led to intensive legislation on product labelling which seeks to protect consumers on the one hand and to convey information on the other. There are a number of important questions which may be raised by buyers and sellers alike, for example, the fat content of cheeses and hamburgers sold in supermarkets, the alcohol content in wine as well as the origin of products. These do not always indicate quality. Some wine growers believe that the alcohol content should not be put on the wine label. By doing so, alcohol is given an importance and a relevance to wine quality which it does not, in their opinion, have. Cheeses, of all sorts, vary over the year and, therefore, the fat content of the milk is really a relative measure (to the time of the year in which it was produced as well as relative to the origin of the milk used in its production). In the case of Normandy Camembert, there is further confusion since there are not enough cows in Normandy to produce even a fraction of the Camembert sold under this label! In other words, even a label of origin can be misleading. In the early 1950, for example, some Japanese products, suffering from a poor reputation, had a label of made in USA, meaning the Japanese city of Usa. To simplify the labelling of products, coloured labels are also used. A red label for chickens in a supermarket is a mark of quality, but under such labels there can be a wide variety of chickens which need not have a uniform quality (even though they are all labelled with the same colour). In fact, a chicken 'color' may stand for similar origins, similar growing or feeding conditions, or perhaps just cooperative marketing.

Although uncertainty is not a property which defines quality, the measurement and perception of quality are directly affected by uncertainty. For this reason, an operational and economic definition of quality (which is the relevant one for businesses) is necessarily sensitive to uncertainty. Due to the importance of this topic, we shall return to it subsequently. Next, we consider manufacturing quality, which seeks to define the attributes of quality by the manufacturing processes. Such characterization is essential to appreciate the potential and the limits of quality control in industrial and operations management.

1.4 Quality in manufacturing

Manufacturing quality, unlike the general concept of quality we sought to define above, is well defined in terms of attributes *which are associated to and required by a manufacturing process to operate faultlesly.* In this sense, quality is a characteristic and a requirement of the industrial apparatus. For example, a factory floor with machines that break down often, machinery that is unable to operate at the required levels of precision, or uniformity of operations, and general manufacturing systems with a propensity to produce highly heterogeneous quality products are an expression of a manufacturing *unquality.* Management of operations and quality control are thus the means used to 'produce' and control quality in manufacturing.

There may be several dimensions along which such manufacturing quality may be defined, including:

(a) The propensity to maintain the manufacturing process in control, i.e. operating according to agreed on standards of manufacture.

(b) The propensity of the manufacturing process to produce items or products faultlessly.

(c) The propensity to maintain (and or reduce) the manufacturing process variability, i.e. limit process instabilities by maintaining the process repetitivity.

Thus, *agreed on standards, faultless production and repetitivity and control of variations* are used to define manufactured quality. In practice, manufacturing quality is easier to measure 'negatively'. In other words, it is a reflection of a negative performance (rather than a positive one, which is, or should have been, the standard). As a result, the ideas underlying the management of quality in manufacturing relate to the management of the process and not to the design of the product. This measure of quality is defined in terms of characteristics which are important and related to the management of the manufacturing process. In this sense, *the measurement of quality is also an incentive for the control of quality.* Of course it is possible, through appropriate integration of both product design and the manufacturing process, to let one facet of quality management (its conception and design) affect the other (the process of manufacturing the product). Although this is increasingly recognized as an important activity known as 'producibility', or 'concurrent engineering', it has not yet fully matured (albeit, it is the topic of intensive research today). In a conventional sense, a process in control would evidently results in products of a better quality than a process which is not in control. As a result, by improving the controls, we will be able to increase the propensity to manufacture products of better quality.

For example, in the manufacturing of certain high precision metallic items, there may be many objective attributes which could be measured and tested for deviations from acceptable manufacturing standards. These may include the location of holes, their sizes (which often require extremely high precision), concentricity, symmetry, and so on. These attributes are measured for the purpose of controlling the processes which are used in making up a product! In other words, *measurements (tests) are made to detect causes of malfunction needed to control the manufacturing process.* For these metallic parts, there may be many causes which contribute both to defective manufacturing or to excessive variations from manufacturing standards. Lack of geometric perfection, stress factors, materials stability, the ambient temperature, lack of perfect rigidity, etc. may be some of these factors. The measurement and detection of sub-standard performance provides the incentive for control and correction.

Thus, just as conceptual or design quality, manufacturing quality is a complex concept which should be clearly understood before seekink to manage it. A comparison of several aspects of quality are given in Table 1.1 to provide some further comparisons between manufacturing and design quality.

Table 1.1: Design and manufacturing quality.

Design quality	Manufacturing quality
Durability	Reliability
Esthetics	Conformance to standards
Attributes' desirability	Process variability
Objective performance	Consistency
Intangibles	Tangibles

A manufacturer concerned with the production of quality products or services uses various tools, statistical and otherwise, as we shall see later on. Statistical tools are used in particular when uncertainty has an important effect on the manufacture of quality. In such cases, poor quality is usually produced due to variations and uncertainties regarding the process operations and performance. When performance variations are totally random, unaccounted for by any malfunction or cause, they reflect a characteristic of the manufacturing process, the type of materials used and the process at hand. When product quality or their attributes do not deviate from a purely random pattern, the manufacturing process is said to be out of control. In this sense, the management of quality in manufacturing consists of determining departures from a state of perfect randomness. As we shall see in Chapters 5, 6 and 7, techniques called Statistical Quality Control (SQC) and Statistical Process Control (SPC) are used to elaborate and apply tests of randomness of various sorts to measure and *predict* departures from this state of perfect randomness.

The increased need to control statistical variations, and thereby the need to control a manufacturing process and its environment, have been ushered in by production concepts developed in the first industrial revolution. These concepts, although complex and numerous, *presume that production standards and producing up to these standards are essential to guarantee the substitutability of parts used in a mass production system. Taking responsibility away from workers and their alienation at the beginning of the century in particular has led to the necessity to control their work through work sampling and other methods used to predict and manage the statistical variations which occur in manufacturing.* These basic tenets of quality management have recently been subject to scrutiny, motivated by a concern for a broader view of quality management, a view which takes account of the whole manufacturing system, distribution, service and business processes, and seeks to produce quality rather than to control some process variations (although this is also an important part of this broader view). This emerging approach is called Total Quality Management. In addition, and more recently, a 'quality trauma' has been ushered in by the increased power of consumers, and by the fact that there can no longer be any justification- economic, managerial and technological- for producing poor quality. Japanese inroads into quality control techniques made in the last two decades have been an example to this effect, and it has led firms to re assess their priorities in terms of the control and management of quality. Based on such premises, we can appreciate the inroads made towards improved quality by corporate boards, and its integration into business strategies. *Quality is Free* (Crosby, 1979, 1984) and *Quality on the Line* (Garvin, 1981, 1988) are samples of work which highlights a growing concern for re-valuing and re-evaluating the place and contribution of quality in manufacturing and its control.

As a result, basic and past tenets regarding quality in manufacturing have been questioned and revised. For example, it is currently believed that:

- Quality is not only a cost, it is also a potential benefit, a value added to the manufacturer which can be translated into added sales and profitability. There are, however, still difficulties in measuring the potential benefits of quality which are essential in inducing managers to take the proper courses of action to improve quality.
- Quality is not only process-specific, but is a total concept, involving everybody! This is the message of Total Quality Control (TQC). In other words, the problem is not only the control of statistical variations in a manufacturing process, but the basic question of producing quality in its broadest sense.

In other words, the re-evaluation of quality in terms of its costs, tractability and integration has created an opportunity to re-design and re- position quality, quality improvement and control where they were always supposed to be. This transformation has, of course, brought quality to people, to the organization, to processes, to services and, in the process, it is transforming production management, both in design objectives and in operational procedures. For example, from a 'robotics notion of people' to one based far more on motivations and incentives to perform; from de-responsabilization to responsabilization. A reminder from Michelin's workers' book on profit sharing:

> The care brought by each worker in his work is the essential capital of the factory
>
> (*Book of Profit Sharing, Michelin 1898*)

implies and recognizes (already prior to the turn of this last century) that quality is a function of a worker's involvement in the work process and the responsibility he is assuming, not only with respect to his own work (i.e. his auto-control), but also with respect to the collective (i.e. Total Control). In a practical sense, the reconciliation, concordance and coherence of 'auto and collective controls' underlie approaches to the control of quality.

The emerging re-definitions of quality are of course leading to new objectives in process and product design. Terms such as *robustness* are also becoming much more fashionable and appropriate. A robust design will, for example, safeguard a standard operating performance against departures from pre- specified conditions. In this vein, a product's quality cannot be assessed in terms of its performance in a laboratory environment, but in the 'real world', while it is being used by people who may or may not how best how to use the product. Then, robustness is a measure of the latitude of conformance of the product to the user, and not to that of the process! For these reasons, quality in manufacturing is a fast changing concept which today seeks greater robustness in the definition of what we ought to look for to improve and produce quality products and services.

The broader view of quality and the complexity of modern firms, combined with a commensurate need to define measures of quality, have of course led to an expansion of the dimensions along which the manufacture of quality ought to be considered. Presenting an integrated view, Garvin (1988) suggests eight dimensions: *Product performance*, *Product Features*, *Reliability*, *Conformance*, *Durability*, *Serviceability*, *Aesthetics* and *Perceived quality*. For the management of quality it is essential to translate these dimensions into economic values and Costs Of Quality (COQ). These will include direct and indirect effects. For example, in Chapter 2, we shall consider various approaches to costing quality. Some internal costs we might consider include: *Planning and Training quality programs; Inspection and Testing; Failure–Scrap and Rework-Repair; Inventory added due to poor quality; Process and delay costs due to stoppages; Capacity losses; Human relations related costs.* External costs might include: *Warranty and liability costs; Servicing; Goodwill and sales; and finally, Costs due to regulatory agencies interventions.*

These costs, properly assessed and combined with the operational costs of manufacture and the potential contribution of quality to the firm competitiveness, provide notions of manufacture quality which must be understood and valued. It is through such comprehension and valuation that we can affect every facet of the firm and thereby make it possible for quality to become strategic and be managed. These problems are of immense importance, so we shall return to their study in far greater detail in subsequent chapters.

1.5 Quality and services

Quality in services exhibit special characteristics. Some of these characteristics include:

- The quality of service generally involves not one but *multiple* services. For example, a gas station provides several services beyond the supply (usually at a regulated price) of fuel. Hotels provide a room and various associated services.

- Services are mostly intangible, often subjective, and are therefore difficult to define.
- Unlike quality in manufacturing, the quality of services depends both on the 'server' and the 'serviced'. Poor service is usually defined by the dissatisfaction of the latter. Further, service delivery, either good or faulty, need not be consistent. Comparable notions of server breakdowns in industry such as machine breakdown or improperly performed functions (and the storability of poorly performed operations) are not applicable in services, as the former is tangible, expressed in some characteristics which are measurable objectively.
- The quality of service and its measurement are dependent. A server who is inspected might improve the quality of service delivery, for example, while a server who feels there are no controls might provide poor service. Such behaviour introduces a natural bias in the measurement of service efficiency and its quality.
- A service is not storable, unlike products that can be sampled and tested for quality.

Figure 1.1: Dimensions of service quality

For these reasons, the definition of service quality is elusive. There are several approaches, as we shall see next. The American Society for Logistics (ASLOG) suggests that service quality be defined in terms of Communication, Time, Organization, Flexibility, Reliability and Post Sales Service. *Communication* might be measured by the opportunity for errors, document errors, billing, client follow through and information exchange. *Time* relates to delays of various sorts (supply responses, routing, conformance and distribution). *Organization* includes the range of services delivered and agreed upon, security in transport and stocking, as well as organizational forms such as subcontracting and franchises. *Flexibility* is the potential to meet demands under various circumstances, and to adapt to a broad range of operational and service conditions. *Reliability* refers to the consistency of the service supplied, its timing and so forth. Finally, *Post Sales Service* applies to maintainability, repairability, service proximity and availability as well as response time to post sales failures (these notions will be defined in greater detail in Chapter 3 however).

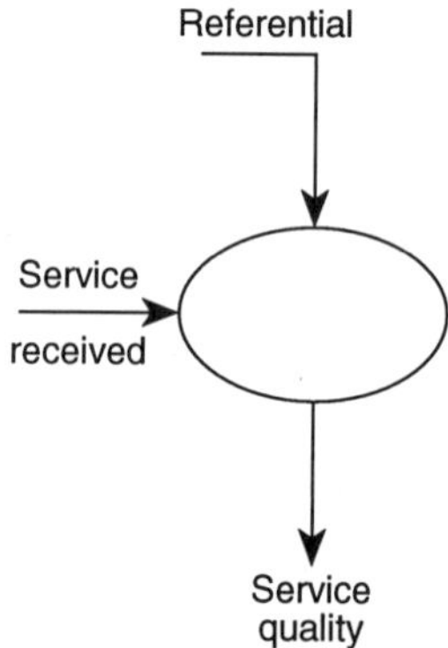

Figure 1.2: Expectations of service and quality

Using a large number of post-consumption evaluation studies, perception and expectation of the service have been identified as essential factors that define the quality of service. In particular, Gronroos (1983) points out that *it seems reasonable to state that the perceived quality of a given service will be the outcome of an evaluation process where consumers compare their expectations with the service they perceive they have got, i.e. they put the perceived service against the expected service.* In this sense, a product or firm's image depends solely upon the consumers' perception. In the same spirit, and based on extensive statistical studies, Parasuraman, Zeithaml and Berry (1985) concluded that *service quality as perceived by consumers results from a comparison of perceived service with expected service.* Focus group interviews also revealed ten dimensions of service quality by which a consumer evaluates the quality of a service. These dimensions were later empirically validated and reduced to five dimensions: Tangible, Reliability, Responsiveness, Assurance and Empathy. Although 'perceived quality' seems dominant in many marketing studies, there are difficulties in following such an approach. First, it only emphasizes the customer, regardless of what the objective of the service is. Second, competition and the competitive effects of quality are ignored. Third, services as well as customers are usually heterogeneous, therefore service quality should be much more difficult to pinpoint. Finally, while 'perceived quality' overcomes the traditional marketing concern for 'search quality' and 'experience quality' in products (and predominant in services), it underplays the role of 'credence quality'. By definition, these qualities cannot be perceived by the customer; instead, the customer relies on indicators such as reputation, price and physical evidence.

Following the definition of quality in business, in services *quality is fitness to use.* A deviation from that 'standard' is an 'unquality'. Of course, it is possible to consider expectations as standards such that any deviation from an expectation is equivalent to a deviation from the standard.

A third approach is based on social psychological concepts, focusing on the interaction between the firm, its employees and its customers. Accordingly, service quality has different levels, comparable to Maslow's pyramid of needs (Klaus, 1991, pp. 261-263):

- Congruence of employees' and customers' behaviours (interlocking behaviours), such as the proper degree of politeness, hand shaking and other ceremonial acts.
- Perceived degree of satisfaction combined with technical services which can be observed and measured objectively (such as an airlines' flights arriving on time)
- Degree of emotional satisfaction (such as a feeling of inclusion and belonging).

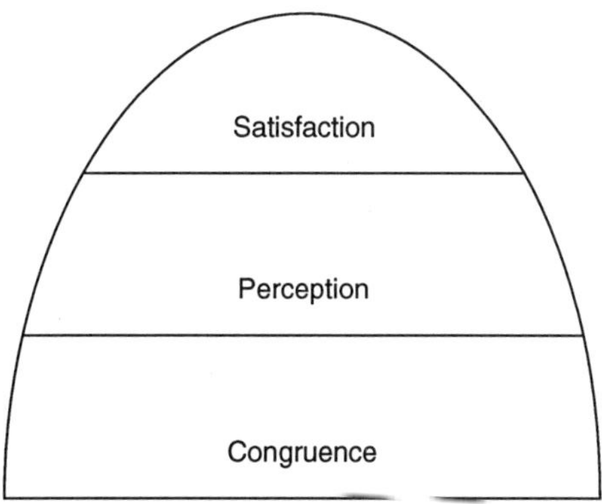

Figure 1.3: Levels of service quality awareness

Similar to Maslow's hierarchy, higher levels of quality (emotional) can be achieved only if lower levels are satisfied first. The social-psychological approach, based on extensive 'human relations' theories, has unfortunately been neglected in the management of quality, although in practice it is essential. For example, the buzz words 'Moment of Truth', are evidence that success depends in many instances upon the moment when customers and employees interact (the moment of truth!).

Below we consider two approaches to service quality, one based on logistical needs and the other on the needs for health care delivery. As we shall see, different needs will necessarily lead to widely differing views of what service quality may mean.

Service quality in logistics systems

Logistics is the 'management of means which are required for some end'. That is, it manages operations to make it possible for a manager, an entity, a work station, and so forth, to perform its function when it is required to do so. Thus, transportation, the delivery of goods, warehouse and stock management, maintenance and supplies and materials handling are some of the basic functions associated with logistics. The quality of service in logistic systems is difficult to define, however. Lambert and Stock (1982) claim that quality is the yield of the logistic system, measuring the improvement of a consumer utility of time. Others claim that service quality is the potential to respond effectively to complaints, to be polite, to welcome clients and to provide information. In industrial situations, Christopher, Schary and and Skjott- Larsen (1979) provide a number of variables which can be used to define service quality. These include (a) the cycle time of an order, (b) the propensity to meet delay requirements, (c) the availability of products, (d) order precision, (e) the number of returns, and (f) the size of orders.

In business, logistics deals with the interface between production and marketing management. As a result, it provides an important link between the market and its industrial base. For this reason, there are several phases in a logistic transaction where there can be causes of non-quality. First, at the pre-logistic phase where the product is finished, tested and passed on to stores or to storage. Second, at the intra-logistic phase where the product is transported, stored and handled. And finally, at the post-logistic phase where the product has been delivered and there is still a need to maintain an ongoing relationship with the customer (e.g. because of installation, repair and replacement, maintenance and operational expertise). Given the increasing share of logistics costs in the management of operations, it is imperative that quality be well defined and improved.

For example, the Customer Service Department of Federal Express began in 1983 to compile its 'hierarchy of horrors', a list of the service failures most critical to Federal Express' customers. Subsequently, this hierarchy became a numerical index of customers' satisfaction. The twelve components of the company-wide SQI (Statistical Quality Index), and the weights attributed by customers, are listed below (Stoner and Werner,

1993). Of course, the need to associate weights to facets of the quality process is meant to simplify and provide an operational and quantitative definition of quality.

Similarly Deming (1982), reporting on a study by Quantas Airways on passenger needs, has listed a number of key items. Some of these items are: Loss of luggage, Clean toilets, Comfortable chairs, Leg room, Quality meals, Stewards' and stewardesses' quality service, Delays and On schedule.

Table 1.2

Indicator	Weight
Abandoned calls	1
Complaints reopened	5
Damaged packages	10
International	1
Invoice adjustments requested	1
Lost packages	10
Missed pick-ups	10
Missing proofs of delivery	1
Overgoods (lost and found)	5
Right day late deliveries	1
Traces	1
Wrong day late deliveries	5

Service quality in health care

The Institute of Medicine in the US suggests the following definition: *Quality of care is the degree to which health services or individuals and populations increase the likelihood of desired health outcomes and are consistent with current professional knowledge.* The concern for quality and the control of quality in health care is indeed one of the greater challenges of this (and the forthcoming) decade. The growth of health care delivery and maintenance costs, making it an essential item of the GNP composite, is now a critical factor addressed in most developed nations' social agendas. This also provides an opportunity for applying the management of quality and its control in health care. The transformation of health care, from a back door cottage industry to a complete and massive 'industrial activity', is also an added motivation to alter the traditional means of management and controls of health care delivery. Brown, Lefkowitz and Aguera-Areas (1993) point out that today all health care's major players are placing quality at the top of their priorities, each for different reasons:

- For hospitals, ambulatory surgical centres and other patient care sites, quality is the goal of patient care and a competitive advantage that will differentiate them in a highly competitive market.

- For physicians, nurses and other professionals, quality is the goal of medical practice and the standard by which they will be measured by peers, patients, regulators and malpractice attorneys.
- For major employers, insurance companies and managed networks of health systems, quality is the primary criterion for selecting doctors and hospitals when price is not a factor.
- For government regulators and health advocacy groups, quality is the means of protecting the public welfare and responding to voter and consumer blocks. (Coile, 1990)

The multiplicity of parties (hospital administrators, government, doctors, patients), each clinging to a definition of quality in health care, introduces some confusion of what quality is in the first place, and therefore how to measure it in a real and practical sense. These are extremely important problems we shall return to in Chapter 2 and subsequent chapters.

1.6 A Historical evolution of quality approaches

To go higher, faster, to perform better and always to improve all underlie an Occidental ethic which has sought and prized valued change. Although this is and remains a principal endeavor, underlying the design of quality, the desire to 'control' the process of quality production and its management through an organized activity is fairly new. Table 1.3 provides a brief outline of how the control of quality has evolved starting in the 19th and 20th century. Prior to the 20th centuries, production was not as organized and as massive an activity as it has grown into with the beginnings of the industrial revolution. Prior to that time, *production was an art and quality a measure of this art.* Each unit produced was 'special', in the sense that no two units were really the same. Further, for items, demand outstripped production capacity so much that quality was of no necessary concern. At the beginning of the 20th century, when the industrial revolution was ushered in by Frederick Taylor and his co-workers, production lines were used, and an increased need for rationalization, the division of labour and standardization became evident. Such needs led to another organization of work, to newly defined principles for 'good management', but also to the 'depersonalization' of work and the work content of products. Production was no longer an art but a process. Products were the outcome, the consequences of such a process. The notion of 'art' was no longer relevant but counter-productive to the operation of the production line. Inventiveness, creativity, improvements and learning were in fact (if not in words) discouraged. Rather, uniformity, and the assurance of product uniformity, consistency, repetitivity and the control of statistical variations, became needed. However, it was only in the 1930*s*, following the seminal papers of Shewart, that the use of statistical principles for the control of product uniformity and process controls became accepted. In this sense, the modern approach to quality control really started with Shewart. Since then the field of quality control has matured and grown very quickly. To this day, Shewart's and R.A. Fisher's work on the design of statistical experiments are the classical tools of quality control, appearing under various names such as SQC (Statistical Quality Control) and SPC (Statistical Process Control) and Experimental and Robust Design. These approaches dominated the field of quality management, until attempts to control and deal with the whole rather than just the parts were made. During all these years, this field has remained unscathed by technology or by innovation.

The need for standardization and conformity for materials, processes and products arising from the depersonalization of manufacturing has thus led to 'Standard Associations' which created both the standard for certain items (such as electrical appliances, building construction standards, etc.) as well as the procedures to follow which, it was deemed, were needed to maintain such standards. Further, even if quality control procedures were known, they were rarely viewed as an integral part of the production process. Industry did not always implement the quality tools needed to ensure the proper control of processes and even less design the production system and implement management procedures which are needed to maintain quality. Thus, until recently, the field of production management has been concerned primarily with the management of physical quantities and not quality.

A great effort was initiated during World War II, essentially due to the awesome procurement problems and the amount of materials and equipment needed for allied forces. Deming, Dodge, Juran and others, today standard names of quality in quality control and its management, began their career in such an environment. In 1942, the concept of **acceptance sampling** was devised: a battery of tests which appear under MIL-STD-XXXX, meaning Military Standard no. xxxxx, were required by suppliers to the army, and a broad range of mathematical- statistical tools required to test the acceptance of production lots were devised. After World War II, the expertise gained in production became taken for granted. Corporate efforts were diverted to marketing, the age of affluence was rising and corporate managers invested their efforts in convincing consumers to consume ever more. Post-war rebuilding, baby-booms and no competition from Europe and the Far East, as their economies were reduced to shambles, induced the American industrial apparatus into a state of over-confidence. There was no challenge to Industria Americana. In this environment, American industry, equipped with an over-confidence gained out of the ashes of WWII and the comparative advantage it obtained while the rest of the world's industries were in a shamble, saw its 'House of Quality' gradually deteriorate relative to other countries. This was, of course, true for car manufacturing, but not only for cars. Cameras, once produced by Bell and Howell, are now produced by Canon; mass Motorbikes production has been completely taken over by firms such as Honda and Kawasaki. Although Harley Davidson has returned, at least in spirit, it has carved a small market share compared to the massive imports of Japanese motorbikes.

Attempts by the 'quality controllers' Deming, Juran and others (Deming, 1982, Juran *et al*, 1974; Juran, 1980; Wetherhill, 1977) to create a greater awareness of such problems in industry did not succeed in the US, but they were heeded in Japan. Quality control was viewed as a production, or at best, an engineering problem which, from a managerial viewpoint, was taken for granted. These were non-problems! At this time, while Japan was attempting to re enter the industrial world and gain recognition for its consumer products, Deming, Juran and others found a 'crowd' willing to listen, learn and improve. Japanese manufacturers also understood that quality and its control transcend the mere problem of process control or product assurance. They recognized the need for quality not only in terms of assurance, but 'true' quality, which is inherent in the design, production and overall operations of a firm. Japan became the country 'where quality really matters' (Wheelright, 1981), because it was recognized more important than just assurance and product standardization. While US firms concentrated their efforts on the reduction of product variability (i.e. producing products that were as uniform as possible), Japanese manufacturers focused on product quality improvement through a 'Total' effort for quality control (Feigenbaum, 1983). In a sense, the Japanese, equipped with 20th century technology and tools, returned the concept of quality to that which prevailed at the beginning of the century and refurbished it. Quality has again become the measure of the art of production, but in a more structured way. Quality and its control became Total Quality Control, and its management became Total Quality Management. Quality became everybody's business: the supplier, the distributor, each worker and management. A meeting point was needed, communications were opened, mechanisms to redirect inventiveness were created and production processes were improved continuously. A wide variety of approaches were then devised. Quality circles, in various forms, were used; 'Zero-Defects' goals were stated and, in the process, the basic approaches to the management of production were altered. The need for quality production was both fuelled and fuelling this tremendous transformation of the production process in almost every industrial and service sector. For example, technology, robotics, automation and flexible manufacturing must be appreciated both on how they have transformed the potential for quality and, at the same time, how they have become a by-product for the need for quality.

Technology has amplified the need for quality and its control. The complexity of manufacturing processes and the potential for higher levels of precision and integrated controls have created an environment which has not been appreciated to its full extent by production management. In such an environment, quality management transcends the traditional statistical approach, and is embedded in an emerging philosophy which recognizes quality and its management as a central part of the process of management. In this sense, quality becomes strategic. The application of Just in Time management concepts, their intolerance to breakdowns and reworks, and their structured and controlled production environment, have also led to a production practice which is much more sensitive to the effects of non-quality production. By the same token, Flexible Manufacturing Systems (FMS), which consist of manufacturing cells linked by AGVs (Automated Guided Vehicles), or some other mechanisms for routing parts between machines and cells, and computer systems have greatly increased the complexity of production. As a result, the problems of non-quality have commensurably become much greater.

Finally, Just in Time as well as an economic environment in which contracts are used to ensure quality, are also creating the need for other novel approaches to the management of quality. Franchises, subcontracting, distributors and intermediaries of various sorts, and in general decentralization of the work place, require controls which are sensitive to the conflicting environment within which business is operating. The freedom by employees, salesmen and firms to choose and follow a policy which is best for them has to be recognized and accounted for in devising incentive schemes which will induce the delivery of quality and quality performances. It is for these reasons that it is essential to devise a contractual approach to quality management. Recent topics on Principal-Agency theory, game theory and repeated games with information asymmetry can be important means to study such problems (as we shall see in Chapter 9). In this environment, the suppliers producers context can be understood and control schemes devised to respond to an ever increasing number of problems which are encountered when operational and service functions essentials to the business process are contracted out.

The globalization of business, increased competition and technology, feeding and fed by the process of management in all its facets, have also led to the emergence of quality as a variable to reckon with. Quality has thus come of age. It has become a topic which it is important to study and manage. Quality has thus become strategic. This will be the topic of Chapter 10 however.

Problems

1. Contrast the concept of manufacturing quality to concepts of quality based on consumer satisfaction. How are these concepts affecting the need for statistical quality control (SQC) and total quality control (TQC)?

2. Discuss: Production is an art and quality is the measure of this art!

3. Contrast the notions of 'quality is the proof of the pudding', it is 'the search of excellence' and it is a 'value added'.

4. Why didn't the total quality approach evolve with the growth of Taylorism, and why is it today a necessity?

5. Discuss: What are the effects of uncertainty on (a) quality perception and definition, (b) the control of quality? How does the uneven distribution of information between a supplier and a producer affect the need for the control of quality.

6. Consider the following products and services: a car, an aeroplane, a bicycle, a secretarial pool and a consultancy business. For each of these, define quality for the firm producing the product or delivering the service and the firm (or consumer) receiving the product or service. Then, define five variables for each of the products (services) of the following categories: attributes, operational performance, reliability-availability, security and the image (or subjective facets) of quality. How would you use scores for each of these variables and in each category to obtain a quantitative measure of quality?

7. Discuss the effects of consumerism and the concern for environmental quality on the concern for quality and the production of quality.

8. Much has been said about consumer protection and its effect on quality. Discuss the need for vendor protection and its direct and indirect effects on the production of quality?

9. Compare two notions of quality of your own choice, and how they affect the production (or service) strategy.

10. Compare the definitions of quality in manufacturing and in services.

Table 1.3 : Evolution of quality management and control
(until the 1960s)

Time	Event
Prior to 20th Century	Quality is an art Demands overcome potential production An era of workmanship
F. Taylor 1900's	The scientific approach to management resulting in rationalization of work and its breakdown leads to greater need for standardization, inspection and supervision
Shewart 1930's	Statistical beginnings and study of quality control. In parallel, studies by R.A. Fisher on experimental design The beginnings of control charts at Western Electric
Late 1930's	Quality standards and approaches are introduced in France (Darmois) and Japan. Beginnings of SQC, reliability and maintainability engineering
1942	Seminal work by Deming at the Ministry of War on quality control and sampling Working group set up by Juran and Dodge on SQC in US Army Concepts of Acceptance Sampling devised
1944	Dodge and Deming seminal research on Acceptance Sampling
1945	Founding of the Japan Standard Association
1946	Founding of the ASQC (American Society for Quality Control)
1950	Visit of Deming in Japan at invitation of K. Ishikawa
1951	Quality Assurance increasingly accepted
1954	TQC in Japan (Feigenbaum and Juran), book published 1956
1957	Founding of European organization for the control of quality (France-AFCIQ, Germany, Italy, Holland, England)
1950's	Growth for the study and application of experimental design and response surface methodology in designing quality

Table 1.3 (continued) : *Evolution of quality management and control* (after the 1960s)

Time	Event
1961	The Martin (Marietta) Co. introduces the zero defects 'approach' while developing and producing Pershing Missiles (Crosby). Quality motivation is starting in the US and integrated programs are begun
1962	Quality Circles are started in Japan
1964	Ishikawa publishes book on Quality Management
1970	Ishikawa publishes the book on the basics of Quality Circles and the concept of Total Quality is affirmed and devised in Japanese industries
1970 to 1980	Just in Time and Quality become crucial for competitiveness. A large number of US and European corporation are beginning to appreciate the advance of Japan's industries. Taguchi popularize the use of experimental design to design robust systems and products
1980+	Facing the rising sun challenge in quality management. Development and introduction of FMSs and greater dependence on supplier contracts.
	Growth of Economic based quality control, information software packages
1990+	The Management of Quality has become a necessity which is recognized at all levels of management. Increasing importance is given to off-line quality management for the design of robust design of manufacturing processes and products. The growth of process optimization

References

Coile R.C. Jr. (1990) *The New Medicine: Reshaping Medical Practice and Health Care Management,* Aspen Publishers, MD.

Scary, Christopher M.P. and Skjott-Larsen, T. (1979) *Customer Service and Distribution Strategy,* New York, Wiley, 152.

Crosby P.B. (1979) *Quality is Free,* McGraw Hill.

Crosby P.B. (1984) *Quality without Tears,* McGraw Hill.

Deming E.W. (1982) *Quality, Productivity and Competitive Position,* MIT Press, Cambridge MA.

Feigenbaum A.V. (1988) *Total Quality Control,* McGraw Hill (3rd edition).

Garvin David A. (1981) Quality on the line, *Harvard Business Review,* July- August, 56-66.

Garvin David A. (1988) *Managing Quality,* The Free Press.

Grant E.L. and R.S. Leavenworth (1988) *Statistical Quality Control*, 6th ed., McGraw Hill.

Gronroos C.H. (1984) A service quality model and its marketing implication, *European J. of Marketing,* **4**, 36-44.

Gronroos C.H. (1990) *Service Management and Marketing: Managing the Moment of Truth in Service Competition*, Lexington Books, Lexington, MA.

Ingene, Charles A., and M.A. Hughes (1985) Risk Management by Consumers, *Research in Consumer Behavior,* volume 1, 103-158.

Jacoby, Jacob and Leon Kaplan (1972) The Components of Perceived Risk, in M. Venkatesan (Editor), *Proceedings: Third Annual Conference, Atlanta Association for Consumer Research*, 382-393.

Juran J.M. et al. (1974) *Quality Control Handbook*, 3rd edition, McGraw Hill.

Juran J.M. (1980) *Quality Planning and Analysis: From Product Development through Use,* McGraw Hill.

Klaus P. (1991) Die Qualitat von Bedienungsinterakionen, in M. Bruhn and B. Strauss,(Eds.), *Dienstleistungsqualitat: Konzepte Methoden Erfahrungen*, Wiebaden.

Lambert D. and J. Stock (1982) *Strategic Physical Distribution Management,* R.D. Irwin Inc., IL, 65.

Parasuraman A, V.A. Zeithmal and L.L. Berry (1985) A conceptual model of service quality and its implication for further research, *Journal of Retailing,* Fall.

Parasuraman A, V.A. Zeithmal and L.L. Berry (1988) SERVQUAL, A multiple item scale for measuring customer perceptions of service quality, *Journal of Retailing,* **64**, 13-7.

Stoner J.A. and F.M. Warner (1993) Finance in the quality revolution-Adding value by integrating finance and Total Quality Management, Series in Innovative Management, Financial Executive Research Foundation, Morristown, NJ.

Wetherhill G.B. (1977) *Sampling Inspection and Quality Control*, Chapman and Hall, New York.

Wheelright S. (1981) Japan-Where operations are strategic, *Harvard Business Review,* **59**, 67-74.

Zeithaml V., A. Parasuraman and L.L. Berry (1990) *Delivering Quality Service*, Free Press, New York.

Appendix 1.A : Glossary of Quality Terms (ISO 3534, 8402)

Quality: The totality of features and characteristics of a product or service that bear on its ability to satisfy stated or implied needs

Grade: An indicator of category or rank related to features or characteristics that cover different sets of needs for products or services intended for the same functional use.

Quality spiral: Conceptual model of interacting activities that influence quality of a product or service in the various stages ranging from the identification of needs to the assessment of whether these needs have been satisfied.

Quality policy: The overall quality intentions and direction of an organization as regards quality, as formally expressed by top management.

Quality management: That aspect of the overall management function that determines and implements the quality policy

Quality assurance: All those planned and systematic actions necessary to provide adequate confidence that a product or service will satisfy given requirements for quality.

Quality control: The operational techniques and activities that are used to fulfil requirements for quality.

Quality system: The organizational structure, responsibilities, procedures, processes and resources for implementing quality management.

Quality manual: A document setting out the general provisions taken by an organization in order to obtain the quality of its products or services.

Quality plan: A document setting out the specific quality practices, resources and sequence of activities relevant to a particular product, service, contract or project.

Quality audit: A systematic and independent examination to determine whether quality activities and related results comply with planned arrangements and whether these arrangements are implemented effectively and are suitable to achieve objectives.

Quality surveillance: The continuous monitoring and verification of the status of the procedures, methods, conditions, processes, products and services and analysis of recprds in relation to stated references to ensure that specified requirements for quality are being met.

Surveillance: Activity carried out within the framework of a defined assignment. It should not be restricted to a comparison with perequisite data.

Quality system review: A formal evaluation by top management of the status and adequacy of the quality system in relation to quality policy and new objectives relating from changing circumstances.

Design review: A formal, documented, comprehensive and systematic examination of a design to evaluate the design requirements and the capability of the design to meet these requirements and to identify problems and propose solutions.

Inspection: Activities such as measuring, examining, testing, gauging one or more characteristics of a product or service and comparing these with specified requirements to determine conformity.

Operator control: Inspection mode in which an inbdividual performs his own inspection on the result of his work according to a set of rules formally specified in quality assurance or quality management provisions.

Inspection plan: A document setting out the specific provisionbs implemented to carry out the inspection of a given product or service.

Inspection status: Documented status of a product or service relating to its location in the implementation of the inspection plan.

Traceability: The ability to trace the history, application or location of an item or activity, or similar items or activities, by means of recorded identification.

Reliability: The ability of an item to perform a required function under stated conditions for a stated period of time.

Product liability (service liability): A generic term used to describe the onus ona producer or others to make restitution for loss related to personal injury, property damage or other harm caused by a product or service.

Nonquality: Overall discrepancy found out between the targetr quality and the quality actually achieved.

Nonconformity: The nonfulfilment of specified requirements.

Defect: The nonfulfilmment of intended usage requirements.

Anomaly: Departure from what is expected.

Concession (waiver): Written authorization to use or release a quantity of material, components or stores already produced but which do not conform to the specified requirements.

Production permit (deviation permit): Written authorization, prior to production or provision of a service, to depart from specified requirements for a specified quantity or for a specified time.

Specification: The document that prescribes the requirements with which the product or service has to conform.

CHAPTER 2

Total Quality Management

2.1 Introduction

Total Quality Management (TQM) is a revolutionary concept in the management of quality. Foremost, it is a recognition that quality not only depends upon tangible investments in machines, processes or facilities, but also on intangibles such as the integration and management of these resources, the corporate and cultural environment, personnel motivation, etc. Thus, TQM results in a new management order, based on lateral integration, a coherent and continuous improvement of the 'global' performance of the firm in the short-term and in the long-term. In its end result, TQM is viewed as a total (social, organizational and operational) commitment to manage a firm's resources to achieve the highest levels of performance in everything in which the firm is involved. This may include a vendor's relationships, the productivity and efficiency of the manufacturing process, manufacturing yields (or reliability), services and customer satisfaction. While there is an agreement regarding the ends of TQM, there may be some confusion regarding the 'how'. In this chapter we shall consider several approaches to TQM, each emphasizing a structured approach to integrated and total quality management (see Figure 2.1).

The effects of TQM are profound, altering work practices and management. For example, while traditionally production and its control were two separate functions, TQM recommends that the management of quality be integrated laterally and that self-control and regulation be introduced at the point where defects can occur. This implies far greater responsibility and authority for workers, greater incentives and multi-tasking, a new set of rules in managing shop floors as well as a *counter status quo order* which values permanent improvement of processes, work practices and productivity. In other words, the classical managerial notions of learning, spec's and procedures take on another tune, amplified and far more structured.

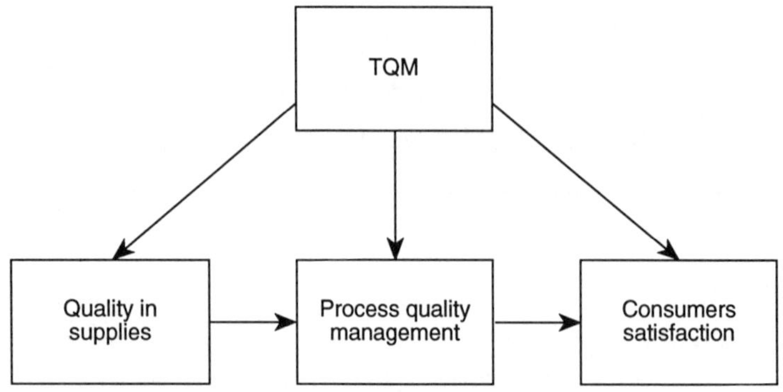

Figure 2.1: The scope of TQM.

The growth of TQM can be attributed to many reasons. Of course, competition from Japan has no small part, but there is much more. First, this is an idea whose time has come. The traditional notion that quality is defined in terms of conformance to standards has run its course. The notion of product quality, traditionally defined by the producer, has been shattered, with quality defined by what consumers want and say it is. This require that Western enterprises break at last from long held habits acquired through an industrial revolution and two world wars in the same century. Second, increased specialization and functionality has led to the evolution of vertical organizational structures which isolate individuals, and have emphasized the management of tangibles and neglected intangibles. These were too difficult to manage, therefore it became for more convenient to ignore their existence. Thus, while it is simpler to understand and manage the problems of production scheduling, it is much more difficult to understand what makes quality happen. Third, the power of firms over national markets has been seriously reduced through the globalization of business and technology and generally the breakdown of barriers to competition. This has transformed production to being far more productive on the one hand, and reducing barriers to entry in most markets on the other, thereby augmenting the necessity of being competitive. In such an environment, past production management practices can no longer be the guide for the future, and something else is needed. TQM seeks to provide part of the answer by focusing greater attention on quality, and by developing a new intentionality, an intentionality based on the following premises:

- Reduce the complexity of systems through simplification and increased manageability. Process and flows simplification, internal coherence, communication, training, lateral forms of management, and so on, are some of the means used to reduce the complexity of systems. More importantly, it is the recognition that complexity increases the probabilities of malfunction and the will to break the infernal cycle of complexity growth that stands at the heart of the concern for simplification.
- Be market oriented, by listening to the consumer, satisfying his real needs, through a 'needs sensitive' quality. Provide a service, an assurance of product spec's both at the time the product is acquired and at the time it is being consumed. In this sense, quality is defined 'downstream' but managed beginning 'upstream'.
- Be people oriented, by increasing awareness through participation, innovation and adaptation to problems when they occur. In a sense, while machines may be all we need to produce quantities, we require people to produce quality and activate a process of improvement, inventiveness and reliability growth. In addition, in most situations malfunctions arise due to human errors, so if these errors can be prevented or corrected when they occur, the system potential for quality can be realized.

In practice, TQM can mean something else to some firms. It is not so much a matter of substance, but of form, however. For example, a marketing firm might be more sensitive to consumer wants and thereby focus on the satisfaction of these wants. A firm producing high precision tools might concentrate on manufacturing quality, however (although both aspects, quality production and satisfying buyers' needs, are important). Overall, in TQM, all firms share a common concern for the following:

- Sensitivity to suppliers' potential and needs, to assure reciprocity and the supply of quality parts and materials upstream which are essential to the production of quality in the factory. Then, synchronization, feedback, conformance, contract negotiation and clauses, desirable price/quality ratios for parts, cooperative and joint development efforts, mutuality, are some of the activities a TQM approach might imply.
- Sensitivity to clients and to consumers' needs and wants, in the present and in the future and through post-sales services. Through quality products, satisfaction, follow-through and follow-ups, it is deemed likely that the consumer will become more loyal to the firm and thereby maintain sales growth in the present and in future. For this reason, quality production and quality post-sales services become far more integrated and relevant to one another. Thus, the concern for quality

'reverses' the traditional approach from 'means' to 'ends' to 'ends' to 'means'.

- An urge for zero defects, which need not mean that zero defects can be attained. Rather, zero defects is established as a means to stimulate a process of continuous improvement. In this sense, the traditional concern for defining and producing according to some standard is revised. There is no standard for producing defects, except the no defects standard!
- A culture for continuous improvement which requires among others: optimization of processes, flexibility/adaptivity, innovation, education, responsabilization, incentives, mobility, belonging, competence, security, clear delineation of authority and responsibility.
- A concern to educate, train and augment the level of employees and all those involved with the firm. This concern underscores the importance of people and the capacity to deal with the continuous change that must be instituted in the firm.
- A concern to measure quality and display it. This is very important, for measurement becomes the 'trigger' for identifying sub-standard performance and focusing attention on it through agreed on measures, display and subsequent control and quality improvement. In this sense, measurement not only informs but also induces the firm to act and communicate.
- Participation of all the actors and the agents of quality. It is through participation that agreements can be reached, attention focused on major problems and proper measures implemented.
- Quality *apriori*, in-the-product, rather than just *aposteriori*. This means that proactive rather than reactive management is required. Operationally, this is translated into preventive measures and a concern for robust design (a built-in insensitivity to unexpected external variations or errors specification is a parts or system spec's).
- Recognition of the added value obtained through quality and not just costs. Further, it is increasingly agreed that the costs of non quality are far broader than traditionally presumed. These costs involve not only short term and direct costs, but indirect and long-term costs as well.
- A prominent role for management and its commitment to quality is deemed essential. Management's role is thus recognized as vital to problem recognition, maintenance of effort in improving quality and in the integration of the efforts related to the management of quality. Quality 'begins at home', it is a function of the administration procedures, production and service processes and how these are carried out. These are, of course, primarily, the responsibility of management.
- Emphasis on prevention rather than just inspection. This concern is based on the understanding that upstream costs of non-quality are

much smaller than downstream costs. As a result, a small investment in prevention can reduce large costs downstream, while saving on such investment can induce large costs downstream.

- Lateral organization, cross disciplinary organization and the integration of a process management are important. It is through organizational design that communication, incentives and management can become more efficient.
- Focus on processes rather than products.

These points are summarized in Figure 2.2 for convenience. These concerns lead to extremely important and difficult problems. While they may seem obvious to some, the implementation of a TQM concept to deal with such problems is far less obvious. These problems require an integrative approach regarding all facets of quality, from sourcing to consumer satisfaction to adopting a multi- disciplinary and cross-functional approach. These are no longer problems of strategic choice, but of implementation strategy which require the full support of management, at its highest levels.

The commitments and effort needed to implement a TQM program can be substantial. As a result, such programs can be implemented when there is a need and overwhelming substantial support from top management. This concern, whatever its origin, leads to the growth of quality objectives and the TQM process, concentrating on clients, processes, managerial coherence and amelioration and to an organic view of the firm process, where the whole is far more than the sum of its parts (rather than just mechanistic).

Once the need for a TQM framework is recognized, its realization is a long process. The transition from Statistical Quality Control (SQC), to Total Quality Management (TQM) is difficult and often misunderstood. Rather than TQM replacing SQC, there is a need for both approaches, and in a far greater intensity. It is a 'cultural transition' from 'process control' to 'systems control', from 'local to global optimization', thereby involving a far greater number of issues, problems and a far greater range for each of these problems and issues. For example, while the traditional quality approach would emphasize the control of an individual process (to ensure its standard operating performance), the total management approach would emphasize the effects of the process on other elements as well, which are essential to the firm's goals (such as response to consumers, industrial buyers, clients, and the stakeholders of the firm).

The application of TQM in practice involves many difficulties, mostly related to the management of complex organizations and dealing with widely distributed and conflicting interests within the firm. Explicitly, some of the problems include:

- Coordination and management problems.
- Communication problems which result in misunderstandings.

- Desire 'too much, too soon with too little'.
- Uncertainty regarding outcome.
- Incapability in dealing with intangibles.
- Lack of incentive for change.

Furthermore, lateral integration and coherence in TQM are not without pitfalls. Applied inordinately, it can lead to a growth of organizations and to over centralization, defeating the original intentions. In many instances, TQM failed precisely because of organizational growth and the overzealous activity of some managers to measure, coordinate and then control everything they can. In this sense, TQM may, if not carefully applied, provide the seeds for its own demise.

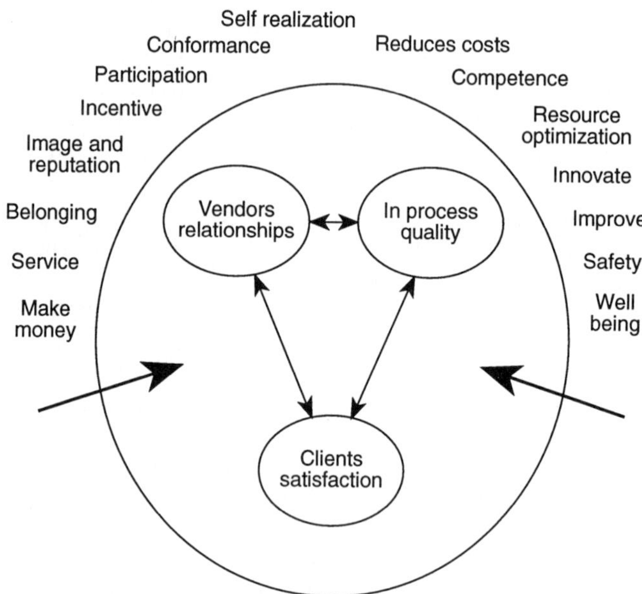

Figure 2.2: The themes of TQM.

2.2 Measurements and controls in TQM

To produce quality, it is essential to state what are 'the ends', and define the measures (or goals) with respect to which quality will be defined, measured, displayed, controlled, monitored and analysed to attain the optimal level of (economic) quality performance/conformance. For such purpose, measurements are very important, and have become an essential part of the TQM approach. It is through them that critical problems can be revealed, communicated and agreed upon. They can then be used to motivate and induce the actors of quality and set up the means for the control and evaluation of quality growth programs. To apply a TQM approach, it is thus necessary to determine what it is that we should measure. There are several issues to bear in mind, however.

First, define the ends (or some intermediate ends). This might include: (1) the measurement of customer needs and satisfaction, (2) the measurement of the firm's performance in terms of these goals, (3) the measurement of 'stakeholders' goals, the actual performance and satisfaction (such as vendors, regulators, interest groups, environmental quality monitors and so on). Practically, TQM managers, use 'broad-goals-slogans' to motivate and induce an environment of quality improvement. Measurement is thus no longer focused on *quality conformance,* but on *quality performance.* In this vein, the means applied to the management of quality, are far more extensive (see Figure 2.3), involving greater competence, coherence, robustness, consistency, perpetual improvement, flawless flows, motivation-participation and so on.

Second, when quality is intangible, the problems is: *What to measure?* This is in many cases the core problem. If we were sure what quality meant, it could be measured and yardsticks with 'sticks and carrots' devised to guarantee its proper manufacturing or delivery at the optimal level. In this sense, the management of quality necessarily involves the management of ill-defined and complex situations. The structured approach on which TQM is based can then be measured in terms of this ability to 'adapt and respond' as the firm evolves through a charted course which awaken 'latent problems and long held beliefs' and in the process changes its goals.

For example, for a customer whose objectives are small supply delays and a small percentage of defectives in a lot, each of these 'goals' is well defined and can be measured easily. In this simple case, quality is the measure of the relevant variables which constitute the customer's objective. They then become elements which make up the Cost Of Quality (COQ), and provide the means to evaluate economically the desired (standard) level of quality expected by the customer. If the customer's objectives are intangible, such as 'satisfaction', an elusive definition of the customer's happiness, and so on, it becomes much more difficult to measure both quality and its cost. In this case, quality is defined implicitly through other variables which, it is believed, are signals to the true quality. For this reason, in such situations, the measurement of quality can be always improved. In practice, we must settle down with a definition which can be used, that is, provide qualitative and quantitative information which can be transformed into economic and operational terms required for management's action.

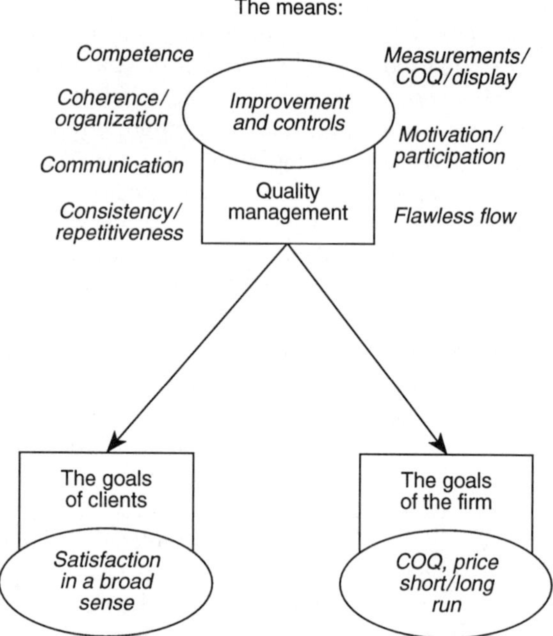

Figure 2.3: Measurements and TQM.

Third, *the measurement of quality is not neutral.* Measurements (or the lack thereof) have an effect on the firm, its stockholders, its managers and its employees. Measurements provide an incentive for action. Underestimating the costs of quality perpetuates non-quality, and *viceversa*; overestimating the costs of quality through inappropriate measurements would generate non-economic solutions to quality (augmenting production costs which cannot be recuperated through better quality for example). In such situations, there may be problems of principle to resolve. Should quality be measured, 'costed' and valued to induce change, or should it be objective, truly reflecting its economic effects? These are difficult and unavoidable issues to deal with when quality is intangible. Management must then arbitrate between the short-term and long-term effects these measurements will have on quality and on the firm's performance. Once these problems have been resolved, or at least recognized, we can turn to defining: (1) measurable objectives, (2) measurable non-conformance, (3) measurable costs of non quality, and finally, (4) measurable benefits of quality. Below, we consider some examples.

Problem

Discuss the use of the '7-zeros': Zero breakdown, Zero rework, Zero returns, Zero delay, Zero stocks, Zero defects and Zero papers as ends for quality management, and what are their effects on a firm's managerial orientation.

Examples: Measurement and the definition of quality

(1) The measurement and definition of quality are intimately related. For example, in a New York Times article (March 311994, p. B8) regarding health care, it was reported that many consumer groups supported the Administration's proposal for report cards to ensure some measure of accountability. But some experts believe that the reports will be of limited value for many years because of problems in gathering useful data. Even with a few local progams scattered across the country, "right now, most H.M.O.*s* know that a patient visited a doctor and the date of the visit ... They don't know the diagnosis. They don't know the procedure or medication prescribed. And they don't know why the patient visited in the first place. The H.M.Os also don't know if the treatments helped the patients or harmed them". The ability to see a doctor quickly is certainly an important measure of patient satisfaction, but subjective benchmarks like satisfaction can be misleading, and some experts warn that health plans may also simply redeploy their resources to score high marks.

(2) The European main office of Otis, an elevator manufacturer, imposed on its European branches a method for establishing a PONC (price of non conformity), which is divided into two parts. The cost of a badly performed job and the costs associated with the management and the control of quality. The costs of non-quality used by Otis have included: reprocessing and rework, special handling, special services, computer reruns, breakdowns, warranties, clients' complaints, after sales services and accounting corrections. Cost of management and control included: controls, verification and inspection, quality training, revisions, tests and experiments, implementation of quality related processes, process testing, prevention and inspections. These were also the elements measured and reported for the purpose of managing quality (Magne, 1989).

(3) Nissan's assembly plant in England, boasting a very high productivity, claim that its 'secret' consists in measuring its performance numerically, even when performance is hard to define. As a result, every activity has an associated numerical objective. In Sunderland (England), for example, they use STR (Straight Through Ratio) to calculate the rate at which cars are assembled without any further need for repairs or adjustments. Further, the NTR (No Touch Ratio) is reduced by the minimization of handling of pieces. Nissan claim that initially, the NTR and STR were 15% and 80% but are now 50% and 95%, respectively. The objective for 1993 was a further 75% for the NTR and 99% for the STR. Of course,

such quality performance should not, according to the Sunderland plant, imply a reduced productivity, but exactly the contrary. To realize such gains and motivate its personnel, Nissan claims that for the Sunderland plant, 'Production' is the 'Centre of Gravity' of the business, and everything else is a means to provide support. Once this is recognized, production is transformed into a number of activities, which are carefully measured and monitored. Derek Amour, the Production manager at Nissan Sunderland, claims that Nissan's obvious but important lesson is summarized by *To measure is to know.* (*Les Echos*, June 30, 1993, p.17).

(4) Grant and Leavenworth (1988) evaluate a health clinic along five performance measures: *Content, Process, Structure, Outcome and Impact.* Content is a measure of medical practice. Measures can include a review of medical records for conformance with national standards of medical care. Process is the sequence of events in the delivery of care and the interaction between patients and medical staff. Measures are a questionnaire of patients, both in process and at the exit of the system. Structure relates to physical facilities, equipment staffing patterns, and the qualifications of personnel. Measurements for such performance are numerous, however, including the time taken for patients to see a doctor, the ratio of doctors to nurses, bed occupancy, the utilization of equipment and certain services. Outcomes describe the change in a patient's health status as a result of care. Measures are again numerous, including the number of deaths, the number of patient complaints, the number of organs removed in surgery and the number of errors. Finally, Impact relates to the appropriateness and the effect of the health clinic on the community. Measures for such performance can include the number of patients turned away because of a lack of insurance, a lack of financial resources and travel time to the clinic (for additional study see de Geynt, 1970, for example).

The cost of quality

Say that quality is defined by the degree of conformance to expectations by customers. In other words, if $(x_1^*, \ldots, x_N^*)$ denote a customer expectations (defined by an advertised set of characteristics, for example), then if performance of the product is some other set of outcomes, say $(y_1, y_2, ..y_N)$, the non-conformance is a measure of the differences $(y_i - x_i^*), i = 1, 2, ..N$, while the Cost Of Quality (COQ) is the economic valuation of this non-conformance. There are, of course, many ways in which to compute non-conformance and translate them into economic values. Nonetheless, this is extremely important, and provides the first and most essential decision to reach when constructing a quality management program. The cost of quality can be broken down into three essential categories:

- Appraisal and measurement costs
- Prevention costs

- Nondetection costs including
  - Internal costs and
  - External cost

Appraisal and measurement costs include inspection, testing, work stoppage costs, materials, direct and indirect labour, delay times, and so on. Prevention costs include maintenance costs, quality and planning, training, reliability improvement, management costs, verification, experimentation, administration and simulations costs. Non-detection costs include the internal costs borne directly by the firm (such as materials, rework, capacity loss due to loss of men and machine time, administrative costs, special dispatches), and external costs (such as handling complaints, warranties, replacements, product liability, returns and allowances, loss of goodwill and its effect on future sales, etc.).

Table 2.1: Typical quality costs

Prevention

Quality engineering, Quality circles, Quality training, Supervision of prevention activities, Pilot studies, Systems development, Process controls, Technical support provided to vendors, Analysis of in-house processes for the purpose of improving quality, Auditing the effectiveness of the quality system.

Appraisal

Supplies used in test and inspection, Test and inspection of incoming materials, Component inspection and testing, Review of sales order for accuracy, In-process inspection, Final product inspection and testing, Field inspection at customer site prior to final release of product, Reliability testing, Supervision of appraisal activities, Plant utilities in inspection area, Depreciation of test equipment, Internal audits of inventory.

Internal Failure

Net cost of scrap, Net cost of spoilage, Disposal of defective product, Rework and labour overhead, Reinspection of reworked product, Retest of reworked product, Downtime due to quality problems, Net opportunity cost of products classified as seconds, Data re-entered due to errors, Defect cause analysis and investigation, Revision of in-house computer systems due to software errors, Adjusting entries necessitated by quality problems.

External Failure

Cost of responding to customer complaints, Investigation of customer claims on warranty, Warranty repairs and replacements, Out-of-warranty repairs and replacements, Product recalls, Product liability, Return and allowances because of quality problems, Opportunity cost of lost sales because of bad quality reputation.

In a study sponsored by the National Association of Accountants (US), on *Measuring, Planning and Controlling Quality Costs*, Morse, Roth and Poston (1987) found that quality (costing) information is important to managers for a number of reasons: (1) dollars can be added meaningfully across departments, and thereby also provide a good basis for comparisons; (2) because dollars can be added, they are more meaningful than disaggregated data, especially to top management; (3) quality cost information helps management identify quality problems and opportunities; (4) quality cost information helps managers evaluate the relative importance of quality problems, and provides a guide as to which to tackle first; (5) quality costs can be used to demonstrate the financial viability of quality improvement programs and obtain the necessary funding; (6) quality costs can be used to evaluate a department's effort in achieving quality objectives. In Tables 2.1 and 2.2, typical cost items are summarized and a simple example for a large firm is given. Note in particular that for the large firm, data can be analysed across departments, and therefore provides the means to concentrate 'the bangs where the bucks are'. On the basis of this data it is, of course, possible to compare departments and concentrate management time and attention on those facets of quality costs where they will do the most good. Further, following these costs from month to month provides the means to measure improvement or deterioration in the quality performance of each of the departments.

Table 2.2: Summarizing quality costs across organizational segments. (Figures in $)

	Dept.1	*Dept.2*	*Dept.3*	*Dept.4*
Prevention				
Quality engineering	4,000	1,000	500	5,500
Quality training	2,000	800	0	2,800
Systems development	3,000	600	0	3,600
Supervision	1,200	400	0	1,600
Subtotal	10,200	2,800	500	13,500
Appraisal				
Inspection	12,200	5,000	2,000	19,000
Testing	2,200	500	0	2,500
Supervision	2,500	600	400	3,500
Subtotal	16,500	6,100	2,400	25,500
Total	*26,700*	*8,900*	*2,900*	*38,500*
Internal Failure				
Scrap	3,700	2,500	500	6,000
Rework	2,700	2,200	1,000	5,900
Reinspection	600	400	200	1,200
Retest	300	200	0	500
Subtotal	6,600	5,300	1,700	13,600

Table 2.2: Summarizing quality costs across organizational segments. (Figures in $) (continued)

	Dept.1	*Dept.2*	*Dept.3*	*Dept.4*
External Failure				
Warranty	400	1,200	12,000	13,600
Allowances	0	0	4,000	4,000
Replacements	600	1,000	8,000	9,600
Subtotal Failure	1,000	2,200	24,000	27,200
Total Quality Cost	**34,300**	**16,400**	**28,600**	**79,300**

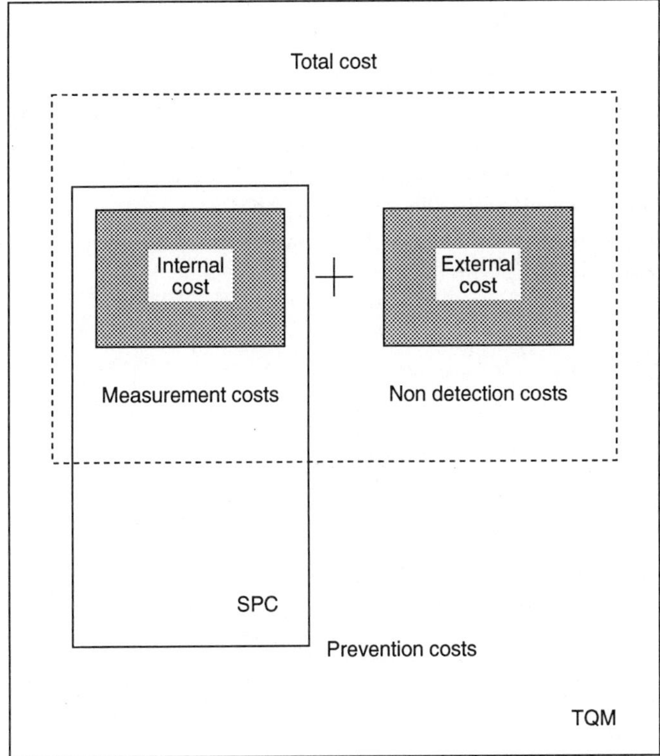

Figure 2.1: The scope of costs in SPC/SQC and TQM.

Traditionally, the lion's part of accounted costs of quality were defectives' costs. TQM, however, recommends that an increased share of the costs should be allocated to prevention, augmenting on the one hand the cost of quality, but reducing it on the other. The underlying belief of this approach is that prevention costs reduce the Total COQ. When COQ is difficult to define, we can use 'standards of reference'. These could be standards of production, industrial standards, or perhaps 'competitive bench marking'. In this latter approach, the standard is what the competition can do.

Example

The COQ can also be used to determine which quality level is optimal. To see how this might work, consider Q, a parameter of quality; the bigger it is, the better is the quality. If we consider both the cost of producing quality, denoted by $P(Q)$ and the COQ(Q), both a function of Q, then the optimal level of quality can be defined as that minimizing the total cost, or:

$$\min_{Q \in \Phi} TC(Q) = P(Q) + COQ(Q)$$
$$COQ(Q) = PC(Q) + DC(Q) + AP(Q)$$

where Φ denotes the set of potential qualities and PC = Prevention costs, DC = Defective costs and AP = Appraisal costs. A solution will depend upon the behaviour of the functions $P(.)$ and COQ(.) If the COQ(.) is decreasing in Q while $P(.)$ is increasing in Q, as seen in the Figure 2.5, then there is some level Q^* which minimizes the total cost TC. This level is the optimal level of quality.

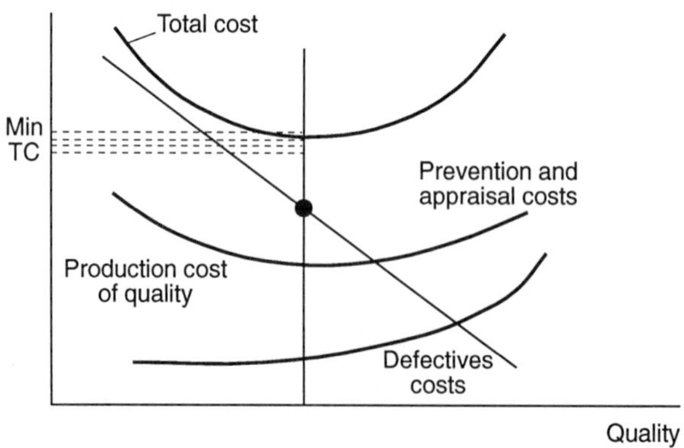

Figure 2.5: The optimal cost of quality

Example: Measuring COQ in a non-economic fashion

Define quality as a set of "standards" and assume that the firm performance is registered. Non-conformance can then be defined by a measure of difference between the standard and the registered performance. In some cases, it might be possible use the difference, or a function of this difference, as a measure of non quality. Typical cases include (a) Quadratic costs, (b) Nonlinear costs. A graphical depiction of these costs is outlined below in Figure 2.6.

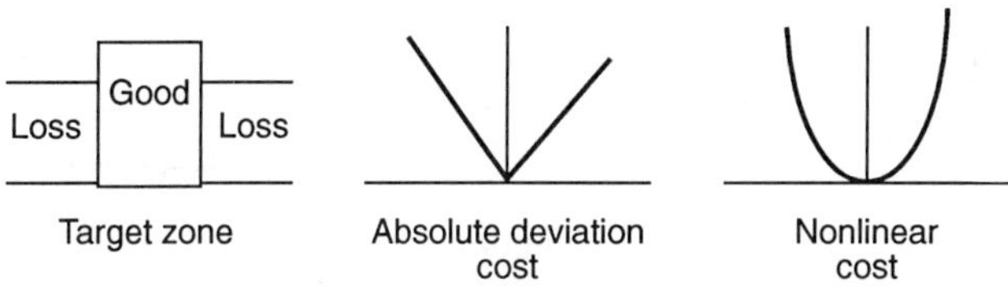

Figure 2.6: The functional costs of quality

Problem

A department store monthly sales and shortages encountered in the course of the month are given below. Using the data below, and assuming that supply delays are one week, devise a measure of quality for the store inventory management performance. Is the performance of the store improving over time?

Table 2.3

Month	Orders	Shortage	Ending Stock
January	2219	119	170
February	1885	50	150
March	1544	27	160
April	1791	10	202
May	2305	11	180
June	1620	4	160
July	1314	10	170
August	1831	4	120
September	1655	11	80
October	2043	2	60
November	1369	1	70
December	1144	8	50

Examples

(1) Medical clinics and laboratories, even with computerization, automation, increasing efficiency and increasing precision of administered tests, has not altogether done away with errors. In fact, in an article in the *Wall Street Journal* (February 2 and 3 1987), it is claimed that medical labs, which are trusted as largely error free, are far from infallible. Overwork, haste, misuse of equipment and specimen mix up afflict even the best of labs. Faulty diagnostics, erroneous reports and so on can sometimes lead to disastrous results for the patient and the hospital lab involved. The costs incurred are numerous, measured both in terms of dollars (as would be expected in insurance premium fees, court settlements etc.) as well as in hospital reputation (goodwill). The assurance of 'quality results' in a lab

and hospital setting are therefore paramount to its name and the quality of health care delivery it provides. The development and the use techniques and procedures for controlling the 'quality' of lab results, assuring that no careless or avoidable errors are made, are therefore of paramount importance. In a laboratory setting, some of the errors encountered include: (1) tests variation, (2) physiological variation and (3) sampling errors. These errors involve many costs that are difficult to assess. They are, nevertheless, needed to respond to some of the following questions:

- What is the probability that a reported test result will be faulty?
- What control procedures are necessary to ensure that an error will be reduced to a predetermined risk (probability) level?
- What are the effects of instituting control procedures as an integral part of the testing activity of the lab? How will such added activity alter staffing requirements, capacity (of equipment) utilization, and so on?
- How can we keep track of results, learn and improve the laboratory's performance?

These are topics which have been the subject of intense research and practice in the clinical and medical profession.

(2) The measurement of service quality is usually measured in terms of several measures of performance which makes the evaluation of the COQ very difficult. Simple questionnaires seeking customers' opinions are often used. There can be more sophisticated approaches, however. SERVQUAL, for example, is such a questionnaire, which is based on a multivariate statistical analysis (Parasuraman, Zeithmal and Berry, 1985, 1988; Zeithmal, Parasuraman and Berry, 1990). Essentially, it is based on a study of a questionnaire with 97 questions (items) regarding quality. Since its construction, SERVQUAL has been reduced to 22 essential items. The conclusions of this study are that service quality is expressed essentially in terms of 'Service differentiation' and that 'Service quality is a perception resulting from the expectation of service and its performance'. Any deviation from expectations will thus induce a cost of service. Further, any differentiation from the best will also incur a quality cost. Formally, we can presume that if the service has a random performance ξ then the quality of service is a measure of the difference $E(\xi)-\xi$, where E is the expectation operator. As a result, the variance $\text{var}(\xi)$, which measures the variation about how expectations in service can be applied, measure some aspect of the cost of quality in services. Based on these observations, SERVQUAL suggests that we measure quality along five dimensions:

Dimension 1: Tangibles such as equipment, personnel attributes (look, neatness, etc.), the physical environment, etc.

Dimension 2: Reliability or the propensity to meet clients' expectations.

Dimension 3: Responsiveness or the propensity to respond to clients' requests.

Dimension 4: 'Assurance' or the potential to induce a sense of security for the client.

Dimension 5: Empathy or the special attention given to the client. This therefore relates to issues of personnel, and represents a sort of implicit valuation of such personnel.

SERVQUAL has been used intensively in marketing studies. Nevertheless, its primary importance resides in its identification of the key factors that affect the definition of quality. For a relationship between these factors and their combination (i.e. service systems design), it is necessary to turn to other methods.

2.3 Approaches to TQM and quality improvement

There are many approaches to TQM and Quality Improvement (QI), as many as there are quality gurus. Throughout their approaches, there seem to be some common and recurring messages. Some of these include:

- A downstream sensitivity for the definition of quality
- An approach to cross-functional management and a growth of lateral functions and communication within firms.
- An emergence of pre- and post-industrial logistics and production management which emphasizes producer supplier relationships, post sales service and management, exchanges, support functions and coordination
- A structural change to simplify organizational flows, reduce manufacturing operational complexity, eliminate bottlenecks and devise a system which is coherent, flexible and sensitive to the environment, and yet which performs well.
- An integration with the business strategy, fed and feeding this strategy. As well as the involvement of higher levels management echelons.

Samples of such approaches are highlighted below, including precepts expounded by Deming, Juran, Crosby, Shingo and others. The use of tools such as SPC/SQC, project follow through and other tools will be considered in great detail in subsequent chapters but are essential for the application of TQM.

Deming

Deming (1975, 1982, 1986) focuses on the improvement of products and service conformance to specifications by reducing uncertainty and variability in designing and manufacturing the product. For this purpose, Deming proposes that we follow an unending cycle –Deming's wheel– which consists of the following (see also Figure 2.7) : (1) Design the product, (2) Plan its manufacture, (3) Collect data, test it, control the process, (4) Record and follow sales performance, (5) Perform survey and research regarding consumer tastes and finally repeat the design of the product.

According to Deming, a quality orientation leads to higher productivity and thereby to lower costs. Thus, Deming proposes that top management 'works on the system' by improving it and by inducing a structural change needed for greater coherence of the organization and its operational effectiveness. Further, Deming asserts that most quality problems are not the workers' fault but management's. The Cost Of Quality (COQ) currently used in most industrial firms is viewed by Deming as too crude a measure. Rather, some attempts should be made to measure the indirect costs and benefit effects of quality. The tools mostly recommended by Deming are Pareto analysis, Ishikawa (fishbone) diagrams and histograms. These tools are presented in the next chapter.

To control the manufacturing process, Deming points out that there are two sources for improvement: first, reduction of systemic recurring errors such as poor design, faulty BOM (Bills of Materials), inadequate training and their like which give rise to common cause problems (as will be presented in greater detail in Chapter 6), and second, elimination of special causes which are associated with specific materials, individuals and machines. The distinction between these errors will become far more evident when we introduce control charts in Chapter 6.

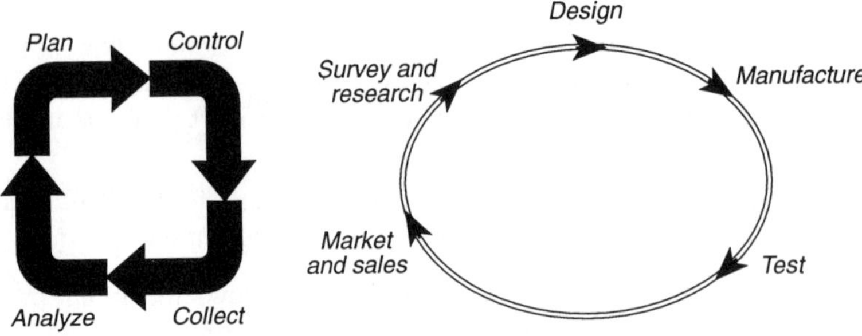

Figure 2.7: Deming's wheel

Juran

Juran (1974, 1988) suggests an organizational approach which focuses on management at two levels. A first level, oriented towards top management, emphasizes *quality as the fitness for use by consumers*, while a second level consists of a breakdown of first level quality missions into missions oriented towards departments in the firm. For these departments, it is then necessary to work in accordance with specifications designed to achieve the fitness for use. The key aspects of the first quality level involve, according to Juran: (1) Product design, (2) Conformance to specification, (3) Availability, (4) Reliability, (5) Maintainability and (6) Serviceability.

To achieve it, however, Juran recommends that we also follow an unending cycle which is given by (see also Figure 2.8) : (1) Market research, (2) Product development, (3) Design, (4) Manufacture and Planning, (5) Purchasing, (6) Production process control, (7) Inspection, (8) Tests, (9) Sales and finally feedback through market research. For Juran, top management is important as it is an essential actor in the everlasting process of market research to manufacture to sales. For the quality management process, Juran proposes three phases:

The Control Sequence, which seeks to solve sporadic problems. This is in essence the function of quality control. Here statistical techniques as well as tolerance fool proofing are used.

The Breakthrough Sequence, which consists of quality improvement by solving chronic problems. To do so, Juran recommends that we use the 'Universal Process' for quality improvement, consisting of: Study the symptoms, Diagnose the causes and Apply remedies. In this sequence, Juran advocates a project-by-project improvement. At any time, many such projects are ongoing simultaneously. The breakthrough sequence requires a breakthrough in attitudes (in addition to a knowledge breakthrough). *Institutionalization of the review process over the quality management process.* In such a program, short and long-term goals are made explicit, priorities are set up and relationships between the firm and the quality strategy are drawn.

Throughout these phases, Juran recommends that training be given a top priority.

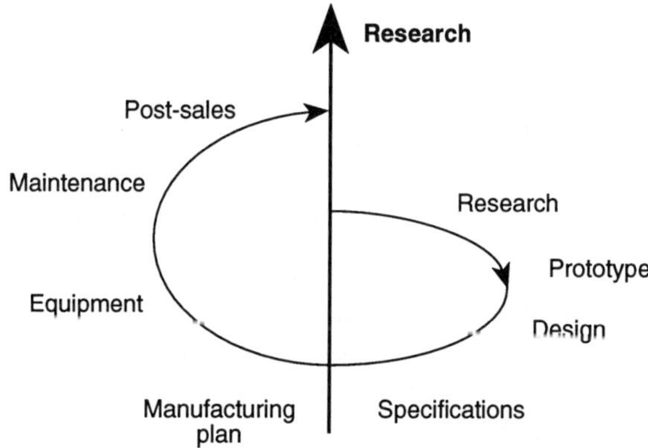

Figure 2.8: Juran's spiral of quality

Crosby

The Crosby approach (1979, 1984) is based on the definition of 'absolutes of quality management' which define quality and the standards required to achieve quality, and prescribes the basic elements of improvement. There are 14 such basic steps: *Management commitment*, *Quality improvement team development*, *Quality measurement*, *Cost of quality evaluation*, *Quality awareness*, *Corrective action*, *Zero-defects committee establishment*, *Supervisors training*, *Zero defects day*, *Goal setting*, *Error cause removal*, *Recognition*, *Quality councils* and *Do it over again*.

Crosby's absolutes, are defined by the following:

> *Absolute 1*: The definition of quality is conformance to requirements which are established by management.
>
> *Absolute 2*: Quality is reached through prevention. It is therefore necessary to understand the process and eliminate all opportunities to make errors. It is recommended to use quality control tools such as control charts and other tools that we shall study in later chapters.
>
> *Absolute 3*: The performance standard is zero. Thus, even if we do not reach it, it is important to strive towards zero defects.
>
> *Absolute 4*: The measurement of quality is the price of nonconformance. For this reason, data is important so that attention is focused on the true magnitude of the cost of nonconformance.

Crosby also recommends an unending cycle. The basic tenets of this cycle are that:

- Quality improvement is an everlasting process.
- Quality education and its philosophy begins at the top.
- Quality control departments should believe in zero defects.
- Quality education and training should be excellent.
- Management is patient and never ceases in concern for quality.

Crosby, perhaps more than Deming and Juran, emphasizes the need for a corporate culture change, so that it can embed the values of quality and its improvement in the organizational process. Furthermore, Crosby's emphasizes zero-defects and preventive measures to attain it.

The approach to Quality Management in Japan

The 'Japanese' approach to the management of production and quality refers to a complex set of organizational procedures for managing plants based on simplification, on the reduction of stocks, on quality improvement and on producer supplier cooperation and synchronization. This is often summarized by application of the Just in Time production approach. Technology, as expressed in the use of computers and automation in production, can find its 'natural place' in the 'Japanese model' once the production system has been simplified into well defined and well controlled operations. Further, exchange between suppliers and producers, labour and management, and generally, the actors of production, is based on cooperation and mutuality rather than coercion. Although it is important to learn from the Japanese experience, it is equally important to appreciate the basic factors that have encouraged the development of the so-called 'Japanese model' and what are the characteristics that have made it efficient in manufacturing and quality. Through such appreciation, it is possible to draw lessons which can be helpful for devising production management concepts tailored to the production environment faced in Europe and the USA. The most important aspect of this lesson is noting that the process of management and the management of quality are intimately integrated. These are, therefore, one and not two separate functions!

Japan's cultural environment and social systems through the ages have imbued the Japanese with a sense of order, mutual dependence and organization. The relative size of the Japanese islands, their large population and limited natural resources have created an environment where frugality and efficiency are essential for survival. As a result, the concern for productivity is not only a goal of economic pursuit, but a purpose strongly embedded in ethical values. Combining these basic tendencies with an 'appropriate organization' integrating the economic means for producing and competing worldwide have rendered Japanese firms formidable competitive opponents.

The Japanese 'model', embedded naturally in a favourable cultural environment and with a history accustomed to organization, guidance, controls and mutual dependence, sets up the stage for efficient and controlled production systems. Factors such as:

- A 'social contract' between employees and firms, based on 'industrial kinship' rather than a 'conflict approach' as in US, Europe labor management negotiating postures
- A clear definition of hierarchy and an understanding of goals (from top to bottom of the organization), with a process (albeit lengthy) of reaching a consensus prior to action. This in contrast to a multiplicity of goals encountered in European and US firms and a confusion regarding the formal and informal structures of the organization.
- A distribution of responsibility down the line, leading to an effective and decentralized implementation system, instead of a concentration of power and responsibility at the top.
- Employees' participation in productivity and quality enhancement programs (through quality circles and self-involvement).

- The on-line solution of problems as they occur.
- The coordination reached at all levels of the organization, which resolve the natural difficulties encountered in interfacing and integrating disparate activities.
- An ability to learn and endogenize quickly the use of equipment and automation in production.

These meaningful characteristics provide an environment which can favour a competitive edge in cost efficiency, as well as create the atmosphere needed for improving quality. At the same time, it does not necessarily encourage inventiveness and can be rigid (due to the internal processes for reaching a consensus and making a decision). These factors are, nevertheless, favourable to the implementation of TQM systems.

Schoenberger (1982), in particular, has studied Japanese work practices and summarized them into a number of lessons, generally associated to JIT (Just in Time) manufacturing (see also Hall, 1983). These are: (1) *Fewer Suppliers,* (2) *Reduced Parts Counts,* (3) *Focused Factories or narrow lines of products/technologies,* (4) *Scheduling to a Rate Rather than by Lot,* (5) *Fewer Racks,* (6) *More Frequent Deliveries,* (7) *Smaller Plants,* (8) *Shorter Distances,* (9) *Less Reporting,* (10) *Fewer Inspectors,* (11) *Less Buffer Stocks* and (12) *Fewer Job Classifications.* Further, although JIT is believed mostly to be based on the reduction of inventories (through the use of Kanbans) and pull scheduling, its more important aspects are also related to TQM. Essentially, the JIT approach will induce production management to:

- Reveal and identify problems and thus enforce their solution.
- Control variations through statistical process control.
- Reduce external interventions in process operation and thus favour greater auto-controls and built in inspection.
- Emphasize quality at the source since the effects and costs of non- quality in process are extremely large.

Enforced problem solving is reached through participative management and quality cost consciousness, which motivate the workers to explore the cause of poor quality and voluntarily implement the improved solutions. In essence, since JIT renders the process much more transparent and sensitive to failures, there is overall a far greater awareness of quality problems. In traditional production systems, some defects are acceptable if lots meet quality standards, while in JIT zero defects is the standard.

Further, through the intensive use of statistical process control, root causes are identified and eliminated. Some defect sources including materials, workmanship, design and processes, are assessed, and statistics are used to maintain processes in control. These tests, however are applied to the process, and not on lots produced, to identify causes and infer percentage defects. The two essential purposes are then continuous improvement and prevention and not just data collection. When quality progresses, inspection may at last disappear. In this sense, the Japanese approach introduces controls as an interim phase, with the purpose of getting rid of them! Once quality is mastered, the Japanese go on to process optimization to attain higher levels of performance. In fact, increased attention is given in Japan to robust design, as we shall see in Chapter 7.

Differences between the US, Japan and Europe are eroding. Globalization of businesses has brought Japanese firms to the US and Europe, and *vice versa*, joint ventures and manufacturing in Japan by leading US and European firms has created sufficient technology transfer to transform both the Japanese and US/Euro models. Nevertheless, such a distinction, perhaps exaggerated, is needed to highlight the fact that there are indeed important differences. Further, although the Japanese use most of the ideas expounded by Deming and Juran in the early 1950's, we should be aware that thay have developed these ideas further and have integrated them into a production strategy, the JIT approach being one example. Ishikawa and Shigeo Shingo are some specific names who have left their imprint on the management of quality. Concepts summarized by Poka Yoke and Kaizen and others are also used to focus attention on quality.

The Poka-Yoke, or Shigeo Shingo's Shop Floor

Poka-Yoke stands for 'resistant to errors'. It is an approach which seeks to render the work place mistake proof. By reducing the opportunity to make errors, the work place is simplified into a stream of activities which will have a propensity to produce 'zero defects'. A Poka-Yoke system can at times institute a full (100%) control if some problems are detected. In this case, there is instantaneous feedback for corrective action. The problem is that the Poka-Yoke system is reactive when a default is detected, for this reason, it is combined with a control upstream to reduce the chances of errors of being detected downstream, once it is too late. The basic steps which are implied by the Poka-Yoke are based on common sense, and include:

- Control upstream, as close as possible to the source of the potential defect as possible.
- Establish controls in relation to the severity of the problem.
- Think smart and small.
- Do not delay improvement by prior over analysis.

Poka-Yoke was developed (at Matsuhita Electric and Toyota) in conjunction with the JIT approach which seeks to render manufacturing as a flawless flow process while at the same time reducing dramatically the level of stocks (which we will discuss in greater depth later on). In JIT, we shall see that the cost of quality is far greater, since 'there are no buffer stocks', and therefore each problem has an effect on the production line as a whole. For these reasons, the management of quality in a JIT production philosophy is a necessity to implementing JIT successfully.

The position of controls in a production process, as Poka-Yoke states, is both important and obvious. Sony Alsace (France), for example, claims that the cost of components failure increases dramatically when it is detected downstream rather than upstream. That is, the COQ is necessarily a function of the position where the quality problem originates and is detected. The closer the detected problem to consumers (downstream), the greater is this cost. A control position upstream, at the time materials enter the process, has a COQ which is the smallest. As we move downstream, the COQ increases, since it involves cumulative costs of machine time, personnel and so on, working on defectives. Further, the costs of prevention are smallest upstream and increase importantly when we move downstream (since in-process production and control is quite complex, and they require both sophisticated equipment and intensive managerial efforts). Although these costs of measurement and prevention could theoretically decline once we approach the state of a finished product, the total costs of quality remain higher. For this reason, it is natural to concentrate quality management effort at the point at which it is least costly and can prevent the most damage (which is the upstream stage).

Kaizen

Kaizen is another Japanese term, meaning *improvement*, improvement as a way of life, both personally and collectively. As a result, it seeks to go 'higher' and 'faster', and reach one's own full capacities and potential. Kaizen stresses the need to combat the *status quo*. Each practice, each goal, should be put in question, so that there must be a way to do it better. It is, of course, simple to ignore Kaizen due to its obviousness, but one should also be aware that Kaizen conveys a mobilizing message which is needed to move towards a TQM approach, for a total approach to quality cannot be reached without a total mobilization (see Masaaki Imai, 1990 for further study, however).

Quality circles

Quality circles have been started in Japan in 1962, as a follow-up effort to ongoing quality improvement. In the US it was introduced at the beginning of the 1970s and in France in the early 1980s. Basically, these are voluntary working groups sharing a common concern which is related to quality improvement. These circles generally include generally a group leader, are of limited duration and involve periodic meetings in or out of working hours (this depends upon the country where it is applied). Experience with quality circles is mixed. In some cases, when they are well structured, part of an overall TQM program, they can be effective. In such cases, they relate to participative approaches of management which seek to sensitize employees prior to introducing change. More importantly, however, quality circles can be used to induce individuals to act and reach 'collective' achievements. In some situations, they can deteriorate into a focus group for disenchantment and gripes within the firm.

Quality circles can be constructed and used for various purposes since *they provide an explicit and implict incentive for work group learning and apprenticeship based on the induction of a collective responsibility and spirit, participation for another approach and more effective way to work.* To succeed, the following procedures may be followed: (a) Emphasize the volunteer character of the group (which means that it ought not to be realized during working hours). As such, it calls for creativity, responsibility and the will to make a difference. (b) The size of the quality circle should be manageable, and should not consist of an assembly where everyone cannot express his opinions. (c) There should be a group leader with potential to stimulate participation and collective reflection on the problem at hand. (d) Emphasize participative styles of management. (e) Problems should not be imposed on the quality circle. Rather, management should be receptive, listen and appreciate the range and the problem's priority devised by members of the quality circle. (f) The group shoud adopt a rigorous procedure to conduct its deliberations. Otherwise, it may miss its essential purpose, to converge and provide quality improving suggestions and programs. For this reason, the use of quantitative measures by quality circles is extremely important. On the one hand, it focuses attention on real measurable problems, and on the other provides a yardstick for measuring improvements. Finally, (g) the quality circles should be conceived as an organizational and structural ingredient of the industrial and business firm, whose survival is independent of members of the quality circle.

There are other practices (aside of Poka-Yoke, Quality Circles, etc.) which were given special names, due to their importance in some firms. For example, there is the 5S:

SEIRI: to distinguish between the useful and the less useful

SEITON: everything which is important must be available for use

SEISOU: for cleanliness and security

SEIKETSU: to respect the 3S to establish a proper work environment

SHITSUKE: to maintain the discipline

Other so-called Japanese 'methods' such as HEIJUNKA (to maintain a coherence and harmony), GEMBA (for the creation of value added at expressed by clients needs) or MUDA/MURA/MURI relating to wastes, disequilibrium and overcapacity, can be found in Ishikawa (1976), Schoenberger (1982), Ouchi (1981) and are used in various proportions to construct approaches to the management and the control of quality. For example, the Total Production System (TPS) of Toyota uses a large part of these methods for the production of quality.

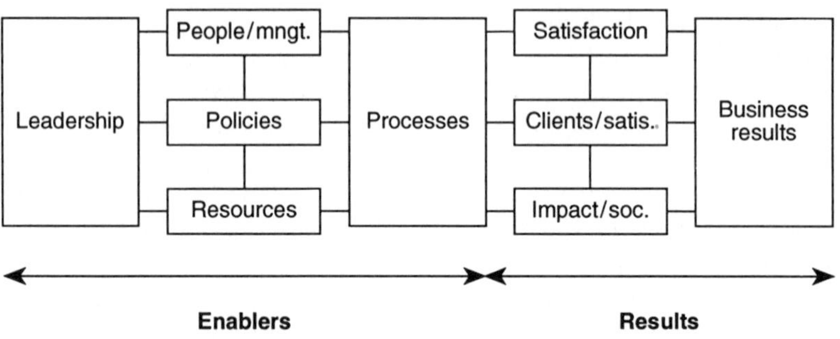

Figure 2.9: The European model.

The 'European model'

The European Foundation for Quality Management has suggested a model which presumes that processes are the means by which the organization harnesses and releases the talents of its people to produce results. In other words, the processes and the people are the *enablers* which provide the *results.* This is represented graphically in Figure 2.9. Essentially, the model implies that: *Customer satisfaction, people (employee) satisfaction and impact on society* are achieved through: *Leadership driving, policy and strategy, people management, resources and processes leading ultimately to excellence in business results.*

Each of these elements is a criterion that can be used to appraise the organization's progress towards TQM. The results are concerned with **what** the organization has achieved and is achieving. The enablers' aspects are concerned with **how** results are achieved. The Euro strategy for TQM is intimately related to the implementation of the ISO–9000 – 9004 standard however and will therefore be presented below. For further study, consult some of the following documents (Magne, 1990, AFCERQ, 1988, AFNOR, 1986*a*, 1986*b*, EFQM, 1992).

Traditional and TQM approaches presented here differ fundamentally. Table 2.4, based on the models outlined here highlights these differences.

Table 2.4: The traditional and TQM approach.

Traditional	TQM approach
Emphasizes production	Emphasizes consumer needs
Emphasizes control	Emphasizes prevention
COQ limited to explicit costs	COQ includes indirect costs as well
Maintains the *status quo*	Counter *status quo* culture
Quality is assurance	Quality is integrated in operations
Quality: a cost to avoid	Quality: deals with global perform.
Static, specific	Process improvement approach
Functional organization	Cross functional organization
Centralized authority	Decentralization and participation
Conformance	Imagination and creativity
Little training in SQC	Intensive training
Many inspectors	Few well trained inspectors
Emphasizes materials, errors	Emphasizes processes and management
Individuality	Group synergy
Interfaces unattended	Manage interfaces

2.4 Certification and ISO 9000/9004

According to Standard ISO 8402 (for the definition of terms), *Quality Assurance* is a set of pre-defined and systematic procedures performed to assure the client that the firm has installed a system of controls which can satisfy the required standards. Such procedures are summarized by five standards ISO 9000, 90001, 90002, 90003 and the comprehensive ISO 9004, which seek to establish a Total Quality Control Certification. These standards were established to ensure that the process of quality management is strongly embedded in the procedures used by the organization in its operations and management. These procedures are regrouped in categories ISO-9000, ISO-9001, ISO-9003 and ISO-9004 spanning the conception, production and control of products and processes, as well as their overall integration (through ISO 9004, which is implemented in the procedures of ISO 9000) as shown in Table 2.5.

ISO-9000 is a general (and comprehensive) standard whose purpose is twofold. First, clarify the basic concepts and the management of quality, and second, outline the broad framework within which quality management (internally and externally) will be applied through the ISO system. The problem areas highlighted include:

- The complexity of the process design.
- The control of designs.
- The complexity of the production process.
- The fundamental characteristics of a product or service.

- Product or service security.
- Economic considerations.

In addition, ISO-9000 outlines the requirements for documentation and the demonstration of the compatibility of quality and the ISO standard. As a result, ISO-9000 calls for a quality audit, which is in practice a necessary but major undertaking. Under ISO-9000, the audit should be conceived to:

- Define the parameters of quality and the requirements of quality.
- Determine conformance (or non-conformance) relative to standards and requirements, and thereby reveal problem areas within the firm.
- Provide sufficient information to verify whether the process is effective or not, and an opportunity for 'house cleaning'. In the process, it may reveal some of the problems long buried due to habit and past practices.
- Outline targets and projects for quality improvement.
- Provide a better grasp for the process of managing quality, meet ISO-9000, obtain certification and project an image of TQM.

Quality audits, even though they may be difficult to implement, are extremely important. They may be applied to suppliers, to the product, the process, management and controls.

A second group consists of ISO 9001 – 9003. ISO-9001 deals with the design, development, production and installation of a distribution and delivery system and, finally, with post-sales service management. ISO-9002 is more specifically tuned to problems of production, suppliers and logistics. ISO-9003 is the framework for tests and final controls for the firm and its suppliers.

The third group, ISO-9004, describes the set of elements which allows the implementation of an internal control and management system. Topics covered in ISO-9004 include the costs, the risks, the advantages, management's responsibilities, principles of the audit, documentation of quality, economic factors, marketing, the definition of design quality, suppliers' quality and quality production, the control of equipment and measures, nonconformance and the corrective actions to follow, maintenance and post-manufacturing procedures, personnel, reliability, security and statistical tools. In ISO-9004, not all elements need to be implemented, as the needs and implementation mode will vary from firm to firm.

Table 2.5: The components of the ISO standard.

ISO 9001	*ISO 9002*	*ISO 9003*
Design/Development Production/Installation Post sales support	Production Installation	Control and Final tests
Design	**Process**	**Controls**

Table 2.6: ISO procedures

Procedure followed for ISO Certification
Letter of intention sent to the General Secretary/ISO
Questionnaire received by the firm
Optional visit by ISO organization and evaluation report
ISO Committee requirements: Contract Reference guide and preliminary information Preliminary questionnaire Examinationand evaluation of submitted documents
ISO Audit Audit report submitted to firm Response by firm In some case, additional audit
Evaluation and Certification by ISO Committee
Certification, for three years
Periodic visits
Contract renewal

Certification is important because it conveys a signal that the certified firm is operating in a structured manner for quality improvement and TQM. Certification can be obtained by the AFAQ (Association Française pour Assurance Qualité) in France but other national and comparable institutions exist in England, Germany and throughout Europe and the US. Each national organization has, of course, special committees such as Chemistry, Electronics, and so on. If American companies want to compete in Europe and the EU, this is likely to be an essential standard. Already, over 50% of major European companies have been certified, while only a dozen US companies such as Dupont, General Electric, Corning, Eastman Kodak and a few others have met the ISO standard. In the UK alone, 20,000 are already certified and the remaining 200,000 will have to do so by the year 1996. Companies that are certified must meet a set of 20 criteria spanning problems relating to contract review, design control, purchasing standards, quality records and corrective action. To meet the ISO standard, it is necessary to understand what exactly the standard means: by setting up a steering committee, conduct an audit and diagnostic of the firm's quality policy and how far/close it is from the ISO standard, check documents and prepare written documents wherever needed, and finally, apply for certification. Table 2.6 points out the necessary steps a firm will have to follow to reach such certification.

Table 2.7: Motivation and perceived advantages

	Motivations	*Advantages*
Personnel mobilization	19%	37%
Reduces audits	15%	5%
Formalizes quality management	9%	
Evaluation of the current quality approach	15%	11%
Subsidiaries and group demands	17%	
Recognition of the importance of quality	25%	
Demanded by clients and greater credibility	17%	31%
Required to penetrate new markets	26%	8%
No opinion	10%	11%
Greater Internal efficiency		32%
Better image		26%

The motivations and advantages in obtaining an ISO quality certification are varied. In a questionnaire distributed to a large number of firms, the answers summarized in Table 2.7 clearly highlight some variety. Thus, an ISO certification has many purposes. For firms seeking to implement a TQM approach, it provides a structured (albeit difficult) approach to quality improvement, a yardstick to evaluate in-house TQM procedures. In some cases, it can be used for re-engineering, to motivate and re-orient workers and improve client supplier relationships. Furthermore, since an ISO certification is often needed by large and public enterprises, such certification is required to qualify for some contracts (and thereby improve the firm's competitive position). For management however, it is helpful to select suppliers without too much regard for quality management procedures, and thus reduce the audits and tests needed to keep an ongoing and profitable relationship with suppliers. Extensive information is available for firms seeking to obtain an ISO certification through a nation's standard and normalization associations.

Implementation of ISO certification can be administratively cumbersome. A firm involved in food processing and seeking to implement ISO-9002 has evolved from an apparently simple structure to the control of quality to a complex one. Although it improved the quality and uniformity of its produce, it went through an important and costly restructuration to satisfy the ISO requirement.

Problems

1. Explain how TQM brings greater efficiency in human relations and in communication, and induces new organizational forms which are more open to communication and exchanges.

2. Explain how ISO 9000 provides a structured approach to the introduction of TQM, and how it provides for management a set of 'standards' operating procedures in everything it does (for example, use the fact that TQM imposes on firms the need to codify their activities relating to the management of quality and its control).

3. What is the difference between ISO-9004 and ISO-9001, 2 and 3? How important are these?

4. What is the difference between national standards specifications and ISO standards? How are these different, and how complementary. In particular, discuss the use of standards for technical and security purposes, and the use of standards for operating procedures and quality management.

5. Discuss the importance of an ISO quality certification in the light of European integration and the globalization of markets.

2.5 Examples and applications

(1) 'I have never met a quality guru I didn't like' says Richard Buetow, director of quality at Motorola, an American Telecom giant (*The Economist*, April 1992, p.55). This mirrors Motorola's concern for quality which set a target for 1992 (made in 1987) to achieve a defect rate of 3.4 per million components manufactured. Although today it stands at 40 defects per million, this is *far* better than the 6000 defects per million of just five years ago. The current target is 1 defect per million by the turn of the century! To do so, Motorola has emphasized the following concepts:

- Quality is in the eye of the customer.
- Robust quality (which we study in Chapter 7).
- Reduce the learning cycle due to a shorter product life cycle.
- Built in redundancy to increase the reliability.
- Pushing responsibility down the line.

Quality is not all that is needed to compete, however. As freely admitted by Motorola, quality is not 'winning the game', but just a ticket to the game. Product development time, production delays, selling prices and so on are only some of the areas in which firms compete once quality production has been attained and taken as a matter of fact.

(2) Magne (1989), in his appreciation of TQM in Switzerland, presented the practice of TQM in Gendre-Otis, a well known elevator manufacturer. They focused their attention on ten processes, three of which were selected due to their importance on the firm's operations and their economic weight. These include:

- Preparation of order forms from their inception to product delivery.
- Procedures for installing new products or renovated existing ones.
- A follow-up of operations until billing.

According to Magne large multinationals have introduced quality programs to Swiss industries. IBM, for example, in 1983 focused on 10 processes which required quality attention. These include (1) the management of contracts and billing, (2) Order processing, (3) In process orders, (4) Management of salesmen's commissions, (5) Spare parts management, (6) Stocks, (7) Administration and payments by quotas, (8) Accounting and reports, (9) Product distribution and finally, (10) New product introduction. At IBM, general managers in all countries are trained and informed about the quality objectives and process improvements. This takes the form of certification levels which represent steps at which an assessment and review of quality programs can be made. It is at these steps that resource allocation is made and that methodologies are critically assessed and selected. In this sense, IBM defines seven critical levels of certification:

- Processes are clearly defined and delineated.
- Responsibilities are assigned.
- Quality councils group departments related to a process.
- Sub-processes (projects) are defined and assigned.
- The needs of suppliers and customers are identified and quantified.
- Documentation is prepared regarding processes so that sufficient understanding of functional and individual responsibilities are clearly made.
- Results are inspected and controlled through statistical means.

(3) ATT (Surette, 1986) is a major international telecommunication and information firm. ATT perceives its position worldwide, with costs to quality ratio being the essential denominator of its competitive positioning. In addition, ATT is subject to a highly dynamic market with a great deal of technological innovation. In this sense, ATT has adopted a total quality philosophy which is based on the following assumptions:

- Differentiating their product.
- Strengthening of its quality image.
- Improving and moving towards zero defects.
- Reducing costs through quality improvement.
- Acting on the organization as a whole.

ATT has also adapted Garvin's eight characteristics of quality and the presumption that it is consumers who define what characteristics are the most important for quality. In this sense, quality is market driven, valued by market questionnaires. The essential functions of the ATT quality system are based on a program for quality planning, a quality review (an audit) and finally a feedback process whose purpose is to improve quality. Feedback, which acts as an incentive to improve quality includes surveys of consumer satisfaction, quality costs tracking, field performance tracking, failure mode analysis, and an internal quality information system. Such information is then used to improve productivity, optimize processes, provide system coherence, set up priorities and eliminate problems causes. James E. Olson, the COE of ATT in ATT Quality Policy Management Focus (July 15, 1985), states clearly that quality excellence is the foundation for the management of ATT, and in implementing the quality strategy of ATT each line-of-business/entity head is responsible for:

- Communicating the quality to each employee.
- Clarifying specific responsibilities for quality.
- Developing and reviewing strategic quality plans and objectives on an on-going basis.
- Implementing a quality management system to carry out the plans and achieve objectives.
- Monitoring and continually improving the level of customer satisfaction.
- Monitoring and continually improving the defect and error rates of internal processes and systems.
- Developing joint quality plans with suppliers and other business partners.
- Implementing, funding, and reviewing specific quality improvement program.
- Providing education and training in quality disciplines for all employees.

(4) TRW is a US conglomerate in aerospace, electronics and car parts manufacturing. In the early 1980s, quality became a topic of particular importance. Broadly, TRW defines quality as the degree of total conformance of the product or service to a customer's needs. TRW defines four essential aspects of quality, each subdivided into elements which are directly associated with 'responsibility areas'. These are reproduced in Table 2.8, and can be compared to ATT's seven aspects for quality improvement and Phillips' four aspects.

Table 2.8 : Key aspects for quality improvements.

TRW: Price (basic price, discounts, credits, warranties, payment terms)

Delivery performance (promised delivery, conformance to promised delivery, correctness of items)

Support Quality (Customer design support, customer sales and service, after sales service, assurance documentation etc).

Product Quality (design quality, product specification features characteristics, conformance to product specification at time of delivery, performance after delivery, reliability, maintainability, durability, etc.)

ATT: Performance, Reliability, Conformance, Life time, After sales, Esthetics, Perceived Quality

Phillips: Repair Time, Response Time, Reliability, Equipment availability, Response Time

TRW also uses customer questionnaires for measuring consumer satisfaction. But, in addition, a comparative analysis is performed with competition. A comparison is then made with respect to annual sales (market share), design product specification, delivered conformance, post-delivery performance, overall product quality, price premium and customer opinion. Through such analysis, simple subjective statements are used (worse, average, best, joint best). Internally, TRW (in 1982) had quality costs of $391 millions, 19% of which accounted for total prevention (including test and inspection planning, prevention and qualification tests), 46% accounted for total appraisal (incoming and source inspection, in-process and final inspection, test and inspection equipment) and 35% for total failure costs (including rework, scrap and external failure).

(5) A major car manufacturer in France sought to devise a TQM approach. To do so, it devised a string of principles which were used across the firm's departments. It is based on three elements 'The Objective', 'The Condition' and 'The Means'. The objective is the consumers' satisfaction, and tying the firm's potential competitive position to this satisfaction. 'The Objective' was then broken down into a number of measures including price, supply delays to customers, quality and the variety of cars the firm can offer consumers. 'The Condition' for the TQM, and thereby the firm's competitive position, is based essentially on the motivation of human resources and the firm's ability to establish incentives for effective operation. There are five principles of which each of the departments must be aware: Competence, Autonomy, Motivation, Working Group and Information. The methods used to breed competence and participation include the actions of management and the messages they convey, broadening responsibilities, multi-tasking, education, quality circles, service contracts, suggestions and a communication environment

which incites exchanges rather than stiffles them. Finally, 'The Means' consists of industrial organization and structure based on zero defects, zero breakdown, zero stock, flexibility, Just in Time and Value Added. While these are stated as principles motivating the application of methods which can lead towards such performance, the actual methods explicitly include Suppliers' Quality Assurance (to be studied later), intra-firm quality assurance, analysis of production and materials flows, Poka-Yoke, re-engineering of work stations, maintenance, focused production, fast tool exchange (also called SMED), on line control, Just in Time supplies and communication in real time. This TQM plan, heralded throughout the company, has thus stressed the increased importance of production and the quality strategies into a whole and integrated approach to the management of quality.

(6) Mersha and Adlakha (1992) compared a number of measures of service quality in several sectors. These measures were based on a questionnaire given to mature graduate MBA students. Scores are based on a scale of 1 = unimportant to 5 = extremely important. These are summarized in Tables 2.8 and 2.9. Note that the number following the comma indicates the rank of these scores.

Table 2.8: The importance of criteria of good quality.

Attribute of service	Physician	Retail Banking	Auto Maint.	College/ Univ.	Fast Food
Knowledge	4.89, 1	4.49, 4	4.74, 2	4.46, 2	3.15,10
Thoroughness and accuracy	4.87, 2	4.56, 2	4.73, 3	4.21, 3	3.53, 6
Consistency/Reliability	4.83, 3	4.51, 3	4.63, 4	4.12, 4	3.49, 8
Errors correction	4.80, 5	4.84, 1	4.81, 1	4.48, 1	3.99, 2
Reasonable costs	4.06, 10	3.98, 7	4.35, 5	4.06, 5	3.90, 3
Timely/prompt service	4.26, 6	4.24, 5	4.32, 6	3.78, 7	4.22, 1
Courtesy	4.12, 9	3.84, 8	3.44,10	3.61,10	3.65, 5
Enthusiasm/Helpfulness	4.15, 8	3.77, 9	3.55, 8	3.87, 6	3.25, 9
Friendliness	3.95,12	3.64,10	3.21,11	3.48,11	3.49, 7
Observance of Bus. Hours	4.16, 7	4.23, 6	3.89, 7	3.70, 9	3.05,11
Post-sales follow up	4.35, 5	2.88,12	3.50, 9	3.14,12	2.08,12
Pleasant environment	3.97,11	3.32,11	2.3312	3.77, 8	3.69, 4

(7) Services often involve the measurement and control of human resources. This is perhaps the most important facet of service management which requires a sensitivity to people, organization design and management. The importance and the extent of these problems require further attention and study. Nevertheless, with this concern in mind, discuss the evaluation of human resources in services, particularly in job performance. Emphasize how one would proceed to ascertain the following: (a) the reliability of job performance, (b) the reliability of measurements of such performance, (c) the relevant selection of attributes (characteristics) of the service

performance, and (d) the effects of uncontrollable external factors which cannot be attributed to the server. For further study, refer to Harris and Chaney (1969).

Table 2.9 Importance of criteria of poor quality by service type

Attribute	Physician	Retail Banking	Auto Main.	College/ Univ.	Fast Food
Lack of knowledge	4.80, 1	4.25, 3	4.63, 2	4.15, 3	3.27, 1
Employees indifferrent	4.60, 3	4.28, 2	4.25, 5	4.17, 2	3.85, 5
Reluctance to correct errors	4.67, 2	4.55, 1	4.64, 1	4.23, 1	3.85, 4
Rudeness	4.29, 6	4.13, 5	3.96, 7	3.97, 4	3.97, 3
Inconsistency	4.65, 5	4.06, 7	4.30, 4	3.87, 6	3.69, 7
Sloppy service	4.58, 4	4.19, 4	4.45, 3	3.89, 5	4.01, 1
High costs	3.74, 12	3.57, 10	3.95, 8	3.67, 9	3.49, 8
Slow response	4.14, 8	4.01, 8	3.97, 6	3.73, 8	4.01, 2
Impersonal or cold Treament of customers	4.24, 7	3.94, 9	3.67, 9	3.80, 7	3.71, 6
Failure to announce business hours	4.03, 10	4.07, 6	3.76, 9	3.61, 10	3.47, 9
No after sales service	4.10, 9	2.88, 12	3.28, 11	3.00, 12	2.26, 12
Inconducive environment	3.83, 11	3.36, 11	2.87, 12	3.53, 11	3.44, 10

(8) There are two complementary approaches in health care to the management of quality: Quality Assurance and Quality Improvement. Lohr (1990) lists four major purposes for a quality assurance program, including: (a) the detection of providers of unacceptable care with the intention of preventing them from maintaining their level of care or third party payers from reimbursing such services; (b) to identify providers of unacceptable care with the intention of improving such practices and increasing the quality of service; (c) to increase the average level of care delivered by a given group or providers, and to prevent the degradation of existing acceptable levels of care; and finally, (d) to motivate providers to ever higher levels of service. Further, due to the complex structure of health care delivery organizations, inherent information asymmetries (between providers and receivers), and the difficulty of establishing a price for health care quality, Lohr (1990) and Brown *et al.* (1993) emphasize the need for TQM-Continuous Improvement methods which have been successfully applied in industry, to be applied in health care as well. There are eight key aspects of continuous quality improvement as it applies to health care:

- Emphasis is on external customers or recipients of care, for the benefit of the patient.
- All facets of health care that underlie the benefit to patients (for example, facilities, equipment, providers, support, staff and

organizational policies) must be involved in a relentless, systematic and cooperative effort to improve care.

- The PDCA cycle (planning, doing, checking and acting) makes it possible for all to apply continuous improvement methods to daily work with responsiveness to patients' needs.
- The work of individuals and departments is recognized as interdependent. Internally, many departments are each other's suppliers and customers.
- Emphasis is placed on systems and processes. Organizations are seen as interrelated networks.
- The opinions of both customers and employees are continually incorporated into a program of review and improvement.
- Commitment at the highest levels of an organization is crucial. Successful implementation of continuous quality improvement methods requires a change in the corporate culture that must be sanctioned and supported.
- The process uses practical analysis tools such as flowcharts, line graphs, decision matrices, Pareto analyses and scatter diagrams, which have been adapted from decades of use in industrial quality control and which we will study in the next chapter.

2.6 Total Productive Maintenance (TPM)

TPM involves the application of traditional productive maintenance augmented by total participation. It was defined in 1971 by the Japan Institute of Plant Engineers (JIPE), the forerunner of the Japan Institute for Plant maintenance, as follows:

> TPM is designed to maximize equipment effectiveness (improving overall efficiency) by establishing a comprehensive productive maintenance system covering the entire life of the equipment, spanning all equipment-related fields (planning, use, maintenance, etc.) and, with the participation of all employees from top management down to shop floor workers, to promote productive maintenance through 'motivation management' or voluntary small group activities (Tsuchiya, 1992).

It focuses on the prevention of losses, including those resulting from breakdown, setup and adjustment, minor stoppages, speed, quality defects and rework and yield losses. When applied appropriately, it can prevent machines breakdowns significantly. At the Nishio pump factory of Aishin Seiki in Japan, prior to TPM implementation in 1979, Aishin Seiki experienced more than 700 equipment breakdowns per month; from May 1982 to 1984 (the year this particular reference was first published) there were *no* equipment breakdowns! The level of quality at the factory has been exceptional. For every one million pumps produced, there are a mere eleven defects (a defect rate of 0.000011%) (Nakajima, 1988). To achieve these results, TPM borrows intensively from and complements the TQM approach. TPM is equipment-directed, however, and lays an educational groundwork that trains as many workers as possible in the fundamental and key components of the equipment they use (Tsuchiya, 1992), together with total involvement of employees in production, maintenance and plant engineering. The objectives and basic activities of TPM are summarized in Table 2.10 and can be considered as complementary with TQM in establishing prevention programs. Further reading regarding this topic can be found in the references at the end of this chapter (Fumio and Masaji, 1992; Seeichi Nakajima, 1982; Steinbacher and Steinbacher, 1993; Tsuchiya,1992).

Table 2.10 Total Production Maintenance (TPM)

The Objectives	The Activities
A disciplined work place	Auto maintenance and the 5S
Efficient production lines	Planned maintenance
Reliable production lines	Equipment improvement
Agreeable production lines	MQP-Machine Quality People management to reduce defects
Training for equipment use	
Create a workplace to achieve these objectives	Preventive maintenance for cost saving and trouble free equipment startup
	Cross train workers, multi tasking
	Management by objectives

2.7 Reengineering and TQM

The multi trillion dollar plus investment of the 1980*s* in Information technology (IT) throughout Europe and the United States has changed the potential for productivity and quality. Until recently, business has emphasized the incremental growth of productivity and quality as a means to justify these investments on the one hand and augment competitiveness on the other. The TQM approach was devised and implemented throughout the 1980*s* and to this day has emphasized continuous improvement, rather than a dramatic breakthrough in business procedures. Cumulative and marginal changes have created business and industrial systems of great complexity however where improvement is difficult to achieve, and in many cases can become counter-productive, augmenting business unmanageability. At the same time, IT has augmented the capabilities of individuals to be more productive, has changed the work place, and the potential to network and work in groups. The changes heralded by the investment in IT is not only induced by computer speed and software versatility, but by the cultural environment of the market place, business and the work place. A marginal improvement, a requirement deeply imbedded in managerial practice, is no longer relevant, leading to industrial and business structures out of tune with their potential and their technology. Instead, breaking loose from past practices and procedures and treating the past as sunk costs has led successful firms to seek 'new ways' to redesign their business process. This led some consulting and some leading firms to experiment with another approach: 'Reengineering' or BPR (Business Process Redesign). These are imbedded in industrial engineering concepts and tools developed on the factory floors of the 1980*s* that have integrated IT and improved productivity dramatically. They seek to redesign business processes in order to provide quantum leaps in process capability through IT. BPR's essential premises are that IT can unleash innovation and motivate employees, it can provide greater traceability of everything the firm is involved with (and thus greater controls over work practices and their results), greater 'responsabilization' through decentralization, greater communication and integration. Its objectives are all encompassing involving at the same time cost reduction, time reduction, output quality and the quality of the work life (Davenport and Short, 1990). The effects of reengineering and BPR on current practice are also impressive. Leading-edge companies such as IBM, Xerox, Ford, Kodak and Hallmark have sought to reengineer, showing the way to the many firms that are reengineering, through simplification, organizational redesign (although often associated with downsizing and de-layering which is not, of course, the purpose of BPR), and through the integration of IT in the firm's business process (Hammer and Champy, 1993; Davenport, 1993).

Davenport (1993), for example, identifies nine capabilities IT can be used for to augment the potential of the business process and, at the same time, improve quality. These include: (1) *Automation,* (2) *Better, precise and timely information,* (3) *Alternate sequencing,* allowing the business to 'operate in parallel' and thus reduce the time consumed in everything the firm does, (4) *Tracking,* improving controls and traceability, which are essential for the management of quality and for quality management, (5) *Analysis* through speedier and effective tools, demystifying methods that were up to now the province of the experts, (6) *Geographic dispersion*, allowing a true decentralization while maintaining effective controls, (7) *Integration*, improving the coordination between tasks and processes, (8) *Intellectual,* augmenting and realizing the potential of 'brain power', (9)

Disintermediation, removing the need for intermediaries such as sales personnel, public exchanges, delayering of management and other activities.

There are many practical examples to support these capabilities. Mrs Fields Cookies was able to project their management control systems into over 400 stores by using a PC-based tool for sales support, personnel training and evaluation, and daily planning. This set of applications, networked to the headquarters location, enabled lower labour costs while increasing revenues and control over the work done at the geographically dispersed locations. Likewise, advances in telecommunications technology has enabled many companies, such as the Otis Elevator Company, Apple Computers, American Express and USAA to consolidate national and, in some cases, international customer support functions in single call-centre based location. The efficiencies achieved through the creative use of technology was often translated into increased customer satisfaction and thereby better quality (Pearlson and Whinston, 1993).

Reengineering has, of course, many similarities with TQM. Both are downstream oriented (whether that be an output, a consumer or a user), they emphasize auto-controls by letting decisions be taken at their information source, they maintain a global vision of the process and thus seek *global optimization rather than just local optimization of the business objectives*, and they follow some of the TQM procedures (see also Hammer and Champy, 1992). In practice, reengineering is difficult to realize, for it involves major disruptions and an investment in and expectation of extremely large and mostly ill-defined payoffs. For these reasons and because many firms who have reengineered did not succeed in their efforts, it is premature to call reengineering a technique, but rather, it is still an art to blend organizational design, IT tools and the experience gained through TQM to produce two digit growth in productivity, efficiency, quality and, most of all, in profitability.

2.8 Implementation

It is through successful implementation of TQM that hoped for benefits are realized. To succeed however, the respective role of management and its relationship to the many facets implied in implementing a TQM approach is necessary. Total Quality Management favours a lateral view of the process; the key problems are simplification, integration, coordination, communication and smoothing interfaces so that a coherent and flawless work environment is created. Therefore, this requires a great sensitivity to the parties involved, and the ability to communicate. Several approaches can be used, emphasizing 'internal or external consultants', 'incitative communication', 'persuasion with various degrees of power which can be exercised', and 'participative styles of management'. Each of these involves role playing, personalities, the situation at hand and of course a compatible organizational and managerial environment. So there aree no simple or quick answers that can lead to the successful implementation of a TQM culture or to a process of continuous improvement. Juran, Deming, Crosby, the Japanese, the ISO standards and so on have addressed these problems. While they all have the same intentions, they do differ with respect to the implementation process.

We should recognize that implementation is a dynamic process, occurring over a period of time and, in some cases involving risks and conflicts. Martin K. Starr, on the basis of past studies and experience, has indicated some conclusions regarding the 'hows', 'when' and 'where' of implementation. These conclusions encompass

- The dynamics of implementation which recognize implementation as a time dependent process where both the risks and rates at which plans are introduced are to be accounted for. A change from simple to complex models cannot be sudden, but must be smooth, minimizing the friction and conflicts that a given solution or change induces within the organization or firm.
- The coupling of managerial style and organizational structure to the implementation strategy. For example, centralizing implementation in a decentralized organization may encounter some difficulties, since it can be in conflict to the 'organization's culture'. Therefore, responsibility for implementation will best be imposed on those elements in the organization that are most responsible for change, namely management (but not exclusively management).

In these approaches emphasis is put on the qualitative characteristics of the management process and how the 'solution' reinforces the basic intentions (i.e. the goals of TQM) of this process. Some of the following guidelines may be helpful:

- Emphasize simplicity and transparency.
- Recognize that management is an essential part of the process.
- Reduce and simplify administrative procedures.
- Be sensitive to people's needs and their environment.
- Seek robust solutions which are insensitive to false assumptions or unexpected change.

These criteria are by no means exhaustive. They remind us, however, that problem solving is not an end in itself, but a means.

Problems

1. Define TQM. How is your definition different or similar to good management practices?

2. What procedure would you recommend in implementing a TQM program in a hospital, a factory and a restaurant? How would you define, in each case, the goals and the procedure to follow?

3. Compare the goal stated by the CEO of HP (Hewlett Packard), John Young, $10X$ (which means tenfold improvement in defect reduction in 10 years) versus Motorola's Chairman Bob Galvin of 6σ (reducing defects to 3.4 ppm, parts per million), and finally, versus Xerox, Ricoh and NEC, who establish as goals the reception of Deming's award.

4. Devise measures of performance for an R&D project for developing a new product. What tools would you use to select the essential variables to concentrate on and design the product?

5. Discuss the similarities and the differences between TQM and reengineering. Discuss in particular their level of change, their starting point, the frequency of change, the time required to gain an amelioration, management participation in the process of change, their market orientation, their emphasis on sourcing policies, the scope of the activity and its orientation, the risks implied, the primary enablers (for example, SPC, IT, Participation, Human Resources and so on), and finally the type of organizational and cultural change that is implied by TQM and reengineering.

6. Customer/user satisfaction is a function of the program's maintainability, customer/user support effectiveness, reliability, safety and usability. Each of these, in turn, is influenced by a number of factors. For maintainability, structure simplicity, modularity, and so on, are important. For usability, requirements traceability, validation and interface suitability are needed. Safety is affected by testing effectiveness, fault tolerance and robustness. Reliability is determined by testing effectiveness and performance measurement. Finally, customer/user support effectiveness is a function of delivery control (variability), help line and bulletin boards, problem fix and cycle time. On the basis of this information, construct a fishbone diagram in the case of problems with customer/user satisfaction.

7. Define the concept of quality in education. How does the concept vary when viewed from the educators', parents' and society's points of view? What are the similarities and what are the differences? Give five measurements that can be used to measure the quality of education of a school. Is there a way to reconcile their differences and apply the TQM approach to quality education? (for further reading see Glasser, 1990; Herman, 1992; Melvin, 1991).

References

AFCERQ (1988) Le *Guide de la Qualité,* Editions d' Organization.

AFNOR (1986a) *Gérer la Qualité,* Normes Afnor, Edition AFNOR, Paris.

AFNOR (1986b) *Réussir l'Audit Qualité,* Edition AFNOR, Paris.

Brown B.S., S.F. Lefkowitz and J.D. Aguera-Areas (1993) Continuous quality improvement in health care services, IC2 Institute, Austin, Texas.

Coile R.C. Jr. (1990) *The New Medicine: Reshaping Medical Practice and Health Care Management,* Aspen Publishers, MD.

Collignon E. and M. Wissler (1988), *Qualité et Competitivité des Entreprises, 2e edition,* Economica, Paris.

Crosby P.B. (1979) *Quality is Free: The Art of Making Quality Certain,* McGraw. Hill

Crosby P.B. (1984) *Quality without Tears,* McGraw Hill.

Davenport T. (1993) *Process Innovation: Reengineering Work Through Information Technology,* Boston, Harvard Business School Press.

Davenport T. and J. Short (1990) The new industrial engineering: information technology and business process redesign, *Sloan Management Review,* Summer, 11-27.

Deming W.E. (1975) On Some Statistical Aids Towards Economic Production, *Interfaces,* vol 5, no.4, 1-5.

Deming E.W. (1982) *Quality, productivity and competitive position,* Cambridge, MA, MIT Press.

Deming E.W. (1986) Out of the Crisis, MIT Center for Advanced Engineering Study, Cambridge, MA.

EFQM (1992) Total Quality Management, The European Model for self-Appraisal, guidelines for identifying and adressing total quality issues, *The European Foundation for Quality Management,* 5612 AA Eindhoven, The Netherlands.

Feigenbaum A.V. (1993) *Total Quality Control,* McGraw Hill (3rd edition).

Fumio Gotoh and Taliri Masaji (1992) *TPM Implementation-A Japanese Approach,* New York, McGraw Hill.

Geyndt De. Willy (1970) Five approaches for assessing the quality of care, *Hospital Administration,* Winter, 21-42.

Glasser W. (1990) *The Quality School, Managing Students without Coercion,* New York, Harper and Row.

Grant E.L. and R.S. Leavenworth (1988) *Statistical Quality Control*, 6th ed., McGraw Hill.

Hall R.W. (1983) *Zero Inventories,* Homewood, ILL Dow Jones-Irwin.

Hammer M. and J. Champy (1993) *Reengineering the Corporation*, New York, Harper Collins.

Harris D.H. and F.B. Chaney (1969) *Human Factors in Quality Assurance,* New York, Wiley.

Herman J.J. (1992) Total quality management basics: TQM comes to school, *School Business Affairs,* **58**, 4, 1992, 20-28.

Imai Masaaki (1990) *Kaizen: La Clé de la Competitivité Japonaise,* Eyrolles, Paris.

Ishikawa K. (1976) *Guide to Quality Control,* Asian Productivity Organization, Tokyo.

Juran J.M. *et al.* (1974) *Quality Control Handbook, 3rd* edition, McGraw Hill.

Juran J.M. (1988) *Juran on Planning for Quality,* New York, The Free Press.

Lohr K.N. (Ed.) (1990) *Medicare. A Strategy for Quality Assurance,* vol. 1, Washington, D.C., National Academy Press.

Magne Pierre-Joseph (1990) *La gestion de la qualité totale: une nouvelle approche de l'organisation de l'entreprise dans le context économique Suisse,* Editions Universitaire Fribourg Suisse.

Melvin C. (1991) Translating Deming's 14 points for education, *The School Administrator,* **9**, 19-23.

Mersha T. and V. Adlakha (1992) Attributes of service quality: The consumer's perspective, *Int. J. of Service Industry Management,* **3**, 3, 34-45.

Morse W.J., H.P. Roth and K.M. Poston (1987) *Measuring, Planning and Controlling Quality Costs,* National Association of Accountants, Montvale, NJ.

Ouchi W.G. (1981) *Theory Z : How America Business Can Meet the Japanese Challenge,* Addison-Wesley, Reading, MA.

Parasuraman A, V.A. Zeithmal and L.L. Berry (1985) A conceptual model of service quality and its implication for further research, *Journal of Retailing,* Fall.

Parasuraman A, V.A. Zeithmal and L.L. Berry (1988) SERVQUAL, A multiple item scale for measuring customer perceptions of service quality, *Journal of Retailing,* **64**, 13-7.

Pearlson K. and A. Whinston (1993) Customer Support Issues for the 21st Century, *Center for Information Systems Management,* MSIS Department, The University of Texas, Austin.

Schoenberger R. (1982) *Japanese Productivity Techniques,* Free Press, New York.

Seiichi Nakajima (1988) *Introduction to TPM-Total Productive Maintenance,* Productivity Press, Cambridge, MA.

Steinbacher, H.R. and N.L. Steinbacher (1993) *TPM for America, What It Is and Why You Need It,* Productivity Press, Cambridge, MA.

Surette Gerald J. (1986) The ATT Quality System, *ATT Technical Journal,* 21- 29.

Tsuchiya, Seiji (1992) *Quality Maintenance-Zero Defects Through Equipment Management,* Productivity Press, Cambridge MA.

Zeithaml V. A. Parasuraman and L.L. Berry (1990) *Delivering Quality Service*, Free Press, New York.

Additional references

Box G. (1993) Quality improvement-The new industrial revolution, *International Statistical Review,* **61**, 3-19.

Collignon E. and M. Wissler (1988) *Qualité et Competitivité des Entreprises, 2e edition,* Economica, Paris.

Connell L.W. (1984) Quality at the Source: The First Step in Just in Time Production, *Quality Progress,* **17**, 11, 44-45.

Dessler G. and D.L. Farrow (1990) Implementing a successful quality improvement program in a service company: Winning the Deming Prize, *International J. of Service Industry Management,* **1**, 2, 45-53.

Dunaud M. (1987) *Maitriser la Qualite et les Couts*, Masson, Paris.

Harrington J.H. (1987) The Improvement Process, McGraw Hill.

Hradesky John (1987) *Productivity and Quality Improvement,* New York, McGraw Hill.

US Dept of Defense (1965) *A Guide to Zero Defects Quality and Reliability Assurance Handbook,* 4115.12.

Wadsworth H.M., K.S. Stephens and A.B. Godfrey (1986) *Modern Methods for Quality Improvement,* Wiley, New York.

CHAPTER 3

The tools of quality control and its management

3.1 Introduction

At the beginning of the century, when production was an art and quality a measure of this art, the tools of quality were those used by the artist, unique and irreproducible. When production became more systematic and organized, rationalization of work, division of labour, standardization and 'deresponsabilization' of workmanship induced the use of supervision and controls of various sorts. These were needed for two reasons: first, to ensure that parts production was meeting the production standards so that each part could be used as a substitute in a mass production system; and second, to ensure that intended production was also performed according to agreed upon standards. At the beginning of the century, 'sabotage' (when workers would put their sabots wooden shoes into machines to stop or destroy the process operation) was becoming troublesome. Supervision of people and processes were needed. Today, the problems are different and the tools needed have also changed. Quality is a far broader concept, more complex and more difficult to manage and the tools more varied. Quality is, as we have seen earlier, viewed in a broader setting, affected and affecting a large number of factors and variables, which require the handling and control of a massive inflow of information and complex control systems. The management of quality (though still an art) is becoming increasingly dependent on data and statistical analyses. In this chapter we shall introduce some tools for representing and analysing data and problems. These span fishbone (Ishikawa) diagrams, Pareto charts, descriptive schemes such as scatter plots, graphing techniques, statistical analysis and decision making tools. These tools can be used to detect, formulate and analyse problems, as well as provide solutions which, in turn, can be implemented and controlled. These tools are summarized in Figure 3.1. Some of these tools are used by managers and operators alike, and are thus both easy to use and convenient for communication. Subsequently, in Chapters 5, 6 and 7 we consider application of the statistical approach to quality management and control.

Statistics are very important in the management of variations and generally in the management of quality. Basically, it is the science of 'making sense' out of data in order to reach decisions of some sort. To do so, statistics provide procedures to collect, organize, summarize and analyse data in a meaningful way. This is how sampling (Chapter 5) and experiments (Chapter 7) are designed and performed. Graphs can be used as a first approximation to represent trends, provide an intuitive representation of data and so on, but they are not sufficient. Qualitative, quantitative and statistical studies are required to provide insights and solutions which cannot be detected just through visual and simple interpretation of data. The importance of data and their analysis in the management and control of quality cannot, therefore, be understated. Practitioners often measure 'things' and collect data without a prior design and without following proper procedures. There are, as a result, some difficulties in analysing and using the data to reach some decision. For these reasons, statistics and statistical analyses are necessary to improve the management of quality.

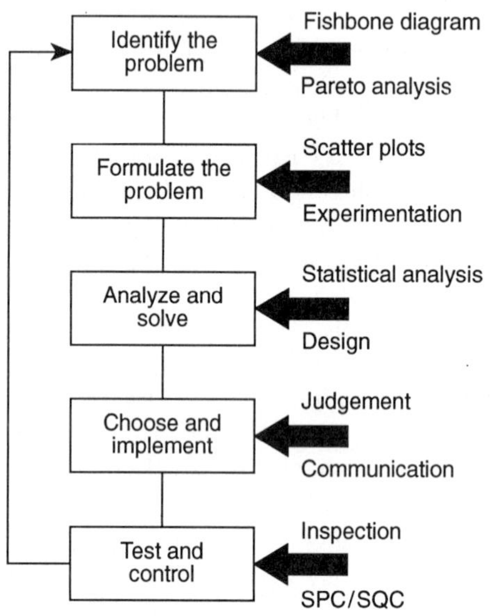

Figure 3.1: The tools of TQM.

3.2 The tools of TQM

Ishikawa (1976), as well as Georges Box (1993), recommend a number of tools which can be used effectively in Total Quality Management. These tools are simple, with the potential of providing important information and insights regarding the main causes of a process or product non-standard performance. They include: brainstorming, tally sheets (or check sheets), histograms, stratification, Pareto diagrams, charts (run, control and Cusum charts), scatter plots, cause-effects diagrams and, finally, various graphs. These are simple tools which do not require much statistical training for their use and are useful to communicate and to deal with the many types of problems we encounter in the management of quality. In Figure 3.1, some of the tools and the problems to which they are applied are outlined. The simple TQM tools are important at the conceptual stages when the important variables and problems to be handled are selected. At this stage, the ability to exchange and communicate are needed to facilitate the successful implementation of the TQM program. Below we briefly consider some of these tools together with some applications. In subsequent chapters, we consider other tools such as statistical sampling, experimental design and robust design.

Brainstorming is used by a group of people involved in the solution of a quality problem to generate ideas freely and to evaluate them. There is no single way to manage such groups. In general, however, it is important to foster imagination, to open communication channels and to generate *simple* ideas. Brainstorming should not be used to hinder creativity or impose a point of view. It should not clutter management with unmanageable alternatives. Rather, simplicity, group discussion seeking to foster a consensus and the motivation to act is needed. Through brainstorming, potential root causes of quality problems can be identified.

Tally sheets are used to count the number of objects (or subjects) in a group that fall into one of a number of classes. How many components were rejected; how many failed; from which process and for what reasons? How many complaints arrived, for what reasons? The idea is simple. On a sheet, we construct rows for the reasons A, B, C and so on. Then we take each complaint and tally the specific cause by entering an indicator in the relevant row. When all complaints have been tabulated, we simply count the number in each row. The data can then be stratified, i.e. it can be refined further into product category, sex of complainants, etc. The underlying theory of tally sheets is 'stratification of data', seeking to construct strata that are internally homogeneous (in the sense that they share a common characteristic). Between strata, though, they exhibit specific and well defined differences (i.e. externally heterogeneous). For example, for the data set in Table 3.1 we can construct a tally sheet by defining five classes (10-12), (12-14), (14-16), (16- 18) and (18-20). The numbers in the third column denote the number of times the data set points fall is a given class category indicated by the tally sheet.

Table 3.1: The data set.

15.7	13.5	15.6	15.3	14.0	16.0	16.2	14.1	16.9	16.5
16.2	13.7	14.8	15.2	10.9	15.1	17.4	14.5	15.5	17.5
15.9	16.7	15.8	12.5	13.3	11.0	14.2	11.8	15.6	14.4
13.6	12.8	14.3	14.7	16.4	15.8	19.0	13.6	16.5	13.7
18.0	13.6	14.4	17.2	15.9	13.4	16.3	16.3	13.5	15.1
16.6	14.5	15.1	14.5	15.1	14.5	18.2	16.4	15.0	14.0
17.2	15.0	15.6	13.4	13.6	15.4	14.8	12.6	16.6	12.1
17.6	14.7	16.8	15.5	12.6	13.1	15.4	13.4	14.8	15.1
16.1	13.6	13.9	15.5	14.3	13.8	13.4	15.0	14.2	15.7
12.7	15.8	18.3	16.1	14.3	18.0	17.2	15.0	17.2	15.5

Scatter plots demonstrate the relationship between two variables so that a visual expression of a pattern (or a lack of it) can be obtained. For example, Figure 3.2. shows such plots. Scatter plots are used in quality studies for several purposes. First they may indicate correlation (positive or negative between variables). Second, they can point to a linear or non-linear relationship between functions. Third, they can detect outliers. Fourth they may point out stratification in the data by graphically showing that certain data points with common properties aggregate together. Finally, when a scatter plot is not evenly distributed, there is some underlying relationship between the variables which we seek to explain.

Histograms are an effective way to organize data and recognize that these are measurements of a characteristic or an attribute which can represent the data set by a number of parameters which *summarize* its basic characteristics. Histograms are then used to process measures of location, measures of variation, and to provide a visual view of the distribution of the characteristic. Measures of location include the mean, the mode and the median, while measures of variation include the variance (or standard deviation), the mean absolute deviation, the range and the coefficient of variation.

Table 3.2: The tally sheet

Classes	Tally	Sum	Freq.	Cum. Freq.
10 – 12	///	03	0.03	0.03
12 – 14	////....	24	0.24	0.27
14 – 16	////.........	45	0.45	0.72
16 – 18	///.....	23	0.23	0.95
18 – 20	/////	05	0.05	1.00
Totals		*100*	*1.00*	

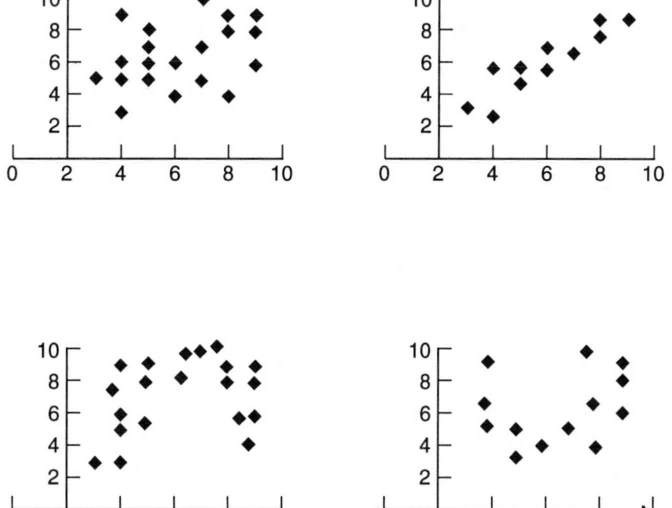

Figures 3.2: Various scatter diagrams.

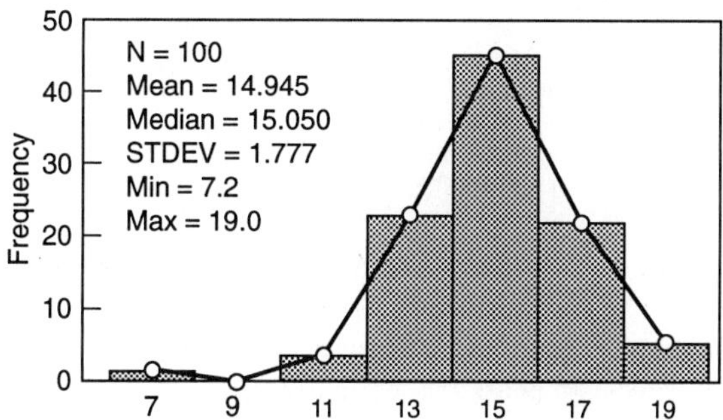

Figure 3.3: A histogram and frequency distribution.

A histogram is a representation of the data set into classes. The number of data points in each class is an indicator of the class probability which we use to construct an empirical probability distribution. Given the data set in Table 3.1 and the tally sheet in Table 3.2 we construct a histogram as shown in Figure 3.3.

Cause-effect or (Ishikawa) Fishbone diagrams are a systematic organization of data to help us distinguish between cause and effect, and relate specific causes to specific effects. Often, symptoms overwhelm the causes, so that it is no longer simple to distinguish which is which. Cause-effects diagrams, combined with Pareto charts, can be helpful in providing a graphical representation of the causes and the effects they induce, and by identifying the basic causes of the underlying problem studied (and not only its symptoms). To construct such diagrams we proceed as follows: (1) Determine the problem to be studied. This is the diagram backbone. (2) Regroup facts on cards and regroup causes, each with its own ID. (3) Then, we select first level causes (but no more than seven). These first levels represent the major bones, all entering the backbone. (4) We then select second level causes, which are middle size bones, entering the major bones. (5) Establish a cause-effect relationship. Then, (6) we repeat steps (4) and (5) on the second level causes (smaller bones) until no more causes can be found. (7) We generalize to first level causes. Finally, (8) we emphasize the principal causes at the second level. These are the *key factors* which will define the problem to study and eliminate.

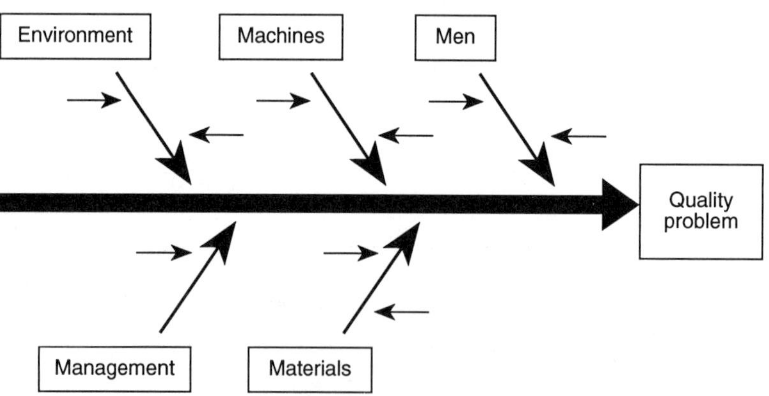

Figure 3.4: An Ishikawa-Fishbone diagram.

The construction of a fishbone diagram is much more difficult than one would at first suspect. It is an art, which requires the ability to distinguish between the many factors that can affect the characteristic under study, and order them causally. In doing so, some causes may have several effects, and there may be complex interactions which might not be revealed by the diagram. Nevertheless, the simplicity of such diagrams makes it a useful and a practical tool to elaborate controllable and non-controllable causal factors in the study of an essential quality characteristic.

Pareto charts are based on classical notions of utility, although they are named after Wilfred Pareto's wealth distribution curve devised in the late 1800s. The number of variables which affect the quality of a product, a process manufacture, service delivery or any other facet of the management process, can be numerous, only a few of which have an important economic effect. There are a 'vital few' of economic impact and a 'trivial many' of no economic impact, as expounded by Juran. As a result, Pareto Charts are constructed as bar graphs (see Figure 3.5) with their cumulative curve, that rank causes of process variation by their effect on quality. Pareto analysis allows one to correlate these causes to the cost/benefits of quality, and thereby obtain obvious indicators for approaching the problems of quality at their source. In this sense, it is possible to:

(a) Elaborate the total number of factors which affect quality.
(b) Provide a cost estimate for each.
(c) Rank each of these factor in a decreasing order.
(d) Define the class 'A' factors as the top.
(e) Define the class 'B' factors as the middle.
(f) Define the class 'C' factors as the bottom.

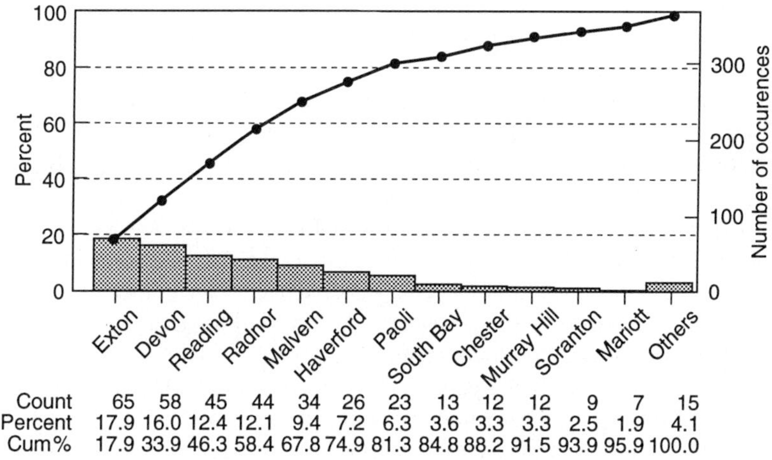

Count	65	58	45	44	34	26	23	13	12	12	9	7	15
Percent	17.9	16.0	12.4	12.1	9.4	7.2	6.3	3.6	3.3	3.3	2.5	1.9	4.1
Cum%	17.9	33.9	46.3	58.4	67.8	74.9	81.3	84.8	88.2	91.5	93.9	95.9	100.0

Figure 3.5: A Pareto chart.

Pareto charts are a rough diagnostic tool which can be helpful in constructing cause-effect diagrams and a useful complement to control charts (studied in Chapter 6). Quoting Price (1984), "This is the usefulness of Pareto analysis; it signals those targets likely to yield maximum results by the deployment of limited effort. In acknowledging that there is little point in frittering away resources through fighting where the battle isn't raging, it pinpoints the most vulnerable areas of the enemy's line, so to speak. It is a technique which finds profitable employment when you are required to sort out a messy quality control situation. When consumer's rejections are bombarding you so thick and so fast that you don't know where to begin, Pareto tells you." To see how this is done we shall consider an example below. Although Pareto charts are widely used, they should be carefully evaluated. We may construct Pareto charts along several criteria, which will make their comparison difficult, therefore reaching 'a decision' based on an over-simplification of the problems at hand may also be costly. Typically, we shall distinguish between Pareto charts of phenomena (such as quality, costs, delivery and safety related variables, for example, and Pareto related causes associated with operators, machines, raw materials management and so on.

To construct a Pareto chart we basically proceed as follows.

- We define what is the problem and what are the factors to study. We define what data is relevant to the problem and how to collect it.
- We construct a Tally sheet where rows denote the factors.
- We use the results thus obtained to draw the Pareto chart.

By ordering the factors by the frequencies through the Tally sheet (or based on some other relevant criterion), we construct the bar chart and draw the cumulative curve.

An application is considered next. Assume that a number of plants have been the source of a number of defects. The data gathered over a given amount of time has indicated the following number for each of the plants investigated: (Paoli, 23), (Malvern, 34), (Exton, 65), (Chester, 12), (Devon, 58), (Reading 45), (Scranton 9), (Coatesville, 2), (Haverford, 26), (Radnor, 44), (Harrow, 4), (Renquyst, 5), (Murray Hill, 12), (Marriott, 7), (South Bay, 13), (Rommert, 4). The Pareto chart for this data is given in Figure 3.6 where we note that four plants account for 58.4% of all defects, while the first eight plants account for 4.8% of defects. Of course, with such information on hand, management time and sources can be focused on plants which produce the greatest number of defects.

Value analysis is used for product design (or redesign) and to cut costs while maintaining the same quality. Similar to Pareto charts, it is essential to concentrate attention on the elements which bring greater added value. Value analysis seeks to justify a product design improvement and the reduction of cost through simple economic analysis, while maintaining a given level of quality. It defines 'cost' as everything which does not contribute to quality, while it defines 'value' as that which contributes to quality. Technically, a value analysis computes the contribution to quality improvement versus the cost of this improvement, or:

$$\text{Value} = \Delta(QI)/\Delta\ (\text{Cost})$$

Given the importance of value analysis, the reader is referred to Ishikawa (1990, p.410) for further study.

FMECA or Failure Mode, Effects and Criticality Analysis, is an approach to evaluate the reliability and safety of a design, a product, a process or a system by considering the potential failures, the resulting effects on the product, process, system and personnel, and the criticality of these effects. It results in a procedure for determining the basic causes of failure and defining actions to minimize their effects. It consists of the identification of problems or critical faults. Namely, by defining the *failure mode* (the hows), in which failure can occur as well as why, through *failure cause analysis.* In addition, *failure effects*, describing the actual results of the failure for each possible failure mode, are obtained together with their criticality, which establishes the category of hazard. Results of FMECA analyses are then applied by devising a program to reduce the probability that a particular problem arises. It emphasizes, as recommended in TQM, developing a preventive approach to problem occurrences through the maintenance of critical effects. FMECA can be used together with Pareto charts and Ishikawa diagrams by assigning probabilities of recurrence to the main causes and in evaluating their effects on quality.

Quantitatively, the application of FMECA requires that each failure mode be defined in terms of its occurrence probability (O), the probability that it is not detected (D) as well as its implication to the user (preferably in terms of costs), denoted by S. The product $O * D * S$ may then be called the index of criticality C, which is used to rank order problems to be attended to:

$$C = (O) * (D) * (S)$$

When a problem has an index which is greater than some critical value C^*, then the problem is dealt with and solved. Its index of criticality is then revised. Throughout FMECA, cross-functional groups are used. FMECA is extremely useful because it is simple to conceptualize, even though the practical definition of probabilities (O), (D) and the calculation of costs (S) to the user, is far from simple.

There are various tools used together with FMECA, for example, *fault-tree analysis* (or logic diagrams). Fault-tree analysis is a useful technique applied in reliability and safety engineering. For example, it measures system safety by determining the probability than an undesired event or fault will occur. It is a graphical representation of the logic that relates certain events or primary failures to an ultimate undesired event. It can use Boolean (0,1) algebra as a modelling tool to represent the flows of system function failures. When systems are complex, based on network-like representations and dependencies, boolean algebra can be used to determine the effect of specific failures (occurring with some known probabilities) on overall or component failure (or their probabilities). The usefulness of fault-tree analysis is extremely varied. It can be used to determine the causes of an accident, to discover failure combinations which otherwise would not have been recognized as causes of the event being analysed and to display system configurations in design review. Failure-tree analysis has long been practiced in reliability engineering (it is believed that it was initiated in the development of the Minuteman Missile), and there are many books and research papers which deal with this topic (Shooman, 1968; Barlow and Proschan, 1965; Kapur and Lamberson, 1977).

Problem

A firm observes a certain type of defects in the course of its manufacturing process. The defects' causes are well defined, and their occurrence recorded. Each defect type incurs a cost to the manufacturer. Assuming that all defects are detected, then the data in Table 3.3 is obtained. In this table, note in particular that the probabilities (O) are calculated by relative occurrence of the events, and that $(D) = 1$ and is therefore not used in our computations. Finally, note that the last column has ranked each of the defect types by their criticality: (a) Assume that defect types are not detected with equal ease. In fact, the probability of detection is presumed to be equal 0.85, except for defect types $(6, 8, 11, 15, 16)$ which have a detection probability of 0.50. On the basis of this information, what should the ranking of defect types be? (b) What is the expected value of a perfect detection method? (c) What is the value of improving the detection probabilities by 1%?

Table 3.3: Data set for FMECA.

	No. of defects	Types	Frequency	Cost $	Expected Cost	Ranking (uncrit.)
1	23	Dent	0.063361	200	12.6722	15
2	34	Poor Seal	0.093664	100	9.3664	14
3	65	*O*-Ring	0.179063	50	8.9532	13
4	12	Finish A	0.033058	25	0.8264	4
5	58	Finish *B*	0.159780	36	5.7521	12
6	45	Dent	0.123967	150	18.5950	16
7	9	Screw A	0.024793	28	0.6942	2
8	2	Connector	0.005510	35	0.1928	1
9	26	*O*-Ring *B*	0.071625	42	3.0083	8
10	44	Scratch	0.121212	14	1.6970	7
11	4	Screw *B*	0.011019	64	0.7052	3
12	5	Connect. *B*	0.013774	75	1.0331	5
13	12	Connect. *C*	0.033058	45	1.4876	6
14	7	Back Dent	0.019284	160	3.0854	9
15	13	Front Dent	0.035813	125	4.4766	11
16	4	Ring	0.011019	350	3.8567	10

Project management is used to coordinate and monitor the performance of many activities which involve repetitive tasks and routine activities, some form of standard reporting system can be setup to facilitate this control. However, when a non-routine, complex and perhaps costly project is to be undertaken, computer aided project management (using CPM and PERT techniques) can be used to organize, control, monitor and allocate resources (time, men, money and materials). Some activities may require time and resources before other activities can start (which will require that we specify the order in which the activities can be done). The methods of CPM and PERT can be helpful by telling us explicitly which tasks are likely to be critical for a quick, economically efficient termination of the project. We refer to CPM when project scheduling is based on activity times which are assumed known and fixed (i.e. all the activity's duration times are deterministic), and we refer to PERT when these activities can at best be defined probabilistically. Then, we provide estimates for the activities' duration times. Project management is as much a pure management tool as a technical aid. A project is defined in terms of a large number of activities or tasks which are interdependent due to precedence constraints, (i.e. one activity must be finished prior to another being started). Since most objectives in project management seek to move as efficiently as possible to the realization of the project, there is also an emphasis on giving greater priority to the management of bottlenecks (which are defined as the activities on the critical path).

The realization of a project uses the following sequences:

- *Plan the project*: *by specifying its activities **by specifying precedence relationships between activities ***by pointing out the appropriate constraints to be imposed on the management of the project, time schedules, resources and so on.
- *Implement and Control*: *by allocation of time **by allocation of resources ***by allocation of moneys
- *Update the Plan: And back to the Plan ... allocations ... implementation....*

Of course, in such a sequence of activities, the managerial challenge and objective is to integrate time, costs, resources (monies, manpower and materials) and carry the project out with the least cost and time. The application of project management is not achieved without difficulty, however. There are many problems, including:

Data problems: it is often difficult to obtain data relating to the time needed to finish an activity, to set up the sequences properly, to pre-specify the resources that will be needed, and so on.

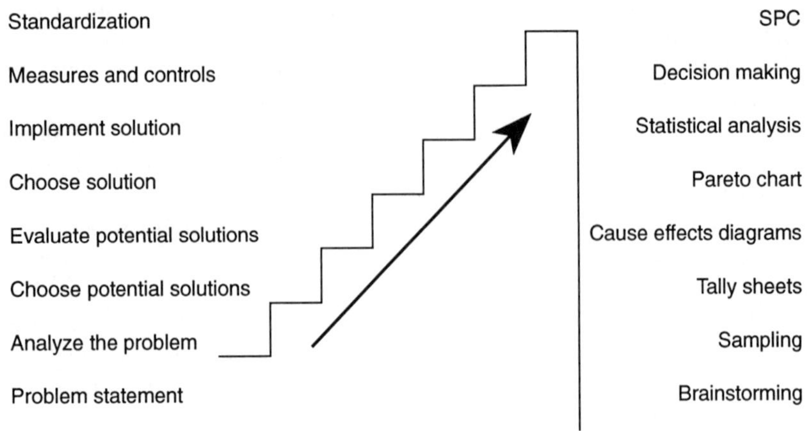

Figure 3.6: The techniques and problems steps.

Forecasts: it is doubtful that a program will evolve exactly according to plan due to variability in the implementation of activities. As a result, monitoring and coordination may be difficult, requiring a continuous update of the plan such that the project will not serve the plan, the plan will serve the project! The study and practice of project management techniques are extensive, and require much further study, which is not considered in this text (even though it is a useful tool in the management of quality). The reader is, therefore, referred to the references at the end of this chapter.

The TQM tools used to detect, study, analyse and implement programs of TQM can be extremely useful. Together they provide a toolkit which can help management deal with each of the problems encountered at each step of the design and realization process. In Figure 3.6, we summarize the essential steps that might be followed. Subsequently, we consider a number of applications.

Problems

1. Consider a trucker whose essential problem involves delivery delays. The set of all relevant factors (defined after brainstorming with drivers and managers) which have contributed to delay include 'Truck breakdown', 'Drivers absenteeism', 'Delivery in traffic hours', 'Weather conditions' and related reasons. We shall denote these factors by the index $1, 2, 3, \ldots, n$. Data was collected representing the number of times a specific factor was at cause in a late delivery. The following Tally sheet, based on 200 such instances was then assembled as in Table 3.4.

Table 3.4: Data tally sheet for delays.

Factor	*Index*	*Tally*	*Total*
Breakdown	1	////////...//	45
Absenteeism	2	////....////	28
Repairs	3	//	2
No communication	4	////...////	12
Weather	5	////	4
Circulation	6	//	2
Time of day	7	////...////	30
..	8	///	5
...	9	////...///	75
....	10	/////	5
.....	11	///...////	12
Total			220

Having constructed the Tally sheet, arrange these factors in an increasing order and then construct the bar chart as well as the chart of cumulative sums. What conclusions can be reached on the basis of these charts?

2. In a production system, rejects over a period of time (for example, one month) have been evaluated and classified following the departments responsible for producing these rejects. A table of results of such outcomes is outlined below (in $1000).

Table 3.5a: Departmental costs.

Dept.	1	2	3	4	5	6	7	8	9	10	12	13	14	15
Cost	100	32	50	19	4	30	40	80	55	150	160	5	10	20

Table 3.5b: Ordered costs.

Dept. no.	Ordered Costs	Cum. Costs	Cum. % Costs
11	160	160	21.2
10	150	310	41.0
1	100	410	54.3
8	88	490	64.9
9	55	545	72.18
3	50	595	78.8
7	40	635	84.0
2	32	667	88.0
6	30	697	92.0
14	20	717	95.0
4	19	736	97.5
13	10	746	98.8
12	5	751	99.5
5	4	755	100.0

Table 3.5c: The Departments ordered.

Class (% of total)	Departments
A, (78.8)	11,10,1,8,9,3
B, (18.7)	7,2,6,14,4
C, (2.5)	13,12,5

To construct a Pareto chart we first construct Table 3.5b which orders departments in decreasing costs order, providing also percentages and cumulative costs. Departments can now be classified into a number of groups (say three) such as A, B and C. The first group, A, accounts for 78.80% (which is the closest to 80%) of the costs. It includes departments $11, 10, 1, 8, 9$ and 3. These departments will be investigated in greater detail, providing the largest potential cost reduction. The proportion for the number of departments involved in this case is $6/14$. The remaining departments are classified in classes B and C, as shown on Table 3.5c. Provide alternative representations based on various distribution of cost and the number of department and thus obtain a number of possible graphs (based on the criteria used in constructing the Pareto charts). Finally, discuss these graphs.

3. A firm has an unusual rate of return due to faulty production, product design, installation and possibly other reasons. Data was collected daily over a week, and the reason for product returns organized into four categories. These are given in Table 3.6.

Table 3.6: The Data set (Problem 3).

	Monday	Tuesday	Wednesday	Thursday	Friday	Total	%
Materials	3	10	0	2	1	16	19
Faulty assembly	2	0	6	2	0	10	11
Faulty design	2	20	6	6	2	36	43
Installation	5	14	2	0	3	24	27
Totals	12	44	14	10	6	86	100

Draw a bar chart which will clearly demonstrate that faulty design and poor installation are the two essential factors accounting for 80% of returns. Note that each of these problems can now be studied further and broken down into subcauses. In fact, we can organize the following data as a cause-effect diagram, with each cause labelled with a 'frequency' of occurrence as well. When economic considerations are included, it is important to associate dollar figures to each of these. For example, say that these costs of failure are as given in Table 3.7. Apply FMECA and compute the average cost of a product return. Discuss the effects of alternative ways to organize and use the information which is collected to investigate a specific problem.

Table 3.7: Data summary.

Factor	Cost	Freq.	Cost×Freq.
Materials	\$700	0.19	133
Faulty assembly	\$1500	0.11	165
Faulty design	\$5000	0.43	2150
Installation	\$500	0.27	135
Totals		1.00	2583

4. A coffee vending machine can have a number of causes for non-standard performance. These include: (1) water too cold, (2) water too hot, (3) polluted water, (4) coffee of poor quality, (5) poor grinding of coffee. Each of these factors can be attributed to a number of causes. Construct an appropriate two level diagram for this problem.

5. A firm producing spare parts for consumer items sold both directly through the firm's outlets and through a number of retailers has decided to install an information system for tracking its image and the quality of its products and services as perceived by its clients and retailers. The firm suggests that there are several dimensions to its products and services: (a) Product performance related; (b) Service related; (c) Price and competitive based factors; and (d) Delay, response and logistic factors. Further, quality has characteristics which are technical, economic and subjective (human). Construct an approach which will identify the indicators (what they could be if it is a firm selling spare parts for European cars), then use Ishikawa, Pareto charts, FMECA and the other tools indicated here to institute the desired program by the firm.

6. For the study of hotels' quality performance, we may use the following variables: service time at breakfast, energy costs, laundry costs, stolen property, litigation costs, reservation errors, turnover of personnel, percent return clients, percent occupancy, percent clients rejected because of full occupancy, number of reservations cancelled, number of complaints, time at which rooms are free and available for clients, and so on. Take these and other potential variables and list those that can be controlled and those than cannot. Then suggest five variables for which some data ought to be collected, and explain why.

7. A firm that produces two complex products, selling each at a price of \$350 and \$950 each, has accumulated statistics over the year regarding the number of defect types per product and the number of units produced in each product category which was defective. The yearly sales volume for each of the products is given by 10,000 and 3000 respectively. The data, including the actual costs incurred for each of the months directly affected to non-quality, is summarized in Table 3.8. On the basis of this table, answer the following questions: (a) Find five graphical representations that would be most revealing for managerial action. To do so specify what would each

graph purport to reveal. (b) Which is the more important product the firm ought to attend to, and motivate your answer? (c) Is there any correlation between the costs of quality and, if so, what is it? What can we conclude if this is the case? (d) Is the period of the year important for the occurrence of non-quality costs?

Table 3.8: Costs over time.

Period	Product 1, No of defects per unit	% Defect	$ cost per unit defect.	Product 2, No of defects per unit	% Defect	$ cost per unit defect.
January	4	2	200	5	1	450
February	2	4	350	7	2	500
March	5	3	150	9	7	150
April	3	7	100	3	4	250
May	6	5	100	8	3	100
June	2	1	200	1	9	550
July	3	2	150	5	2	300
August	2	1	200	7	1	400
September	4	6	400	9	5	250
October	6	4	300	3	6	200
November	7	8	500	8	8	600
December	9	12	600	5	9	300

Graphical reporting of data

Graphical techniques are important. Often a 'simple picture' is worth 'a thousand words'. Their advantage can be summarized by the following:

(a) They provide *visual* means of communication.

(b) They *condense* vast quantities of data into recognizable patterns.

(c) They provide a visual mode of organization for complex problems.

(d) They allow, when properly scaled, an obvious comparison of choices.

In most cases, the effective presentation of a quantitative study will require the effective use of graphical techniques. For example, consider a data set regarding the number of defectives produced for various products over the current year. The problem at hand is how to transmit most effectively a 'message' which will reveal underlying quality problems.

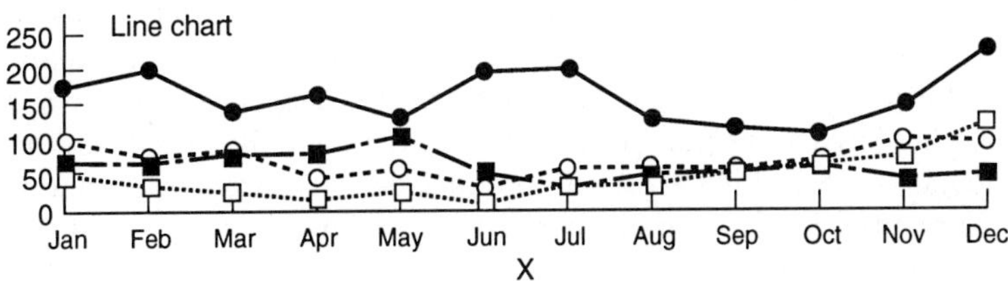

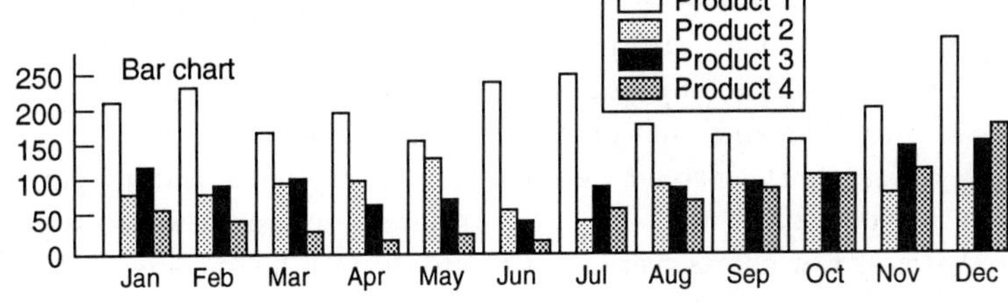

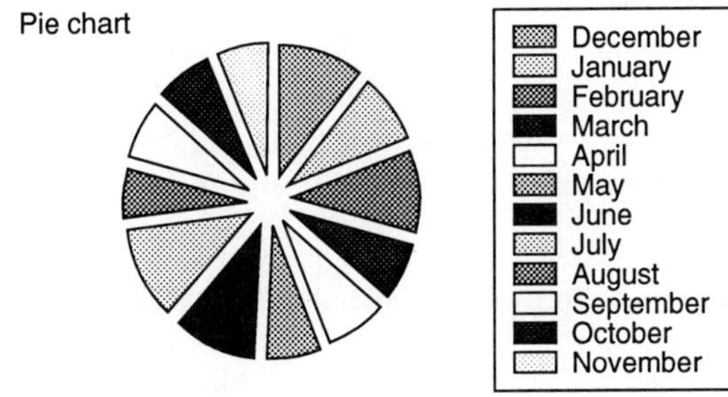

Figure 3.7: Graphical means to represent data.

Table 3.9: The number of defectives per product over time.

Time	Product 1	Product 2	Product 3	Product 4
January	180	70	100	50
February	200	75	80	40
March	150	85	90	30
April	175	90	60	20
May	140	120	70	30
June	210	60	50	20
July	220	50	75	50
August	150	75	75	60
September	140	80	80	75
October	130	90	90	90
November	170	70	120	100
December	250	75	130	150

Line charts: In a line graph, we can represent this data by letting one of the axes represent *time* (the months of the year), while the other axis represents the *defectives* level. The plot of defectives for each product, with a line connecting any two neighbouring points in time, is called the line graph. In particular, note in Figure 3.7 the product defectives 'going up and down' almost together! What does it mean? Is this related to the time of the year or to the number of units sold, or perhaps to the proportion of defectives for each of the products (or is it a potential relationship between the defectives produced in each product)? To answer these problems, preliminary insights can be obtained through the graphical representation of the data, although further insights can be obtained only through statistical analyses.

Bar charts: The information in a line graph can also be represented through a bar chart. Instead of using points to denote a data point, we can use a 'whole bar'. Each bar, appropriately designed, would represent another series. Bar charts were used to graph both histograms and Pareto charts.

Pie charts: For a product, consider the defectives production over a whole year, and assume that this is represented by 100% of a pie. In such a pie, we can represent monthly defectives as slices of the pie.

These are by no means the only graphical means to represent information. Previously, we used scatter plots and other means to represent data and construct models.

Problem
The Speedy Transport company involved in fast delivery has been plagued by complaints and poor service. For this reason, it decided to follow and record its transport activities for a full working week. During the week it discovered that there are basically three factors accounting for the quality problems of the company: the number of delays; the number of false deliveries; and the number of times delivered goods were damaged. In fact, Table 3.10 represents the occurrence of these factors each day of the week, and the average costs associated to each event.

Table 3.10: Weekly data collection.

Factor	Mon.	Tues.	Wends.	Thurs.	Fri.	Av Cost
No. of delays	4	7	3	8	12	$30
False delivery	10	6	8	4	2	$80
Damaged goods	5	1	2	0	2	$200

Represent this data in four visual forms. How would you organize the data to emphasize the differences between the effects of these factors and their comparative costs? Finally, use Pareto charts to show what are the most prominent factors necessary for the firm to concentrate on improving the situation.

3.3 A statistical refresher

A *sample space* S defines the set of all relevant and potential events. A product sample space can be defined, for example, by 'good' or 'bad', or in terms of its exhaustive attributes. In the former case, the sample (attributes) has only two possible observations (good, bad). We can, of course, associate to each observation a number such as '0' for good and '1' for 'bad', in which case the sample space is $\{0, 1\}$. These numbers are also called the *elementary events* of the sample space, usually denoted by letters $w_i, i = 1, 2, 3, ..n$, where n is the number of elements in the sample space. For elementary events we have necessarily a mutual exclusion and exhaustive relationship, which is expressed by

$$w_i w_j = 0 \text{ for } i \neq j \text{and } S = w_1 + w_2 + \ldots + w_n$$

where '+' is used as a union sum (meaning that all elementary events belong to the sample space), and $w_i w_j = 0$ mean that events i and j are non-overlapping. We can associate a real number with each elementary event. This defines a function called a *random variable.* In other words, we can define a function $X(w)$, the random variable, which can take on events $w_1, w_2, \ldots, w_n$ and, for each value w_i, we have a real number $X(w_i)$ which is a probability distribution. In our case, we can associate to a 'good' product a weight 0.9, and to a 'bad' product 0.1, therefore (0.9, 0.1) can be defined as a probability distribution. In the general case, a probability distribution is formulated as an affectation, therefore it is necessarily a function with particular characteristics.

If a random variable takes on discrete values $w_i \in S, i = 1, 2, .., n$, in the sample space S with probabilities p_i, with

$$p_i \geq 0, \sum_{i=1}^{n} p_i = 1,$$

then this defines a discrete probability distribution whose graph can be a histogram, and for which we can calculate the mean, the variance and other moments. When a random variable assumes continuous values in a range $R, w \in S$, then the affectation is defined by a continuous function $f(w)$, which is called the probability density function, given by

$$f(w) \geq 0, \text{ and } \int_S f(w)dw = 1$$

where integration is over all values of the sample space S whose range is R. Now, say that underlying a data set there are two probability distributions $f_1(x)$ and $f_2(x)$. In other words, there is a proportion belonging to the first distribution and a data set belonging to the second. Let p be the proportion belonging to the first data set. In this sense, the data set can be conceived as having a mixture probability distribution which we can write as follows:

$$f(x) = \begin{cases} f_1(x) & \text{with probability} \quad p \\ f_2(x) & \text{with probability} \quad 1-p \end{cases}$$

or

$$f(x) = pf_1(x) + (1-p)f_2(x).$$

Probability distributions are, of course, used intensely in the management of quality. For this reason, we shall consider a number of often used distributions.

The binomial pdf

Say that the daily production volume of a product is 100 units. The probability of producing a defective unit is known and constant, and given by $\theta = 0.15$. In any one day, what is the probability distribution of obtaining r defectives? Assuming that production is statistically independent and maintained each day, this is given by the binomial probability distribution:

$$P(R=r) = \binom{n}{r} \theta^r (1-\theta)^{n-r}, n = 100, \theta = 0.15.$$

This distribution allows, assuming that the parameters are correctly assessed, calculation of the number of defectives. Let n be a sample size, thus in such a sample the number of defectives, say r, can be observed.

The binomial distribution has the following mean and variance:

$$E(r) = n\theta, \text{var } (r) = n\theta(1-\theta).$$

When θ, the process parameter, is not known for sure, it can be represented by a probability distribution, say $f(\theta)$. The resulting (mixture) distribution of the outcomes r is then a mixture, and is given by the following:

$$P(R=r) = \int_0^1 \binom{n}{r} \theta^r (1-\theta)^{n-r} f(\theta) d\theta.$$

In this case, for *all* distributions $f(.)$, these are called Lexian distributions and they have the property that their mean and variance are given by:

$$\begin{aligned} E(R) &= nE(\theta), \\ \text{var}(R) &= nE(\theta)[1-E(\theta)] + n(n-1)\text{var } (\theta). \end{aligned}$$

The cumulative binomial distribution is denoted by

$$F(k) = \sum_{i=0}^{k} P(i) = \sum_{i=0}^{k} \binom{n}{i} \theta^i (1-\theta)^{n-i},$$

which can be represented by the following chi-square integral, as we shall see later on and is used often for numerical computations of the binomial distribution:

$$F(k) = n\binom{n-1}{k-1}\int_0^{\theta} t^{k-1}(1-t)^{n-k}dt.$$

Example

The defective rate of an IC (Integrated Circuit) manufacturing process is assumed to be $\theta = 0.25$. A number of chips is tested every day, say $n = 20$, and for reasons to be seen in Chapter 5, the quality manager has stated that any number of defectives over the mean $n\theta = (20)(0.25) = 5 = c$ should lead to a process stoppage. In this case, we note that the probability of defective ICs in a lot of size $n = 20$ is binomial with:

$$b(r \mid n, \theta) = \binom{n}{r}\theta^r(1-\theta)^{n-r} = \binom{20}{r}(0.25)^r(0.75)^{20-r}.$$

Since stoppages of the manufacturing process occur if $r > 5 = c$, we have

$$\text{Prob [No stoppage]} = \sum_{r=0}^{5}\binom{20}{r}(0.25)^r(0.75)^{20-r} = 0.3912,$$

while the probability that there is a stoppage is:

$$\begin{aligned}\text{Prob [Stoppage]} &= 1 - \text{ Prob [No stoppage]} = \\ &= \sum_{r=6}^{20}\binom{20}{r}(0.25)^r(0.75)^{20-r} = \\ &= P(r \leq 5 \mid p = 0.25) = 1 - 0.3912 = 0.6088,\end{aligned}$$

which is usually calculated using tables of the binomial distribution. The probability of no stoppage is thus the probability that we accept the process operating performance, assuming that 0.25 is the acceptable operating standard. Note, however, that we reject the process operating performance with probability 0.3912, *even though* it also produces defect rates at 25%. Thus, for every procedure or decision which is specified by management, there is a risk of taking the wrong decision. Of course, if we vary the decision parameter c, specified by management, from 5 to 4, we would alter this risk. This will be the topic of the next section, however. As an exercise, perform calculations for $c = 1, 2, 3$ and 4, and compute the risks of stopping the process wrongly.

Example

We can distinguish between US/Europe and Japanese approaches to quality management by the priority they give to: (a) Improving a process performance (say by reducing the defect rate). (b) Reducing the variability of the process. Which approach is right and important and when? A partial answer can be seen through the use of the binomial distribution. Consider again the IC manufacturing problem, and assume that the process defect rate is not exactly 25%, but it varies because the production process is complex involving many variables, some of which cannot be controlled. In other words, instead of $\theta = 0.25$ we will have $E(\theta) = 0.25$, while the variance of this rate is some value var(θ). Consider now the defectives' output r for a daily production of $N = 1000$ ICs. Ideally, the control objective ought to be the minimization of both the defectives output and its variance, or

$$\text{Min}[E(r), \text{var}\ (r)].$$

Thus, if $N = 1000$, the total daily output is

$$\begin{aligned} E(r) &= NE(\theta) = 1000(0.25) = 250 \text{ and} \\ \text{var}\ (r) &= NE(\theta)[1 - E(\theta)] + N(N-1)\text{var}\ (\theta) = \\ &= 250(.75) + 999{,}000\text{var}\ (\theta). \end{aligned}$$

It is apparent that the mean defectives can be reduced if $E(\theta)$ is reduced (as the Japanese would recommend). But what good is such a reduction if the variance of θ is significant leading to an extremely large variance for r, with disastrous post sales performance? In this sense, it is misleading to believe that an approach is right or wrong, for each has emphasized a problem which has its greater priority in a given context. Therefore, to properly reach a conclusion, the full range of direct and indirect costs and benefits must be assessed and on this basis priority for one or the other reached. Of course, if N, the daily production rate, also denotes the production lot size, we can see that the variability is a squared function of this lot size. By reducing the lot size (as attempted in Just in Time systems), it is clear that the variability is reduced, *even if the production process variability* (σ^2) *is large.* In this sense, process improvement and lot size reduction seem to be combined policies which can deal with the problems of process quality.

Problem

Automatic versus manned systems can also be compared using the mixture binomial model. All things equal, an automatic system has a repetitive potential, and therefore the parameter θ (whether acceptable or not) remains fairly stable and would thereby reduce the process variability. This is in comparison with manned systems where θ might be 'better' but the variability of manned performance may be large. In this case, construct a case for a production strategy which would be based either on excellent manned production or on complete automation. Are there any alternatives, such as better manufacturing controls?

The binomial probability distribution can be generalized and approximated in several ways. For example, generalizations include the multinomial and multivariate binomial distributions which are multi-variable forms of the binomial distribution (an extensive definition and characteristics can be found in Johnson and Kotz, 1970). Approximations include the Poisson and normal distributions. When θ is small, then $n\theta$ is used as the parameter of a Poisson distribution. When n is large, a normal approximation is also possible. It is then given by a distribution whose mean is $n\theta$ and its variance is $n\theta(1-\theta)$. In other words, for a Poisson approximation

$$\lim_{n\theta\to} \lambda P(r) = e^{-\lambda}\lambda^r/r!, r = 0,1,2,3,\ldots, E(r) = \lambda$$

while for the normal approximation

$$\begin{aligned} \lim_{n\to\infty} P(r) &= \frac{1}{\sqrt{2\pi}\sigma} \exp\left[-\frac{(x-\mu)^2}{\sigma^2}\right], \\ x \in (-\infty, +\infty), \mu &= n\theta, \sigma^2 = n\theta(1-\theta). \end{aligned}$$

Both distributions are extremely important, and will be studied in detail.

Problems

1. The probability of producing a non-defective unit is 0.98; what is the probability of producing 10 non-defectives and two defectives in a lot of 50? What is the probability of producing fewer than three defectives in a production lot of 150?
2. A process is in control with a probability 0.8 and out of control with a probability 0.2. When the process is in control, it produces a defective with probability 0.02, and when it is out of control, the probability of producing defectives is equal to 0.3. Calculate the expected number of defectives and its variance in a lot of size 20.

The Poisson distribution

Consider a process counting the number of arrivals to a store, the number of complaints in a day or the number of employees arriving late to work. Some of these processes, provided they satisfy a set of required assumptions, can be defined by a Poisson distribution. This distribution is given by:

$$P(n) = \exp(-\lambda)\lambda^n/n!, n = 0,1,2,3,\ldots.$$

where n is the number of arrivals, the number of complaints, and so on, and $P(n)$ is the probability distribution of n. The mean and variance of this distribution are equal and given by

$$E(n) - \lambda, \text{var}\,(n) = \lambda.$$

This is an important distribution which will be the subject of many applications.

Problems

1. A group of knitting machines operate continuously. The number of needle

breaks varies from time to time, however. Management has tabulated the following needle breaks in a typical day using 15 minute intervals. (a) Present a histogram of needle breaks. (b) What is the mean number of needle breaks? (c) What is the mean time between breaks? (d) Can you represent the occurrence of needle breaks by a Poisson distribution? If so, at what mean? (e) Assuming that the Poisson distribution is an appropriate choice, what is the theoretical probability that there will be more than three breaks in 15 minutes? What is the probability that there will be four breaks in half an hour? What is the probability that there will be at most two breaks in a15 minute period?

Table 3.11: Time record of needle breaks.

Time Hours	Needle Breaks	Time Hours	Needle Breaks
0801 – 0815	12	1001 – 1015	15
0816 – 0830	14	1016 – 1030	13
0831 – 0845	16	1031 – 1045	10
0846 – 0900	17	1046 – 1100	8
0901 – 0915	18	1101 – 1115	5
0916 – 0930	19	1116 – 1130	3
0931 – 0945	18	1131 – 1145	2
0941 – 1000	17	1146 – 1200	0

The parameter λ of the Poisson distribution may also be subject to random variations. Say that λ denotes the mean number of complaints in any given day. Complaints vary from day to day, however, with a distribution which is given by $f(\lambda)$. Then, the unconditional probability distribution of the number of complaints is

$$\pi(r) = \int_0^\infty f(\lambda)\pi(r \mid \lambda)d\lambda = \int_0^\infty (\lambda)(\lambda^r e^{-\lambda}/r!)d\lambda.$$

This integral has no general solution, but for many probability distributions $f(\lambda)$, it can be calculated.

2. To study and improve the quality of service provided to its customers, the US-Northwest phone company has estimated, on the basis of 600 directory assistance calls in six hours, that call inter-arrival times follow an exponential distribution with mean $1/\lambda = 6/600 = 0.01$ hours (between calls). Do you agree with such an assumption? In particular, justify your answer based on the behavioural hypotheses which might be reasonable in constructing a process for telephone calls assistance.

3. The number of complaints arriving at a firm regarding poorly installed appliances is, on average, 12 per day. It is believed (on the basis of past experience and data which was collected and appropriately tested) that it is reasonable to assume that complaints have a Poisson probability distribution. What is the probability that there are less than 10 complaints

in one day? What is the probability that there are more than 8 and less than 14 complaints in a day? What is the probability that there are less than 50 complaints in a six- days week?

4. The number of machines breaking down in any month is shown to be best described by a Poisson distribution. Managerial procedures seeking to control machine breakdowns have been instituted with an observable change expressed by a lower mean breakdown rate as well as variance lower than the mean. What are the implications of such an observation?

The normal distribution

The normal probability distribution is a cornerstone of statistical theory and practice. Abraham de Moivre was probably the first to obtain this distribution as an approximation for the binomial distribution (De Moivre, 1718), although the distribution is mostly attributed to the famed mathematicians Gauss and Laplace. For a binomial distribution with parameters (n, p) we can approximate it by a normal one with mean $\mu = np$ and variance $\sigma^2 = np(1-p)$ if n is large. The Poisson distribution can also be approximated by a normal distribution. In its standard form, the normal distribution is given

$$f(z) = (1/\sqrt{2\pi})\exp[-z^2/2], -\infty < z < +\infty$$

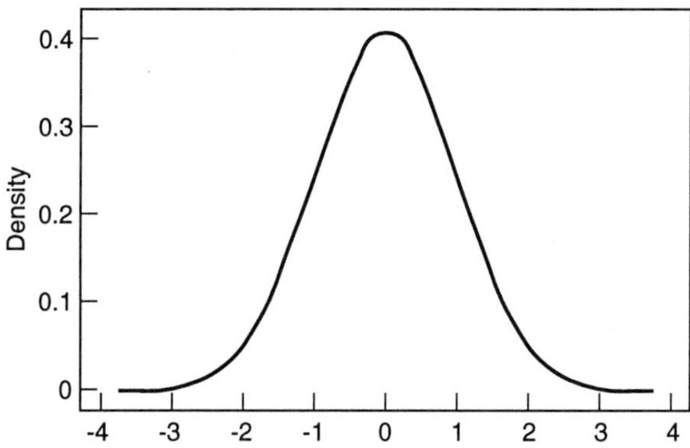

Figure 3.8: The normal probability distribution.

which is a bell shaped distribution with its mean (which equals the median and its mode) equaling zero and its variance 1. This is a distribution which is defined over the real line (i.e. from minus infinity to plus infinity). It has two parameters (μ, σ^2), with mean μ and variance σ^2.

Tables of the standard normal distribution are extremely useful; since for any normal distribution, it is possible through a linear transformation to obtain an equivalent standard normal which has zero mean and unit variance. For any value $x, x = \mu + \sigma z$ or $z = (x - \mu)/\sigma$. Of course, it is easily verified that $E(z) = E(x-\mu)/\sigma = (\mu-\mu)/\sigma = 0$ and that $\text{var}(z) = \text{var}[(x-\mu)/\sigma] = \text{var}(x)/\sigma^2 = \sigma^2/\sigma^2 = 1$. Explicitly, the normal probability distribution with mean μ and variance σ^2 is given by

$$f(x) = (\frac{1}{\sqrt{2\pi\sigma}}) \exp[-\frac{(x-\mu)^2}{2\sigma^2}], -\infty < x < +\infty$$

while its cumulative is:

$$F(x) = (\frac{1}{\sqrt{2\pi\sigma}}) \int_{-\infty}^{x} \exp[-\frac{(x-\mu)^2}{2\sigma^2}]dy.$$

The normal distribution has additional properties which are extremely useful in quality management. These are:

- The reproducible property, and
- The law of large numbers.

The sum of two or more random variables, each independently and normally distributed also has a normal distribution. In particular, if $x_i, 1, 2, \ldots n$ are normal random variables each with parameters $(\mu_i, \sigma_i), i = 1, 2, \ldots n$, then the sum is also normal with mean M and variance Σ^2

$$M = \sum_{i=1}^{n} \mu_i, \Sigma^2 = \sum_{i=1}^{n} \sigma_i^2.$$

This is in essence the reproducible property. The law of large numbers, on the other hand, states that the sum of independent random variables with arbitrary distributions converges to a normal random variable when the sum of variables increases. As a result, for large samples, we can justifiably use the normal distribution to represent characteristics which involve the sum of large samples (independently distributed). For example, if we collect a 'sufficiently large number' of samples, then the average,

$$\bar{x} = \sum_{i=1}^{n} x_i/n$$

involves a sum, and for n sufficiently large (usually over 30) the average has (by the law of large numbers) a normal probability distribution with mean μ-the population parameter and variance σ^2/n, which was calculated earlier.

Problem

The normal probability distribution has been tabulated with great precision. Further, and as seen earlier, any distribution with mean μ and variance σ^2 can be transformed to the standard form by a linear transformation. Let $x \simeq N(\mu, \sigma^2)$, and let $z \simeq N(0, 1)$. Then the following relationship between x and z holds: $z = (x - \mu)/\sigma$, or $x = \mu + \sigma z$. In this case, compute (using the table and the numerical procedure suggested) the following values:

$$P[-1.96 \leq z \leq 1.96], P[0 \leq z \leq 0.8], P[z \leq 1.5].$$

Further, if x has a mean of 10 and variance 4, then calculate, $P[4 \leq x \leq 12]$, $P[8 \leq x \leq 10], P[x \leq 14]$. To do so, use the tabulated normal probability distribution which is included in the appendix.

Other distributions of importance include the sampling distributions: *Chi- Square*, t and F distributions. Motivation for the chi-square distribution arises when we consider the sum of a number of squared random variables each of which is iid (meaning identically and independently distributed) and normally distributed. Namely, if $z_i, i = 1, 2, \ldots, n$ are n standard normal random variables, then the sum

$$Z = \sum_{i=1}^{n} z_i^2$$

is said to have a χ_n^2 (chi-square) distribution with n degrees of freedom. The student t distribution is mostly used in hypotheses testing in normal regression curves. Say that we have two random variables Y and Z where y is normally distributed and z has a chi square distribution with n degrees of freedom. Then, the ratio

$$t = \frac{y}{\sqrt{(z/n)}}$$

is said to obtain the student t distribution. This distribution is well tabulated and can be found in the appendix. Consider now two random variables z_1 and z_2 each of which have chi-square distributions with n_1 and n_2 degrees of freedom. Then, the ratio

$$F = \frac{z_1/n_1}{z_2/n_2}$$

is said to have the F-Snedecor, $F(n_1, n_2)$, distribution with n_1 and n_2 degrees of freedom.

Confidence intervals

Consider a probability distribution $f(x)$, defined over some random variable $x \in \Omega$. Then, by definition

$$P[x - dx/2 \leq x \leq x + dx/2] = f(x)dx.$$

By the same token, if we take two bounds, a lower one 'a' and an upper one 'b', then the probability that some value x is between a and b is given by the sum (integral) of the probabilities from a to b, or:

$$P[a \leq x \leq b] = \int_a^b f(z)dz.$$

The integral therefore defines a probability interval, represented in Figure 3.9. Say that for some values a and b that $P[a \leq x \leq b] = 95\%$. This means that the probability of obtaining any measure x which is between a and b is equal to 0.95. By the same token, a $(1-\alpha)$ confidence interval is the $(1-\alpha)$ probability that an observation x will be in the interval (a, b). When the underlying probability distribution is not specified, confidence intervals can be approximated using Tchebychev's inequality,

$$P[\mid x - E(x) \mid > K] \leq \frac{\sigma^2}{K^2}$$

where $E(x)$ is the mean of the distribution of x and σ^2 is its variance.

Example
The mean number of clients arriving at a supermarket equals 200, while its standard deviation is 25. Staffing of the supermarket is made on the basis of a number of clients of 200 ∓ 25. What is the probability that the supermarket will be understaffed (and thereby the quality of service poor)? Assume first that the probability distribution is normal. Then assume that this distribution is not known, and find the upper bound probability.

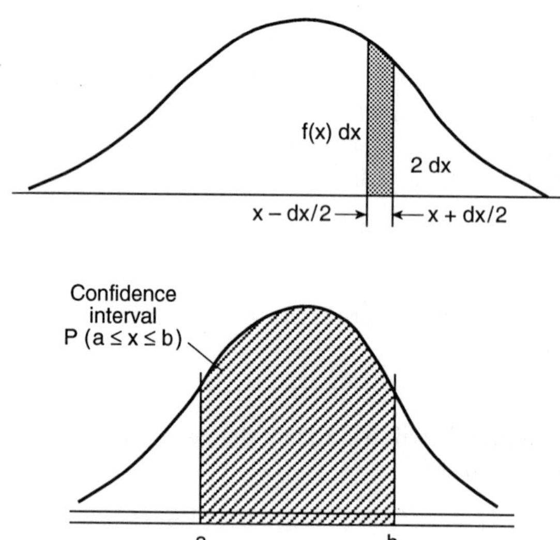

Figure 3.9: Probability intervals.

When a random variable has a normal probability distribution with mean μ and variance σ^2, then its transformation to a standard normal variable yields

$$z = \frac{x-\mu}{\sigma} \simeq N(0,1)$$

and therefore a confidence interval expressed in terms of a and b is

$$P[a \leq z \leq b] = \int_a^b \frac{1}{\sqrt{2\pi}} \exp(-z^2) dz$$

This is equivalent to:

$$\begin{aligned} P[a \leq z \leq b] &= P[a \leq \frac{x-\mu}{\sigma} \leq b] \\ = P[a\sigma \leq (x-\mu) \leq b\sigma] &= P[\mu + a\sigma \leq x \leq \mu + b\sigma], \end{aligned}$$

where a and b are deviations from the mean expressed as the number of standard deviations. For example, say that $a = -1.96$ and $b = 1.96$, which corresponds to a 0.025 probability of being to the right of $b = 1.96$ and 0.025 probability of being at the left of $a = -1.96$. Of course $0.025 + 0.025 = 0.05 = \alpha$ which corresponds to $1 - \alpha = 0.95$, or a 95% confidence interval, explicitly written

$$P[x - 1.96\sigma \leq \mu \leq x + 1.96\sigma] = 0.95.$$

A sample of computations are reproduced in Table 3.12, while complete results are obtained in the Standard Normal Table at the end of the chapter.

Table 3.12

a	$\alpha/2$	a	$\alpha/2$	a		a	$\alpha/2$
0.0	0.5000	0.6	0.2743	1.2	0.1151	1.8	0.0359
0.1	0.4602	0.7	0.2420	1.3	0.0968	1.9	0.0287
0.2	0.4207	0.8	0.2119	1.4	0.0808	2.0	0.0228
0.3	0.3821	0.9	0.1841	1.5	0.0668	2.1	0.0179
0.4	0.3446	1.0	0.1587	1.6	0.0548	2.2	0.0139
0.5	0.3085	1.1	0.1357	1.7	0.0446	2.3	0.0107

When we use the sample data to estimate the confidence interval of a sample average the standard deviation is $\sigma/\sqrt{n}$, and therefore

$$P[\bar{x} - 1.96\sigma/\sqrt{n} \leq \mu \leq \bar{x} + 1.96\sigma/\sqrt{n}] = 0.95.$$

Generally, $(1-\alpha)$ confidence intervals are computed by $Z_{\alpha/2}$ in normal tables, which measure, as stated above (but denoted by a), the number of standard deviations from the mean, such that the left (or right tail) accounts for $\alpha/2$ of the probability of the distribution. In other words,

$$P[\bar{X} - Z_{\alpha/2}\sigma/\sqrt{n} \leq \mu \leq \bar{X} + Z_{\alpha/2}\sigma/\sqrt{n}] = 1 - \alpha.$$

Of course, our ability to calculate this confidence interval depends upon the knowledge of σ. If this is not the case, the probability of the standard deviate $(x - \mu)/\sigma$ is no longer normal, since it is necessary to replace σ by its estimator s (which is also a random variable). In this case, the probability distribution of the average is no longer normal but has the t-student distribution with $(n - 1)$ degrees of freedom. Namely, for the standard deviate t, and a sample of size n which is used to estimate both $\bar{X}$ and s, we have:

$$t_{n-1} = \frac{\bar{X} - \mu}{s/\sqrt{n}}$$

and

$$P[\bar{X} - t_{\alpha/2,n-1}s/\sqrt{n} \leq \mu \leq \bar{X} + t_{\alpha/2,n-1}s/\sqrt{n}] = 1 - \alpha,$$

where $t_{\alpha/2,n-1}$ is the student$-t$ distribution with $n - 1$ degrees of freedom, and $\alpha/2$ corresponds to the area to the right of t. For example, for a 95% confidence interval, we have the t values shown in Table 3.13, expressed in terms of the sample size n. Thus, if $n = 12$, a confidence interval for the sample average is

Table 3.13

n	04	08	12	20	∞
$t_{0.025,n-1}$	3.18	2.36	2.20	2.09	1.96

$$P[\bar{X}(\mp)2.20(s/\sqrt{12})] = 0.95$$

In other words if some study yields an average of 4 and a standard deviation of 2, then a 95

$$\mu \in [4 - 2.20(2/\sqrt{12}), 4 + 2.20(2/\sqrt{12})] \text{ or } \mu \in [2.873, 5.127].$$

By the same token, we can construct confidence intervals for the sample variance. Noting that $(n-1)s^2/\sigma^2$ has a chi-square distribution with $n - 1$ degrees of freedom, we can construct a $1 - \alpha$ confidence interval by,

$$P[\chi^2_{1-\alpha/2,n-1} \leq (n-1)s^2/\sigma^2 \leq \chi^2_{\alpha/2,n-1}] = 1 - \alpha,$$

and therefore,

$$P[\frac{s^2(n-1)}{\chi^2_{\alpha/2,n-1}} \leq \sigma^2 \leq \frac{s^2(n-1)}{\chi^2_{1-\alpha/2,n-1}}] = 1 - \alpha$$

where $\chi^2_{1-\alpha/2,n-1}$ is the area under the curve of the chi-square distribution. For example, the numbers in Table 3.14 are calculated using the chi-square tables.

Table 3.14

n	α	$\chi^2_{\alpha/2,n-1}$	$\chi^2_{1-\alpha/2,n-1}$
04	0.05	9.35	0.213
08	0.05	14.4	1.690
12	0.05	21.9	3.820
18	0.05	30.2	7.560
20	0.05	32.9	8.910
30	0.05	45.7	16.00

Thus, if $n = 12$, the sample standard deviation is equal to three, and $\alpha = 0.05$, and the 95 percentile confidence interval for σ^2 is given by

$$P[s^2(11)/21.9 \leq \sigma^2 \leq s^2(11)/3.82] = 0.95$$

or

$$P[0.50228s^2 \leq \sigma^2 \leq 2.8795s^2] = P[4.5205 \leq \sigma^2 \leq 25.9155] = 0.95.$$

Problem

A process specification for the production of a certain type of tubes used in research is 60 mm for the tubes diameter. Tolerances are from 59.8 to 60.2 mm. A number of tubes were collected and measured. The data set is given below:

60.1	59.8	60.0	60.0	59.7	59.4	60.15	60.2	60.35	58.8
60.3	60.1	60.3	58.9	59.7	60.1	59.95	59.7	59.80	60.0

Assuming diameters are normally distributed, what is the probability that a unit produced will not be accepted? What is the probability that it will be due to the unit being under specified? or being over specified? What is the probability that two successive units will be under specified, over specified and being within the specified tolerances? Construct a 95% confidence interval for the mean diameter based on the data gathered. Finally, construct 95% and 80% confidence intervals for the variance.

Now consider two independent random variables, each distributed with a normal probability distribution with mean and variances given by μ_i and $\sigma_i^2, i = 1, 2$, respectively. These parameters are assumed unknown, however. Our purpose is to construct a confidence interval for the variance ratio σ_1^2/σ_2^2. Let s_1^2/s_2^2 be the ratio of the samples' variances, each of size n_1 and n_2, respectively. Then, since s_1^2 and s_2^2 have each a chi square distribution, their ratio has an F distribution with $n_1 - 1$ and $n_2 - 1$ degrees of freedom. The confidence interval for the ratio of the variance is thus

$$\frac{s_1^2}{s_2^2} F_{1-\alpha/2}(n_1 - 1, n_2 - 1) \leq \frac{\sigma_1^2}{\sigma_2^2} \leq \frac{s_1^2}{s_2^2} F_{\alpha/2}(n_1 - 1, n_2 - 1).$$

Of course, once the F distribution with $n_1 - 1$ and $n_2 - 1$ degrees of freedom is calculated, we can then calculate a $(1 - \alpha)$ confidence intervals for the ratio of variances.

Problems

1. Two processes for the production of ball bearings are being considered. Process variabilities are to be compared using the processes' variances. A first firm, selling the first process, claims that its precision variance is equal to 0.0001, while the competing firm claims that its precision variance is only 0.00015. The machines are tested over two samples. A first sample of nine units uses the first process, while a second sample of 16 units uses the second process. The sample variance in both cases turns out to be equal to 0.00013 and 0.00016. What is the probability that these processes are different, as the first firm has claimed, and what is the probability that the precision of the firms' processes are different? (Note: compare the sample standard deviations and construct confidence intervals using the appropriate probability distribution).

2. A firm advertises that its product is guaranteed to work without any failure for a number of years (say 2). Product design and manufacturing processes point out that 'theoretically', the product can perform its function for an average of two years with a standard deviation of six months. (a) What is the probability that the cost of the guarantee will be null? (b) If failure occurs before the end of the guarantee, the cost to the firm is \$100. What is the expected cost of the guarantee if we can use the normal distribution as a first approximation to the time to failure? (c) Construct a 95lifetime of the product using both the normal and the Weibull probability distributions. (d) Finally, after the product has been marketed, product returns under the guarantees have pointed out that the firm may have underestimated the cost of the guarantees. A sample of 30 products that have failed at some time (both under the guarantee and out of it) were collected. On the basis of this sample, management has asked to construct a 95 percent confidence interval for the mean time to a first failure as well as a confidence interval for its variance assuming a normal probability distribution. If no distributions were given, how would you proceed by application of Chebychev's formula? In addition, management has requested that an estimate for the cost of the guarantees be given. The data set is:

2.1	1.5	3.0	2.1	0.8	1.4	1.7	2.3	0.5	1.9	1.7	2.8	1.0	1.6	2.9
1.7	1.4	0.6	2.5	2.6	1.3	1.9	2.1	2.0	1.6	1.8	1.4	1.0	2.4	3.2

Confidence interval on a proportion

Consider a binomial probability distribution with parameters (n, p). If we can approximate the binomial distribution by a normal with mean np and variance $np(1-p)$, then a $(1-\alpha)$ confidence interval is given by

$$\text{Prob}\ [n\hat{p} - Z_{\alpha/2}\sqrt{n\hat{p}(1-\hat{p})} \leq np \leq n\hat{p} + Z_{\alpha/2}\sqrt{n\hat{p}(1-\hat{p})}] = 1-\alpha,$$

where $\hat{p}$ is the population proportion parameter and $\hat{p}$ is the sample estimate.

For convenience, set

$$\hat{\sigma}_p = \sqrt{\hat{p}(1-\hat{p})/n}.$$

Then a confidence interval for the ratio p is given by,

$$\text{Prob}\ [\hat{p} - Z_{\alpha/2}\hat{\sigma}_p \leq p \leq \hat{p} + Z_{\alpha/2}\hat{\sigma}_p] = 1-\alpha.$$

By the same token, we can construct a confidence interval for the difference between two proportions. Say that there are two samples, each with a binomial distribution with parameters $(n_i, p_i), i = 1, 2$. Let the difference be approximated by the normal distribution whose mean is $n_1p_1 - n_2p_2$ and variance $n_1p_1(1-p_1) + n_2p_2(1-p_2)$. Thus, a $1-\alpha$ confidence interval is given by

$$\text{Prob}\ [\hat{p}_1 - \hat{p}_2 - Z_{\alpha/2}\hat{\sigma} \leq p_1 - p_2 \leq \hat{p}_1 - \hat{p}_2 + Z_{\alpha/2}\hat{\sigma}] = 1-\alpha$$

where

$$\hat{\sigma} = \sqrt{\hat{p}_1(1-\hat{p}_1)/n_1 + \hat{p}_2(1-\hat{p}_2)/n_2}.$$

Consider, for example, the proportion of defectives in two lots, one of size $n_1 = 30$ and the other of size $n_2 = 50$. Let the proportion of defectives in each of the lots be $\hat{p}_1 = 0.07$ and $\hat{p}_2 = 0.05$, and therefore $\hat{p}_1 - \hat{p}_2 = 0.02$. Then a 95 percentile confidence interval for this difference is given by,

$$\text{Prob}\ [0.02 - 1.96(0.05585) \leq p_1 - p_2 \leq 0.02 + 1.96(0.05585)] = 0.95,$$

and therefore,

$$\text{Prob}\ [0.089466 \leq p_1 - p_2 \leq 0.1246] = 0.95.$$

Hypothesis testing

A statistical hypothesis is a proposition about the parameter of a probability distribution which is presumed to represent the behaviour of a random variable. The procedure followed consists of:

- Asserting a statement (formulating the hypothesis).
- Collecting the data.
- Selecting criteria for testing the assertion (the hypothesis).

The decision to reject a hypothesis is based on the construction of a decision rule. This decision rule is optimized by minimizing some objectives, typically the risks of making an error or some economic criteria. We consider essentially two types of errors, Type I and Type II errors.

A *Type I error* expresses the risk (expressed as a probability) of rejecting the hypothesis when it is in fact true. For example, in acceptance sampling the probability of a type I error corresponds to the producer's risk, because it expresses the probability that a producer will reject a lot when it is in fact good. A *Type II error* expresses the risk of accepting the null hypothesis when it is false. Accepting a lot when its quality is unsatisfactory corresponds in acceptance sampling to the consumer's risk. There are therefore four possibilities represented in Table 3.15.

Table 3.15: The table of errors

The Hypothesis is:	Accept	Reject
True	No error	Type I
False	Type II	No error

Table 3.16: The α and β errors

H_0	Accept	Reject
True	$1-\alpha$	α
False	β	$1-\beta$

The probabilities associated to these risks are denote by α and β, respectively. The tables above, expressed in terms of these probabilities is thus as shown in Table 3.16, and $(1-\beta)$ is called *the power of the test.* The hypothesis testing problem then consists of setting a null hypothesis, denoted by H_0, which is tested against an alternative, denoted by H_1. This is written as follows:

H_0: Assertion

H_1: Alternative

By definition,

$$
\begin{aligned}
\alpha &= \text{Prob[Reject } H_0 \mid H_0 \text{ istrue]} \\
\beta &= \text{Prob[Accept } H_0 \mid H_1 \text{ istrue].}
\end{aligned}
$$

The probability of accepting the hypothesis is then expressed in terms of the OC (Operating Characteristic) curve which is given in Figure 3.10.

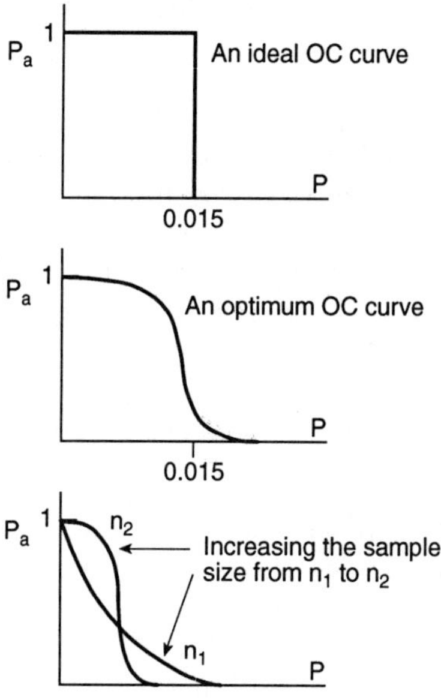

Figure 3.10: The power of a test.

There are various approaches to performing such hypothesis testing problems, depending on the formulation of the tests and the hypotheses' probability distributions. We consider several problems which are often used in the management of quality. For further study, the reader should consult any standard statistical text.

Examples

1. (Chatfield, 1970, p. 134). Suppose that the strength of a steel wire made by an existing process is normally distributed with mean $\mu_0 = 1250$ and standard deviation $\sigma = 150$. A batch of wire is made by a new process, and a sample of 25 measurements gives an average strength of $\bar{X} = 1312$. We assume that the standard deviation of the process does not change. The problem we are faced with is to decide whether the difference $\bar{X} - \mu_0$ is strong enough evidence to justify changing the process. Common sense suggests that the larger the difference $\bar{X} - \mu_0$ the more likely is the new process to yield greater strength for the wires. Since the standard deviation for the new process is known to be σ, we can characterize the probability distribution of the average by a normal probability distribution; in standard variate form

$$z = (\bar{X} - \mu_0)/(\sigma\sqrt{n}) = (1312 - 1250)/(150\sqrt{25}) = 2.06.$$

Thus, using the standard normal probability table, the probability that z is greater than 2.06 is

$$\text{Prob}\,[z > 2.06] = 1 - F_N(2.06) = 0.0197.$$

This means there is 1.97% chance of getting a more extreme result. If this result is deemed unlikely, we can be inclined to reject the null hypothesis that these are similar process, $(H_0 : \mu = \mu_0)$ and accept the alternative $(H_1 : \mu > \mu_0)$ that there was an improvement.

When the standard deviation of the new process is not known, we can replace it by the sample standard deviation estimate

$$t_{n-1} = \frac{(\bar{X} - \mu_0)}{s/\sqrt{n}}, \quad s = \sqrt{\sum_{i=1}^{n} \frac{(x_i - \bar{X})^2}{(n-1)}}.$$

But in such a case, the probability distribution of standard variate value t provides another statistic. Say that $s = 130$, then

$$t_{n-1} = (\bar{X} - \mu_0)/s\sqrt{n} = (1312 - 1250)/(130\sqrt{25}) = 0.0953.$$

From the t distribution tables (with $\alpha = 0.05$), $t_{24,0.05} = 1.711$ and, since $0.0953 < 1.711$, the null hypothesis cannot be rejected.

2. According to agreed upon standards, the percentage of fat in hamburgers should be 12%. To test the fat content of incoming meat, we analysed nine different shipments to see if fat content measurements differ significantly from 12%. The null hypothesis is thus:

$$H_0 : \mu = 0.12.$$

The alternative hypothesis can be formulated in two manners. We could state that

$$H_1 : \mu \neq 0.12.$$

in which case, if shipments were of a lower fat content, that would lead to rejection of the hypothesis (since it will be better than the null hypothesis). Alternatively, we can formulate the alternative hypothesis as

$$H_1 : \mu > 0.12,$$

in which case the null hypothesis will be rejected only if the fat content is greater than the specified 12%. The first alternative leads to a two-sided hypothesis, meaning that both 'above and below' limits of the hypothesis are to be considered. For example, if $\alpha = 0.05$, then for a two-sided hypothesis we consider as a test statistic the values which correspond to $\alpha/2 = 0.025$. For the second alternative, we have a one sided test which will mean that we consider the statistic that corresponds to $\alpha = 0.05$.

Assume that the standard deviation of fat content is known to be 0.03. For the nine samples, we obtain 14% fat content. Thus, the statistic Z, is

$$Z = (0.14 - 0.12)/(0.03/\sqrt{9}) = (0.2)/(0.09) = 2.222.$$

Thus, for the first alternative, we have a two-sided hypothesis which means that $Z_{\alpha/2} = Z_{0.025} = 1.96$ and, since $2.222 > 1.96$, we reject the hypothesis. For the second alternative, it is a one-sided alternative and, therefore, $Z_\alpha = Z_{0.05} = 1.645$ and, since $2.222 > 1.645$, we reject the hypothesis.

3. In a similar manner, we can construct tests for comparing several means and variances. All that is needed are the sampling probability distributions. Say that we want to compare the difference between two samples. Then we can write

$$H_0 : \mu_1 - \mu_2 = 0; H_1 : \mu_1 - \mu_2 \neq 0.$$

We have at present two sets of samples, with averages $\bar{x}_1$ and $\bar{x}_2$. The variances are known for each set of samples and given by σ_1^2 and σ_2^2. Thus, the difference has a mean $(\bar{X}_1 - \bar{X}_2)$, while the variance (when n_1 and n_2 are the samples sizes of the first and second set, respectively), is

$$\text{var } (\bar{X}_1 - \bar{X}_2) = \sigma_1^2/n_1 + \sigma_2^2/n_2,$$

and, therefore, the test statistic is again (due to the normality of the difference), a two-sided test, with

$$z = \frac{(\bar{X}_1 - \bar{X}_2)}{\sqrt{\text{var } (\bar{X}_1 - \bar{X}_2)}} = \frac{(\bar{X}_1 - \bar{X}_2)}{\sqrt{(\sigma_1^2/n_1 + \sigma_2^2/n_2)}}$$

For example, if $\bar{X}_1 = 10, \bar{X}_2 = 8, \sigma_1^2 = 4, \sigma_2^2 = 6, n_1 = 10, n_2 = 16$, then

$$z = (10 - 8)/\sqrt{(4/10 + 6/16)} = 2/1.1105 = 1.800,$$

and therefore, if $\alpha = 0.05$, we have $Z_{\alpha/2} = Z_{0.025} = 1.96$, which leads to the conclusion that we cannot reject the hypothesis.

When the parameters σ_1^2 and σ_2^2 are not known as well, then we can use the sample estimates of the variances. If the samples have the same variance, i.e. $\sigma_1^2 = \sigma_2^2$, the combined estimator of this variance is

$$s^2 = \frac{(n_1 - 1)s_1^2 + (n_2 - 1)s_2^2}{n_1 + n_2 - 2}, \text{ where}$$

$$s_i^2 = \sum_{i=1}^{n_1} \frac{(x_i - \bar{X}_i)^2}{(n_i - 1)}.$$

In this case, we again use the t statistic, which is given by

$$t = \frac{(\bar{X}_1 - \bar{X}_2)}{s\sqrt{1/n_1 + 1/n_2}}.$$

If we wish to establish hypotheses on the variance, then is sufficient to know that the ratio

$$(s^2/\sigma^2)[n_1 + n_2 - 2] = [(n_1 - 1)s_1^2 + (n_2 - 1)s_2^2]$$

has a chi-square distribution with $[n_1 - 1 + n_2 - 1]$ degrees of freedom and proceed as above.

4. (Messina, 1987) On a manufacturing line for microelectronic circuits, one of the processes consists of attaching the leads of the circuit to a substrate. This process will be tested by a lead frame pull test. This test will determine the amount of force necessary to pull the leads off the frame. The manufacturing manager would like to know with 95% confidence the upper and lower limits of this pull-strength test. The variance of the process is known from recent studies to be $\sigma^2 = 0.05lb/\text{in}$. In this study, 10 microelectric circuits were bonded to 10 different substrates and pulled off. The results of this study are given in Table 3.17. From this data, $\bar{x} = 5.64$. Since a two-sided confidence interval is required, we have the following interval:

$$P[5.64 \mp 1.96(0.05)(1/\sqrt{10})] = 0.95,$$

and therefore the 95% confidence interval is given by, $5.33 \leq \mu \leq 5.95$. Now assume that the variance is not known. In this case, the standard deviation is estimated by

$$\begin{aligned} s^2 &= [(5.6 - 5.64)^2 + (4.8 - 5.64)^2 + (6.2 - 5.64)^2 \\ &+ (6.0 - 5.64)^2 + (5.8 - 5.64)^2 + +(5.6 - 5.64)^2 + (5.4 - 5.64)^2 \\ &+ (6.0 - 5.64)^2 + (5.8 - 5.64)^2 + (5.2 - 5.64)^2]/9 \end{aligned}$$

or

$$s^2 = 0.176,$$

and therefore the 95 confidence interval is (using the t distribution with $n - 1 = 9$ degrees of freedom, $t = 2.262$)

$$P[5.64 \mp 0.95(1/\sqrt{10})] = 0.95 \text{ or } 5.34 \leq \mu \leq 5.94.$$

Table 3.17

Circuit No.	*Pull strength (lb/in^2)*	*Circuit No.*	*Pull strength (lb/in^2)*
1	5.6	6	5.6
2	4.8	7	5.4
3	6.2	8	6.0
4	6.0	9	5.8
5	5.8	10	5.2

3.4 The reliability function

Classical reliability was developed in response to a need for very high performance, which is needed in the management of complex systems. Consider a part, a product or a system, and say that $f(t)$ is the probability that the part is failing in a small time interval Δt. In other words, the event that the part fails in the time interval $(t, t+\Delta t)$ is $f(t)\Delta t$. The probability that it fails in a time interval $(0, t)$ is given by its cumulative distribution

$$F(t) = \text{Prob}(\tau < t).$$

Thus, the probability that *it will not fail in this interval* is $1 - F(t)$, which is called the *reliability*, or

$$R(t) = 1 - F(t).$$

As a result, reliability relates to the life of a product, a unit or a system after it has been put to use. The greater its reliability, the more likely it will continue to perform properly. There are various models to represent reliability, for it provides a description of a process' potential quality operation over time (which can be a function of a number of conditions). In logistics, for example, reliability and a broad number of performance measures derived from the reliability function are used to characterize the quality operation of the logistic system. For example, this might include the operation of a car, a fleet of cars or planes, or the availability of spare parts in an inventory system.

Consider the fatigue of metal, the fatigue of an attendant in a restaurant, the time a car is put to use without maintenance, the time to failure of a product, the process of reliability growth, and so on. These processes are often represented by models which we use to assess their quality performance. Some of these characteristics include the hazard rate, the process availability, mean residual lifetime, the Mean Time Between Failures (MTBF), maintainability and others. These are defined below.

(a) The hazard rate $h(t)$

Say that a system breaks down at some future time T, and let t denote the present time. The the hazard rate is defined by the conditional probability rate of failure in a subsequent time interval Δt,

$$\begin{aligned} h(t) &= \lim_{\Delta t \to 0} (1/\Delta t) P[t \leq t + \Delta t \mid T > t], \text{ or} \\ h(t) &= \frac{f(t)}{\bar{F}(t)} = \frac{f(t)}{1 - F(t)} = -\frac{dR(t)/dt}{R(t)} \end{aligned}$$

where

$$f(t) = dF(t)/dt = -dR(t)/dt$$

is the probability distribution of the process life. Processes can be distinguished by the behaviour of the hazard function $h(t)$, which can be increasing, decreasing or be piecewise increasing and decreasing, depending on the functional form of the reliability function. An increasing hazard rate function would model a deteriorating process, while a decreasing hazard rate would model an improving-over-time process.

(b) *The mean residual lifetime*

The mean residual lifetime is the expected remaining lifetime, or

$$\begin{aligned}\mu(t) &= E(T-t \mid T>t) = \int_t^{\infty} \bar{F}(x)dx/F(t) \\ &= \int_t^{\infty} x\bar{F}(x)dx/F(t) - t = \int_t^{\infty} R(x)dx/(1-R(t)).\end{aligned}$$

If $t = 0$, then $\mu(0)$ is the mean life time of the part (product or system) while $\mu(t)$ is an indicator or the remaining useful life (or time to failure, for example, of the process) at a given instant of time t.

(c) *The mean time between failure (MTBF)*

The MTBF is defined by

$$\begin{aligned}\text{MTBF} &= \int_0^{\infty} tf(t)dt = -\int_0^{\infty} t(dR(t)/dt)dt \\ &= -tR(t)\mid_{t=0}^{t=\infty} + \int_0^{\infty} R(t)dt = \int_0^{\infty} R(t)dt,\end{aligned}$$

where $f(t)$ is the probability distribution of the first time to failure of a part, component or a system.

(d) *Process availability*

The point availability $A(t)$ is the probability that the system is in an up state at time t. If $z(t) = 1$ denotes an up state and $z(t) = 0$ when the system is down, then

$$E[z(t)] = A(t).$$

Interval availability in $[0, T]$, however, is defined by the average

$$AV(T) = (1/T)\int_0^T A(t)dt.$$

When T becomes very large (tending to infinity), we define the long-term average availability. These measures are often used in logistics to compare spare parts inventory policies, maintenance and repair policies. For this reason, these are often used as the measures of quality of such systems.

(e) *Maintainability*

System maintainability is a design characteristic which expresses the probability that a part, product or system is restored to specified conditions within a given period of time when maintenance action is performed in accordance with prescribed procedures and resources. Maintainability is thus a measure of a system's downtime (needed to compute the system availability). Thus, if $g(t)$ is the probability density function that a failed system returns to operation, then by some time T,

$$\Pr\left[\text{Downtime } \leq T\right] = \int_0^T g(t)dt,$$

which is the maintainability equation. Of course, depending on the assumptions made regarding the distribution $g(t)$, we obtain various models. Let MTTR be the mean time to repair of a down unit. Then, of course, the ratio $\frac{\text{MTBF}}{\text{MTBF+MTTR}}$ can be used to measure the mean availability of the unit. The more efficient the repair facilities the shorter the time to repair and the greater the MTBF, and the better the unit.

These functions provide a broad range of potential measures of systems performance which are both acceptable and commonly used in logistics management. We consider next two examples based on the exponential and the Weibull distribution.

Example: Exponential reliability

The (memoryless) exponential distribution we discussed is given by $f(t) = \lambda \exp[-\lambda t]; \lambda > 0, t \geq 0$ and therefore, $F(t) = 1 - \exp[-\lambda t]$. The reliability is thu, $R(t) = \exp[-\lambda t]$ and the hazard rate is $h(t) = h = \lambda$, where λ is the mean lifetime. The Mean Time Between Failures (MTBF) is

$$\text{MTBF } = \int_0^\infty tf(t)dt = -\int_0^\infty t(dR/dt)dt = -tR(t)\mid_0^\infty + \int_0^\infty R(t)dt$$

and therefore,

$$\text{MTBF } = \int_0^\infty \exp[-\lambda t]dt = 1/\lambda.$$

Interestingly, this distribution has a constant rate. Thus, if it were to be used to evaluate the operational performance of lamps, it would mean that its failure probability when it is new and when it has already been used for some time will be the same! Clearly, this assumption can sometimes be misleading. It is thus necessary to be careful in selecting such models. The Weibull life distribution generalizes both the exponential distribution and, at the same time, can have an increasing or decreasing hazard rate.

Example: Reliability of the Weibull life distribution

The Weibull life distribution is

$$f(t) = \alpha\lambda^{\alpha}t^{\alpha-1}\exp[-(\lambda t)^{\alpha}], \lambda > 0, \alpha > 0, t \geq 0.$$

Thus, the reliability function is given by $R(t) = \exp[-(\lambda t)^{\alpha}]$, while the hazard rate $h(t)$ is $h(t) = \alpha\lambda^{\alpha}t^{\alpha-1}$. If $\alpha > 1$ then the hazard rate increases over time, while for $\alpha < 1$ it is decreasing. For $\alpha = 1$, the hazard rate is constant and we obtain the exponential model. Finally, for the MTBF, we have

$$\text{MTBF} = \int_0^{\infty} \exp[-(\lambda t)^{\alpha}]dt = \lambda^{-1/\alpha}\Gamma((1+\alpha)/\alpha).$$

The Weibull distribution is often used because of its convenient analytical structure.

References

Barlow R. and F. Proschan, *Mathematical Theory of Reliability* (1965) Wiley, New York.

Box G. (1993) Quali improvement-The new industrial revolution, *International Statistical Review,* **61**, 3-19.

Chatfield C. (1970) *Statistics for Technology,* London, Chapman and Hall (1975, Second Edition).

Ishikawa K. (1976) *Guide to Quality Control,* Asian Productivity Organization, Tokyo.

John Peter M. (1990) *Statistical Methods in Engineering and Quality Assurance,* New York, Wiley-Interscience.

Johnson N.L. and S. Kotz (1969) *Discrete Distributions*, New York, Houghton Mifflin.

Johnson N.L. and S. Kotz (1970a) *Continuous Univariate Distributions-1*, New York, Houghton Mifflin.

Johnson N.L. and S. Kotz (1970b) *Continuous Univariate Distributions-2,* New York, Houghton Mifflin.

Kapur K.L. and L.R. Lamberson (1977) *Reliability Engineering in Design,* Wiley, New York.

Messina W.S. (1987) *Statistical Quality Control for Manufacturing Managers,* New York, Wiley.

Price F. (1984) *Right First Time: Using Quality Control for Profit,* Gower Publ. Co., Brookfield, Vermont.

Rau John G. (1970) *Optimization and Probability in Systems Engineering,* New York, Van Nostrand.

Shooman M.L. (1968) *Probabilistic Reliability: An Engineering Approach,* McGraw Hill, New York.

Appendix 3.A

Distributions of potential interest are numerous. References and surveys can be found in Johnson and Kotz (1969, 1970a, 1970b). Below, we consider the Negative Binomial Distribution (NBD) with parameters P and N, defined by

$$\Pr[x=k] = \binom{N+k-1}{N-1}(P/1+P)^k(1/1+P)^N, k=0,1,2,3,\ldots$$

whose mean is NP and variance is $NP(1+P)$. It can be represented equivalently as the number of independent trials necessary to obtain n occurrences of an event which has a constant probability θ of occurring at each trial. If x denotes the number of necessary trials, we then have

$$\Pr[x=n+k] = \binom{n+k-1}{n-1}\theta^n(1-\theta)^k,$$

which is the NBD with parameters $N=n$ and $P=\theta/(1-\theta)$. For example, say that we test products coming off a production line. We assume that the probability that a unit will be defective is θ. Then the number of units to test until a certain number n is found defective has a negative binomial distribution with mean and variance given by $n(1-\theta)/\theta$ and $n(1-\theta)/\theta^2$. When n is large and $(1-\theta)n$ tends to a constant λ, we approximate the NBD distribution by a Poisson whose parameter is λ. The NBD also arises from the mixture of the Poisson distribution. In particular, if a random variable has a Poisson distribution with mean λ and the parameter λ has itself a gamma probability distribution with parameters α and β, given by

$$f(\lambda) = [\beta^\alpha\Gamma(\alpha)]^{-1}\lambda^{\alpha-1}\exp[-\lambda/\beta], \lambda>0, \alpha>0, \beta>0,$$

then the probability of the unconditional Poisson distribution is

$$\begin{aligned}
P(k) &= \int_0^\infty [\lambda^k e^{-\lambda}/k!][\beta^\alpha\Gamma(\alpha)]^{-1}\lambda^{\alpha-1}\exp[-\lambda/\beta]d\lambda \\
&= [\beta^\alpha\Gamma(\alpha)]^{-1}\int_0^\infty [1/k!]\lambda^{k+\alpha-1}\exp[-\lambda(1+1/\beta]d\lambda \\
&= \binom{\alpha+k-1}{\alpha-1}[\frac{\beta}{(1+\beta)}]^k[\frac{1}{(1+\beta)}]^\alpha,
\end{aligned}$$

which is the NBD with parameters α and β.

Appendix 3.B: Statistical tables

Binomial Probabilities (with $p = 0.05$)

$n = 4$	.0100	.0200	.0300	.0400	.0500	.0600	.0700	.0800	.0900
0	.9606	.9224	.8853	.8493	.8145	.7807	.7481	.7164	.6857
1	.0388	.0753	.1095	.1416	.1715	.1993	.2252	.2492	.2713
2	.0006	.0023	.0051	.0088	.0135	.0191	.0254	.0325	.0402
3	.0000	.0000	.0001	.0002	.0005	.0008	.0013	.0019	.0027
4	.0000	.0000	.0000	.0000	.0000	.0000	.0000	.0000	.0001
$n = 5$									
0	.9510	.9039	.8587	.8154	.7738	.7339	.6957	.6591	.6240
1	.0480	.0922	.1328	.1699	.2036	.2342	.2618	.2866	.3086
2	.0010	.0038	.0082	.0142	.0214	.0299	.0394	.0498	.0610
3	.0000	.0001	.0003	.0006	.0011	.0019	.0030	.0043	.0060
4	.0000	.0000	.0000	.0000	.0000	.0001	.0001	.0002	.0003
5	.0000	.0000	.0000	.0000	.0000	.0000	.0000	.0000	.0000
$n = 6$									
0	.9415	.8858	.8330	.7828	.7351	.6899	.6470	.6064	.5679
1	.0571	.1085	.1546	.1957	.2321	.2642	.2922	.3164	.3370
2	.0014	.0055	.0120	.0204	.0305	.0422	.0550	.0688	.0833
3	.0000	.0002	.0005	.0011	.0021	.0036	.0055	.0080	.0110
4	.0000	.0000	.0000	.0000	.0001	.0002	.0003	.0005	.0008
5	.0000	.0000	.0000	.0000	.0000	.0000	.0000	.0000	.0000
6	.0000	.0000	.0000	.0000	.0000	.0000	.0000	.0000	.0000
$n = 7$									
0	.9321	.8681	.8080	.7514	.6983	.6485	.6017	.5578	.5168
1	.0659	.1240	.1749	.2192	.2573	.2897	.3170	.3396	.3578
2	.0020	.0076	.0162	.0274	.0406	.0555	.0716	.0886	.1061
3	.0000	.0003	.0008	.0019	.0036	.0059	.0090	.0128	.0175
4	.0000	.0000	.0000	.0001	.0002	.0004	.0007	.0011	.0017
5	.0000	.0000	.0000	.0000	.0000	.0000	.0000	.0001	.0001
6	.0000	.0000	.0000	.0000	.0000	.0000	.0000	.0000	.0000
7	.0000	.0000	.0000	.0000	.0000	.0000	.0000	.0000	.0000
$n = 8$									
0	.9227	.8508	.7837	.7214	.6634	.6096	.5596	.5132	.4703
1	.0746	.1389	.1939	.2405	.2793	.3113	.3370	.3570	.3721
2	.0026	.0099	.0210	.0351	.0515	.0695	.0888	.1087	.1288
3	.0001	.0004	.0013	.0029	.0054	.0089	.0134	.0189	.0255
4	.0000	.0000	.0001	.0002	.0004	.0007	.0013	.0021	.0031
5	.0000	.0000	.0000	.0000	.0000	.0000	.0001	.0001	.0002
6	.0000	.0000	.0000	.0000	.0000	.0000	.0000	.0000	.0000
7	.0000	.0000	.0000	.0000	.0000	.0000	.0000	.0000	.0000
8	.0000	.0000	.0000	.0000	.0000	.0000	.0000	.0000	.0000

The Standard Normal Table

z	0.00	0.01	0.02	0.03	0.04	0.05	0.06	0.07	0.08	0.09
0.00	0.500	0.496	0.492	0.488	0.484	0.480	0.476	0.472	0.468	0.464
0.10	0.460	0.456	0.452	0.448	0.444	0.440	0.436	0.429	0.429	0.425
0.20	0.421	0.417	0.413	0.409	0.405	0.401	0.397	0.394	0.390	0.386
0.30	0.382	0.378	0.374	0.371	0.367	0.363	0.359	0.356	0.352	0.348
0.40	0.345	0.341	0.337	0.334	0.330	0.326	0.323	0.319	0.316	0.312
0.50	0.309	0.305	0.302	0.298	0.295	0.291	0.288	0.284	0.281	0.278
0.60	0.274	0.271	0.268	0.264	0.261	0.258	0.255	0.251	0.248	0.245
0.70	0.242	0.239	0.236	0.233	0.230	0.227	0.224	0.221	0.218	0.215
0.80	0.212	0.209	0.206	0.203	0.200	0.198	0.195	0.192	0.189	0.187
0.90	0.184	0.181	0.179	0.176	0.174	0.171	0.169	0.166	0.164	0.161
1.00	0.159	0.156	0.154	0.152	0.149	0.147	0.145	0.142	0.140	0.138
1.10	0.136	0.133	0.131	0.129	0.127	0.125	0.123	0.121	0.119	0.117
1.20	0.115	0.113	0.111	0.109	0.107	0.106	0.104	0.102	0.100	0.099
1.30	0.097	0.095	0.093	0.092	0.090	0.089	0.087	0.085	0.084	0.082
1.40	0.O81	0.079	0.078	0.076	0.075	0.074	0.072	0.071	0.069	0.068
1.50	0.067	0.066	0.064	0.063	0.062	0.061	0.059	0.058	0.057	0.056
1.60	0.055	0.054	0.053	0.052	0.051	0.049	0.048	0.047	0.046	0.046
1.70	0.045	0.044	0.043	0.042	0.041	0.040	0.039	0.038	0.038	0.037
1.80	0.036	0.035	0.034	0.034	0.033	0.032	0.031	0.031	0.030	0.029
1.90	0.029	0.028	0.027	0.027	0.026	0.026	0.025	0.024	0.024	0.023
2.00	0.023	0.022	0.022	0.021	0.021	0.020	0.020	0.019	0.019	0.018
2.10	0.018	0.017	0.017	0.017	0.016	0.016	0.015	0.015	0.015	0.014
2.20	0.014	0.014	0.013	0.013	0.013	0.012	0.012	0.012	0.011	0.011
2.30	0.011	0.010	0.010	0.010	0.010	0.009	0.009	0.009	0.009	0.008
2.40	0.008	0.008	0.008	0.008	0.008	0.007	0.007	0.007	0.007	0.006
2.50	0.006	0.006	0.006	0.006	0.006	0.005	0.005	0.005	0.005	0.005
2.60	0.005	0.005	0.004	0.004	0.004	0.004	0.004	0.004	0.004	0.004
2.70	0.003	0.003	0.003	0.003	0.003	0.003	0.003	0.003	0.003	0.003
2.80	0.003	0.002	0.002	0.002	0.002	0.002	0.002	0.002	0.002	0.002
2.90	0.002	0.002	0.002	0.002	0.002	0.002	0.002	0.001	0.001	0.001
3.00	0.001	0.001	0.001	0.001	0.001	0.001	0.001	0.001	0.001	0.001

The Student–t distribution.
The two tails, $1 - P(-t \leq x \leq +t)$

$n \backslash p$	.90	.50	.30	.20	.10	.05	.02	.01
1	.158	1.00	1.963	3.078	6.314	12.706	31.821	63.657
2	.142	.816	1.386	1.886	2.920	4.303	6.965	9.925
3	.137	.765	1.250	1.638	2.353	3.182	4.541	5.841
4	.134	.741	1.190	1.533	2.132	2.776	3.747	4.604
5	.132	.727	1.156	1.476	2.015	2.571	3.365	4.032
6	.131	.718	1.134	1.440	1.943	2.447	3.143	3.707
7	.130	.711	1.119	1.415	1.895	2.365	2.998	3.499
8	.130	.706	1.108	1.397	1.860	2.306	2.896	3.355
9	.129	.703	1.100	1.383	1.833	2.262	2.821	3.250
10	.129	.700	1.093	1.372	1.812	2.228	2.764	3.169
11	.129	.697	1.088	1.363	1.796	2.201	2.718	3.106
12	.128	.695	1.083	1.356	1.782	2.179	2.681	3.055
13	.128	.694	1.079	1.350	1.771	2.160	2.650	3.012
14	.128	.692	1.076	1.345	1.761	2.145	2.624	2.977
15	.128	.691	1.074	1.341	1.753	2.131	2.602	2.947
16	.129	.690	1.071	1.337	1.746	2.120	2.583	2.921
17	.128	.689	1.069	1.333	1.740	2.110	2.567	2.898
18	.127	.688	1.067	1.330	1.734	2.101	2.552	2.878
19	.127	.688	1.066	1.328	1.729	2.093	2.539	2.861
20	.127	.687	1.064	1.325	1.725	2.086	2.528	2.845
21	.127	.686	1.063	1.323	1.721	2.080	2.518	2.831
22	.127	.686	1.061	1.321	1.717	2.074	2.508	2.819
23	.127	.685	1.060	1.319	1.714	2.069	2.500	2.807
24	.127	.685	1.059	1.318	1.711	2.064	2.492	2.797
25	.127	.684	1.058	1.316	1.708	2.060	2.485	2.787
26	.127	.684	1.058	1.315	1.706	2.056	2.479	2.779
27	.127	.684	1.057	1.314	1.703	2.052	2.473	2.771
28	.127	.683	1.056	1.313	1.701	2.048	2.467	2.763
29	.127	.683	1.055	1.311	1.699	2.045	2.462	2.756
30	.127	.683	1.055	1.310	1.697	2.042	2.457	2.750
∞	.1257	.6745	1.0364	1.2816	1.6449	1.960	2.3263	2.5758

The percentage points of the chi-square distribution

$\nu \backslash \alpha$	.995	.990	.975	.950	.500	.200	.100	.05	.025	.01	.005
1	0.000	0.0002	0.001	0.0039	0.45	1.64	2.71	3.84	5.02	6.63	7.88
2	0.010	0.020	0.051	0.103	1.39	3.22	4.61	5.99	7.38	9.21	10.60
3	0.072	0.115	0.216	0.352	2.37	4.64	6.25	7.81	9.35	11.34	12.84
4	0.207	0.30	0.484	0.71	3.36	5.99	7.78	9.49	11.14	13.28	14.86
5	0.412	0.55	0.831	1.15	4.35	7.29	9.24	11.07	12.83	15.09	16.75
6	0.676	0.87	1.24	1.64	5.35	8.56	10.64	12.59	14.45	16.81	18.55
7	0.989	1.24	1.69	2.17	6.35	9.80	12.02	14.07	16.01	18.48	20.28
8	1.34	1.65	2.18	2.73	7.34	11.03	13.36	15.51	17.53	20.09	21.95
9	1.73	2.09	2.70	3.33	8.34	12.24	14.68	16.92	19.02	21.67	23.59
10	2.16	2.56	3.25	3.94	9.34	13.44	15.99	18.31	20.48	23.21	25.19
11	2.60	3.05	3.82	4.57	10.34	14.63	17.28	19.68	21.92	24.72	26.76
12	3.07	3.57	4.40	5.23	11.34	15.81	18.55	21.03	23.34	26.22	28.30
13	3.57	4.11	5.01	5.89	12.34	16.98	19.81	22.36	24.74	27.69	29.82
14	4.07	4.66	5.63	6.57	13.34	18.15	21.06	23.68	26.12	29.14	31.32
15	4.60	5.23	6.26	7.26	14.34	19.31	22.31	25.00	27.49	30.58	32.80
16	5.14	5.81	6.91	7.96	15.34	20.47	23.54	26.30	28.85	32.00	34.27
17	5.70	6.41	7.56	8.67	16.34	21.61	24.77	27.59	30.19	33.41	35.72
18	6.26	7.02	8.23	9.39	17.34	22.76	25.99	28.87	31.53	34.81	37.16
19	6.84	7.63	8.91	10.12	18.34	23.90	27.20	30.14	32.85	36.19	38.58
20	7.43	8.26	9.59	10.85	19.34	25.04	28.41	31.41	34.17	37.57	40.00
21	8.03	8.90	10.28	11.59	20.34	26.17	29.62	32.67	35.48	38.93	41.40
22	8.64	9.54	10.98	12.34	21.34	27.30	30.81	33.92	36.78	40.29	42.80
23	9.26	10.20	11.69	13.09	23.34	28.43	32.01	35.17	38.08	41.64	44.18
24	9.89	10.86	12.40	13.85	23.34	29.55	33.20	36.42	39.36	42.98	45.56
25	10.52	11.52	13.12	14.61	24.34	30.68	34.38	37.65	40.65	44.31	46.93
26	11.16	12.20	13.84	15.38	25.34	31.79	35.56	38.89	41.92	45.64	48.29
27	11.81	12.88	14.57	16.15	26.34	32.91	36.74	40.11	43.19	46.96	49.64
28	12.46	13.57	15.31	16.93	27.34	34.03	37.92	41.34	44.46	48.28	50.99
29	13.12	14.26	16.05	17.71	28.34	35.14	39.09	42.56	45.72	49.59	52.34
30	13.79	14.95	16.79	18.49	29.34	36.25	40.26	43.77	46.98	50.89	53.67
40	20.71	22.16	24.43	26.51	39.34	47.27	51.81	55.76	59.34	63.69	66.77
50	27.99	29.71	32.36	34.76	49.33	58.16	63.17	67.50	71.41	76.15	79.49
60	35.53	37.48	40.48	43.19	59.33	68.97	74.40	79.08	83.30	88.38	91.95
70	43.28	45.44	48.76	51.74	69.33	79.71	85.53	90.53	95.02	100.43	104.2
80	51.17	53.54	57.15	60.39	79.33	90.41	96.58	101.88	106.63	112.33	116.3
90	59.20	61.75	65.65	69.13	89.33	101.05	107.57	113.15	118.14	124.12	128.3
100	67.33	70.06	74.22	77.93	99.33	111.67	118.50	124.34	129.56	135.81	140.2

CHAPTER 4

Decision theory and the management of quality

4.1 Introduction

Typically, we face the prospect of having to make a decision when some of the information needed to reach that decision is not available. Statistical decision theory deals with such problems. It defines rational procedures for reaching with such decisions in a consistent manner, and based on something more than intuition and personal subjective judgment (which is important when quality is intangible and hardly measurable). The modern theory of decision making under uncertainty has evolved in four phases, starting at the beginning of the 19th century. In the beginning, it was concerned with collecting data to provide a foundation for *experimentation and sampling theory.* These were the times when surveys and the counting of populations of all sorts began. The theories of quality inspection, statistical production and process controls (SPC/SQC) are a direct application of these statistical theories.

Subsequently, statisticians such as Karl Pearson and R. A. Fisher studied and set up the foundations of *statistical data analysis*, which deals with the assessment of the reliability and accuracy of data. They provided the elements which seek to represent large quantities of information (as given explicitly in data) in an aggregated and summarized fashion, as probability distributions and moments (mean, variance), and to state how accurate these representations are.

The next step, expounded and developed primarily by R.A. Fisher in the 1920s, went one step further by *planning experiments.* This approach is now an essential tool for the design and control of quality in complex situations (when many variables are involved and must be controlled).

A third phase, which expanded dramatically in the 1930s and the 1940s, consisted of the construction of *mathematical models* which sought to bridge the gap between the process of data collection, and the need of such data for specific purposes like as decision making. At that time, classical models for decision making under uncertainty included the well known models for inventory management, maintenance of equipment, failure, aging processes, fatigue and reliability models.

It was only in the 1950s and the 1960s that the modern theory of *decision making under uncertainty* took hold. In important publications, Raiffa, Luce, Schlaiffer and many others provided a unified framework which integrated some of the problems relating to data collection, experimentation, model building and decision making. In addition, the theory of decision making under uncertainty was intimately related to typical management problems in industry, business and other areas. Problems such as the assessment of the value of information, methods of collecting it, the amount to pay for it, the weight of intuition and subjective judgment (as often used by managers), became relevant and integrated into the theory. Currently, these are an important part of the tools of management, and can be used profitably to manage and control quality. Their practical importance cannot be understated, for it provides a structured approach for reaching decisions under uncertainty and complexity. In a complex and competitive environment, this approach can be used profitably for decision making in general, and for the economic management of quality in particular.

In decision theory, a state of uncertainty is characterized in terms of:

(a) Knowledge of the states of nature and their numbers.

(b) Knowledge of the probabilities associated with each state of nature.

Given the states and their probabilities, decision problems require:

1. A number of alternatives, one and only one of which will be selected.
2. The conditional consequences of selecting a specific alternative
3. An objective which expresses the relative desirability of outcomes and the decision maker's attitude toward risk.

For example, in quality control, alternatives may include decisions on whether to inspect a lot, to select one from a number of alternative sampling techniques, or to select one supplier from a number of alternative suppliers. Conditional consequences are the outcomes which occur for sure, once uncertainty regarding the occurrence of a state is removed and a specific decision is selected.

4.2 Formulation of problems under uncertainty

Assume that an objective is given, the states that a system can take and their probabilities are known, and finally, assume that conditional consequences are appropriately measured. There are two ways to represent such information: using payoff tables and decision trees.

The payoff table

Conditional consequences are expressed in a table format where the rows designate the alternative actions that can be taken, and the columns the set of possible states, each accompanied by the state's probability. Entries in the table are costs, payoffs and generally outcomes. These outcomes can be deterministic, or random. The sample Table 4.1 given below specifies n states numbered $1, 2, 3, 4, \ldots.., n$, and m alternative acts $A_1, A_2, \ldots, A_m$. When alternative $A_i (i = 1, ..m)$ is taken and, say, state j occurs (with probability $p_j, j = 1, ..n$), then the cost (or payoff) is c_{ij}. Thus, in such a decision problem, there are:

n potential, mutually exclusive and exhaustive states

m alternative actions

nm combinations which define the conditional consequences.

Table 4.1: The payoff table.

States Probabilities	1 p_1	2 p_2	......	n p_n
Alternative 1	c_{11}	c_{12}		c_{1n}
Alternative 2	c_{21}	c_{22}	.	c_{2n}
Alternative 3	c_{31}	c_{32}	..	c_{3n}
.....	...	...	...	...
.....	...	...	....	...
Alternative m	c_{m1}	c_{m2}	.....	c_{mn}

Example

The buyer of a used car may have three alternatives when purchasing the car. First, accept the car as is. Second, take the car to a specialist who will perform a number of tests to check whether it is worth buying. And three, the buyer can buy a service contract and warranty for a certain amount of time which is offered by the used car salesman. The potential states are defined by the quality state of the car. It can be in good condition, as the used car salesman may have claimed, or may be hiding some defects (resulting from a past accident). Finally, the conditional consequences (payoff less costs, for example) would be the value the buyer derives from a good (or bad) car, less its price and the costs sustained under each alternative (take a chance, pay the specialist or buy the service contract). Assume the payoff matrix in Table 4.2.

Table 4.2: Numerical payoffs.

States: Probabilities:	Good 0.9	Bad 0.10
Accept as is:	1000	-900
Seek specialist:	800	-200
Buy contract:	700	400

If the car is good and the buyer accepts the car as is, there is no cost but a profit of \$1000. If a specialist is called in whose cost is \$200, then the profit is \$800 if the car is good. If it is bad, then the only cost is that of having brought in the specialist. A service contract costs \$300, and therefore if the car is good, the profit is $1000 - 300 = \$700$ and less if the care is bad (to account for the nuisance). The expected profit for each of the alternatives is thus:

Accept as is: $EP_1 = (0.9)(1000) + (0.10)(-900) = 900 - 90 = 810$

Seek Specialist: $EP_2 = (0.9)(800) + (0.10)(-200) = 720 - 20 = 700$

Buy contract: $EP_3 = (0.9)(700) + (0.10)(400) = 630 + 40 = 670$

If the manager's decision objective is to select the largest expected profit, then obviously the decision to adopt is to accept the car as is (we shall return to the problem of objective selection later on).

The opportunity loss table

Instead of considering payoffs, we can consider the opportunity loss associated with each action. Say that event j occurs and we select alternative i. In this case, the payoff is π_{ij}. If we were equipped with this knowledge *prior* to making a decision, it is possible that another decision could have brought a greater payoff. Let the maximum payoff decision yield a payoff $\text{Max}_j[\pi_{ij}]$. The difference between this max payoff and the payoff obtained by following any of the other alternatives is called the 'opportunity loss'. Denote this loss by l_{ij}, then:

$$l_{ij} = \max_i [\pi_{ij}] - \pi_{ij}.$$

The opportunity loss table is as shown in Table 4.3.

Table 4.3: The opportunity loss table.

States	1	2	......	n
Probabilities	p_1	p_2		p_n
Alternative 1	l_{11}	l_{12}		l_{1n}
Alternative 2	l_{21}	l_{22}	.	l_{2n}
Alternative 3	l_{31}	l_{32}	..	l_{3n}
.....	...	...	...	...
.....	...	...	....	...
Alternative m	l_{m1}	l_{m2}	.....	l_{mn}

Consider again the previous car buyer example. If the buyer knew that the car was good, he would accept it as is, since this is the maximum profit alternative. In this case, the opportunity loss for each of the other alternatives is $1000 - 800 = 200$ as well as $1000 - 700 = 300$. If the buyer knew that the car was bad, then the best alternative is to buy a contract and, as a result, the opportunity loss for each of the other alternatives is: $400 + 900 = 1300$, and, $400 - (200) = 600$, as shown in Table 4.4.

Table 4.4: Numerical losses.

States:	Good	Bad
Probabilities:	0.9	0.10
Accept as is:	0	1300
Seek specialist:	200	600
Buy contract:	300	0

The expected cost (opportunity loss) under each of the alternatives is thus

Accept as is: $EL_1 = (0.9)(0) + (0.10)(1,300) = 130$

Seek specialist: $EL_2 = (0.9)(200) + (0.10)(600) = 180 + 60 = 240$

Buy contract: $EL_3 = (0.9)(300) + (0.10)(0) = 270$

As a result, the best decision is clearly, again, to accept the car as is. Note in particular that for each strategy we have:

Accept as is: $810 + 130 = 940$

Seek specialist: $700 + 240 = 940$

Buy contract: $670 + 270 = 940$

This is not a coincidence, and will be studied in detail in Section 4.4. Although opportunity loss matrices are rarely used in decision making problems, they are important in the management of quality because they are a measure of what could be economically gained, in an expected sense, if we were to exert full control of a process, fully test a production lot, etc. (and thereby all uncertainty-variability). This will be discussed later on.

4.3 Examples and applications

We consider next some problems which are important for the study of quality problems and their control.

The two actions problem

In two actions problems (inspect/do not inspect, control/no control, buy-lease, for example) there are only two alternatives, one of which has to be selected. Let z_{1j} and z_{2j} be the outcomes when an event j occurs. For example, $j = 1$ may represent a defect free order which is delivered with probability $p_1, j = 2$ the event that a unit is defective with probability p_2, etc. Define for each alternative i, a fixed decision cost K_i, and let k_i be the variable cost associated with the outcomes $z_{ij}, i = 1, 2$. The prior probabilities of states j are p_j. The decision table is given in Table 4.5. The outcomes faced under each strategy are random, given by,

$$\begin{aligned} u_i &= K_i + k_i z_{ij} w.p. p_j, i = 1, 2; j = 1, \ldots n \\ p_j &\geq 0, \sum_{j=1}^{n} p_j = 1 \end{aligned}$$

Table 4.5: Alternatives-states probabilities.

States	1	2	3	..	..	..	n
Probabilities	p_1	p_2	p_3	..	..	..	p_n
Alternative 1	z_{11}	z_{12}	z_{13}	..	..	..	z_{1n}
Alternative 2	z_{21}	z_{22}	z_{23}	..	..	..	z_{2n}

where w.p. is used to denote the statement 'with probability'. The two actions problem consists of comparing the two costs u_1 and u_2. If the objective can be expressed by the expectation of costs, and if U_i is this expectation, then

$$U_i = Eu_i = \sum_{j=1}^{n} u_{ij} p_j = K_i + k_i \sum_{j=1}^{n} z_{ij} p_j, i = 1, 2.$$

Alternative strategy 1 is 'preferred' to 2 in an expected cost sense, if

$$U_1 \leq U_2 \text{ or } K_1 + k_1 \sum_{j=1}^{n} z_{1j} p_j \leq K_2 + k_2 \sum_{j=1}^{n} z_{2j} p_j$$

and therefore,

$$K_1 - K_2 \leq \sum_{j=1}^{n} (k_2 z_{2j} - k_1 z_{1j}) p_j.$$

If we further simplify the problem, to a two states problem, with

$$p_1 = p \text{ and } p_2 = 1 - p,$$

alternative 1 is preferred to 2 if:

$$\begin{aligned} K_1 &- K_2 \leq (k_2 z_{21} - k_1 z_{12}) p + (k_2 z_{22} - k_1 z_{12})(1 - p) \\ &= [k_2(z_{21} - z_{22}) - k_1(z_{12} - z_{11})] p + (k_2 z_{22} - k_1 z_{12}) \end{aligned}$$

which is equivalent to:

$$p^* = \frac{K_1 - K_2 - (k_2 z_{22} - k_1 z_{12})}{k_2(z_{21} - z_{22}) - k_1(z_{12} - z_{11})} \leq p.$$

In other words, if p denotes the probability of failure and if this probability $p \geq p^*$, then alternative 1 is preferred to 2. Of course, the probability p can be objective, based on a complex analysis, or it may be subjective and thus based on expert estimates of various sorts. The potential subjective nature of the prior probability underlies the Bayesian approach to decision making. Finally, it can be based on experience acquired through testing, which can be costly, however, and thus can affect the propensity to want to make such tests! Although the above decision framework is simple, it is useful as it provides a direct relationship between the state of uncertainty (the states probabilities and their estimates) and the recommended action a rational decision maker will follow.

A numerical example

A decision problem is defined in terms of two *alternatives*: inspect and do not inspect. There are also two states: a lot is good (state $j = 1$) or bad (state $j = 2$). The costs table for each of the alternatives is given in Table 4.6.

Table 4.6: The conditional outcomes.

States:	Good	Bad
Inspect:	10	-150
No Inspect:	0	200

Using the previous example, inspection will be performed if only the expected cost of inspection is smaller than the expected cost of no inspection. In other words,

$$\begin{aligned}
\text{EC (inspection)} &= 10p - 150(1-p); \\
\text{EC (No inspection)} &= 200(1-p) \text{ and} \\
\text{Inspection occurs if} &: 10p - 150(1-p) < 200(1-p) \\
\text{or } p &< 350/360
\end{aligned}$$

Example with decision trees

A manager must satisfy an order for a quantity of special purpose computer chips designs. The manufacture of these chips involves the use of a seldom employed process and pieces of equipment. The company owns a rather old technology production line which may break down before the order of the special chips is complete. Were it to be used and some breakdown were to occur, there would be no time to repair it. Instead, a new piece of equipment would have to be acquired at a cost of \$5000. In addition, a further cost of \$1000 would be incurred in overtime costs to make up for lost time. Alternatively, the new piece of equipment could be bought initially at the same cost of \$5000. It is believed that the new technology machine would not break down during the production run for the chips, but might require some adaptation to the production process. If needed, this adaptation would cost \$500. What is the manager to do? The various components of this problem are, of course, to use the old machine or buy the new one. The *sources of uncertainty* include whether the old machine would fail or not, and whether the new machine would need adaptation. As a result, *the conditional consequences* associated with each action are:

If alternative (a) is selected:

(i) Old machine does not breakdown;

(ii) Old machine fails; the new machine needs no adaptation.

(iii) Old machine fails; the new machine needs adaptation.

If alternative (b) is selected:

(i) New machine needs no adaptation.

(ii) New machine needs adaptation.

In this problem, note that there are several decisions and events, each depending on the other. To represent the sequence of decisions and their events, we use the *decision-tree* format. This is a diagrammatic depiction showing the various actions, outcomes and sources of uncertainty, and the order in which decisions and outcomes happen. How do we construct and 'grow' such decision trees? First we organize decisions and their events following their natural sequence, *Decisions* $\rightarrow$ *Outcomes*.

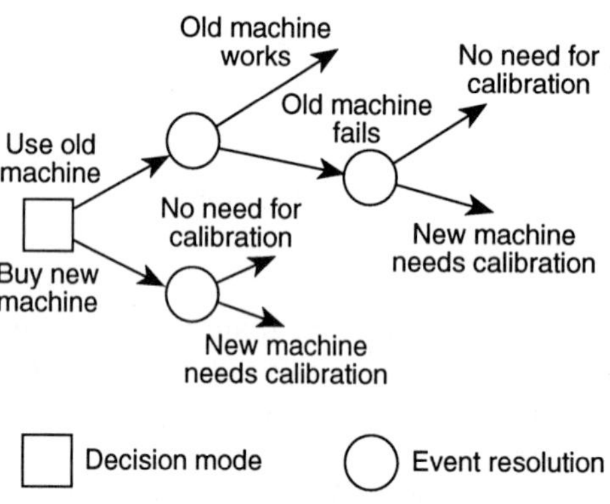

Figure 4.1a: The decision tree.

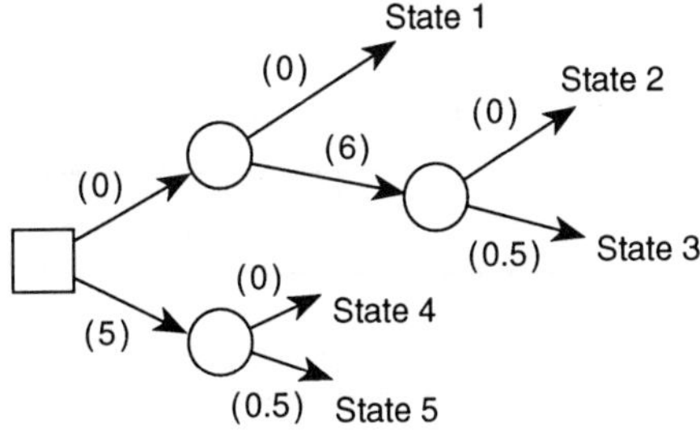

Figure 4.1b: The decision tree costs.

For convenience, we use a square symbol to denote a *decision point* such that at this point the number of outgoing lines equals the set of alternative decisions, as shown in Figure 4.1a. Here we note that the outcomes are represented as branches which evolve from the decision point. There are two sets of states of nature: first, the old machine breaking down or not; which leads to the other events of the new machine needing adaptation or not.

Having defined a problem in terms of its decision tree, how is an action to be selected? For this example, the total cost associated with each outcome is easily computed. These costs, expressed in dollars, can conveniently be entered at the end points of the decision-tree. The numbers (in parentheses) on the branches are the costs associated with the corresponding action or event. The end point costs are then the total costs, being the sums of costs on all branches leading to them.

The next step is to cope with uncertainty. On the one hand, we have a prior assessment of the probabilities of each event occurring. On the other, we should consider how to reduce the uncertainty before making a decision (for example, by seeking additional information regarding the potential events and their probabilities of occurrence through sampling or other means).

Suppose for the moment that only prior information is available. This is expressed by the probabilities that the events considered will occur. In particular, say that the probability of the old technology equipment failing is assessed to be 0.6 while the probability of the new technology machine needing adaptation to the process is judged to be 0.2. The probabilities are usually entered alongside the branches for each uncertain event. The probability of reaching each final outcome is then simply the product of the probabilities of each event branch leading to it. Therefore, the problem statement can be summarized as seen in Figure 4.1b.

If the manager were to select the first option (keep the old technology), the potential outcomes he will face and their probabilities are given as shown in Table 4.7a.

Table 4.7a: The outcomes probabilities

Outcomes	\$0	\$6	\$6.5
Probabilities	0.40	0.48	0.12

If the manager were to select the second option (buy the new technology immediately), then the potential outcomes and their probabilities are given as in Table 4.7b.

Table 4.7b: The outcomes probabilities

Outcomes	\$5.0	\$5.5
Probabilities	0.8	0.2

On the basis of the outcomes-probabilities associated with each alternative, which alternative should the manager select? This is a question one can respond to once the preferences of the manager are well-stated, and a decision rule is adopted to compare the outcomes-probabilities each alternative generates.

Decision trees may involve more than one decision point. In particular, decisions may depend upon outcomes that are uncertain at a given decision time. This leads to general 'multi-stage decision trees' which are more difficult to analyse. For example, a two-stage decision tree problem of special importance in decision theory consists of linking information acquisition together with the actual decisions being entertained. Say that information relating to a problem can be acquired. Then, the decision tree format can be expanded. Such a decision problem would involve the following phases:

(a) Phase 1: Collect information or not; and if so, how much (such as survey data and sampling inspection).

(b) Assess the 'conditional consequences' of such data on the uncertainty faced by the manager while reaching a strategic decision.

(c) Phase 2: Reach a strategic decision

(d) Assess the conditional consequences of this decision not only in terms of potential and realizable outcomes, but also in terms of the costs of the strategic decision and the costs of collecting the information used in reaching the strategic decision.

Note here that the second phase decision will depend upon the first decision (since by being better informed a 'better' strategic decision can be reached). This procedure renders the decision making process slightly more complex, but still tractable. Graphically, Figure 4.2 represents the two phases of the information collection and decision making problems. Although these problems can still be analysed, they are a little more difficult.

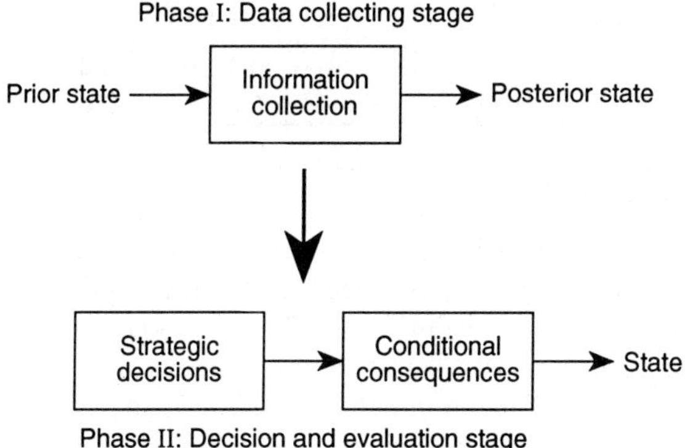

Figure 4.2: Decision phases.

As long as some uncertainty remains in a decision problem, it can be treated only by specifying a 'criterion of choice'. That is, the manager specifies a rule through which he will select an action from among those available and will take into account the uncertainties. Such a rule will express an attitude toward the risk inherent in the problem.

4.4 Decision rules

There are several approaches we can follow to reach a decision. They depend upon both the prior knowledge and the decision maker's attitude towards risk, which is implied by making a decision under uncertainty. We consider the essential situations below.

The expected value criterion

This consists of selecting the largest Expected Monetary Value (EMV) yielded by the various alternatives. The EMV is, we should point out, a special case of the more general expected utility criterion we shall present subsequently (and in this chapter's mathematical appendices). If the matrix entries are Opportunity Losses (OL), we compute the Expected Opportunity Loss (EOL) and choose the alternative with the least value. Invariably, *when either the EMV or EOL criterion is used, the same decision is reached.* This is not a mere coincidence but an important property of decision theory. For the example, verify that:

Expected cost (alternative a) $= 0\text{x}.4 + 6\text{x}.48 + 6.5\text{x}.12 = 3.66$

Expected cost (alternative b) $= 5\text{x}.8 + 5.5\text{x}.2 = 5.1$.

where the cost table is given in Table 4.8.

Table 4.8: Probabilities and expectations.

Probabilities	.12	.48	.08	.32	Expectation
The States	1	2	3	4	
Keep old Tech	6.5	6.0	0.0	0.0	*3.66
Acquire new tech	5.5	5.0	5.5	5.0	5.10

The probabilities (0.12, 0.48, 0.08, 0.32) define an information state regarding the states which can be improved through sampling and other types of information. Alternatively, we can buy some service contracts or warranties, and invest some effort in controlling the equipment, which would alter the expected value of the decision to be taken (although it will probably incur a cost as well). A problem of considerable interest in this context is assessing the maximum expected benefit which is to be gained by moving to a state of full knowledge (or alternatively, to full control). This value is given by,

Value of Information= Objective Value (with Information/Control)

Less

Objective Value (without Information/Control)

Less

Collection, Processing and Control Costs

In this case, information and control are valued in the same manner, as that improving the attainable expected objective. Sampling, for example, becomes an 'investment' (a cost) whose potential benefit is *a priori* unknown (the information it will generate). Further, unlike investment theory, the value of a sampling plan depends upon the valuation of outcomes revealed by the information, which is in itself a difficult problem.

There are several concepts and measures which are useful in measuring the economic value of information and control. We shall consider first the Expected Profit Under Perfect Information (EPPI) (or under perfect control) and subsequently the Expected Value of Perfect Information (EVPI) (or perfect control). Remember that an opportunity loss arises because we have either less than full information, or we do not control the randomness surrounding the process. Thus, we are uncertain about which state will, in fact, occur. If we had full information (a state of complete certainty), then we would not incur this loss and, as a result, our expected payoff would be that much greater. As a result, the EPPI simply equals the sum of the EMV and the EOL, or for each strategy,

$$\text{EPPI} = \text{EMV} + \text{EOL}.$$

However, since this is also true for the optimal strategy, with values denoted by stars, we also have

$$\text{EPPI} = \text{EMV}^* + \text{EOL}^* = \text{EMV} + \text{EOL},$$

which means that the EPPI will be the same for each strategy.

The EVPI (or perfect control) measures how much more valuable our decision would be if it were based on perfect information (or full control). In other words, if we select an optimal strategy with EMV*, and if the EPPI is given, then the most we will be willing to pay will be the difference between this EPPI and the current optimal EMV*. Thus,

$$\text{EVPI} = \text{EPPI} - \text{EMV}^* = \text{EOL}^*.$$

In other words, reducing the effects of uncertainty on a system and always taking the best decision whenever uncertainty is resolved cannot be more costly to achieve than the EVPI (or EOL*). In this sense, the control of process variability, as sought in modern production systems of the JIT type, has a *direct* value which is bounded by the EVPI/EOL*. This bound is also the maximum amount we would be willing to pay for introducing controls of such process variability. Explicitly, if the cost of full information (or the cost of control) was, say, $\$C$, then we would 'buy it' (exercise it) if only,

$$\text{EVPI} - C \geq 0,$$

in which case, we can improve our objective by, at most,

$$\text{EVPI} - C = \text{EPPI} - \text{EMV}^* - C = \text{EOL}^* - C.$$

If the cost of control equals the EVPI, then we would be indifferent about exercising it. In this sense, the EVPI is the most we can hope for whenever we institute a quality improvement program (assuming that the problem is indeed well defined). If a production manager has recurrent problems in a factory with breakdowns occurring with probability $\theta > 0$, how much can be gained by instituting a zero-defects program? The answer is, again, the EVPI, since there is no possibility to gain more if we we institute full control.

When full information or full control (such as zero defects) cannot be attained economically, we can resort to partial information and controls. In this case, we can use the Expected Value of Sample Information (EVSI) (or partial controls). This measures how much more valuable our decision would be if it were based on the information we can draw from a sample, an audit, a survey of consumers and competition, or other information source and controls can be implemented to affect the states probabilities. Thus, if we define a particular decision problem (without the sample information or partial control) and let the EMVs for each situation be EMV*and EMV**, then the EVSI is the expected value gained by improving the EMV, or

$$\text{EVSI} = \text{EMV}^{**} - \text{EMV}^*.$$

Of course, if C is the cost of the sample (or partial control), then the net value of the sample information (partial control) is EVSI$-C$. If some consulting firm were to sell a survey at a cost of C, then we would only buy it if the EVSI is larger than the sample or survey cost. Later on, we shall consider several examples and applications of this problem.

Problem

Using the payoff Tables 4.9a,b, compute (a) the the expected values, (b) the opportunity loss table as well as the opportunity losses and (c) the EPPI and the EVPI.

Table 4.9a: Case 1–The payoffs table.

Probability	0.2	0.3	0.5
State	1	2	3
Alternative			
Alt. 1:	1000	2000	3000
Alt. 2:	2500	1500	2800
Alt. 3:	6000	5000	1000

Table 4.9b: Case 2–The payoff table.

Probabilities	0.05	0.20	0.15	0.30	0.30
States	1	2	3	4	5
Alternatives:					
Alt. 1:	100	50	-260	200	-50
Alt. 2:	0	875	55	-70	140
Alt. 3:	25	50	-25	60	-90
Alt. 4:	900	180	-300	-160	200
Alt. 5:	400	200	150	45	-80

Other objectives

Other approaches to determining a decision criterion include the *minimax cost (or maximin payoffs) criterion.* This consists of letting the best alternative be the one that *minimizes the maximum loss.* For the computer chips example discussed earlier, the maximum loss is incurred when the old machine is kept, and it equals 6.5, while the maximum loss incurred if a new machine is acquired would be 5.5. Hence in applying a minimax criterion, the 'best' action would be to acquire the new technology, which is different from the result obtained by using the expected value criterion! The minimax criterion is appropriate if we seek protection against the worst outcome. In certain situations, such as testing very dangerous drugs, this might be the proper criterion to use. Alternatively, we might consider the *maximax payoff (or the minimin cost).* This criterion seeks the maximax payoff (or the minimin cost) among all alternative actions. It is also called the *optimist criterion.* In our problem: if we use the old machine, the least cost would be zero dollars, which assumes that the machine will work. If we acquire the new machine, the least cost is \$5. Thus, the minimum of the two is \$0, and the decision would be to keep the old machine. Clearly, this is based on believing that the best of all events will occur. When both criteria are weighted, we use the *Hurwicz α criterion.* Assume that payoffs are used, and say that we combine the optimistic and pessimistic criteria considered earlier as follows:

$$\text{Hurwicz Criterion} = \alpha\ [\text{largest payoff}] + (1-\alpha)\ [\text{smallest payoff}]$$

If it is a cost problem, we have

$$\text{Hurwicz Criterion} = \alpha\ [\text{smallest cost}] + (1-\alpha)\ [\text{Largest Cost}].$$

Using a coefficient of optimism $\alpha = 0.4$, we have, if we keep the old machine,

$$\text{Hurwicz Criterion} = 0.4 * (0) + 0.6 * (6.5) = 3.9,$$

while if we buy the new technology machine,

$$\text{Hurwicz Criterion} = 0.4 * (5) + 0.6(5.5) = 5.3,$$

and, therefore the decision would be not to acquire the new machine. Another criterion includes the *Minimax Regret* or *Savage's Criterion.* Here we select an alternative by minimizing the maximum drawbacks associated to each of the alternatives. Under complete ignorance, we might use the *Laplace Criterion,* named after Laplace, the famous French mathematician, who postulated the 'Principle of Insufficient Reason' for decision problems under complete ignorance. This principle states that when we do not know what the probabilities of the states of nature are in a given problem, we can assume that all probabilities are equally likely, reflecting a state of utmost ignorance. Thus, to compute a decision objective we apply the expected criterion as if all the states of nature were equally likely! The 'idea' behind this principle is that we adopt a distribution for the states of nature which assumes the least information, and this distribution consists of equal probabilities.

In practical situations, we choose a decision in terms of the measurement of costs (or payoffs) and the criterion of choice which is selected to evaluate these measurements. It is important to understand that *no criterion is the objectively correct one to use. The choice is a matter of managerial judgment.* A major branch of decision theory, known as 'utility theory', provides an approach which is both consistent and rational but often the function is not readily observable. In any event, a problem is solved 'rationally' if we have made all the necessary judgments about the available actions, the potential outcomes, the preferences and the sources of uncertainties, and then combining them in a coherent manner (without contradicting ourselves, i.e. being rational).

It is possible to be 'too rational', or too careful, or too timid. A decision-maker who, for example, refuses to accept *any* dubious measurements or assumptions whatever will simply never make a decision! He would then incur the same consequences as being irrational. To be a practical, but a good decision– maker, one must accept the advice of Herbert Simon and be of 'bounded rationality'. That is to be satisfied merely that one did the best possible analysis given the time, information and techniques available. In the management of quality, where we mostly make decisions regarding ill-defined problems, these are important considerations to keep in mind.

The expected utility criterion

The expected value criterion is an acceptable criterion for reaching a decision under uncertainty when decision-makers evenly weigh the uncertain outcomes and their probabilities. Such situations presume that the decision maker is risk neutral. When this is not the case, it is necessary to find a scheme which can reflect the decision makers' preferences for outcomes of various probabilities. Two outstanding examples to this effect are gambling in a Casino and the buying of service warranties. If we were to visit Monte Carlo, Atlantic City or Las Vegas, we might see people gambling (investing!) their wealth on ventures (such as putting \$100 on number 8 in roulette), knowing that these ventures have a negative expected return. We may argue, in this case, that not all people value money evenly, or the prospect of winning $36 * 100 = \$3600$ in a second for an investment of \$100 (and with no work!) is worth taking the risk. After all, someone will win, so it might be me!! Both the attitude towards money and the willingness to take risks, originating in a person's initial wealth, emotional state and the pleasure to be evoked in some way, are all reasons that may justify a departure from the expected payoff criterion. If all people were 'straight' expected payoff decision-makers, then there would be no national lotteries, no football, basketball or soccer betting. Even the Mafia might even be much smaller! People do not always use straight expected payoffs to reach decisions however. Their subjective valuation of money and their attitudes towards risk and gambles provide the basic elements that characterize their utility for money and for assuming a gamble. *Utility theory* is the domain of study which seeks to represent how such subjective valuation of wealth and the attitude towards risk can be quantified, so that it may provide a rational foundation for decision making under uncertainty.

Just as in Las Vegas we might derive 'pleasure from gambling our wealth away', we may be also very concerned about losing our wealth, even if this can only happen with an extremely small probability. To help resolve such difficulties there is a broad set of instruments, coined 'risk management' (which includes warranties for products, malpractice insurance for medical personnel, and many others). The purpose of risk management is motivated by the will to avoid large losses which can have adverse effects. For example, maintenance and saving can also be viewed as a means to manage the risk sustained by a firm or a consumer. How much protection should we seek? Of course, this will depend upon how much it will cost, the ability to sustain such losses and our 'attitude toward risk'. Thus, just as with our gambler willing to pay a small amount to earn a very large amount with a very small probability, we may be willing to pay a small amount (through the inspection of a lot or the buying of a warranty, for example) to protect ourself from a loss (whether very large or small). In both cases, the expected payoff criterion breaks down, for otherwise there would be no casinos and no insurance firms. Yet, they are here and provide an important service to society.

Due to its importance, we outline the underlying foundations of utility theory. To do so, consider 'lotteries'. These consist of the following: we are asked to pay a certain amount π which is the price of the lottery (say, \$5). This gives the right to earn another amount, called the reward, R, (which is, say, \$1,000,000!) with some probability, p, (which is, say, $0.5 * 10^{-6}$). If we do not win the lottery, then we lose π. In other words, by buying the lottery we buy the chance of winning $\$R$ (albeit with a small probability p) while losing $\$\pi$. If we use an expected criterion, its value is

$$\text{Expected Value of lottery } = p(R-\pi) - (1-p)\pi = pR - \pi$$

or

$$\text{Expected Value of lottery } = 0.510^{-6}(10^{-6}) - 5 = 0.5 - 5 = -\$4.5.$$

By participating in the lottery, we lose, in an expected sense, \$4.5. Such odds for lotteries are not uncommon, and yet, however irrational they may seem at first, many people play such lotteries. Who plays lotteries? People who value the prospect of 'winning big', even with a small probability, much more then the prospect of 'losing small', even with a large probability. This uneven valuation of money means that we may not be able to compare two sums of money easily. To value these amounts of money equitably we need to find some way to transform their values. Say that you were to scale the value of money by some function, which will be called $U(.)$, such that the larger $U(.)$ the 'better off you are'. More precisely, the function $U(.)$ is a transformation of the value of money which makes various sums which are considered in the lottery, comparable. Thus, the two outcomes $(R-\pi)$ and $(-\pi)$, can be transformed into $U(R-\pi)$ and $U(-\pi)$, and only then can we look upon these newly transformed sums as comparable. The lottery would then be,

$$\begin{cases} U(R-\pi) & \text{w.p. } p \\ U(-\pi) & \text{w.p. 1-p.} \end{cases}$$

Since both transformed values are entirely comparable, we can now take their expected values to compute the value of the lottery. If we call this function $U(.)$, *a utility function,* then by computing the expected utility, by,

$$\text{Expected Utility } = pU(R-\pi) + (1-p)U(-\pi).$$

we obtain an expression which tells you how valuable participation in the lottery is. Denote by EU the expected utility, then,

$$\begin{aligned} \text{If } EU &= 0 \text{ we ought to be indifferent.} \\ \text{If } EU &> 0 \text{ we are better off participating in the lottery.} \\ \text{If } EU &< 0 \text{ we would be worse off by participating in the lottery.} \end{aligned}$$

When would we participate in a lottery? As long as the expected utility of the lottery is at least non-negative (i.e. $EU \geq 0$). What price $\$\pi$ would we be willing to pay for the prospect of winning $\$R$ with probability p? Using the expected utility criterion defined above, we can say now that the most we will be willing to pay is that amount that makes us indifferent (for if we were to pay more we would become worse off, and therefore would not participate in the lottery). This is the price $\$\pi$ which solves $EU = 0$, or

$$EU = 0 = pU(R-\pi) + (1-p)U(-\pi)$$

and numerically,

$$0 = 10^{-6}U(10^6 - \pi) + (1 - 10^{-6})U(-\pi)$$

which is one equation in one unknown.

Problems

Discuss the relationship between the control of variations and the attitude towards risk based on expected utility.

4.5 Bayes rule and Bayesian decision making

Bayes theorem is a probability rule which relates the posterior probability of a state of nature in terms of its prior probability and the conditional probability of that state given the sample information obtained from an experiment. This is represented schematically in Figure 4.3, where information is expressed in terms of an updated knowledge of the posterior probability distribution over all states relative to the prior one. Thus, basically, Bayes theorem states that if we start with an initial probability estimate for some event, and if additional evidence (information) is gathered regarding that event, then a better probability estimate can be obtained by incorporating this new information.

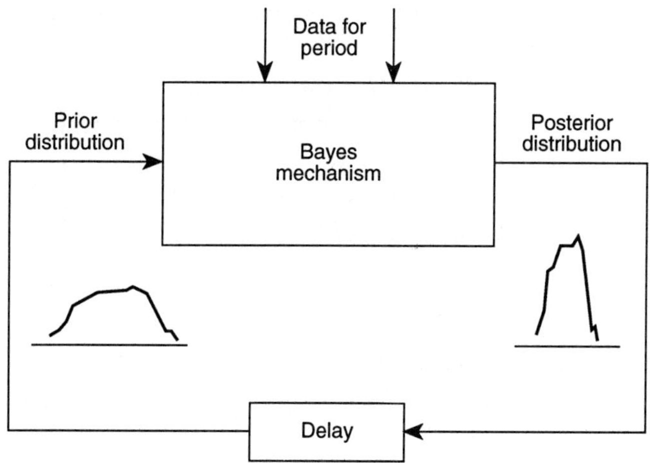

Figure 4.3: The Bayes Mechanism.

With additional data, Bayes theorem obtains a combined estimate which uses all the potential sources of information. For example, these sources may include subjective estimates of managers (based on personal experience, knowledge or any other source of information) together with the 'hard evidence' obtained from sample or survey data. Thus, it is substantially different from the 'average frequency' concept of event prediction (which defines the probability of an event as the fraction of observations in an experiment which led to that event, assuming that the experiment was repeated a large number of times). This different characterization of probability is also appealing to managers, for it integrates their lack of knowledge, expressed by probabilities, with their experience and subjective assessment of these events. In situations where quality is intangible and difficult to measure, this is particularly the case. To demonstrate this approach, we shall consider an example and a number of problems.

Example: Bayes rule and customers' satisfaction

A company is considering whether to perform a sample survey to study the effects on customers' satisfaction of a particular service investment which might be introduced. This service is intended to attend to queries regarding products' malfunctions and repairs after it has been sold. The investment required is $400,000. A Prior estimate points out that such a service will increase the firm's image of quality and will have an effect on future profitability. The prior probability that this is the case is 0.15, while its economic value is calculated to be $3,000,000. If service is not successful, there will be no economic gain. The payoff in both cases is given in Table 4.10.

Table 4.10: A decision table.

Probabilities States of Nature	0.15 Success	0.85 Failure
act 1: No invest.	0	0
act 2: Investment	2,600,000	-400,000

Using an EMV criterion, the value of the post sales service is

$$\begin{aligned}\text{Expected Value (No Investment)} &= (0)(1.0) - 0 = \$0 \\ \text{Expected Value (Investment)} &= (2,600,000)(0.15) + (0.85)(-400,000) \\ &= \$50,000,\end{aligned}$$

and therefore, on the basis of expected monetary value, the firm will go ahead, set up the special quality service and hope that it is recognized as a leader in service and quality.

Survey data can be acquired to improve the probabilities estimate of the service business. The problem faced then is assuming that the planned survey costs $\$100.000 (= \$C)$, should the firm go for it? Since surveys are an imperfect source of information, it is also necessary to specify their reliability. Past experience points out that a survey may be correct or incorrect with some probability, given in Table 4.11.

Table 4.11: The efficiency of indicators.

	Survey Results (information indicators)	Past Outcome A: Satisf.	Past Outcome B: No Satisf.
X:	Satisfactory	0.7	0.1
Y:	Not Satisf.	0.3	0.9

Thus, there are two indicators: consumers will be satisfied by the investment $(= X)$ which will induce the service investment success, or consumers will not be satisfied, thus inducing its failure (Y). These reliabilities are conditional probabilities which are explicitly written by

$$P[X \mid A] = 0.7, P[X \mid B] = 0.1, P[Y \mid A] = 0.3, P[Y \mid B] = 0.9$$

These are the *likelihoods* of the survey, as they point out what the various possibilities are when a clients' survey is used to forecast the investment's success. The *prior probabilities* (without the survey test performed), expressing the current state of knowledge prior to using the client's survey, are given by

$$P[A] = 0.15, P[B] = 0.85.$$

If the firm buys its client's survey it revises its estimate regarding the probability of satisfying clients. Our next purpose is to calculate the revised posterior probabilities using Bayes probability rule. This is represented graphically in Figure 4.4, which shows how to compute the following probabilities technically:

$$P[A \mid X] =? \text{ and } P[A \mid Y] =?; P[B \mid X] =? \text{ and } P[B \mid Y] =?$$

Explicitly, Bayes Rule is given by,

$$P[A \mid Z] = P[A, Z]/P[Z] \text{where } Z = X \text{ or } Y.$$

But, using

$$P[A, Z] = P[Z \mid A]P[A], \text{with } Z = X \text{ or } Y$$

we have

$$P[A \mid Z] = P[Z \mid A]P[A]/P[Z] \text{ with } Z \equiv X \text{ or } Y.$$

But since

$$P[Z] = P[Z \mid A]P[A] + P[Z \mid B]P[B]$$

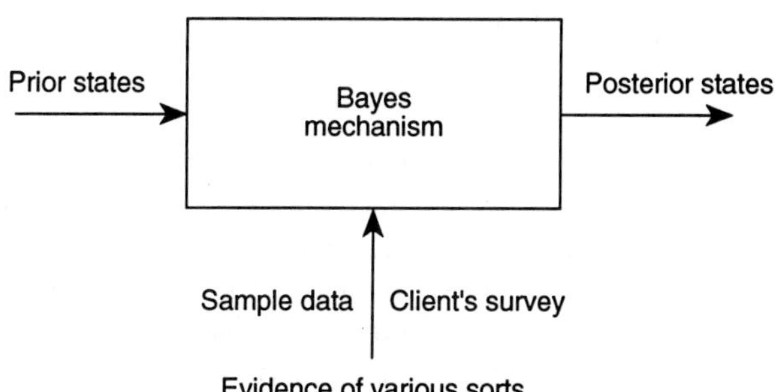

Figure 4.4: The problem's Bayesian mechanism.

this is inserted in the equation above yielding the expression of Bayes rule, or:

$$P[A \mid Z] = \frac{P[Z \mid A]P[A]}{P[Z \mid A]P[A] + P[Z \mid B]P[B]}$$

Using the numbers given in the example,

$$\begin{aligned}
P[A, X] &= (0.7)(0.15) = 0.105 \\
P[A \mid X] &= [(0.7)(0.15)/[(0.7)(0.15) + (0.1)(0.85)] = 0.553 \\
P[B, X] &= (0.15)(0.3) = 0.045 \\
P[B \mid X] &= (0.3)(0.15)/[(0.3)(0.15) + (0.9)(0.85)] = 0.056 \\
P[A, Y] &= 0.045 \\
P[A \mid Y] &= (0.1)(0.85)/[(0.1)(0.85) + (0.7)(0.15)] = 0.447 \\
P[B, Y] &= 0.765 P[B \mid Y] = (0.9)(0.85)/[(0.9)(0.85) + (0.1)(0.15)] = 0.944
\end{aligned}$$

The joint distribution $P[.,.]$ is shown in Table 4.12*a*,

Table 4.12a: The joint distribution

	A	B	
X	.105	.085	.190
Y	.045	.765	.810

where the terms on the right-hand side of the table, as row sums of the joint distributions, denote the posterior distributions once the survey results are taken into account. Basically, note that for the posteriors

$$\begin{aligned} P[A] &= P[A,X]+P[A,Y]=0.105+0.085=0.19 \text{ and} \\ P[B] &= P[B,X]+P[B,Y]=.045+0.765=0.81. \end{aligned}$$

The table of the conditional probabilities is given in Table 4.12b.

Table 4.12b: The conditional probabilities

	A	B
X	.553	.447
Y	.056	.944

The cost of a survey sample is $100,000. An interpretation of the calculated results are as follows. The probabilities of the sample survey indicating satisfaction (indicator 1) is 0.19, while the probability that it indicates no satisfaction is 0.810. If the survey indicates that there is no satisfaction, then the updated probability estimate for satisfaction is 0.553, while the posterior probability that there is no satisfaction is only 0.447. If the survey indicates that there is no satisfaction (with probability 0.810), then the revised (posterior) probability that there is satisfaction is 0.056, while the probability that there is no satisfaction increases to 0.944. The cost and payoff of potential decisions under alternative state realization can also be computed, so that we may select the best decision (to invest in the service system and improve quality, or not). A summary of these calculations is given below. If the survey indicates satisfaction, then one should invest. The payoff is then 1,257,895.0 and its expectation is $239,000 = 1,257,895.0(0.19)$. When the sample indicates no satisfaction, then we should not invest and the payoff collected is null. This leads to an expectation of 239,000. Without the sample information, the expectation is $50,000 (= 0.15 * 2,600,000 - 0.85 * 400,000 = 390,000 - 340,000 = 50,000)$. The value of the sample information is thus 239,000 less $50,000, which equals $189,000. Finally, since the sample costs $100,000, the net value of the sample is: $\$189,000 - \$100,000 = \$89,000$. These computations will be repeated in greater detail below. Using standard computer software (see for example, STORM, 1991), we have the results in Table 4.13.

Table 4.13: Probabilistic analysis

Expected Value of Sample Information - Summary Report.

Indicator	Prob.	Decision	Payoff	Prob.*Payoff
Indictr 1	0.190	Invest	1257895.0	239000.00
Indictr 2	0.810	No invest	0.000	0.00

Expected Payoff	239000.00
Expected Payoff without sample information	50000.00
Expected Value of Sample Information	189000.00
Efficiency of sample information(%)	55.59
Expected Net Gain from Sampling	89000.00

If we had perfect information, then the payoff is $2,600,000, therefore its expectation is $390,000. Since the expected monetary value without the sample is $50,000, then the expected value of full information is $\$390,000 - \$50,000 = \$340,000$.

How is a decision reached? Verify that there are still two alternatives: to invest or not to invest! If we decide to invest, we can then use the expected values updated by the sample results. Say that the decision is to invest, then the expected value will be

> *Profit from the service times the probability that the survey indicates that there is satisfaction times the probability that we will find it to be the case if we invest (based on the sample results)*
>
> *less*
>
> *The loss if we invest and clients are not satisfied times the probability that the survey told us that there will be satisfaction times the probability that there will be satisfaction (based on the sample result).*

Or, in numbers this is equal to

$$2,600,000 * (0.19) * (0.553) - 400,000 * (0.19) * (0.447) = 239,000.$$

Since the value of this strategy without the sample information (SI) is 50,000, we deduce that

$$\text{EVSI } = 239,000 - 50,000 = 189,000.$$

That is, if the cost of the sample information is 100,000, then the sample information net contribution to profits is

$$189,000 - 100,000 = 89,000$$

as shown in the table above.

Pre-posterior analysis

Prior and posterior analyses are both terminal analyses which help us to make a decision. With such analyses we were able to compute:

- The cost of uncertainty.
- The cost (or payoff) associated with each alternative decision.
- The best decision to take, with respect to an appropriate objective function which is chosen by the decision maker.

At the same time, we found that there is a recurring question: Should we collect information first and then make a decision, or reach a decision now without any additional information? If the answer is reach a decision now, then there is no problem; and on the basis of any of the criteria we have set up, we can select a course of action. If the answer is (yes) collect more information, then there are several important and critical questions we must answer first. *How much information should we collect* (that is, the sample size)? *Which information is relevant, and of course, how should we collect this information* (i.e. sampling)? This kind of analysis is called *Pre-posterior analysis.* These questions were answered earlier and separately, although they are important to study together so that a decision can be reached both by being rational (once a criterion of choice has been selected) and by using additional information when it is economical to do so.

Problem

Mr. Ugliel, a quality manager, considers the acquisition of parts from a number of suppliers. The expense involved is $200,000. Suppliers are classified into three risk categories; high risk, medium risk and low risk. Ugliel considered that there is a 30% chance that a supplier is a high risk supplier, a 50% chance that this is a medium risk supplier and a 20% that this is a low risk supplier. If the order is extended, the expected profit for each of these risk categories is $-\$15,000, \$10,000$ and $20,000, respectively. Auditing information regarding the supplier can be obtained at a fee by asking the Dejavu Quality Auditors. The cost of such query is $3000. The conditional probability of each audit rating, given each actual risk, is shown in the Table 4.14.

Table 4.14: Actual auditor's risk.

Auditor's rating	High	Medium	Low
Dejavu's evaluation			
High Risk	1.0	0.10	0.10
Medium Risk	0.0	0.80	0.40
Low Risk	0.0	0.10	0.60

(a) Construct a Decision tree for this problem. (b) Using the decision tree, enter all probabilities. Assuming that Mr. Ugliel seeks to maximize the expected monetary value of the transaction, answer the additional questions as well: (*b*1) Should Ugliel consult Dejavu and give the supplier a medium risk rating? (*b*2) What is the most money that Ugliel would be willing to pay for any additional supplier's audit, even if this were a perfect audit analysis?

Reproducible processes

For some processes, it turns out that the prior and posterior distribution are of the same form! That is, instead of writing the Bayes recursive equation in its explicit form which is difficult to compute, it is possible to represent just the change of the parameters of these distributions in terms of the sample information collected (which is, of course, much simpler and just as revealing). Since most actions and measurements are taken on the basis of moments, it is not necessary to remember the probability distributions, but only the equations tracing the evolution of such parameters. Under such conditions, we have a *reproducible process.* This feature will be used in Chapter 9 when we consider the control of quality in a temporal setting and apply filtering techniques.

Example: The normal process

Assume that a prior probability distribution of consumers satisfied with a given service delivered by our firm is normal with mean $\mu_0 = 480$ and variance $\sigma_0^2 = 31600$. That is,

$$P(s) = C_0 \exp\left[-\left([s-\mu_0]^2/2\sigma_0^2\right)\right], \text{ where } C_0 = (1/\sqrt{2\pi})\sigma_0.$$

Say that we contract a market research firm to study consumer satisfaction. This firm's estimates have in the past proved to be right some of the time and wrong some of the time. That is, let the probability distribution of the estimate $P(x \mid s)$ be normal with mean s and variance 20000. Or $x = s + \epsilon$ where ϵ is the error term assumed to have a mean zero and variance $\sigma^2 = 20,000$. Since,

$$P(x) = \int_{-\infty}^{\infty} P(x \mid s)P(s)ds$$

using Bayes theorem, we have,

$$P(s \mid x) = \frac{P(x \mid s)P(s)}{\int_{-\infty}^{\infty} P(x \mid u)P(u)du}.$$

If we call μ_1 and σ_1^2 the mean and the variance of this distribution, then it can be shown that its mean and variance are

$$\begin{aligned} \mu_1/\sigma_1^2 &= x/\sigma^2 + \mu_0/\sigma_0^2 \\ 1/\sigma_1^2 &= 1/\sigma_0^2 + 1/\sigma^2 \end{aligned}$$

In other words, if $N(s \mid \mu_0, \sigma_0^2)$ is used to denote the normal probability distribution with mean μ_0 and variance σ_0^2, then we can write concisely $P(s) = N(s \mid \mu_0, \sigma_0^2)$ and $P(s \mid x) = N(s \mid \mu_1, \sigma_1^2)$, with μ_1 and σ_1^2 as given above. Assuming that the forecast is $x = 500$, inserting the numerical data given for this example, we obtain a posterior probability distribution for the assaults estimate that has a mean and variance which are obtained by solving

$$\begin{aligned} \mu_1/\sigma_1^2 &= 500/20000 + 480/31600 \\ 1/\sigma_1^2 &= 1/31600 + 1/20000 \end{aligned}$$

or

$$\mu_1 = 5923 \text{ and } \sigma_1^2 = 12248.$$

By the same token, if we collect additional information regarding potential assaults, say a second sample observation x_2, a third one x_3, and so on then with each observation we can update the estimated probability distribution. How? By treating the posterior of the first sample as the prior for the second sample and repeating such a procedure, to obtain an 'evolution' of posterior distributions, depending on the ith sample information, x_i, and the moments of its prior distribution, μ_{i-1} and $\sigma_{i-1}^2, i = 2, 3, \ldots$. Assume that a total of K samples are taken, the posterior distribution after the Kth sample are included is a normal probability distribution with

$$P(s \mid x_1, x_2, x_3, \ldots x_K) = N(s \mid \mu_K, \sigma_K^2)$$

where μ_K, σ_K^2 are obtained by recursion from

$$\begin{aligned} \mu_i/\sigma_i^2 &= x_i/\sigma^2 + \mu_{i-1}/\sigma_{i-1}^2 \\ 1/\sigma_i^2 &= 1/\sigma_{i-1}^2 + 1/\sigma^2 \end{aligned}$$

with $i = 1, 2, 3 \ldots, K$ and initially μ_0 and σ_0^2 are given.

These recursive equations entirely summarize the information which is provided by the sequence of sample observations. The posterior is calculated just by solving these equations recursively. In this case, these are called sufficient statistics, for it is sufficient to know the moments and the sample observations to repeatedly apply Bayes' theorem in computing the posterior distribution.

The beta-binomial model

A lot has a proportion of defectives p with a prior beta probability distribution with parameters a and b, or

$$f(p) = \frac{1}{B(a,b)} p^{a-1}(1-p)^{b-1}, B(a,b) = \frac{\Gamma(a)\Gamma(b)}{\Gamma(a+b)}$$

whose mean and variance are given by

$$p = \frac{a}{(a+b)}, \sigma_p^2 = ab(a+b+1)(a+b)^2.$$

Now, assume that at some time t we consider the decision to inspect or not to inspect the lot. If we inspect, we also 'create information', since by testing the lot we will be able to confirm (or not) the presumed prior of p. Let z be the outcome of sampling and, for simplicity, state that $z \in \{1, 0\}$ with $z = 1$ if the lot is good and $z = 0$ if the lot is not. Now introduce the time index t, and say that 't' denotes 'now' and '$t+1$' denotes the next period. If we have a prior beta distribution and we inspect, then the posterior distribution is also beta (but prior at the next decision period), and will be given by the following parameters:

$$a_{t+1} = a_t + z_t, b_{t+1} = b_t + 1.$$

This result is proved by considering the more general case given next. Say that we inspect a lot of size n, and let r be the number of defectives in the sample when p is the probability of the number of defectives. Namely,

$$P(r \mid p) = \binom{n}{r} p^r (1-p)^{n-r}, r = 0, 1, \ldots, n.$$

Thus, by Bayes theorem,

$$f(p \mid r) = \frac{\binom{n}{r} p^r (1-p)^{n-r} p^{a-1} (1-p)^{b-1}}{B(a,b) \int_0^1 P(r \mid u) f(u) du},$$

and therefore,

$$f(p \mid r) = \frac{p^{r+a-1}(1-p)^{n-r+b-1}}{\int_0^1 u^{r+a-1}(1-u)^{n-r+b-1} du}.$$

But, by the Beta distribution,

$$\int_0^1 u^{r+a-1}(1-u)^{n-r+b-1} du = B(a+r, b+n),$$

and therefore the posterior distribution $f(p \mid r)$ has a posterior distribution with parameters $a+r$ and b+n. Of course, for a bernoulli trial, $n = 1$ and the outcome $r = z = 0, 1$ and the above stated follows directly, since

$$a_{t+1} = a_t + r = a_t + z_t, b_{t+1} = b_t + n = b_t + 1.$$

This relationship, called the beta-binomial process, is useful for many applications in quality control and management, as we shall see in the following chapters.

Selecting a sample size

The problem is how much information, or practically what sample size, should we collect? Assume a sample size $n; x_1, \ldots, x_n$. Such samples may represent the performance of a missile which is tested on a range. Define the average of the sample by

$$\bar{X} = \sum_{i=1}^{n} x_i/n.$$

If each sample has a mean outcome μ and variance σ^2, then the average outcome has mean $\bar{X}$ and variance σ^2/n. The larger the sample size, the smaller the variance, and therefore the greater its informative content. Assume that the distributions are normal. Since the outcome is now $\bar{X}$ rather than x_1, and as the likelihood now has a normal distribution with variance σ^2/n, we have a posterior distribution whose mean and variance is given by μ_1 and σ_1^2 with,

$$\begin{aligned} \mu_1/\sigma_1^2 &= \bar{X}/(\sigma^2/n) + \mu_0/\sigma_0^2 \\ 1/\sigma_1^2 &= 1/\sigma_0^2 + 1/(\sigma^2/n). \end{aligned}$$

Through these moments we can estimate the value of information. On the basis of this value we can also select the sample size. For example, if we let $V(n)$ be the value of information, expressed as a function of the sample size n and if the cost of each sample is c, then the sample size will be determined by solving the following maximization problem

$$\underset{n}{\text{Maximize}}\; V(n) - cn$$

which consists of finding that sample size n which yields the largest next period profit (value $V(n)$ less the sampling cost cn). For example, if $V(n)$ is expressed by the following form $\mu - \rho\sigma^2/n$, then, minimization with respect to n yields

$$n = \sqrt{\rho\sigma^2/c}.$$

This result will mean that the larger the risk aversion, the more we will inspect, the larger the risk aversion, and the larger the process variance while we inspect, the larger the cost of inspection.

References

Belton V. (1986) A comparison of the Analytic Hierarchy Process and a simple multi-attribute value function, *Euro. J. of Operations Research*, **26**, 7-21.

Chankong, V. and Haimes, Y.Y. (1983) *Multi objective Decision Making,* North Holland.

Cogger K.O. and Yu, P.L. (1985) Eigenweight vectors and least distance approximation for revealed preference in pairwise weight ratios, *J. of Optimization Theory and Applications,* **46**, 483-491.

Dyer J.S. (1990) Remarks on the Analytic Hierarchy Process, *Management Science,* **36**, 249-258.

Keeny R.L. and H. Raiffa (1976) *Decisions with Multiple Objectives: Preferecnes and Value Tradeoffs,* New York, Wiley.

Lootsma F.A. (1987) Modélisation du jugement humain dans l'analyse multicritère au moyen de comparaisons de paires, *RAIRO/ Recherche Operationnelle,* **21**, 241-257.

Lootsma F.A. (1988) Numerical scaling of human judgement in pairwise comparison methods for fuzzy multi-criteria deciison analysis. In G. Mitra (Ed.), *Mathematical Models for Decision Support,* Springer, Berlin, 57-88.

Lootsma F.A. (1990) The French and the American School in Multi-Criteria Decision Analysis, *RAIRO/Recherche Operationnelle,* **24**, 263-285.

Roy B. (1985) *Méthodologie Multicritère d'Aide* à la *Décision,* Paris, Economica.

Roy B. and D. Bouyssou (1992) *Aide Multi-Critères* à la *Décision: Méthodes et Cas*, Paris, Economica.

Saaty T. (1980) *The Analytic Hierarchic Process,* New York, McGraw Hill.

Zeleni, M. (1982) *Multiple Criteria Decision Making,* New York, McGraw Hill.

Additional references

Luce R.D. and H. Raiffa (1958) *Games and Decisions*, New York, Wiley.

Morgan B.W. (1968) *An Introduction to Bayesian Statistical Decision Processes,* Englewood Cliffs, NJ, Prentice Hall.

Raiffa H. and R. Schlaiffer (1961) *Applied Statistical Decision Theory,* Boston, Division of Research, Graduate School of Business, Harvard University.

Schlaiffer R. (1959) *Probability and Statistics for Business Decisions,* New York, McGraw Hill.

Winkler R.L. (1972) *Introduction to Bayesian Inference and Decision,* New York, Holt Rinehard and Winston.

Mathematical appendix: *Multiple criteria*

In many situations, quality is evaluated along several criteria. In this case, and to reach a decision which is 'as close as possible' to reaching the best decision, we use multi-criteria decision making. This is a widely practiced set of tools based on both interactive and non-interactive procedures, which seek to reveal a decision maker's preferences. For example, assuming two Pareto charts, each evaluated along different criteria, how should our decisions be based on these two charts? Given a number of desirable operating standards, say x^*, how can we design a process, or a product which is as close as possible to these standards when operating performance is constrained? Let y be the process characteristics, then given the constraint set $f(y) \in Y$, we want 'a solution' which would minimize the deviation $y - x^*$. If we had a single variate y and compared two decisions, say y_1 and y_2, then we could define a criterion, say a function $g(.)$, such that

$$y_1 \text{ is preferred to } y_2 \text{ if } g(y_1) \leq g(y_2).$$

In formal terms, the criterion g is a real valued function defined on a set Y of potential decisions so that a comparison of two decisions, y_1 and y_2, can be reached solely based on the comparison of $g(y_1)$ and $g(y_2)$. More generally, the function $g(.)$ is assumed to construct an ordering scale (that is, establish a preference or indifference relation among the alternative decisions). The construction of a single criterion is not a simple feat. There may be problems of comparability of decisions, a criterion may shift over time, and so on. Of course, when we consider two or more criteria to compare two alternative (or a continuum of) decisions, the problem is much more complex. Authors such as Zeleni (1982), Roy (1985), Saaty (1980), Keeny and Raiffa (1976), Chankong and Haimes (1983) and recently, Roy and Bouyssou (1992) have studied these problems from different points of view, emphasizing both problems of making decisions when the consequences are known or under uncertainty. These approaches fall under several categories, seeking alternative routes in determining an aggregated criterion, or some standards which can be used to compare the alternative solutions. When criteria are not conflicting with respect to the choice of a decision, this leads to one criterion dominating other criteria, which is thus a single criterion problem. When some of the criteria are conflicting, we can use weights to provide a subjective (or objective) desirability of these criteria (and then aggregate them). Some well known procedures include goal programming, consisting of transforming a problem based on the minimization of absolute deviations into a constrained optimization problem. Similarly, the Analytic Hierarchic Process (AHP) developed by Saaty (1980) uses a paired comparison to evaluate a finite number of decision alternatives $A_1, \ldots, A_n$, under a finite number of conflicting performance criteria $C_1, \ldots, C_m$, by a single decision maker or by a decision making body. In the basic experiment there are two alternatives under a particular criterion, and the decision maker is requested to express his indifference between the two. There are then several answers, including very strong, strong, strict, weak or indifference. With this information on hand, AHP uses the elicitation of preference intensities to derive a set of weights which is applied for each decision and overall criteria to derive a unique index. AHP has been subject to considerable theoretical research and applications. Nonetheless, it has also been subjected to some criticism on several grounds. First, because of difficulties inherent in the quantification of human preferences in terms of numerical scales. Second, it estimates the impact scores of the alternatives by the Perron-Frobenius eigenvector, which consists of transforming the scores matrix collected (over decisions and criteria) into eigenvalues. And concentrating on the largest eigenvalues), and thirdly, because it calculates the final scores of the alternatives via an arithmetic-mean aggregation rule. This criticism has not fundamentally attacked the approach suggested by Saaty, but has instead stimulated interest and focused attention on being far more sensitive to subjective judgements and preferences over a number of issues and their quantification. To a large extent, these are also some of the problems we face in applying quantitative tools in measuring the intangible factors of quality and quantifying them (for further study on the AHP, see also, Belton, 1986; Cogger and *Yu*, 1985; Dyer 1990; Lootsma, 1987, 1988, 1989).

Multi-criteria techniques have not been widely applied to quality management and control problems. It is generally important for the reader to be aware of this important and practical field and pursue its study, however.

CHAPTER 5

Inspection and acceptance sampling

5.1 Introduction

The purpose of acceptance sampling is to provide for the user some assurance that the risks associated with accepting a lot are within specified limits. To do so, it is necessary to specify these risks, state clearly how sample data will be collected and measured, and state for what purpose it will be used and how to reach some conclusion (such as reach a decision to accept or reject the lot, or conclude whether the sample evidence is inconclusive). In this chapter we shall consider these issues, and provide a broad managerial approach to inspection and acceptance sampling.

We use inspection and acceptance sampling for many purposes. Some of these include

- *Testing for reliability*: used to control a process, to detect faults and to correct them. It is applied extensively when a product is new, when the quality manager deems it necessary, typically following complaints or the detection of problems once the product has been sold (usually returning to the producer in the form of complaints, excess warranty payments and services). In these cases, fault detection is assigned to either materials, workmanship, product design or process operations, and usually an in-depth study of the problems detected follows. When problem causes are removed and no special problems are detected, reliability testing is reduced.
- *Special tests* following clients' complaints, the introduction of new technologies or new products. In such cases, inspection tests are performed by sampling finished product lots.
- *Preventive inspection* is used when there is uncertainty regarding a process continued operating performance. Inspection is then used to improve the information available to management and detect problems before they occur. Furthermore, when the costs of non-quality are large, preventive measures can be efficient, detecting problems prior to system breakdown. Such inspection is becoming increasingly important due to the growth of preventive measures in TQM.
- To assure customers that 'proper procedures' have been followed in ensuring that a lot shipped to the customers conforms to pre-specified standards (and thus both provide a signal for quality operation and

reduce the chance that the seller-supplier will face punitive damages of various sorts if this were not the case).

- To rectify potential defects prior to a lot's shipment. This is often important in complex assembly products which require integration tests after their final assembly.

Of course, the motivation for inspection and assurance will determine both the stringency of risk specifications as well as the procedures followed in implementing them. The environment, the subject/object being tested, statistical and economic considerations and the sampling techniques are also some of the important considerations in designing inspection and acceptance sampling programs. For example, testing incoming parts and materials can be performed to control suppliers and shippers, testing output may be performed to rectify the average outgoing quality and reduce the chance that defective lots are shipped to buyers. A process is tested to control deviations from agreed on performance (quality) standards. In the same vein, firms use survey samples to monitor the perception and quality of their products. Testing is performed because it is important and useful. If the cost of testing was negligible then a firm would logically apply full inspection to everything it does and there would be, as a result, no uncertainty regarding performance and manufactured quality. The problem arises, however, because inspection testing is costly and there is 'intolerable' uncertainty regarding some facet of the quality, manufactured, serviced or sold. As a result, exhaustive testing might on the one hand be impractical, but partial sampling might remove some of the uncertainty faced by management, on the other.

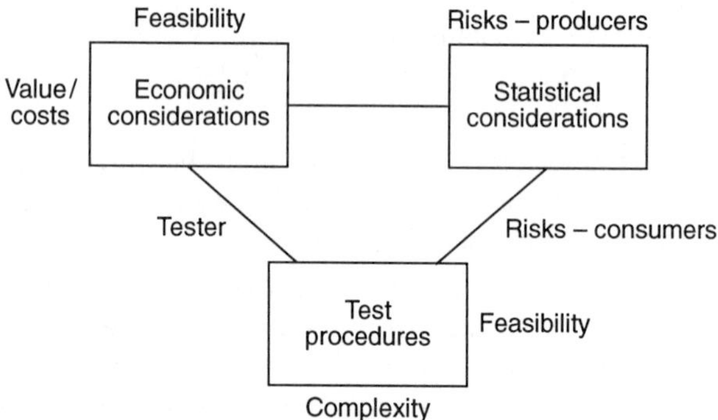

Figure 5.1: Multiple considerations in statistical sampling.

Risk may be specified in several ways by statistical and economic approaches. The statistical approach consists in specifying the risks of reaching a wrong decision (for both the producer-seller and the consumer-buyer). Such risks are traditionally expressed by the type I and II errors of a statistical test seen in Chapter 3. Increased use is made of the Average Run Length (ARL) needed to reach some decision under one or a number of hypotheses (which will be developed further later on), as well as economic and decision theoretic considerations. Statistical considerations are also needed to specify the sampling techniques to use. We shall consider here a number of techniques, each with a varying degree of complexity and including the binomial sampling model, curtailed sampling, double and multiple stage sampling and, finally, the Sequential Probability Ratio Test (SPRT) of Wald. These techniques differ by their ease of implementation (i.e. their complexity), by their mathematical tractability in computing the risk protection they can provide, and by the underlying statistical hypotheses they can handle. In acceptance sampling, the importance of these methods arises due to the fact that they can, in some circumstances, provide *the same risk protection with less sampling*, thereby reducing the required cost of sampling. Inspection costs are, of course, only one of the elements to consider in assessing the economic value and costs of sampling the value of information obtained through inspection. Increasingly, the integration of inspection techniques with management problems, and costs such as maintenance, warranties, servicing, machine scheduling, learning and quality improvement are yielding designs which are more sensitive to the costs and benefits of inspection, and to the problems of management. In this sense, inspection testing and acceptance sampling are quickly changing, becoming much more in tune with the process of management.

5.2 Acceptance sampling

Acceptance sampling provides statistical criteria for accepting or rejecting a lot. For example, it is applied to test incoming materials to a manufacturing process. When a lot is 'rejected', it may induce some corrective action and/or a process verification which are needed to control the process (see Figure 5.2). When it is 'accepted', however, it does not mean that the lot is necessarily good (although there may be a good chance that it is), but only that there is insufficient evidence to warrant its rejection. There are various types of procedures according to whether:

(a) We sample by attributes (i.e. classify the units tested into one of a number of qualitative states, such as good versus bad).

(b) We sample by measuring a quantitative characteristic of sampled units. For example, the width of a tube, the fat content of meat and so on, are such quantitative values.

(c) We sample continuously or at some periodic times.

(d) We use random or stratified samples based on prior observations regarding the attributes or quantitative variables being sampled.

(e) We reach a decision on single or multiple samples.

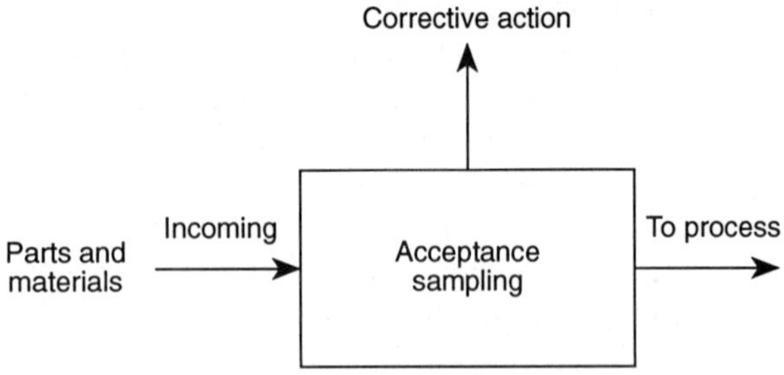

Figure 5.2: Acceptance sampling

Each of these procedures has specific statistic or economic characteristics. The design of acceptance sampling plans recognizes both the statistical and economic environment within which operations (or services) are performed, and then formulates the optimization problem which is adapted to the situation at hand.

Application of acceptance sampling in general proceeds as follows: products are grouped into lots of certain sizes and a sample is drawn from each lot to test the quality. Then, the sample is tested and a decision, based on some pre- specified criterion, is either accepted or rejected. If all lots are of the same quality, the sampling plan may accept some lots but reject others. Accepted lots, as stated above, need not be better than the rejected ones however. Since inspected units are only a small portion of the lots, direct improvement by removal of defectives is insignificant. In Figure 5.3, the procedure usually followed in acceptance sampling is summarized. Such a procedure will be used if:

(a) Inspection is destructive and therefore full sampling is not realistic.

(b) The COQ is high.

(c) Full inspection is not economical.

(d) There are potentially important product liability risks

(e) Vendor monitoring is needed for the assurance of contract compliance.

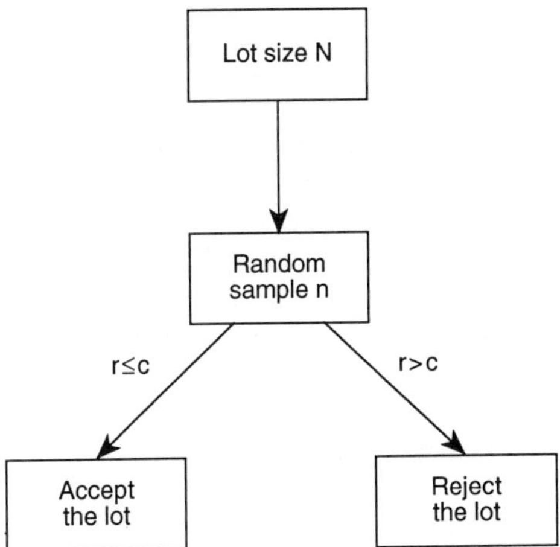

Figure 5.3: Lot acceptance sampling.

Standards have been devised in practice to help the quality manager select an appropriate acceptance plan. For example, MIL-STD 105D (to be discussed later on), as well ISO $2859 - 1, 2$ and 3, ISO 8422, ISO 8423, ISO DTR 8550, are some practical references for industrial users.

Attribute sampling

Say that we receive a lot of size N, D of which are presumably defective. Sampling inspection will help us 'predict' the number of defectives and 'control' will be instituted when the sampling outcomes do not conform to the 'predictions'. To do so, say that we select a sample of size $n < N$ which is tested for defectives. The number of defectives sampled is counted and found equal to r (function of N and D). The larger D/N, the greater the probability that r is large. The observation, r, is thus a 'predictor' of D. The smaller D, the smaller we can expect r to be. If an unexpected large r is observed, we can then 'guess' that, perhaps, we 'erred' and the number of defectives is perhaps larger than D. In other words, the 'surprise' encountered is indicative of some anomaly which requires 'control'. The sample size, the definition of 'what constitute a surprise', etc. are determined by statistical, economic and decision theoretic criteria.

For a sample of size n, the sampling inspection probability yields the probability of observing r defectives if N and D are the population parameters of the lot. In this special case, assuming that the *n sampled units are not replaced,* (in which case, successive samples are not statistically independent), the sample distribution is the hypergeometric distribution, or

$$f(r \mid n, N, D) = \frac{\binom{D}{r}\binom{N-D}{n-r}}{\binom{N}{n}}$$

The hypergeometric distribution is appropriate when n/N is not small, which is the case when N, the lot size, is small (as in Just in Time systems, which are based on small lot sizes). When n/N is very small, i.e. if $N >> n$, or if we sample with replacement (meaning that the sample probability is not altered from one experiment to another), then the hypergeometric distribution can be reduced to a binomial distribution, with parameters $(\theta, n), \theta = D/N$ and,

$$b(r \mid n, \theta) = \binom{n}{r}\theta^r(1-\theta)^{n-r}, r = 0, 1, ..n.$$

To reach the decision on whether to accept a lot, it is necessary to specify a decision procedure and its parameters. For the current situation, we shall reach a decision as follows. Let the number of outcomes observed be r, and let c be a decision parameter such that

If $r \leq c$, the lot is accepted,
If $r > c$, the lot is rejected (or some sort of action is taken).

Acceptance sampling design consists in this case of selecting the parameters (n, c). There are various ways to do so. Below, we shall first specify the risks sustained by 'producers' and 'consumers' if the parameters (n, c) are to be selected.

The producer and consumer risk

When tests are expressed as a function of the risks to be borne by a producer and a consumer, or the risk sustained by transacting parties, we then seek inspection plan parameters compatible with these prior risk specifications. A producer risk is defined by the probability that the producer will reject the lot when it is in fact of acceptable quality. The consumer risk, however, is defined as the probability of accepting a lot when it is in fact bad. 'Good' and 'bad' are, of course, relative terms, and therefore defined in terms of an AQL and an LTFD as follows:

AQL = The acceptable quality level of a lot which measures the fraction of defectives that the producer is willing to accept.

LTFD = The lot tolerance fraction defective level, which is the proportion of defectives (quality) that the consumer will not accept.

The AQL is a 'measure of quality' which the producer will be willing to accept most of the time, while LTFD is a measure of non-quality which the consumer will be rejecting most of the time. Thus, if θ is the probability of fraction defectives, we can construct a sampling plan by specifying the risks that both the producer and the consumers will be willing to tolerate. Specification of the AQL depends upon a number of factors, such as the importance of the fault being tested (measured economically or in terms of its effects on the process) and the amount of inspection. Some firms, for example, follow a MIL standard approach with three sorts of inspection which depend upon the size of the sample and the stringency requirement of the test. For example, we can define tolerant inspection, normal inspection, and strict inspection.

Table 5.1: (n,c) Inspection table.

	Tolerant			Normal			Strict		
Lot sizes	n	c	d	n	c	d	n	c	d
2 – 150	3	0	1	8	0	1	13	0	1
151 – 280	5	0	1	13	0	1	13	0	1
281 – 500	13	0	2	20	0	2	32	0	2
501 – 1200	13	0	2	32	1	2	50	1	2
1201 – 3200	20	0	2	50	2	3	50	1	2

Strict inspection, for example, would require larger sample sizes n and/or smaller critical parameters c than, say, a tolerant inspection plan. SONY Alsace for example, uses tests based the required stringency of the test. If N denotes the lot size, n the sample size, c the critical number (below which the lot is accepted) and d is the critical rejection number (above which the lot is rejected), then the tests used at SONY Alsace for product testing are defined as in Table 5.1.

The LTFD is determined by using a set of similar considerations, but using the consumer point of view. The selection of an LTFD can have an important effect on a firm's long-term profitability, since dissatisfied customers may switch to competition, while satisfied ones will be loyal. Suppose that θ_1 is the proportion of defectives of a good lot, while θ_2 is the proportion of defectives of a bad lot; the AQL and LTFD are then an expression of the risk which is sustained by both the producer and consumer. For example, if the producer is making the decision to inspect a lot, it is debatable whether he 'knows' what is the consumer risk he ought to use in his calculations. This is a particularly important problem in supplier/producer problems, and will be considered in Chapter 8. Here, we adopt the conventional approach, which presumes that such risks are known and can therefore be used in the design of an inspection plan. Define two competing hypotheses by

$$\begin{aligned} \text{The Null hypothesis } H_0 &: \theta \leq \text{ AQL and} \\ \text{The Alternative hypothesis } H_1 &: \theta \geq \text{ LTFD,} \end{aligned}$$

let α be the probability of a sampling plan rejecting a lot with an AQL fraction of defectives. This corresponds to the producer's risk, which is the probability $P[\text{Reject } H_0 \mid H_0 \text{ is true}]$ of rejecting the null hypothesis when it is true. If P_a is the probability of accepting the lot, then the statement 'Lot quality≥AQL' is equivalent to '$P_a \geq 1 - \alpha$'. For the consumer, set β, the probability of accepting a lot which has a fraction of defectives is greater than the LTFD. This probability corresponds to the consumer's risk, which is $P[\text{Accept } H_0 \mid H_0 \text{ is false}]$. If P_b is the probability of accepting a bad lot, then the statement 'Lot quality≤LTFD' is equivalent to '$P_b \leq \beta$'. Equivalently, if a sampling plan has sample size n and test number c, then the conditions

$$P_a \geq 1 - \alpha, P_b \leq \beta$$

correspond to a plan whose producer's risk is α and whose consumer's risk is β. We can write these conditions explicitly as follows:

$$\begin{aligned} P_a &= \sum_{r=0}^{c} \binom{n}{r} (\text{AQL})^r (1 - \text{AQL})^{n-r} \geq 1 - \alpha \\ P_b &= \sum_{r=0}^{c} \binom{n}{r} (\text{LTFD})^r (1 - \text{LTFD})^{n-r} \leq \beta. \end{aligned}$$

Thus, given the producer's and consumer's risk (α, β), as well as the AQL and LTFD, an acceptable inspection plan (n, c) satisfies the two inequality conditions above. Tables for the solution of such inequations have been devised. Of course, it is a straightforward exercise to devise a computer program which can select parameters n and c which will satisfy the above conditions for known AQL, LTFD, α and β. Alternatively, we can use economic criteria (such as inspection effort and COQ minimization) and optimize them subject to these 'risk' constraints.

When the binomial is approximated by a Poisson distribution, we have

$$\begin{aligned} P_a &= \sum_{r=0}^{c} \exp\ (\text{-nAQL})(\text{nAQL})^r / r! \geq 1 - \alpha \text{ and} \\ P_b &= \sum_{r=0}^{c} \exp\ (\text{-nLTFD})(\text{nLTFD})^r / r! \leq \beta. \end{aligned}$$

These equations can of course be solved using appropriate mathematical manipulations, or by using tables provided by SQC societies for this purpose.

Problems

1. Let AQL $= 0.04$, LTFD $= 0.12, \alpha = 0.05$ and $\beta = 0.10$. Find an appropriate sampling plan (n, c). To do so, use both the statistical tables of the chi– square distribution as well as a computer program you can write.

Finally, assume a sampling plan of $n = 12$ and $c = 2$, find the corresponding α and β.

2. Let a sample size be $n = 30$, the AQL 4% and the critical acceptance parameter $c = 1$. Show that the probability of acceptance is 0.661 if we use the binomial distribution and 0.663 if we use the Poisson approximation. How would these probabilities change if we use instead a sample size of 20? If, for such a test, 1-AQL = 0.96, LTFD = 0.03, and if $\alpha = 0.10$ and $\beta = 0.05$, what are the parameters of the sample test (n, c)? Repeat your calculation using the Poisson approximation and compare your results.

Computations can be simplified further if we can approximate the binomial distribution by the normal distribution (when the sample size n is large) whose mean and variance are:

$$\begin{aligned} \mu_1 &= n\ (\text{AQL}),\ \sigma_1^2 = n\ (\text{AQL})(1\text{-AQL}) \\ \mu_2 &= n\ (\text{LTFD}),\ \sigma_2^2 = n\ (\text{LTFD})(1\text{-LTFD}). \end{aligned}$$

In this case, the prior risk constraints are

$$\begin{aligned} P_a &= \int_{-\infty}^{c} N(y \mid \mu_1, \sigma_1^2)dy \geq 1 - \alpha \\ P_b &= \int_{-\infty}^{c} N(y \mid \mu_2, \sigma_2^2)dy \leq \beta \end{aligned}$$

where, $N(.,.)$ is the normal probability integral

$$N(y \mid \mu, \sigma^2) = \frac{1}{\sqrt{2\pi}\sigma} \exp\left[-\frac{1}{2}\left(\frac{y-\mu}{\sigma}\right)^2\right], -\infty < y < \infty.$$

To obtain explicit results, it is necessary to find a plan (n, c) which satisfies these two inequalities. Of course, similar arguments can be used for other sampling distributions. In practice, an approximate plan can be obtained by one of the distributions above. Then through sensitivity analysis of the parameters, the solution for the actual sampling distribution can be found. We shall consider some examples below. By transforming the normal distribution $N(y \mid \mu, \sigma^2)$ to its standard form, a simpler expression for (n, c) can be found. Note that

$$\int_{-\infty}^{c} N(y \mid \mu_1, \sigma_1^2)dy = \int_{-\infty}^{u} N(z \mid 0, 1)dz = \mathbf{N}(u), u = (c - \mu_1)/\sigma_1,$$

where $N(z \mid 0, 1)$ is the standard normal distribution and $\mathbf{N}(u)$ is used to denote the cumulative standard normal distribution. For given n we can compute the least c which satisfies both constraints, or

$$P_a = \mathbf{N}[\frac{(c-\mu_1)}{\sigma_1}] \geq 1-\alpha$$
$$P_b = \mathbf{N}[\frac{(c-\mu_2)}{\sigma_2}] \leq \beta.$$

For example, if AQL= .05, LTFD= 0.15, $\alpha = 0.10$ and $\beta = 0.25$ then

$$\mu_1 = 0.05n, \sigma_1^2 = n(0.05)(0.95)$$
$$\mu_2 = 0.15n, \sigma_2^2 = n(0.15)(0.85)$$

then an inspection plan (n, c) which satisfies

$$\mathbf{N}[(c-0.05n)/(n(0.95)(0.05))] \geq 0.90$$
$$\mathbf{N}[(c-0.15n)/(n(0.15)(0.85))] \leq 0.05$$

can be calculated using standard normal tables or by writing an appropriate computer program which would repeat calculations by incrementing n until an appropriate solution is found. In our case, $n = 95$ and $c = 7$ provides an adequate solution to the risk specifications. The closer the AQL and the LTFD, the harder it is to discriminate between them and thus the larger the sample size required for assurance. For example, if AQL $= 0.05$ and LTFD $= 0.15$ then for a fixed $\alpha = 0.01$ and $\beta = 0.20$, the required sample size is 37. If AQL is increased to 0.06, while maintaining the remaining parameters at their former value, then we note that the required sample size will increase to 77, 95 and 122, respectively. Some results are summarized in Table 5.2, and clearly highlight this relationship.

Table 5.2: Sampling plans (α, β, AQL, LTFD).

AQL	LTFD	α	β	n	c
0.01	0.15	0.10	0.20	37	1
0.04	0.15	0.10	0.20	77	5
0.05	0.15	0.10	0.20	95	7
0.06	0.15	0.10	0.20	122	10
0.05	0.12	0.10	0.20	112	8
0.05	0.17	0.10	0.20	67	5
0.05	0.15	0.05	0.20	113	9
0.05	0.15	0.08	0.20	97	7

Of course, if we treat the inequality constraints above as equalities, an assurance plan can then be defined by solving for n and c. Or

$$\frac{(c-\mu_1)}{\sigma_1} = Z_{1-\alpha},$$
$$\frac{(c-\mu_2)}{\sigma_2} = Z_\beta$$

and therefore,

$$\begin{aligned} c &= Z_{1-\alpha}\sigma_1 + \mu_1 = Z_\beta \sigma_2 + \mu_2 \\ \text{or } c &= Z_{1-\alpha}\sigma_1 + \text{ nAQL } = Z_\beta \sigma_2 + \text{nLTFD} \end{aligned}$$

which leads to,

$$\begin{aligned} n &= [Z_{1-\alpha}\sqrt{\text{AQL(1-AQL)}} - Z_\beta \sqrt{\text{LTFD(1-LTFD)}}]^2/(\text{LTFD-AQL})^2, \\ c &= Z_{1-\alpha}\sqrt{\text{nAQL(1-AQL)}} + \text{nAQL}. \end{aligned}$$

Problem
Compute the (n, c) sampling plan if AQL $= 0.05$, LTFD $= 0.15, \alpha = 0.10$ and $\beta = 0.20$.

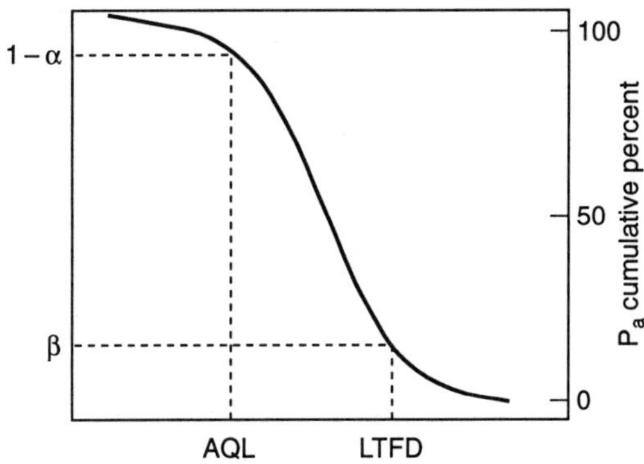

Figure 5.4: The OC curve.

Throughout the problems treated above, note that the acceptance probabilities are a function of n. An explicit relationship can be noted by writing $P_a(n)$, which is also called the OC (Operating Characteristic), curve which has been tabulated intensively by statisticians and quality controllers alike. Its importance resides in the fact that it establishes a clear relationship between the sample size and the risk specifications (α, β) of a sampling plan.

To construct the OC curve, two pointa are particularly important. A first point (AQL, $1 - \alpha$) defines the probability of acceptance of a lot, set at the $1 - \alpha$ level, when the proportion of acceptable quality is equal to the specified AQL. A second point (LTFD, β) defines unacceptable quality level LTFD which is acceptable at the low probability β(the consumer's risk). This is represented in Figure 5.4 where the points along the curve are similarly computed when the proportion defectives in a lot varies.

Other attributes sampling plans

When the sampling plan is changed, the sampling distribution necessarily changes as well. The following sampling plans, although more difficult to implement, have the advantage of reducing the expected amount of sampling (and thereby reduce inspection costs). The sampling plans studied include the curtailed, double stage and the multi-stage SPRT test.

(a) Curtailed sampling

Consider again a lot of size N with an unknown number of defectives. Curtailed sampling consists of the selection of a sample size n. Then, the first time k defectives are detected, the lot is rejected. Otherwise, the lot is accepted. This has the advantage of reducing the amount of inspection when the lot unexpectedly has many defectives. For example, if $k = 1$ and θ is the probability of a defective, then the probability of accepting the lot (not detecting even one defective) is

$$P_a = (1-\theta)^n.$$

If the lot is rejected, this will happen as soon as a defective is obtained. In this case, the probability of the number of units sampled is a truncated geometric distribution, given by

$$g(m \mid n) = \begin{cases} \theta(1-\theta)^{m-1} & \text{if} \quad m = 1, 2, \ldots, n-1 \\ (1-\theta)^{n-1} & \text{if} \quad m = \text{n}. \end{cases}$$

The expected number of units sampled through curtailed sampling, also called the *Average Sample Number* (ASN), is thus (see the appendix for the mathematical development):

$$\text{ASN } (n, 1) = \frac{1-(1-\theta)^n}{\theta} < n.$$

The risk implications of such a sampling plan are then defined by considering the statistical hypotheses

$$H_0 : \theta \le \theta_0; H_1 : \theta > \theta_0.$$

For a producer risk α, we require that $P_a \ge 1-\alpha$ or $(1-\theta)^n \ge 1-\alpha$. As a result, $\alpha = 1-(1-\theta)^n$, or the sample size n compatible for such a risk is

$$n \ge \frac{\ln(1-\alpha)}{\ln(1-\theta)}.$$

The advantage of such a sampling technique compared to the binomial sample approach is that in some cases we can obtain similar risk satisfaction, and with smaller ASN, thereby providing inspection cost economies.

Consider the following hypotheses:

$$H_0 : \theta = \theta_0; H_1 : \theta = \theta_1$$

and suppose that we use an (n,k) sampling technique with ASN calculated in the appendix. Further, specify the error risks as follows: under the null hypothesis the ASN is at least 100, while under the alternative we can detect the defective lot (in the mean) in at most an ASN = 5 sample, then this means that

$$\text{ASN}\ (\theta_0) = E(m \mid \theta_0, n, k) \geq 100, \text{ASN}\ (\theta_1) = E(m \mid \theta_1, n, k) \leq 5,$$

which leads to the following set of inequalities:

$$\begin{aligned}
\text{ASN}\ (\theta_0) &= [\frac{(k+1)}{\theta_0}]\sum_{j=0}^{k}\binom{n+1}{j}\theta_0(1-\theta_0)^{n+1-j} \\
&+ [\frac{(n-k)}{(1-\theta_0)}]\sum_{j=0}^{k}\binom{n+1}{j}\theta_0(1-\theta_0)^{n+1-j} \geq 100 \\
\text{ASN}\ (\theta_1) &= [\frac{(k+1)}{\theta_1}]\sum_{j=0}^{k}\binom{n+1}{j}\theta_1(1-\theta_1)^{n+1-j} \\
&+ [\frac{(n-k)}{(1-\theta_1)}]\sum_{j=0}^{k}\binom{n+1}{j}\theta_1)^j(1-\theta_1)^{n+1-j} \leq 5.
\end{aligned}$$

A solution of these two inequations for n and k will provide the appropriate sample test using the (n,k) curtailed sampling plan. Of course, to solve this problem it will be necessary to use either tables or a computer program which can calculate repetitively the ASNs until an acceptable solution is found. Wrting such a computer program is left as an exercise, however.

Problems

1. Say that under the null hypothesis the ASN_0 is 100 while under the alternative it is $\text{ASN}_1 = 8$. Assuming that a good lot has at most 0.05 defectives while a bad lot has over 15% defectives; what is the curtailed sampling plan compatible with these risk specifications? Compare this plan to the (n,c) binomial sampling plan.
2. For a producer risk α and a consumer risk β, a curtailed sampling plan is being designed. That is $P_a(\theta_0) \geq 1-\alpha, P_b(\theta_1) \leq \beta$. Show that $\log(1-\alpha)/\log(1-\theta_0) \leq n \leq \log\beta/\log(1-\theta_1)$. Calculate the ASNs for this test under the null and the alternative hypotheses.

(b) Double sampling

When sample evidence is not conclusive, further sampling might be required to reach a decision. This leads to multi-stage sampling plans where the number of stages corresponds to the number of times sampling results are inconclusive and inspection is continued. The rationale of such tests is that they can reduce the average inspection cost required for a given risk specification. The application of these tests is more complex, however, and involves a larger number of parameters. *Double sampling* has the advantage of giving a second chance to 'doubtful' results. For example, we might first use a sample size n_1 with two critical parameters c_1 and d_1. If the first sample results in r_1 defectives, $r_1 \leq c_1$, the decision to accept the lot will be taken, while if $c_1 \leq r_1 \leq d_1$, the decision might be to continue sampling, say by taking an additional sample size n_2 on the basis of which a decision will be necessarily taken (see Figure 5.5). Daudin and Trécourt (1990), for example, compute explicitly the probabilities of acceptance and rejection using such a sampling plan. The decision process is given at the first stage by

$$\begin{aligned} \text{If } r_1 &\leq c_1, \text{ accept the lot,} \\ \text{If } c_1 &< r_1 \leq d_1, \text{ collect a second sample of size}_2 n \\ \text{If } r_1 &> d_1, \text{ reject the lot.} \end{aligned}$$

At the second stage when the lot size is n_2, the number of defectives is r_2, a decision is reached as follows:

$$\begin{aligned} \text{If } r_1 + r_2 &\leq c_2, \text{ accept the lot} \\ \text{If } r_1 + r_2 &> c_2, \text{ reject the lot.} \end{aligned}$$

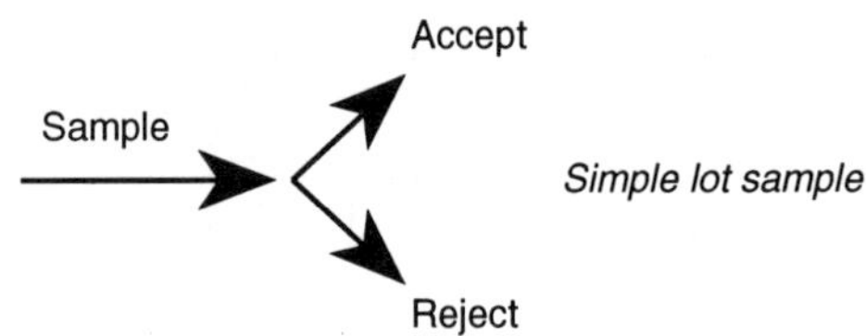

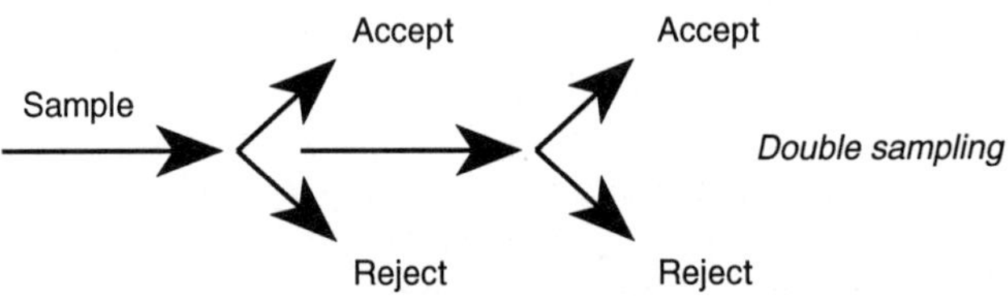

Figure 5.5: Simple and double sampling.

The parameters of the plan can be computed following any of the methods used earlier. There are also generalizations to multiple sampling plans, consisting in a set of successive and conditional plans, each depending on accrued and prior evidence. Although these plans have a smaller ASN than single stage plans, they can be difficult to administer.

If the AQL, the LTFD, the α error and β error are specified by the following probabilities,

$$\begin{aligned}\alpha &= P(r_1 > d_1) + P[(c_1 \le r_1 \le d_1) \cap \le (r_2 + r_2 > c_2)] \\ &= P(r_1 + 1 \ge d_1 + 1) + P[(c_1 + 1 \le r_1 \le d_1) \cap (r_1 + r_2 \ge c_2 + 1)] \\ &= P(r_1 \ge d_1 + 1) \\ &+ P[(r_2 \ge c_2 - r_1 + 1) \mid c_1 + 1 \le r_1 \le d_1)]P(c_1 + 1 \le r_1 + d_1)\end{aligned}$$

and

$$\begin{aligned}\beta &= P(r_1 \le c_1) + P[(c_1 < r_1 \le d_1) \cap \le (r_2 + r_2 \le c_2)] \\ &= P(r_1 \ge c_1) + P[(c_1 + 1 \le r_1 \le d_1) \cap (r_1 + r_2 \le c_2)] \\ &= P(r_1 \le c_1) + P[(r_2 \le c_2 - r_1) \mid c_1 + 1 \le r_1 \le d_1)]P(c_1 + 1 \le r_1 + d_1).\end{aligned}$$

In other words, the two stage sampling plan is defined by the following distributions:

$$\begin{aligned}\alpha &= \sum_{i=d_1+1}^{n_1} \binom{n_1}{i} (\mathrm{AQL})^i (1 - \mathrm{AQL})^{n_1} \\ &+ \sum_{i=d_1+1}^{n_1-1} \binom{n_1}{i} (\mathrm{AQL})^i (1 - \mathrm{AQL})^{n_1} \\ &* \; [\sum_{s=c_2-i+1}^{n_2} \binom{n_2}{s} (\mathrm{AQL})^s (1 - \mathrm{AQL})^{n_2}] \\ \beta &= \sum_{i=0}^{c_1} \binom{n_1}{i} (\mathrm{LTFD})^i (1 - \mathrm{LTFD})^{n_1} \\ &+ \sum_{i=c_1+1}^{d_1-1} {}^{n_1}\{\binom{n_1}{i} (\mathrm{LTFD})^i (1 - \mathrm{LTFD}) \\ &* \sum_{s=0}^{c_2-i} \binom{n_2}{s} (\mathrm{LTFD})^s (1 - \mathrm{LTFD})^{n_2}]\}.\end{aligned}$$

These equations can then be used to select the plan's parameters, as we have shown above. If the objective is to minimize the expected amount of inspection (i.e. the ASN), then it can be shown that the problem definition is

$$\min \mathrm{ASN} = n_1 + n_2 \sum_{i=d_1+1}^{c_1-1} \binom{n_1}{i} p^i (1 - p)^{n_1} \le n_1 + n_2,$$

where p is the average fraction of defectives. The numerical solution of this problem can be based again on tables (as calculated by Daudin and Trecourt, 1990, for example) or using a computer program, searching iteratively for a solution. Based on numerous examples, Daudin and Trécourt claim that this generalized approach provides less expensive inspection schemes and at least the same risk protection.

(c) The sequential probability ratio test (SPRT)

Often, the information gained through one or more samples is not conclusive, as was the case while presenting the double sampling approach. In such cases, it might be appropriate to continue sampling. At the limit, if all sample sizes are treated as units, Wald's SPRT test (sequential probability ratio test) might be used. We shall consider its essential form. Sample information is collected sequentially over time. At each time, given a producer and consumer risk (α, β), there are three possibilities. First, we can accept the lot (i.e. accept the statistical null hypothesis that is used by the test). Second, we can reject it; and finally, we may be uncertain and therefore continue sampling. This is defined by acceptance, rejection and uncertainty regions, which are delineated by boundaries that can be calculated. The boundaries are in fact two lines, as shown in Figure 5.6. The first line delineates the rejection region while the second delineates the acceptance region. The remaining part of the plan defines the 'uncertainty region' (which prescribes to continue sampling). If we inspect a proportion, for example, and assume that the AQL, LTFD and (α, β) are known, Wald has shown that these lines are given by

$$\text{Rejection Line: } R = a_R + bn$$
$$\text{Acceptance Line: } A = -a_A + bn$$

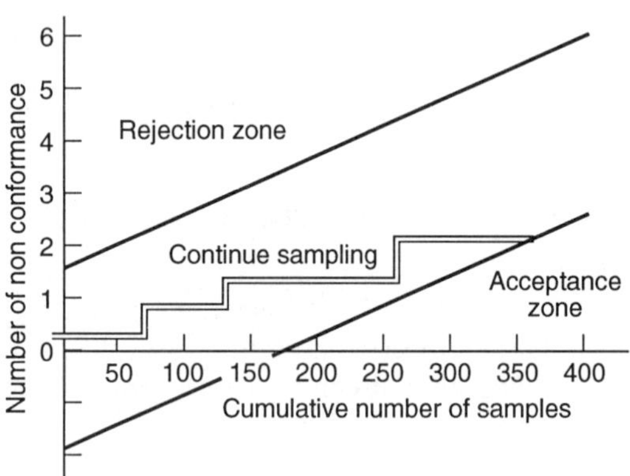

Figure 5.6: Sequential sampling with the SPRT test.

where n is the aggregate samples collected and the test parameters a_R and a_A are required to satisfy the following:

$$a_A = \frac{\ln[(1-\alpha)/\beta]}{\ln\left[\text{LTFD(1-AQL)}/\big(\text{AQL(1-LTFD)}\big)\right]}$$
$$a_R = \frac{\ln[(1-\beta)/\alpha]}{\ln\left[\text{LTFD(1-AQL)}/\big(\text{AQL(1-LTFD)}\big)\right]}$$
$$b = \frac{\ln\left[\text{(1-AQL)/(1-LTFD)}\right]}{\ln\left[\text{LTFD(1-AQL)}/\big(\text{AQL(1-LTFD)}\big)\right]}.$$

The proof of this result is somewhat involved, however. Sequential and multiple sampling tests are more difficult to study, and will be discussed in Chapter 9 from a theoretical standpoint. Wald's SPRT ratio generally requires a large number of samples, mainly when the proportion of defectives are tested (values of θ) in a zone of indifference between θ_0 and θ_1.

Example

A lot is being tested by taking one unit at a time. Application of SPRT is required with the following specifications: $\alpha = 0.050, \beta = 0.10$, AQL = 0.0103 and LTFD = 0.0652. To apply such tests, it is first necessary to construct the rejection and acceptance lines. As a result, note that:

$$\begin{aligned}
[(1-\alpha)/\beta] = 9.500 \text{ and } \ln[(1-\alpha)/\beta] &= 0.977724 \\
[(1-\beta)/\alpha] = 18.000 \text{ and } \ln[(1-\beta)/\alpha] &= 1.255273 \\
[\text{ LTFD } (1-\text{AQL })/(\text{ AQL } (1-\text{LTFD }))] &= 6.33010/1.05873 \text{ and} \\
\ln\frac{\text{LTFD}(1-\text{AQL})}{\text{AQL}(1-\text{LTFD})} = \ln\frac{6.330}{1.05873} &= 0.826195 \\
\ln\frac{\text{(1-AQL)}}{\text{(1-LTFD)}} = \ln(1.05873) &= 0.024785,
\end{aligned}$$

and therefore,

$$\begin{aligned}
a_A &= 0.977724/0.826195 = 1.1834058 \\
a_R &= 1.255273/0.8201195 - 1.5194811 \\
b &= 0.024785/0.826195 = 0.0299989.
\end{aligned}$$

As a result, the minimum sample required for acceptance is

$$a_A/b = 39.448 \cong 40,$$

while the minimum required for rejection (all units defectives) is

$$a_R/(1-b) = 1.566 \cong 2.$$

The probability of acceptance as a function of the number of units inspected is

$$\begin{aligned} P_a &= \frac{a_R}{(a_A + a_R)} = \frac{\ln[(1-\alpha)/\beta]}{\ln[(1-\beta)(1-\alpha)/\beta\alpha]} \\ &= \frac{1.1834058}{(1.1834058 + 1.5194811)} = 0.43783, \end{aligned}$$

which is independent of the AQL and the LTFD.

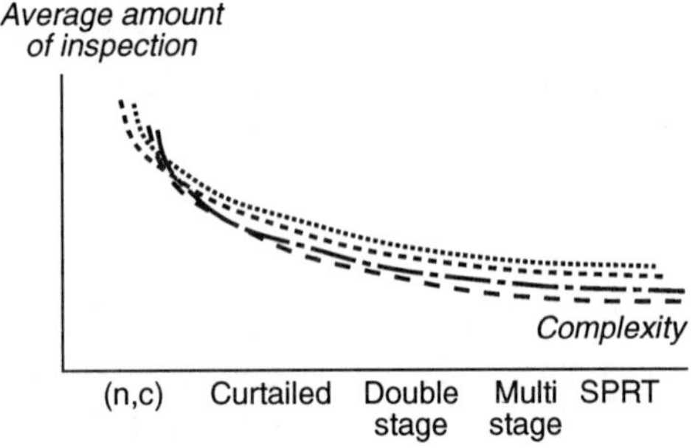

Figure 5.7: Inspection techniques and the amount of inspection.

The choice of a single lot, double, multiple and sequential (sprt) sampling technique is based practically on a number of considerations. On the one hand, the more involved the sampling technique, the more complex it is to implement. On the other, sequential (as compared to single lot) sampling can reduce the average number of inspections to perform, and thereby reduce the direct cost of acceptance sampling. This is represented in Figure 5.7, and is self- explanatory.

MIL standards and tests

According to the DoD *(Department of Defence)* glossary of Quality Assurance (MIL-STD-109B), under the term SPECIFICATION, we find:

> A document intended primarily for use in procurement, which clearly and accurately describes the essential and technical requirements for items, materials or services, *including the procedure by which it will be determined, that the requirements have been met.*

To ensure that these requirements have been met, there is an array of tests and procedures to follow (Kenett and Halevy, 1984). According to MIL-STD-490, these include

(a) Tests and checks of the performance and reliability requirements.

(b) A measurement of comparison of specified physical characteristics.

(c) Verification with specific criteria for workmanship

(d) Test and inspection methods for ensuring compliance, including environmental conditions of performance.

(e) Classification of characteristics as critical, major or minor.

Tests are usually classified in groups (groups A, B, C and D), each group being characterized by the nature of tests, the timing when they are performed and quantitites of items to which they are applied. Several MIL standards, specifying the production process of MIL Spec. items, refer to group $A - B - C$ testing. These groups are descending in the number of tested items, but ascending in the depth of the tests.

It is possible to classify MIL Spec. guidelines for testing into three main categories:

1. Sampling plans based on MIL-STD-105.
2. LTFD sampling plans.
3. Algorithms for sampling procedures with no direct statistical basis.

MIL-STD-105 is used for quality conformance and pre-delivery inspection. It uses groups A, B and C, and describe the tests and sampling plans (specified by following the appropriate tables). In the DoD tables, both the sample size and acceptance number are determined by the AQL and the lot size. Defects are usually classified into two categories; major and minor. Different AQL values are assigned to major and minor defects. Acceptance criteria for minor defects are larger. Typical AQL values for group A are $0.65 - 1\%$ for major defects, $2.55 - 4\%$ for minor defects. Group B is a sub-sample taken from group A or from units which were subjected to and met group A inspection. Typical AQL values are $4.0 - 6.5\%$. Group C sampling is normally not based on MIL-STD-105 tables. Test parameters are grouped into sub-groups, each sub-group receiving detailed instructions as to sample size, frequency of sampling and action to be taken in cases of non-compliance. There are usually $5 - 7$ groups with two units tested in each. As a result, MIL STD 105D requires the specification of:

(a) The AQL.

(b) The LTFD.

(c) The protection level (A, B, C).

(d) Rules for switching from a normal to a reduced control (as in CSP-1).

5.3 Rectifying inspection

Rectifying inspection is a form of preventive inspection. It can be used, for example, to control defective parts in outgoing lots, to reduce (or eliminate altogether) through inspection a sufficient number of defectives and so on. In lot-by-lot sampling, most rectifying inspection plans call for 100 percent inspection of rejected lots. Since 100% inspection is restricted to rejected lots only, the average fraction of total items inspected will be much less than 1, if the average fraction of defectives is small. Basically, sampling plans switch between 100% screening and sampling inspection. During the 100% screening phase, if a predetermined number of consecutive non-defective items are found, the plan switches to sampling inspection immediately. If an unacceptably large number of defectives is found during sampling inspection, the plan switches to 100% screening again. These methods are called 'CSP techniques', and will be considered subsequently. The principle of rectification is far broader, however, since it uses the information gained through sampling to reach a decision. We can use this information equally to reach some other decision, such as scheduling maintenance, replacement of equipment and people. We shall consider later on how this can be done. Nevertheless, it is useful to note that rectifying inspection ties in to some process we wish to manage, and provides an information source for the management of this process.

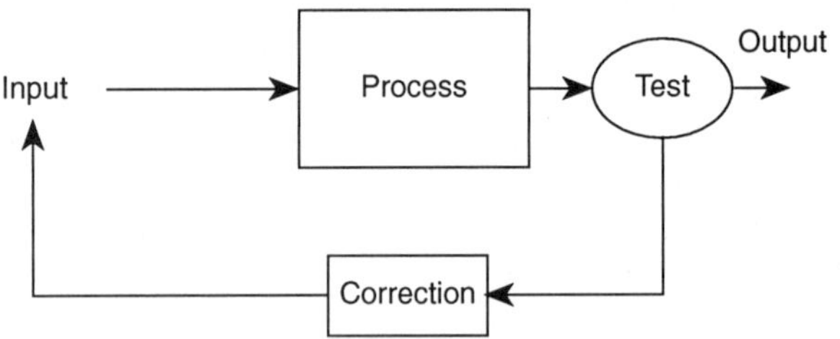

Figure 5.8: rectifying inspection.

Traditionally, rectifying inspection plans are designed using a pre– specified Average Outgoing Quality Limit (AOQL). The Average Outgoing Quality (AOQ) curve shows the relationship between incoming quality and outgoing quality. The maximum ordinate of the AOQ curve gives the worst possible AOQ, which is the AOQL. Given an average product quality, the decision to design a rectifying inspection plan is defined as follows:

Minimize: The total cost of quality

Subject to: $AOQ \leq$ *a specified value*

It is important to point out that in rectifying inspection we replace detected defective items with good ones, without considering the cost of re-production or repair.

Consider an (n, c) plan. If a lot is accepted, then its output is delivered as is, with the sample defectives corrected. If a sample is rejected, then the lot is fully tested and all defectives corrected. As a result, the Outgoing Quality (OQ) fraction of defectives is a random variable given by

$$OQ = \begin{cases} \theta(N-n)/N & \text{w.p.} \quad P_a \\ 0 & \text{w.p.} \quad 1 - P_a \end{cases}$$

where P_a is the probability of acceptance given earlier. Using the binomial sampling distribution, we have

$$P_a = \sum_{r=0}^{c} \binom{n}{r} \theta^r (1-\theta)^{n-r}.$$

The average outgoing quality is thus AOQ$= E(OQ \mid \theta) = P_a\theta(N - n)/N + (1 - P_a)(0) = P_a\theta(1 - n/N)$. For $N >> n, n/N$ is negligible, thus AOQ$= \theta P_a$. Let the required AOQ be given by a, then the 'rectifying' inspection sampling problem is given by

$$\text{Minimize: } C = n \text{ Subject to: } AOQ \leq a.$$

5.4 Variables sampling plans

These plans, unlike attribute plans, do not classify results in terms of *good/bad or defective/not defective*, but measure the degree of conformance of the sample results. These plans are presented in MIL-STD 414 tables (Military Standard MIL-STD 414, June, 1957, Sampling Procedures and Tables for Inspection by Variables for Per Cent Defective, Superintendent of Documents, U.S. Government Printing Office, Washington, D.C.). They can be used to control the fraction of nonconforming units, and to control the mean or the standard deviation with single and double specification limits. The advantage of these variable sampling plans is that measurements are more precise, the samples needed to perform tests are smaller, there is more information per unit sampled and they are more useful for destructive testing. We first consider a life testing example, and subsequently use economic criteria to design variables sampling plans.

Life testing

Say that the desirable life of a good lamp is $x_1 = 12,050$ hours and let the life time of a lamp in an undesirable lot be $x_2 = 11,900$ hours. The life of lamps is approximated by normal distributions with a known standard deviation of 500 hours. We assume $\alpha = 0.05$ and $\beta = 0.10$. Now we wish to construct a test based on a sample size n and a minimal acceptance average life x_a for the bulbs. A solution is found as before by selecting sampling parameters which satisfy prior producer and consumer risk constraints

$(P_a \geq 1 - \alpha, P_b \leq \beta)$. The test parameters are (n, x_a) and the life of bulbs is assumed to have a normal probability distribution. Thus, we can write

$$\begin{aligned} x_a - x_1 &= -Z_\alpha(\sigma)/\sqrt{n} \text{ (the producer's risk constraint)} \\ x_a - x_2 &= Z_\beta(\sigma)/\sqrt{n} \text{ (the consumer's risk constraint)} \end{aligned}$$

where Z_α is the number of standard deviations from the mean corresponding to a producer risk α, while Z_β is the number of standard deviations corresponding to the consumer risk in a standard normal distribution. In our special case, $x_1 = 12,050, Z_\alpha = 1.645, \sigma = 500, x_2 = 11,900$ and $Z_\beta = 1.282$. Therefore,

$$\begin{aligned} x_a - 12,050 &= -1.645(500)/\sqrt{n}; x_a - 11,900 = 1.282(500)/\sqrt{n} \\ (x_a - 12,050)^2 &= [-1.645(500)]^2/n; (x_a - 11,900)^2 = [1.282(500)]^2/n \end{aligned}$$

Further,

$$\begin{aligned} (x_a &- 12,050)/(x_a - 11,900) = -[1.645/1.282] \\ x_a &= \{12,050 + (11,900)[1.645/1.282]\}/[1 + 1.645/1.282] \\ &= 27,319.5/2.28315 \end{aligned}$$

and after some elementary manipulations, we obtain

$$x_a = 11,965.7 \text{ and } n = 95.$$

That is, to perform such a test, we ought to use sample sizes of 95 and calculate the average lamp life. If the average is below 11,965 we reject the lot, otherwise we accept it.

Generally, variables sampling plans are a function of the sampling distributions they are based on (which presume the sampling approach used, knowledge or estimation of some of the parameters). A general treatment of this problem follows using an example, let Q be the measure of average quality calculated using a sample. Let Q_l be the lower quality tolerance limit and Q_u be the upper tolerance limit. Assume that the quality characteristic has a normal probability distribution with mean μ and variance σ^2. Thus, a '$1 - \alpha$' confidence interval for the quality characteristic is

$$P_a = P[Q_l \leq Q \leq Q_u \mid \mu, \sigma/\sqrt{n}] \geq 1 - \alpha.$$

This means that

$$\begin{aligned} \Phi((\mu - Q_l)\sqrt{n}/\sigma)) + 1 - \Phi((Q_u - \mu)\sqrt{n}/\sigma)) &\geq 1 - \alpha \text{ or} \\ \Phi((Q_u - \mu)/\sigma)) - \Phi((\mu - Q_l)/\sigma)) &\leq \alpha. \end{aligned}$$

Assume that a defective lot has mean μ', and suppose that it has the same variance. The consumer risk, which is the probability of accepting a bad lot, is thus defined by

$$P_b = P[Q_l \leq Q \leq Q_u \mid \mu', \sigma/\sqrt{n}] \leq \beta.$$

This means that

$$\Phi((\mu' - Q_l)\sqrt{n}/\sigma)) + 1 - \Phi((Q_u - \mu')\sqrt{n}/\sigma)) \leq \beta,$$

and therefore,

$$\Phi((Q_u - \mu')\sqrt{n}/\sigma)) - \Phi((\mu' - Q_l)\sqrt{n}/\sigma)) \geq 1 - \beta.$$

In other words, an acceptable sampling plan (based on the parameters n, Q_l, Q_u) with α and β risks, must satisfy the two constraints on α and β above.

Problems

1. The average breaking strength of a yarn is usually used a measure of its quality. Let the acceptance quality level for a given use be an average of 90lb, and let the lower tolerance limit be an average of 80lb. The standard deviation of the breaking strength of the particular grade of yarn is 11lb. Design a sampling plan based on sample averages that will yield a 95of accepting yarn of 90lb quality and a maximum chance of 10yarn of 80lb quality or less.

2. A firm may have several types of clients. For example, a shirt manufacturer may stratify clients as speciality shops, department stores and 'seconds stores'. These latter stores usually accept quality products at a lower level but at the same time pay a lot less than specialty stores, who are willing to pay for premium quality. Now assume that a manufacturing process produces products with quality measured on a quantitative scale given by x. Let x be a random variable with mean μ and standard deviation σ. The manufacturer's daily output is N units while the inspection sample is n. The price of a unit product sold to market segment i is p_i while the inspection cost is I_c per unit. A control procedure is established as follows: If z, the average quality of a lot, is smaller than z_0 (a parameter), then the daily output is shipped to market segment 1 (say the seconds stores), if $z \in [z_0, z_1]$, the daily output is sent to market segment 2, and finally, if $z > z_1$, the daily output is sent to the third market segment. On this basis, construct an optimization problem which will help you select both the sample size and the critical parameters z_0, z_1 To do so, proceed in two ways: first, by assuming the consumers' risks sustained by each market segment; and second by assuming the costs implied in shipping substandard units to the market segments. When solutions are obtained, perform a sensitivity analysis with respect to the process standard deviation σ.

5.5 Inspection in a continuous process

A typical continuous control scheme with continuous feedback between the process operating performance and its control is presented in Figure 5.8. For example, NCM (Numerically Controlled Machines) measure and control operating results and deviations from production standards continuously. In many cases, these machines replace machine operators and require continuous controls. Usually, they also have a built-in capacity to:

- Sense the machine status.
- Make logical programmable decisions.
- Communicate with other machines.

In such systems, 'Adaptive Optimization', which seeks to combine measurements, inspection and performance optimization, is becoming increasingly possible. There are three types of processes in such cases. The first is coined 'open loop', in which case all controls are made *apriori* with a feedback based on the position and the velocity used in machine control. The second process uses information (obtained continuously or sampled) to alter the machine's operating controls. These are called 'feedback controls'. Finally, when data is integrated into measures of performance and optimized on line, this is called 'adaptive optimization'. The value of such machines arises for many reasons, most of which relate to their flexible characteristics, precision (and thus quality) and their capacity to auto-control. The criteria used to evaluate the quality performance of these machines include, for example,

- Life of machine, or component.
- Machine accuracy.
- Machine finish.
- Power consumption and maintenance costs.
- Flexibility or reliability while performing a number of functions.
- Software support.
- Training, manpower and control requirements.

Practically, these machines are used in many automatic factories. In such an advanced technology environment of integrated automation, data and control requirements are both extensive and stringent, and require careful attention.

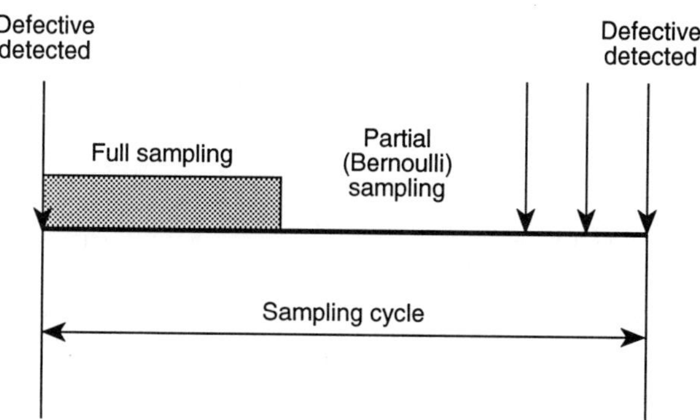

Figure 5.9: The CSP-1 process.

CSP-1, or Continuous sampling procedure

CSP-I is a sampling technique used in the continuous control of processes. CSP-I begins by full (100%) inspection. When n consecutive units are found to be non-defective, full inspection is stopped and it switches to random sampling with probability q until one unit is found defective (see Figure 5.9). The larger n and q, the tighter the controls. Consider a process whose propensity to manufacture defectives is ν, then the probability of sampling is either q or 1, depending on which mode we find ourselves in. Let A be the q-inspection mode and $P(A)$ its probability, with $P(\bar{A}) = 1 - P(A)$. In other words, the fraction inspected FI is

$$FI = \begin{cases} q \text{ w.p. } P(A) \\ 1 \text{ w.p. } P(\bar{A}) \end{cases}$$

while the average fraction inspected is AFI_n,

$$\begin{aligned} \text{AFI}_n &= q \text{ Prob } (A) + (1) \text{ Prob } (\bar{A}), \\ P(A) &= \frac{v}{(u_n + v)}, \quad v = \frac{1}{q\nu}, \quad u_n = \frac{1 - (1-\nu)^n}{\nu(1-\nu)^n}. \end{aligned}$$

In the equation above, v is the mean number of units processed between two detected defective units when the propensity of the process to produce defectives has the fixed probability ν, while u_n denotes the average number of units processed until n consecutive non-defective units are processed, under a full sampling mode. These observations are obtained by noting that the probability distribution of processing n consecutive units prior to processing a defective one is given by the geometric distribution $f(n) = \nu(1-\nu)^n$. Then AFI_n, ϵ_n(the probability of detecting a defective) and

AOQ_n(the average outgoing quality) are given by

$$\text{AFI}_n = \frac{q}{q+(1-q)(1-\nu)^n}, \epsilon_n = \nu \text{ AFI}_n, \text{ AOQ}_n = \frac{\nu(1\text{-AFI}_n)}{1-\epsilon_n}.$$

Explicitly, the AOQ_n is given by

$$\text{AOQ}_n = \frac{\nu\theta}{\theta+(1-\nu)q}, \theta = (1-q)(1-\nu)^n,$$

which provides an estimate of the average outgoing quality as a function of the sample size (prove it as an exercise).

Problem

An acceptable quality level for a part is at most a 2% defective rate. Several inspection plans can be used to test lots of size 1000. The cost of testing a unit is \$5, while the management has specified a producer risk α of 0.05 and a consumer's risk of risk β of 0.02. Formulate the sampling design problems which will select the best binomial sampling plan and the best CSP-1 plan.

5.6 Economic inspection sampling

Economic criteria of various sorts can be used to construct sample tests. The problems are two-fold: first, finding measurable criteria which truly depict the COQ; and second, expressing the performance and the objective measures in terms of the sampling design parameters. We can then optimize the criterion subject to prior risks specification. To demonstrate alternative approaches to sample design using economic criteria, we consider specific examples.

Inspection costs minimization and prior risk specifications

Let the COQ of a manufacturer performing destructive tests consist of the cost of a producer's risk and the cost of inspection. The lot size is N while n is the sample size. The unit production cost is P while the salvage value of a defective unit detected prior to sales is Q. Thus $P-Q$ is the cost of a defective detected in-house (salvaged at Q). In addition, we consider the Post Sales Cost (PSC) which consists of the Direct Cost (DC), the Indirect Cost (IC) and the scrapping cost of the unit detected after it has been used by the consumer (P). In other words, we have, PSC$= P + DC + IC$. Assume that the AQL, LTFD, the producer's risk and consumer's risk are given while the unit inspection cost is c_i. The producer's problem is thus

Minimize TC

$$\text{TC} = n(P+c_i) + (N-n)\alpha(P-Q) + (N-n)(1-\beta)\ (\text{PSC})(\text{LTFD})$$

Subject to;

$$1-\sum_{r=0}^{c}\binom{n}{r}(\text{AQL})^r(1-\ \text{AQL})^{n-r}\geq 1-\alpha$$

$$\sum_{r=0}^{c}\binom{n}{r}\text{LTFD}^r(1-\ \text{LTFD})^{n-r}\leq\beta.$$

A solution to this problem can be found by numerical calculations, first selecting values of n and c which satisfy the constraints above, and then selecting those values that minimize the expected cost.

Non-linear objectives

The definition of the COQ is, as seen in Chapter 2, extremely important. Use of an expected profit or cost objective might be insufficient, ignoring the uneven risks associated with losses of varying sizes. The valuation of losses is a topic of permanent research and will be discussed further in Chapter 7. Moskowitz and Tang (1992), for example, suggest the use of a quadratic and a step-loss function. Suppose that there is an incoming lot of N items for inspection, and let x denote the deviation of the performance variable from the standard-target value of the item. The pdf of the deviation is assumed to be given by a normal distribution with mean μ and variance σ^2. The quadratic loss function is given by

$$\ell(x)=kx^2$$

while the step-loss function is

$$\ell(x)=\begin{cases}0 \text{ if } -\delta\leq x\leq\delta\\ b \text{ otherwise.}\end{cases}$$

Here k, b and δ are parameters. The expectation of these costs is given for the quadratic function by

$$L(\mu,\sigma^2)=\int_{-\infty}^{+\infty}\ell(x)f(x)dx=k[\mu^2+\sigma^2],$$

while for the step-loss function it is given by

$$L(\mu,\sigma^2)=b\{1-\Phi(\frac{\delta-\mu}{\sigma})+\Phi(\frac{-\delta-\mu}{\sigma})\},$$

where Φ denotes the standard normal distribution function. A random sample of size n is drawn from the lot, and let $\bar{x}$ denote its sample mean deviation from the standard performance. Let d_U and d_L be the action limits, where the decision rule is to reject the lot if $\bar{x}>d_U$ or $\bar{x}<d_L$. The problem's parameters are (n, d_U, d_L). Let R be the per item cost of rejection, s be the unit sampling cost, and assume that the prior probability of μ is given by $\pi(\mu)$ and that the sample average distribution is normal

with mean μ and variance σ^2/n. Using these facts, we can construct the optimization problem which will provide the optimum test parameters for both cost assumptions (quadratic and step loss). This is left as an exercise, however.

The Bayesian approach to economic sampling

The Bayesian approach (see Chapter 4 for a review of basic concepts) considers explicitly the costs associated with the decisions to accept or reject inspected lots (rather than through the specification of producer and consumer risks). There are three classes of costs: the inspection cost, the rejection cost and the cost of defectives accepted in a lot. In addition, the decision theory approach provides a managerial approach to the evaluation of sampling information, as we saw in Chapter 4. Below, we consider a generalization of the Bayes risk approach as well as a problem for Bayesian updating of the prior probability of defectives based on sample information. Other problems such as the economic value of unreliable inspectors and inspections, are also considered.

The Bayes risk approach is in principle simple. Given a number of alternatives (hypotheses, decisions, classes to allocate items), there is a cost of making the wrong decision. Explicitly, let $C(x_i \mid x_j)$ be the cost of stating that an item (or lot) belongs to class i when there are M alternative (independent and exhaustive) classes and when in fact it belongs to class j. Further, let $\mathbf{y}$ be a vector of sample information collected in some fashion (objective or subjective). Thus, by Bayes' theorem, the probability that the item belongs to class j, given the 'evidence' $\mathbf{y}$, is given by

$$P(x_j \mid \mathbf{y}) = \frac{f(\mathbf{y} \mid x_j)P(x_j)}{\sum_{i=1}^{M} f(\mathbf{y} \mid x_i)P(x_i)}.$$

Further, assume that there is a decision rule $\delta(\mathbf{y})$, a function of the sample information $\mathbf{y}$. In other words, given $\mathbf{y}$, a decision $\delta(\mathbf{y})$ is reached and the cost incurred is then $C(x_{\delta(y)} \mid x_j)$. For example, given three alternative decisions and four potential states, the matrix in Table 5.3 is obtained.

Table 5.3: The costs of quality.

Decision	Prob. States	$P(x_j \mid \mathbf{y})$ 1	$P(x_j \mid \mathbf{y})$ 2	$P(x_j \mid \mathbf{y})$ 3	$P(x_j \mid \mathbf{y})$ 4
$\delta(1)$	1	$C(x_{(y)} \mid x_j)$	$C(x_{(y)} \mid x_j)$	$C(x_{(y)} \mid x_j)$	$C(x_{(y)} \mid x_j)$
$\delta(2)$	2	$C(x_{(y)} \mid x_j)$	$C(x_{(y)} \mid x_j)$	$C(x_{(y)} \mid x_j)$	$C(x_{(y)} \mid x_j)$
$\delta(3)$	2	$C(x_{(y)} \mid x_j)$	$C(x_{(y)} \mid x_j)$	$C(x_{(y)} \mid x_j)$	$C(x_{(y)} \mid x_j)$

The expected cost associated with a (feedback) decision rule $\delta(.)$ is, therefore,

$$C(\mathbf{y} \mid \delta(.)) = \sum_{j=1}^{M} C(x_{\delta(y)} \mid x_j)P(x_j \mid \mathbf{y}).$$

Now if $\mathbf{y} = (y_1, y_2, \ldots, y_T)$ is a vector of measurements, the expected cost $C(\delta \mid T)$ associated to the decision rule is simply

$$C(\delta \mid T) = \int_{\Omega} C(\mathbf{y} \mid \delta(.))dy_1 dy_2 \ldots .dy_T.$$

The optimal decision rule $\delta(.)$ at time T is therefore found by solving the following problem:

$$\min_{\delta(\mathbf{y}) \in [0,1,..M]} \quad C(\delta \mid T)$$

$$= \quad \int_{\Omega} \sum_{j=1}^{M} C(x_{\delta(y)} \mid x_j) P(x_j \mid \mathbf{y}) dy_1 dy_2 ..dy_T$$

Here the state '0' was added to the decision alternatives to make it possible that the item (lot) does not belong to any of these classes (i.e. it is a rejection alternative). This expression is known as the 'Bayes risk'. The inspection problem in a Bayesian framework thus consists of selecting such a decision rule based on cost specifications. To do so, it is necessary to determine the cost parameters and apply thereafter standard optimization techniques. Of course, when the sample size increases, the probability distribution of states is updated. Explicitly, let $y(T+1)$ be the $T+1$ sample and let $\mathbf{y}'$ be the new augmented sample vector. Then, again applying Bayes theorem, we have

$$P(x_j \mid \mathbf{y}') = \frac{f(y(T+1) \mid x_j) P(x_j \mid \mathbf{y})}{\sum_{i=1}^{M} f(y(T+1) \mid x_i) P(x_i \mid \mathbf{y})}.$$

which provides the updating scheme for the states' probabilities' estimates.

For example, a production output might consist of three levels of quality. Grade A, grade B and grade C. Each grade will fetch a price in the market which is not known *apriori*, although probability estimates are available. The profits realized by shipping a lot of grade A when the market is in 'state 1' is \$50, the profit of a lot of grade B is then \$20, etc. for the other situations represented in Table 5.4a.

Table 5.4*a*.

Prob. Market States	$P(1 \mid \mathbf{y})$ "1"	$P(2 \mid \mathbf{y})$ "2"	$P(3 \mid \mathbf{y})$ "3"
A	50	10	-10
B	20	30	0
C	-20	-10	10

Once a decision is taken, it is possible that the decision selected will turn out not to be optimal due to insufficiency of the prior knowledge. For example, if we have an A grade lot and ship it to market, we will collect 50, and since $50 > 20, 50 > -20$, we have no lost opportunity loss. If we ship an A

lot to a B market, market is in state '2', then the profit is equal to 10, and the opportunity loss is thus $30 - 10 = 20$, which could have been made had we shipped a Grade B product, and so on, for all the other situations. The opportunity losses for each alternative are thus the costs of having taken the wrong decision. Explicitly, for an A grade lot, we have:

Opportunity loss for a Grade A lot sent to the A market$= 50 - 50 = 0$

Opportunity loss for a Grade A lot sent to the B market$= 50 - 20 = 30$

Opportunity loss for a Grade A lot sent to the C market$= 50 - (-20) = 70$

Similarly, repeating calculations for the B and C markets, we obtain the opportunity loss cost matrix in Table 5.4b.

Table 5.4*b*.

	$P(1 \mid \mathbf{y})$ "1"	$P(2 \mid \mathbf{y})$ "2"	$P(3 \mid \mathbf{y})$ "3"
A	0	20	20
B	30	0	10
C	70	40	0

These costs are lost profits due to shipping non optimal grades, while $P(1 \mid \mathbf{y}), P(2 \mid y)$ and $P(3 \mid \mathbf{y})$ are the probabilities that the market will be in states '1', '2' or '3' when the information vector is $\mathbf{y}$. The Expected Profit (EP) and the expected Opportunity Loss (OL) are thus

$$\begin{aligned}
\text{Alternative } A\text{: EP } (A) &= (50)P(1 \mid \mathbf{y}) + (10)P(2 \mid \mathbf{y}) + (-10)P(3 \mid \mathbf{y}) \\
\text{Alternative } B\text{: EP } (B) &= (20)P(1 \mid \mathbf{y}) + (30)P(2 \mid \mathbf{y}) + (0)P(3 \mid \mathbf{y}) \\
\text{Alternative } C\text{: EP } (C) &= (-20)P(1 \mid \mathbf{y}) + (-10)P(2 \mid \mathbf{y}) + (10)P(3 \mid \mathbf{y}) \\
\text{Alternative } A\text{: EOL } (A) &= (0)P(1 \mid \mathbf{y}) + (20)P(2 \mid \mathbf{y}) + (20)P(3 \mid \mathbf{y}) \\
\text{Alternative } B\text{: EOL } (B) &= (30)P(1 \mid \mathbf{y}) + (0)P(2 \mid \mathbf{y}) + (10)P(3 \mid \mathbf{y}) \\
\text{Alternative } C\text{: EOL } (C) &= (70)P(1 \mid \mathbf{y}) + (40)P(2 \mid \mathbf{y}) + (0)P(3 \mid \mathbf{y})
\end{aligned}$$

If, on the basis of the vector $\mathbf{y}$, the prior estimates for grade alternatives A, B and C are equal to $0.6, 0.3$ and 0.1 respectively, then

$$\begin{aligned}
\text{EP } (A) &= 32,\ \text{EOL } (A) = 8,\ \text{EPPI } = 40 \\
\text{EP } (B) &= 21,\ \text{EOL } (B) = 19,\ \text{EPPI } = 40 \\
\text{EP } (C) &= -14,\ \text{EOL } (C) = 54,\ \text{EPPI } = 40
\end{aligned}$$

where EPPI is the Expected Profit under Perfect Information. Since the maximum profit decision is to send all lots to the A market (with expected profit 32), the value of information (i.e. fully sampling the lots and sending the grade lots to the appropriate markets) is the EOL of the this alternative. That is,

$$\text{EPPI - EP } (A) = 40 - 32 = 8.$$

Table 5.4c.

Prob.	$A, P(1 \mid \mathbf{y})$ Profit	OL	$B, P(2 \mid \mathbf{y})$ Profit	OL	$C, P(3 \mid \mathbf{y})$ Profit	OL
A	50	0	10	20	-10	20
B	20	30	30	0	0	10
C	-20	70	-10	40	10	0

In a Bayesian framework, economic considerations are thus introduced by assessing the implications of each potential decision. In many applications, great simplification is reached if we ignore the quantitative impact of costs (which is, of course, impossible in a business environment). For example, say that the cost of making the right decision is null, while that of reaching the wrong decision is 1. That is, $C(x_i \mid x_j) = 1$ for $\forall i \neq j$ and $C(x_i \mid x_j) = 0$ for i =j. Then given $\mathbf{y}$, the expected cost is

$$C(\mathbf{y} \mid x_i) = \sum_{j \neq i}^{M} (1) P(x_j \mid \mathbf{y}) = 1 - P(x_i \mid \mathbf{y}),$$

which is the conditional error of misclassification. Thus, a test can be constructed by minimizing this error. Namely, for each information vector $\mathbf{y}$, selecting the decision which maximizes the likelihood $P(x_i \mid \mathbf{y})$, or

$$e^*(\mathbf{y}) = \min_{i=1,\ldots,M} [1 - P(x_i \mid \mathbf{y})] = e_i(\mathbf{y}).$$

Next assume that there is a cost of rejection, i.e. of reaching the decision '0' when it is in fact wrong to do so. Let the cost of such a decision be C_r. That is $C(x_0 \mid x_j) = C_r$, and therefore the costs of rejecting wrongly, denoted by $C_0(\mathbf{y})$ is

$$C_0(\mathbf{y}) = \sum_{j=i}^{M} C_r P(x_j \mid \mathbf{y}) = C_r.$$

The optimal decision rule then consists of selecting the decision which minimizes

$$\text{Minimize } [C_0(\mathbf{y}), e^*(\mathbf{y})] \text{ or}$$

$$\delta(\mathbf{y}) = \begin{cases} i & \text{if } \quad e^*(\mathbf{y}) = e_i(\mathbf{y}) \leq C_r \\ 0 & \text{if } \quad e^*(\mathbf{y}) > C_r. \end{cases}$$

Problem: Bayes risk with two states

For the two states problem, suppose that the conditional distribution $f(\mathbf{y} \mid x_i)$ is a multivariate normal with mean vector and variance-covariance matrix (μ_i, Σ_i). Then demonstrate that

$$\delta(\mathbf{y}) = 1 \text{ if } \frac{f(\mathbf{y} \mid x_1)}{f(\mathbf{y} \mid x_2)} \geq \frac{P(x_2)(1 - C_r)}{P(x_1)C_r}$$

$$\delta(\mathbf{y}) = 2 \text{ if } \frac{f(\mathbf{y} \mid x_1)}{f(\mathbf{y} \mid x_2)} \leq \frac{P(x_2)C_r)}{P(x_1)(1 - C_r)} \text{else } \delta(\mathbf{y}) = 0.$$

Then calculate the likelihood ratio $\frac{f(\mathbf{y}|x_1)}{f(\mathbf{y}|x_2)}$ for the multivariate normal distribution of the sample information $\mathbf{y}$. For each of these cases, calculate the error probability. Finally, discuss the effects of knowing or not knowing the probability distributions of the likelihoods.

Example: Inspectors' reliability and inspection

Inspections by a person, through a process or through a machine, are not always reliable. There is a need, therefore, to account for this unreliability when a decision is to be based on sample information. In practice, this is an important and acute problem. For example, products submitted to a number of tests may point out that the product is rightly or wrongly defective. Tests have their own particularities which are important to consider. For example, certain (and expensive) pieces of equipment are sold to provide a test for electronic systems integration, which would require otherwise lengthy and sometimes unreliable tests. To what extent is the acquisition of such expensive test equipment justified? How can we consider inspection unreliabilities in the control of quality? These are the kind of questions we propose to deal with in this section. To present the essential ideas, we again consider a simple inspection problem where the probability of a unit inspected has a yield (probability of being good)p which is assumed *apriori* known and given by 0.60. There are two alternatives: send the unit as is to a customer, or submit it to further tests or repairs. Each of these alternatives leads to different outcomes, which are summarized in the revenues table in Table 5.5*a*(with negative values denoting losses). Alternatively, a machine for testing system integration can be used. The machine (the inspector) is unreliable, however. In the past, the machine was known to indicate that the system was in proper operating condition when it was not, and *vice versa*, indicating that it was not in operating order, when in fact it was. These unreliabilities are given in Table 5.5a.

Table 5.5*a*: *Past outcomes or inspection system's unreliability.*

	Indicator	A: Operating	B: Not Operating
X:	Operating	0.85	0.25
Y:	Not Operating	0.15	0.75

There are two indicators: the system will indicate that the unit is good (X) or it is bad (Y). These reliabilities are therefore conditional probabilities $P[X \mid \text{Good}] = 0.85, P[X \mid \text{Bad}] = 0.15, P[Y \mid \text{Good}] = 0.25, P[Y \mid \text{Bad}] =$

0.75. The prior probabilities are as we saw earlier $P[\text{Good}] = 0.60$ and $P[\text{Bad}] = 0.40$. If the special machine's test is applied, recommendation would be denoted X(it is good) or Y(it is bad). By application of Bayes theorem we can obtain the posterior distribution for the unit being good:

$$P[\text{ Good } \mid Z] = \frac{P[Z \mid \text{Good }]P[\text{Good}]}{P[Z]}, Z \equiv X \text{ or } Y$$

$$P[Z] = P[Z \mid \text{ Good }]P[\text{ Good }] + P[Z \mid \text{ Bad }]P[\text{ Bad }].$$

Similarly, for the posterior distribution that the unit is bad. Consider the profits decision Table 5.5*b*, which has two alternatives and two states with prior probabilities (0.6,0.4).

Table 5.5*b: System's integration inspection.*

Row Label	Good	Bad
State Prob	0.6	0.4
Altern 1	200	-140
Altern 2	-100	-50
**********	****	****
Indictr 1	0.85	0.25
Indictr 2	0.15	0.75

Application of the expected value criterion to each of the alternatives leads to selection of the first alternative, as shown in Table 5.5c.

Table 5.5c: Expected value - summary report

Decision	Exp. Payoff
Altern. 1	64.00 *
Altern. 2	-80.00

Consider first the EPPI. It equals 100. Since without perfect information it equals 64, the expected value of perfect information will be the maximum amount we should be willing to pay for full controls, or $100 - 64 = 36$. Now consider the unreliable inspection system. In this case, results are given as follows. If the first indicator points to the first alternative, then the updated probabilities are 0.8361 and 0.1639. In this case, the expected payoffs for both alternatives are 144.26 and -91.80. If the second indicator points to the first alternative, the expected payoff is -61.54. In other words, if inspection is unreliable as stated here, it is pointless to use inspection in the first place.

Table 5.5d: EXPECTED VALUE OF SAMPLE INFORMATION
Detailed report, Indicator 1: Prob. 0.61.

Decision	State	Payoff	Prob	Prob*Payoff	Expect.
Altern. 1	State 1	200.00	0.8361	167.21	
	State 2	-140.00	0.1639	-22.95	
					144.26
Altern. 2	State 1	-100.00	0.8361	-83.61	
	State 2	-50.00	0.1639	-8.20	
					-91.80

Indicator 2: Prob. 0.39

Decision	State	Payoff	Prob	Prob*Payoff	Expect.
Altern. 1	State 1	200.00	0.2308	46.15	
	State 2	-140.00	0.7692	-107.69	
					-61.54
Altern. 2	State 1	-100.00	0.2308	-23.08	
	State 2	-50.00	0.7692	-38.46	
					-61.54

Expected value of sample information - summary report.

Indicator	Pb.	Decision	Payoff	Prob*Payoff
INDICTR 1	0.610	Altern. 1	144.26	88.00
INDICTR 2	0.390	Altern. 2	-61.54	-24.00

Expected Payoff:	64.00
Expected payoff without sample information:	64.00
Expected value of sample information:	0.00
Efficiency of sample information (%):	0.00
Expected net gain from sampling:	-25.00

References

AFNOR (1993) *Statistique, Tome 2, Controles Statistiques de Fabrication et d'Acceptation, 6eme Edition,* Paris.

American National Standards Institution (1980, 1981, 1986) *Sampling Procedures and Tables for Inspection by Attributes,* Z1.4, American Society for Quality Control, Milwaukee, WI.

Daudin J.J., C. Duby and P. Trécourt (1990) Plans de controle double optimaux, *Rev. Statistique Appliquée,* **4**, 45-59.

DoD Handbook, H 53, June (1965) *Guide for Sampling Inspection,* Information Officer, Department of Defense, Pentagon, Washington, D.C.

Dodge H.F. and H.G. Romig (1944) *Sampling Inspection Tables*, New Wiley.

Kenett R. and A. Halevy (1984) Statistical aspects of quality conformance inspection in military standard documents, *Proceedings of the Fifth Intl. Conference of the Isreli Society for Quality Assurance,* Tel Aviv, 23-35 October.

MIL-STD 414 (1957) *Sampling Procedures and Tables for Inspection by Variables and Percent Defectivs,* US Government Printing Office, Washington, D.C.

MIL-STD 1235B (1981) *Single and Multi Level Continuous Sampling Procedures and Tables for Inspection Attributes,* US Government Printing Office, Washington, D.C.

MIL-STD-109B (1969) *Quality Assurance: Terms and Definitions.*

MIL-STD-490 (1968) *Specifications Practices,* 1968.

MIL-STD-105D (1963) *Sampling Procedures and Tables for Inspection by Attributes,* US. Government Printing Office, Washington, D.C.

Moskowitz H. and K. Tang (1992) Bayesian variables acceptance sampling plans: Quadratic loss function and step loss function, *Technometrics,* **34**, 340-347.

Vance L.C. (1980) A Bibliography of Statistical Quality Control Techniques, 1970-1980, *J. Qual. Tech.,* **15**, 2, 59-62.

Wald A. (1947) *Sequential Analysis,* New York, Wiley.

Wetherhill G.B. (1977) *Sampling Inspection and Quality Control,* Chapman and Hall, New York.

Wetherhill G.B. and W.K. Chiu (1975) A review of acceptance sampling schemes with emphasis on economic aspect, *Intern. Stat. Review,* 30, pp. 896-925.

Additional references

Abramowitz M.and I.A. Stegun (1964) *Handbook of Mathematical Functions,* Dover Publications, New York.

Allied Quality Publications, 1 to 13, 1972 to 1983, *NATO Quality Control Requirements for Industry* (Ministry of Defence, London).

Barnard G.A. (1954) Sampling inspection and statistical decisions, *J. of the Royal Stat. Soc. Series* B., **16**, 151-174.

Bowker A.H. and G.J. Lieberman (1959) *Engineering Statistics,* Prentice Hall, Englewood Cliffs, N.J.

Burr, I.W. (1953) *Engineering Statistics and Quality Control,* McGraw Hill, New York.

Campbell, S.K. (1974) *Flaws and Fallacies in Statistical Thinking,* Prentice Hall, Englewood Cliffs, N.J.

Cowden, D.J. (1957) *Statistical Methods in Quality Control*, Prentice-Hall, New York.

Cross R. (1984) PPM-Parts per Million-AOQL Sampling Plans, *Quality Progress,* vol 17, **11**, 28-34.

Dodge H.F. (1943) A Sampling Inspection Plan for Continuous Production, *Annals of Mathematical Statistics,* **14**, 264-279.

Dodge H.F. and M.N. Torrey (1951) Additional Continuous Sampling Plans, *Industr. Qual. Control,* **7**, 5, 7-12.

Duncan A.J. (1974) *Quality Planning and Industrial Statistics,* 4th ed., Irwin, Homewood, IL.

Fetter R.B. (1967), *The Quality Control System,* Richard D. Irwin, Homewood, IL., 25-34.

Freund R.A. (1985) Definitions and Basic Quality Concepts, *J. Qual. Techn.,* **17**, 1, 50-56.

Guthrie D. Jr. and M.V. Johns Jr. (1959) Bayes acceptance sampling procedure for large lots, *Annals of Math. Stat.,* **30**, 896-925.

Hald A. (1981) *Statistical Theory of Sampling Inspection by Attributes,* New York, Academic Press.

Juran J.M. (1944) *Management of Inspection and Quality Control,* New York, Harper Bros.

Juran J.M. and F.M. Gryna (1980) *Quality Planning Analysis,* , 2nd ed., McGraw Hill, New York.

Juran J.M., F.M. Gryna, R.S. Bingham (1976) *Quality Control Handbook,* 3rd ed., McGraw Hill.

Montgomery D.C. (1985) *Introduction to Statistical Quality Control,* Wiley, N.Y.

Sarhan A. E. and B.G. Greenberg (1962) *Contributions to Order Statistics,* New York, Wiley.

Tapiero C.S. and H. Lee (1989) Quality control and product servicing, *Euro J. of Operations Research,* **39**, 261-173.

Appendix 5.A: *Curtailed sampling*

Consider $P_a = (1-\theta)^n$ as stated in the text. Since the probability of the number of units sampled is a truncated geometric distribution given by

$$g(m \mid n) = \begin{cases} \theta(1-\theta)^{m-1} & \text{if} \quad m = 1, 2, \ldots, n-1 \\ (1-\theta)^{n-1} & \text{if} \quad m = n, \end{cases}$$

we have

$$\text{ASN} \quad = \quad ng(n-1 \mid n) + {}^{n-1} \sum_{m=0}^{n-1} mg(m \mid n) = n(1-\theta)$$

$$
\begin{aligned}
&+ \sum_{m=0}^{n-1} m\theta(1-\theta)^{m-1} < n \\
&\sum_{m=0}^{n-1} m\theta(1-\theta)^{m-1} = -\theta\frac{\partial}{\partial\theta}\sum_{m=0}^{n-1}(1-\theta)^m = -\theta\frac{\partial}{\partial\theta}\frac{1-(1-\theta)^n}{\theta} \\
&= \frac{1-\theta n(1-\theta)^{n-1}-(1-\theta)^n}{\theta}.
\end{aligned}
$$

Thus, the ASN for a curtailed sampling plan $(n, 1)$ is

$$\text{ASN }(n,1) = \frac{1-(1-\theta)^n}{\theta} < n.$$

For generalized curtailed sampling, however, with $k > 1$, the acceptance probability is

$$P_a(\theta) = \sum_{j=0}^{k}\binom{n}{j}\theta^j(1-\theta)^{n-j},$$

while the probability distribution of the number of units sampled is:

$$
\begin{aligned}
g(m) &= \binom{m-1}{k}\theta^{k+1}(1-\theta)^{m-k-1} \\
&+ \binom{m-1}{m-k-1}\theta^{m-n+k}(1-\theta)^{n-k}
\end{aligned}
$$

for $m = 1, 2, \ldots$n. As a result, the average sample number is

$$
\begin{aligned}
\text{ASN }(\theta) &= E(m \mid \theta) = \frac{[}{(k+1)}\theta]\sum_{j=0}^{k}\binom{n+1}{j}\theta^j(1-\theta)^{n+1-j} \\
&+ \frac{[}{(n-k)}(1-\theta)]\sum_{j=0}^{k}\binom{n+1}{j}\theta^j(1-\theta)^{n+1-j}.
\end{aligned}
$$

CHAPTER 6

Control charts

6.1 Introduction

Control charts are used for monitoring and controlling repetitive processes over time. They were introduced by Shewart (1931) to control the variability of large volume parts manufacturing. Today they are used extensively to detect and control various sources of variation, including

- Variation due to process during normal operations, or common causes.
- Variation due to special causes.
- Variability patterns such as trends, covariations and jumps in the short- in the long-term.

A control chart is represented in Figure 6.1. The chart has a centre line 'CL' as well as upper and lower control limits, 'UCL' and 'LCL', respectively. The vertical abscissa represents the measurement scale of a variable of interest (which can be quantitative or qualitative), while the horizontal abscissa stands for time. Measurements are recorded by star '*', which provides a visual record of experiments performed over time (positioned with respect to the CL, UCL and LCL). As we shall see later, the frequency as well as the size of the samples used to obtain the recorded observations are important considerations in the design of control charts.

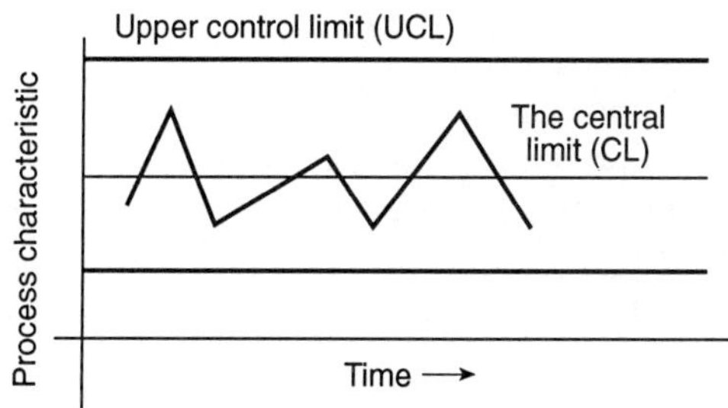

Figure 6.1: The control chart

The distribution of measurements (points) on the control chart can be due to chance variation or (special) assignable causes. Chance variations include the sum of all chance causes acting simultaneously on a process. Any chance cause has an individual and indistinguishable effect on the process, however. For this reason, these are called *common causes*, and are ascribed to reflect inherent 'normal' characteristics of the process. Such variations can be influenced only by changing the process or by introducing a structural change through technology or using new managerial procedures. Assume a normally operating process; control charts can be used to detect unexpected states as well as highlight improved performance when new procedures are introduced. When surprises occur, these are assigned to *special causes* and reasons are sought to explain these 'surprising' observations.

Special causes can result from

- Differences among factors such as machines, workers and materials.
- Differences in each of these factors over time.
- Differences in the relationship of the factors to one another.

For example, a machine operating in standard conditions may have certain operating characteristics. If for some reasons, the machine is no longer operating in the same conditions, then sample information collected to monitor the process may point out to unexpected performances and states and therefore attract special attention. Similarlyl, changes in workers, in service delivery, vendors products, materials and so on and their consistent performance over time can be monitored through control charts.

If samples conform to a statistical pattern that can be reasonably produced by chance variations, then no special assignable causes are present and the process is 'in control'. However, if samples do not conform to a statistical pattern that might be reasonably produced by chance variations, one can conclude that some assignable causes are present and the process is 'out of control'. This may call for intervention of some sort to find the cause and to attend to it.

Common (or environmental) causes of variation are of course numerous. Deming (1975) suggests a partial list:

- Hasty design of component parts and assembly. Inadequate tests of prototypes. Hasty production. Inadequate testing of incoming materials. Specifications that are too stringent, or too loose, or meaningless or waived specifications.
- Failure to know the process capabilities; lack of statistical support for monitoring and control; failure to use charts as a measure of system faults; improper specs of process capability.
- Incompetence of workers; repetition of the same mistakes; reliability of instruments and tests; smoke, noise, dirt, poor light, humidity, confusion.

According to Deming, it is management's responsibility to act and remove as many of the common causes as possible, and thereby render the process more efficient and error free. They can do so 'by working on the system' rather than 'working on the workers' who are not at fault for these common causes. Control charts are an important tool for quality managers but they are limited in scope. They 'do not produce quality' nor improve a process' performance, even though they can help monitor and maintain a process in control. In practice, control charts are used to communicate quality performance targets and induce actions that improve quality. In many cases, control charts, once introduced, exhibited patterns no-one thought of at first, and which led to subsequent questioning and research regarding the consistency of the process. In this sense, control charts provide signals for the quality and consistency of a system's performance.

Control charts have basically two types:

1. Variable control charts.
2. Attribute control charts

Variable control charts use quantitative measures. These include x-bar ($\bar{x}$) charts whose purpose is to control a process average, the R-chart for the control of the range, s-chart for the control of standard deviations, s^2-chart for the control of the variance, and X-chart for the control of individual values. In practice, the x-bar chart and the R chart are used together. The former to monitor the average pattern, while the latter provides an indication regarding the meaningfulness of the x-bar measurements.

Attribute charts measure characteristics which need not be quantitative, such as as the fraction of defectives in a sample, the number of non-conformities, etc. They include the p-chart for the control of fraction defectives, the np-chart for the number of nonconforming units, u-chart for control of the number of nonconformities per unit produced and, finally, the c-chart for the number of non-conformities. Generally, we can apply control charts to monitor a broad set of indicators such as business performance, productivity indices and other measures of performance in both industrial and service settings.

When sample measurements are cumulated they are called CUSUM charts (cumulative sum charts). These are important for the detection of small but persistent shifts in a process and therefore complement the use of ordinary charts, also called Shewart charts (that can detect large shifts in a process). They were developed in the early 1950s(see Page, 1954) and are useful for the rapid detection of small changes (Johnson, 1961; Fellner, 1990). These charts will be studied in greater detail later. Other charts, such as moving average and related charts, will be studied in Chapter 9.

The importance of control charts should not be underestimated, for they have been proved over and over again to be essential to quality control plans by highlighting non-conforming performances, detecting process instabilities and providing a basis on which to reach decisions regarding a management program's or a process' track record. Thus, their importance is both formal and informal (as an incitative, curative tool), as well as educational.

Control charts do not solve problems, but provide information on the basis of which we can reasonably (in a statistical sense) presume that a process is 'in control' or 'out of control'. They can also indicate 'false alarms' (errors that the system is out of control when it is not, also called the type I, α risk) as well as not detect situations which are out of control (i.e. the type II, β risk). There are essentially three approaches to construct control charts. First, use specified statistical characteristics (such as standards); second, use historical data of a process operating over some periods of time in normal operating conditions (when it is known *apriori* that there are no special causes); finally, economic models and criteria can be used to construct charts. The construction of a control chart and its analysis based on a working system is called the *process capability study.* This is the topic of the next section.

Example

Juran extensively uses control charts both as a technical tool and a conceptual tool weaved into a managerial approach to quality management. In Figure 6.2, we use control charts to demonstrate the process of quality improvement. In the initial phase, the old standard is in effect and the number of defectives is fairly large. After the introduction of a quality improvement program (denoted by a discontinuous shift in the process statistical characteristics), we note two types of improvement. First, a mean improvement in the first chart and more stable (less volatile and smaller variance) measurements in the second chart. In other words, control charts can be used to demonstrate various aspects and forms of quality improvement.

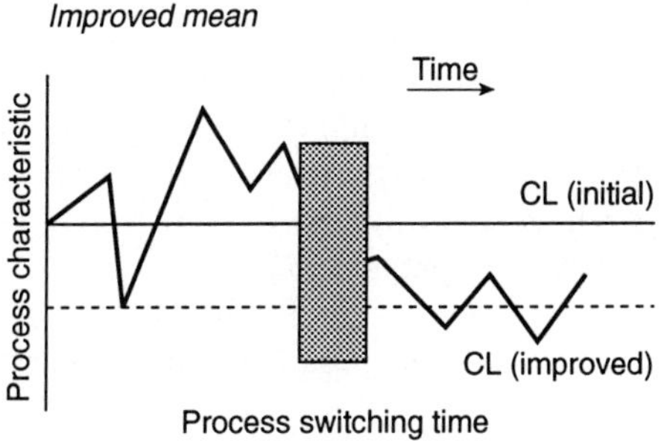

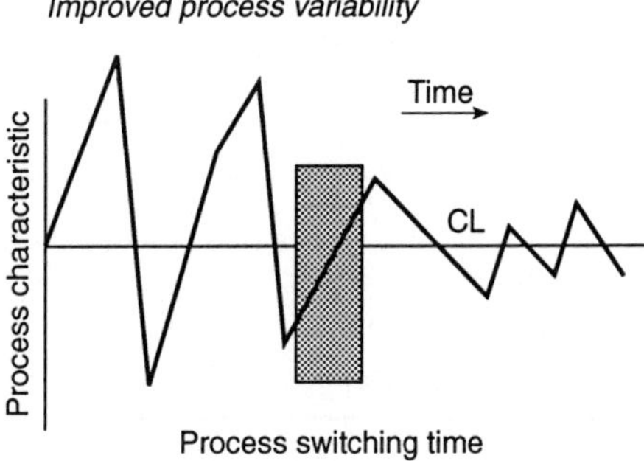

Figure 6.2: Improvement detection through a control chart

Problems

1. Define causes of variation and approaches which might be considered in reducing this variation for each of the following categories: (a) Poor management, (b) Poor products or poor specs., (c) Poor component specs., (d) An inadequate quality system, (e) Faulty material supplies, (f) Employee and operator errors.

2. Classify the following causes of variation and variation reduction techniques: Poor instructions and training, external inspection, lack of sensitivity to statistical measurements, inappropriate definition of basic quality factors, over marketing, too wide tolerances in process manufacturing, lack of coordination of suppliers, too many suppliers, no concurrent engineering, over (or under) fascination with technology, infrequent use of reliability based analyses, no testing of any sort, not reporting information from tests, tests too stringent, and no knowledge of interaction effects.

6.2 Process capability

Process capability studies are conducted to compare the performance of a controlled process to its requirements. Processes, once constructed, whether in theory or otherwise, are subject to variation. To control a process based on a control chart which was improperly constructed can be very costly, causing many unneeded stoppages or accepting operating conditions and output which should be rejected. In Figures 6.3 we note two situations which can lead to poor judgment in interpreting the control chart.

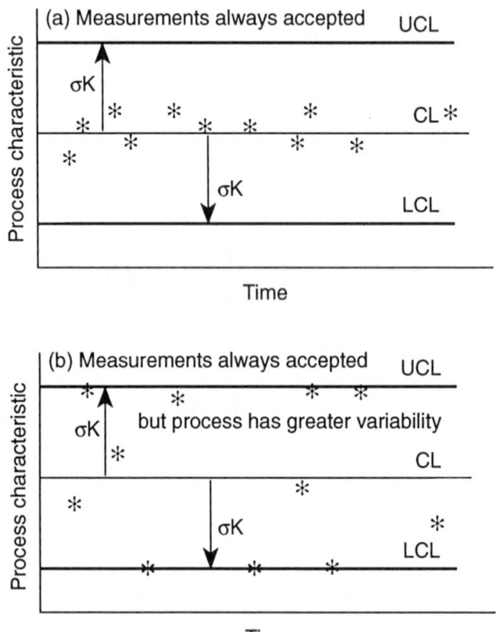

Figure 6.3: Process Mis-specification.

In Figure 6.3*a*, note that measurements are always accepted since they are concentrated near the centre line. This does not mean that the process is in control, but that only the control lines have been mis-specified. If some assignable cause occurs, it might not be detected since measurements might still fall within the upper and lower control lines. In Figure 6.3*b*, we note the opposite situation; almost every measurement in the control chart leads to the conclusion that there is an assignable cause. This may again be erroneous due to the specification of unrealistically tight upper and lower control lines. For these reasons, the prior analysis of what constitutes an appropriate and representative chart is extremely important in practice. A process capability study seeks to avoid such problems and provide an assurance that the chart in use duly represents the normal operating conditions of the process.

Say that a process has a standard specification (denoted by the standard line, SL, in a control chart), and denote by USL and LSL the upper and lower specifications limits (see Figure 6.4a).The USL and LSL explicitly define requirements imposed on the component which is manufactures. Thus, any component outside these specifications cannot be acceptable. This is in contrast to the UCL and LCL which are specifications representing the process propensity to deviate from its expected performance. If the process standard deviation is σ, we define the 'process capability index' C_p as follows:

$$C_p = \frac{\text{USL-LSL}}{6\sigma}.$$

This is a *process potential*, measuring the potential to meet the requirements, if operating properly. Since most processes may turn out to be asymmetric with respect to the standard line, we use a corrected process capability index, C_{pk}, which is defined by

$$C_{pk} = \text{Min}\ \{\frac{\text{USL-SL}}{3\sigma}, \frac{\text{SL-LSL}}{3\sigma}\}.$$

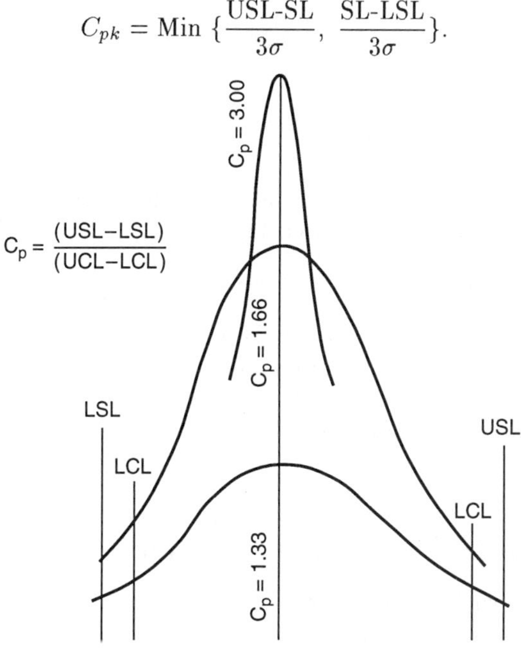

Figure 6.4a: Process capability studies.

If $C_p \geq 2$ or $C_{pk} \geq 1.5$, then this implies that the process specifies a control requirement which is close to zero defects. For a process controlled with this chart, the defect rate is at most 3.4 ppm (parts per millions).

This parameter is also used as a peasure of *process performance.* That is, based on the process parameters (the measures of location and spread), the index tests the process conformance to its specifications.

A 'robust' manufacturing process has evidently a large capability index, since the tolerance range (USL-LSL) which is needed for a component to be of acceptable quality is 'much' larger than the control range (UCL-LCL) of the manufacturing process. In this sense, 'quality production' can be improved either by design increasing the tolerance range of standards specification or by improved controls reducing the control limits (UCL-LCL).

To estimate the parameter σ, a property of the manufacturing process, we collect the data over a reasonable amount of normal operation time. The data, say N samples, is then organized into a number of samples of given size, say m and $n_i, i = 1, 2, \ldots m$, respectively, with $\sum_{i=1}^{m} n_i = N$. For convenience denote by x_{ij}, the jth data point of the ith sample. Then the process SL is the overall average,

$$CL = \frac{\sum_{i=1}^{m} \sum_{j=1}^{K} x_{ij}}{mK},$$

while the process standard deviation estimate using the full data set is

$$s = \sqrt{\sum_{i=1}^{m} \sum_{j=1}^{K} (x_{ij} - CL)^2 / (mK - 1)},$$

We can then represent each data point in a group by the following equation which will represent simple random variation:

$$x_{ij} = CL + s\epsilon_{ij}, E(x_{ij}) = CL, \text{ var } (x_{ij}) = s^2 \text{ var } (\epsilon_{ij}) = s^2,$$

where ϵ_{ij} is the deviation between the CL and the ijth data point. This term is assumed to have a standard normal distribution. If we consider the grouped data (in K samples), there is a between group variation to consider as well. In this case, the ijth data point can be modelled as follows

$$\begin{aligned} x_{ij} &= CL + s_k \xi_i + s\epsilon_{ij}, E(x_{ij}) = CL, \\ \text{var } (x_{ij}) &= s_k^2 \text{var } (\xi_i) + s^2 \text{var } (\epsilon_{ij}) = s_k^2 + s^2, \end{aligned}$$

where s_k is the within group standard deviation and ξ_i is again a standard normal random variable. This is calculated as follows: first the group average is given by

$$x_i = \frac{\sum_{j=1}^{K} x_{ij}}{K},$$

and then the within group standard deviation is found by

$$s_k = \sqrt{\sum_{j=1}^{K}(x_{ij} - x_i)^2/(K-1)}.$$

The group sample average has, however, a variance, which is given by

$$\text{var}\ (x_i) = s_k^2 + \frac{s^2}{m}.$$

Using data, the process capability indices will thus be

$$\begin{aligned} C_p &= \frac{\text{USL-LSL}}{6s}, \\ C_{pk} &= \text{Min}\ \{\frac{\text{USL-SL}}{3s}, \frac{\text{SL-LSL}}{3s}\} \end{aligned}$$

When more complex models are used, it will be necessary to include the variations produced (for example, between samples, within sample) in estimating the process standard deviation.

Example

The design specification for a part used in jet engines is 100 hours of flight time (∓ 6). Therefore, the nominal spec limit is 100 while the USL = 106, LSL = 94. If the parts' life parameters have a mean $\bar{x} = 100$ and standard deviation $\sigma = 2, (\bar{x}, \sigma) = (100, 2)$, then the capability index is

$$C_p = (\text{ USL-LSL })/6\sigma = (106 - 94)/(2 * 6) = 12/12 = 1.0.$$

By the same token, the corrected process capability index is

$$C_{pk} = [\{\frac{\text{USL} - \bar{x}}{3\sigma}, \frac{\bar{x}\text{-LSL}}{3\sigma}\} = \text{Min}\ (3,3)/3 = 1.0.$$

Since $C_p \geq 1$, we can conclude that the process is capable of producing the product within the specification. Similarly, since $C_{pk} \geq 1$, we conclude that the product produced fits within the specifications. Of course, the larger the index the better its performance.

Problems

1. A control chart with the following properties was constructed: $\bar{x} = 0.140, \bar{R} = 0.024$, LSL $= 0.105$, USL $= 0.190$ and sample size $n = 5$. Calculate the capability index C_p. Discuss the difference between processes with a Capability index greater than 2 and those smaller than 1.

2. Calculate the capability index C_{pk} for the process with samples mean equal to 0.738, standard deviation 0.0725 and USL and LSL specifications given by 0.500 and 0.900, respectively (answer: 0.74). If the minimum performance criterion is equal to $C_{pk} = 1$, what can be done to improve

the process and what are the target improvements to implement? What would be the probability of being out of spec once the process has been improved? What is the improvement percentage?

Example

A process sample data set is collected while a process is presumed to be in control. The data set is as given below. On the basis of this data set, a process capability study is required. In other words, the process properties and variabilities are to be estimated. The data set is given in Table 6.1

Table 6.1: A data set.

127, 118, 121, 122, 132, 112, 120, 115, 113, 109, 119, 117, 125, 115,
111, 119, 117, 125, 115, 111, 119, 123, 134, 117, 130, 117, 116, 128,
120, 124, 117, 121, 121, 120, 116, 119, 122, 108, 106, 127, 120, 116,
124, 127, 106, 116, 114, 133, 111, 117, 123, 124, 123, 121, 126, 130,
120, 128, 116, 130, 115, 112, 135, 119, 121, 125, 119, 118, 135, 116,
134, 119, 123, 110, 123, 128, 117, 127, 106, 117, 121, 117, 116, 120,
120, 108, 119, 124, 120, 124, 123, 120, 130, 117, 107, 124, 111, 115,
124, 110, 113, 109, 113, 116, 127, 118, 132, 122, 122, 112, 119

Numerical computations performed to evaluate the statistical properties of this data set (that can be performed using a number of software statistical packages, such as Minitab) lead to the following results, expressed by the data histogram, its frequency distribution and the distribution's properties (see Figure 6.4b).

Problem

A drill is set up to produce parts to a dimension of 3 ∓ 0.005". *A* process capability study reveals that the process limits are at 3.002 ∓ 0.006", i.e. at a minimum of 2.996" and a maximum of 3.008". Improvement of the process by changing one of the parts which was not performing in a satisfactory manner has brought the process limits under control to 3.001 ∓ 0.002". Using this information, calculate the C_p and C_{pk} of the old and the new process (Answers: for the old process, $C_p = 0.833, C_{pk} = 0.5$. For the new improved process, $C_p = 2.5$ and $C_{pk} = 2.0$.)

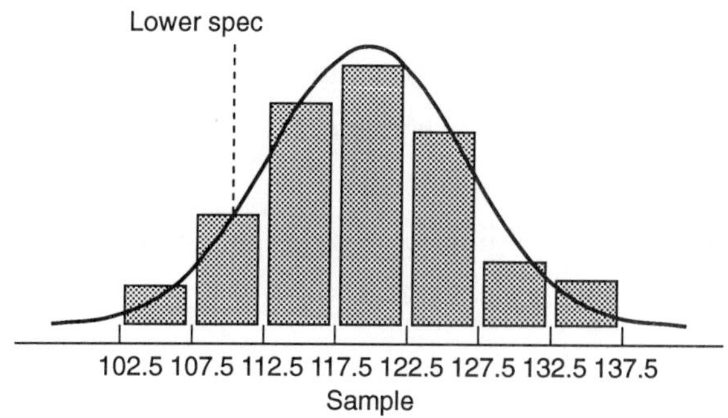

Cp	*	Targ	*	Mean	119.664	%>USL Exp	*	PPM>USL Exp	*
CPU	*	USL	*	Mean+3s	140.248	Obs	*	Obs	*
CPL	0.45	LSL	110.4	Mean-3s	99.080	%<LSL Exp	8.85	PPM<LSL Exp	88476
Cpk	0.45	k	*	s	6.861	Obs	10.40	Obs	104000
Cpm	*	n	125.0						

Figure 6.4b: A computer aided process capability study.

Process capability studies belong to a broad range of problems in the management of quality coined 'measurement assurance'. Essentially, it seeks to construct procedures and tests to ensure that measurements taken are actually representative of the variables or process being measured. The technical Committee (TC 69) of the ISO standards organization has called attention to this problem through subcommittee SC6 for Measurements (see Boulanger, 1993). For capability studies, ISO 5725 provides documentation for 'Accuracy of Measurement Methods and Results'. Other documents include 'Intermediate Measures on the Precision of a Measurement Method' and 'Decision Limit, Detection Limit, Capability of Detection: Terms and Definitions'. For calibration of equipment and control, ISO provides documents such as, 'Linear Calibration Using Reference Materials', ISO/DIS/5725 Part 6 for 'Accuracy of Measurement Methods and Results' which uses Shewart and CUSUM charts. Other documents include ISO 7870 for Control Charts, ISO 7966 for Acceptance Control Charts, ISO 8258 for Shewart Control Charts, and so on (see the references at the end of this chapter). To implement a MAP (Measurement Assurance Program) strategy, Boulanger (1993) suggests that nine steps be taken:

(1) Define measurements, identify the customer, supplier and owner.

(2) Quantify adequacy of measurements from the customers' viewpoint.

(3) Characterize the precision of the measurement process.

(4) Search and correct for systematic errors.

(5) Control the stability of the measurement process.

(6) Assess the uncertainty of measurements.

(7) Evaluate the impact on customers.

(8) Document all sources of information on the measurement process.

(9) Improve the performance of the measurement process.

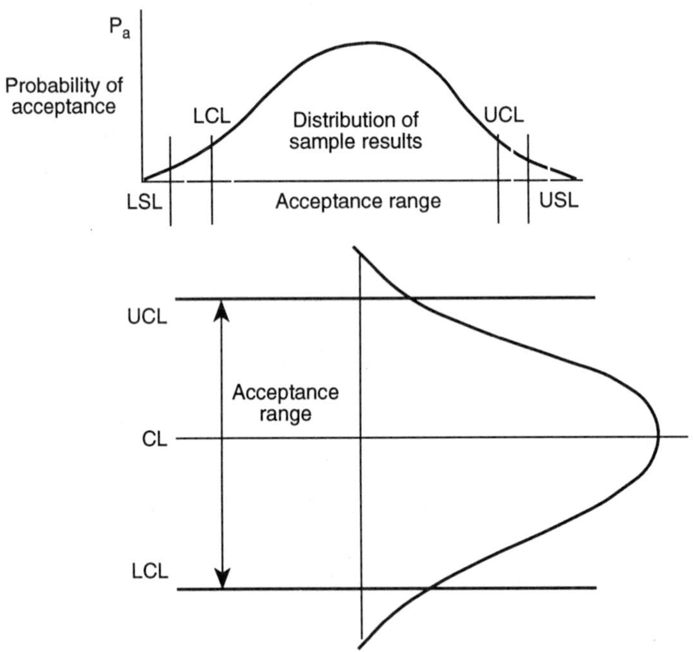

Figure 6.5: The control limits of a chart.

6.3 Constructing control charts

To construct control charts we can either use some pre-specified standards or historical data to test the null hypothesis that the process is in control (i.e. operating in a stable manner between the lower and upper limits, LCL and UCL, as shown in Figure 6.5, with all variations resulting from common chance) against the alternative that the process is out of control (i.e. a potential chance that an observation will fall outside the limits LCL, UCL). Once a process capability study has been performed and we can reliably represent the process parameters when it is operating normally, we can then test for some assignable causes. Namely, we can then test for the hypotheses:

$$H_0: \quad \text{The process is in control}$$
$$H_1: \quad \text{The process is out of control.}$$

If a sample result falls between the UCL and LCL, then the process is in control, otherwise further study of the sample result and the process being controlled might be needed to find an explanation to such (special cause) deviations. Such a chart is given in Figure 6.6, where we detail the probabilities of an observation falling at one, two, three and so on standard deviations away from the centre line. For example, the probability that an observation falls within one standard deviation is equal to $0.34130 + 0.36130 = 0.6920$, within two standard deviations it is $(0.34130 + 0.1360) * 2 = 0.9546$. Similarly, the probability that two consecutive observations fall first within two and then three standard deviations on either sides of the centre lines is equal to $(0.9546)(0.9970) = 0.95173$. These probabilities are, as we shall see later, very important for the interpretation of charts and the control of processes. It is noteworthy that if no current observations fall outside the control limits, and if there is no evidence of nonrandom variation within the control charts limits, this does not mean that no assignable causes are present. Rather, it only means that it will be unprofitable to check for special assignable causes (for the costs of investing in such causes will not result in an improvement which can be justified by improved statistical control of the process). In operating a control chart it is necessary to select three parameters: (a) The sample size; (b) the sampling frequency or the time interval between samples; (c) the control limits for the chart UCL and LCL.

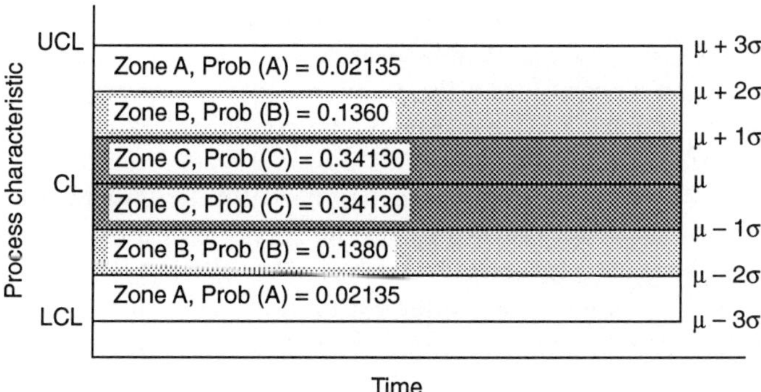

Figure 6.6: The control limits-detailed.

A larger sample size improves the statistical quality of the measurement estimates. In addition, when the sampling probability distribution is difficult to determine, an increase in the sample size makes it possible to apply the law of large numbers (and thereby use the normal distribution). For example, consider a record of means calculated using a sample size n. Since the mean variance is inversely proportional to n, the larger n, the more precise the mean estimate. The sampling frequency provides a temporal record of the process. If measurements are infrequent, a process may be out of control for too long a period of time and/or the increasing and cumulative uncertainty which accumulates between two samples may be intolerable. Both the sample size and the sampling frequency are intimately related. If a process is sensitive to variations of some sorts and the costs of not controlling such a process are great, our propensity will be to sample more often than for a fairly stable 'slow' changing process. Problems related to temporal records such as those encountered in control charts are covered in far greater detail in Chapter 9. For example, when samples are correlated from period to period (for example, see Neuehard, 1987; Yang and Hancock, 1990), their analysis requires special attention for a control chart record to be treated appropriately. Finally, control charts limits UCL and LCL define explicitly 'common causes' (since an observation within the UCL and LCL limits is presumed to be an outcome resulting from a set of complex and non-tractable causes). When a result or a string of results occur and the probability of their occurrence is very small (i.e. they are surprising), this might provide an indication that something specific has occurred. In other words, there may be some 'assignable causes' to explain such outcomes. These causes may be many things, such as differences between machines' performance, differences between materials, which have an effect on the process or variations over time in the working environment. Of course, the sample size, its frequency and the control chart limits should be defined simultaneously, since adopting one will affect the appropriate magnitude and meaning of the other. Practically, it may be important to weigh the advantages of larger and more frequent samples and the costs they incur. Thus, process sensitivities, the measurement (sample) costs, the costs of seeking assignable causes and the costs of a process being out of control (both direct and indirect cost) should be considered in constructing the control chart.

Traditionally, control charts were designed using statistical criteria only. Their performances were measured by OC curves (i.e. in terms of producer and consumer risks). In control charts, however, OC curves indicate the probability of a sample result falling within the control limits given the true value of the characteristics, say the average $\bar{x}$. Specific charts are considered below.

$\bar{X}$-*Chart*

An $\bar{X}$-*chart*, or x-bar chart, expresses the evolution of means from sample to sample, and is therefore a graphical depiction of between-sample variation. These charts are used to detect changes in a process average, and may exhibit shifts (due to improvement or deterioration of the process), cyclical patterns and stratified results due to some assignable cause (such as an operator's performance). By themselves, they are not sufficient to represent a process evolution. For example, while a mean may remain almost constant from sample, to sample indicating that the process is 'stable', it may in fact be unstable, exhibiting extremely large variation within samples. For this reason, we combine the use of x-bar, range (R) and standard deviation (s) charts to investigate within-sample variation as well. To see how such charts are constructed, assume that a firm has collected a data set which is organized in m samples of size n each. Each element of the data set is denoted by x_{ij}, expressing the ith observation in the jth sample. The jth sample average is

$$\bar{X}_j = \frac{1}{n}\sum_{i=1}^{n} x_{ij}$$

while the m samples average is

$$\bar{X} = \frac{1}{m}\sum_{j=1}^{m} \bar{X}_j.$$

If the sample size is sufficiently large, then by the law of large numbers, the average necessarily has a normal probability distribution (otherwise it would be appropriate to use the exact sample distribution). Assume that σ, the population parameter standard deviation, is known, then the sample standard deviation is reduced to

$$\sigma(\bar{X}) = \sigma/\sqrt{n}.$$

Thus, if we construct an α confidence interval for the average, we have by definition for each sample average,

$$\text{Prob}\,[\bar{X} - k\sigma(\bar{X}) \leq \bar{X}_j \leq \bar{X} + k\sigma(\bar{X})] = 1 - \alpha,$$

where k is the number of standard deviations from the mean and α is the producer's risk. Evidently, the confidence interval is a function of the sample, size n since $\sigma(\bar{X}) = \sigma/\sqrt{n}$. For example, let $k = 3$, then $\alpha = 0.003$ and $\alpha/2 = 0.0015, 1 - \alpha = 0.9973$, and

$$\text{Prob}\,[\bar{X} - 3\sigma(\bar{X}) \leq \bar{X}_j \leq \bar{X} + 3\sigma(\bar{X})] = 0.9973.$$

In this case, the CL is $\bar{X}$ while the UCL and LCL are given respectively by

$$\text{UCL} = \bar{X} + 3\sigma(\bar{X}), \;\; \text{LCL} = \bar{X} - 3\sigma(\bar{X}).$$

while the control range UCL-LCL has $6\sigma(\bar{X})$. When the population standard deviation σ is not known, we replace it with its estimate. That is, instead of $\sigma(\bar{X})$ we use $s(\bar{X}) = s/\sqrt{n}$, where s is the estimated standard deviation calculated using the nm data set. Or, as we saw earlier,

$$s^2 = \frac{1}{(nm-1)} \sum_{i=1}^{n} \sum_{j=1}^{m} (x_{ij} - \bar{X})^2.$$

In this particular case, it is appropriate to use t-distribution rather than the normal distribution (see Chapter 3 for Tables of confidence intervals). In most cases, when samples are sufficiently large, the normal distribution is sufficiently precise. In other cases, charts can be constructed using tables which are commonly available, or using SQC/SPC software systems which perform computations automatically.

Example

A manufacturing process produces rings of 60mm diameter, on the average, with a sample deviation of 0.005. Namely $\bar{X} = 60, \sigma(\bar{X}) = 0.005$ while the UCL and LCL are calculated using three standard deviations from the mean, or

$$\text{UCL } = 60 + 3(0.005) = 60.015, \ \text{LCL } = 60 - 3(0.005) = 59.985.$$

The probability that the diameter falls within three standard deviations from the mean is thus:

$$\begin{aligned} 1 - \alpha &= \text{Prob }[60 - 3(0.005) \leq \bar{X} \leq 60 + 3(0.005)] \\ &= \text{Prob }[60.015 \leq \bar{X} \leq 59.985] = 0.9973. \end{aligned}$$

Thus, $\alpha = 1 - 0.9973 = 0.0027$, which is the probability of rejecting the null hypothesis $H_0 = 60$ against the alternative $H_1 \neq 60$ when it is in fact true.

A computer aided example

The Mines Supply Company is a regional supplier for a large number of firms. It has recently been under strong criticism due to poor service, mostly measured by the number of delivery delays and the number of defective units supplied. Over a number of days (125 exactly), data was recorded regarding the number of trips performed by the firm, the number of delays during the day and the number of packages which were damaged in delivery. Trips were organized in 25 samples, each of size $n = 5$. The data is given in Table 6.2, where the first five columns represent the number of trips while the 6th and 7th stand for the number of delays and the number of defective units delivered in the sample.

Table 6.2: Sample data.

Sample	Obs. no.1	Obs. no.2	Obs. no.3	Obs. no.4	Obs. no.5	no. of delays	no. of defects
1	121	122	132	112	120	1	6
2	115	113	109	119	117	7	0
3	125	115	111	119	123	2	0
4	134	117	130	117	116	1	3
5	128	120	124	117	121	0	6
6	121	120	116	119	122	1	3
7	108	106	127	120	116	2	0
8	123	110	123	114	124	6	18
9	124	135	118	113	107	0	6
10	110	119	135	118	124	1	3
11	127	106	117	126	119	2	0
12	117	112	129	121	106	1	3
13	116	114	133	111	117	0	6
14	123	124	123	121	126	0	21
15	130	120	128	116	130	2	3
16	115	112	135	119	121	2	0
17	125	119	118	135	116	1	0
18	134	119	123	110	123	0	15
19	128	117	127	106	117	1	12
20	121	117	116	120	120	2	9
21	108	119	124	120	124	3	6
22	123	120	130	117	107	4	3
23	124	124	111	115	124	5	0
24	110	113	109	113	116	0	3
25	127	118	132	122	122	0	6

First, we construct the $\bar{X}$-bar chart of the number of trips and calculate the samples average. For the 12th sample, for example, we have

$$\bar{X}_{12} = (121 + 122 + 132 + 112 + 120)/5 = 121.4.$$

When the sample average is calculated for all samples, we compute the overall samples average which defines the centre line of the control chart. In this case, we have

$$\bar{X} = (\bar{X}_1 + \bar{X}_2 + \ldots + \bar{X}_{12} + \ldots + \bar{X}_{25})/25 = 119.7.$$

Then, letting the upper and lower centre lines be defined by 1.96 standard deviations from the mean, we have

$$\text{LCL } = 110.4, \text{ UCL } = 128.9.$$

The chart and the sample results for the 25 samples are given in Figure 6.7. We shall interpret and discuss such charts in Section 6.7, and calculate the probabilities of obtaining unlikely outcomes which will provide a warning that perhaps 'something' might be wrong. $\bar{X}$-bar charts, as stated earlier, do not by themselves provide sufficient information to conclude if a process is stable or not. It only provides *between-sample variation. There might be within-sample variation,* which is just as useful to know and complementary to the $\bar{X}$-bar chart. For this reason, in practice, $\bar{X}$-bar charts are used conjointly with range R charts (or s-charts) to indicate within sample variation.

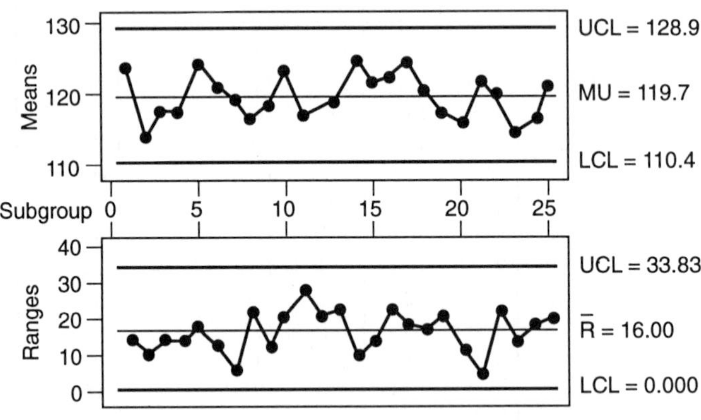

Figure 6.7: The x-bar and R chart.

The R-Chart

Range R-charts, as well as charts based on measures of variation, are used to detect within sample variation. R-charts can be derived from order statistics with control limits calculated by

$$\text{UCL } = \mu + D_1\bar{R}, \ \text{LCL } = \mu - D_2\bar{R},$$

with D_1 and D_2 appropriately calculated based on the sample distribution of ranges. In practice, tables such as those summarized in appendix 3.1 are available. Namely, given one or both or none of the underlying statistical parameters (mean μ, standard deviation σ), the control and the warning limits of the control chart are given. For example, assuming that the standard deviation is not known and has to be estimated from the data, and if the sample size equals $n = 5$, then the control limits are $(0.16\bar{R}, 2.36\bar{R})$. By increasing the sample size, we note that these limits are increasingly stringent. For a sample data set, and similarly for computations of the $\bar{X}$-chart, we calculate the range for each sample. For the 8th and 11th samples in our previous data set for example, we have

$$\bar{R}_8 = 124 - 110 = 14, \bar{R}_{11} = 127 - 106 = 21.$$

Repeating these calculations and computing the overall range average (over the 25 samples), we obtain $\bar{R} = 16.0$, which is the range chart centre line.

To obtain the UCL and LCL for this chart, note that $n = 25$, and therefore for 95% intervals, we have

$$\begin{aligned} \text{LCL} &= \max(0, 16.0 - 18.6322) = 0.0 \\ \text{UCL} &= 16.0 + 18.6322 = 33.83. \end{aligned}$$

The resulting control chart with points inserted is given in Figure 6.7 as well. The more dispersed are the sample points, the greater the samples' heterogeneity. The theoretical framework which justifies the computation of boundaries is given by order statistics. Range charts have been used in the past because they are easier to calculate than standard deviation charts. Further, they are more meaningful when samples are small. It is of little use to interpret an x-bar chart by itself since we require the information for within-sample variation as well which is given through the range chart.

The S and S-squared charts

The S and S-squared charts are important when the sample range information is not satisfactory. Consider a sample of size n with observations $x_i, i = 1, 2, \ldots n$, each distributed according to a normal distribution with mean μ and variance σ^2. The sample variance estimate s^2, when the population mean is μ is given by:

$$s^2 = \frac{1}{m}\sum_{i=1}^{m}(\bar{X}_i - \mu)^2.$$

When the population mean μ is not known, however,

$$s^2 = \frac{1}{m-1}\sum_{i=1}^{m}(\bar{X}_i - \bar{X})^2.$$

Note that $\bar{X}_i$ has a normal distribution with mean μ and variance σ^2/n, while the average $\bar{X}$ has a normal distribution with mean μ and variance σ^2/mn. As a result, if nm is large, the difference is a zero mean normal random variable and s^2 has a chi-squared distribution with $m - 1$ degrees of freedom which can be used to construct the upper and lower limits of the control chart both for the s and s^2control charts. Confidence intervals for the UCL and LCL for the standard deviation can be computed as well. When the population standard deviation is not known, we instead use its estimate.

Consider again the Mines Supply Company and construct the S and S-squared charts for the number of trips. The results are highlighted in Figure 6.8. For the S-squared chart, the bounds are given by the chi-square distribution, and therefore the control limits are calculated by this distribution. This makes it possible to use the appropriate chi-square tables for any type of risk. Of course, tables are also freely available for such computations. Using the same sample sizes as in the previous x-bar and R charts, we have the previous tables to compute the control and warning limits for s-charts.

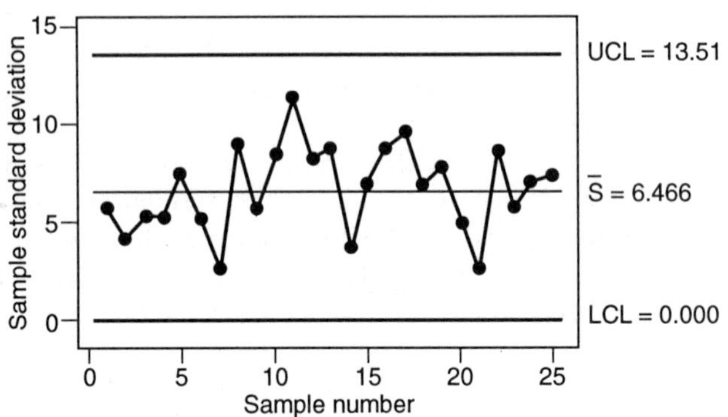

Figure 6.8: The standard deviations chart

The Mines Supply Company S-squared chart can be similarly calculated. Note that it will be asymmetric, since it is truncated from the left by zero (since there is neither negative variance nor negative standard deviations, as seen above).

The np and p-charts

The p-chart is an attribute (qualitative) chart measuring the ratio of non-conforming items per unit sampled. If x is the number of non-conforming units and n is the sample size, then $p = x/\text{n}$. In this sense, p is an estimate of the probability that a unit is defective. The centre line in such charts are the average proportion non-conforming $\bar{p}$ while the variance is

$$\text{var }(x)/n^2 = \bar{p}(1-\bar{p})/n.$$

The control charts limits are, therefore,

$$\text{UCL } = \bar{p}+d\sqrt{\bar{p}(1-\bar{p})/n}, \text{ LCL } = \bar{p}-d\sqrt{\bar{p}(1-\bar{p})/n},$$

where d is the appropriate parameter used for determining the number of standard deviations from the centre line (based on the risk used in constructing the chart and the normal distribution). For demonstration purposes, consider the following data set, which expresses the number of defective units in production lot samples of size 10:

1,7,2,1,0,1,2,6,0,1,2,1,0,0,2,2,1,0,1,2,3,4,5,0,0,
1,2,1,0,0,3,2,4,0,0,1,2,0,1,0,1,2,4,6,2,7,2,1,0,2

Then, the p-chart is given by Figure 6.9. If there are K samples, each with average $\bar{p}_i$, the centre line is calculated by

$$\text{CL} = \bar{p} = \sum_{i=1}^{K} \frac{\bar{p}_i}{K}.$$

The parameter d used to calculate the UCL and LCL is equal to 3 if we construct a 99% confidence interval.

When the sample size is constant, we can also consider the number of defect charts, called the *np*-chart. In this case, the upper and lower bounds are

$$\text{UCL} = n\bar{p} + d\sqrt{n\bar{p}(1-\bar{p})}, \ \text{LCL} = n\bar{p} - d\sqrt{n\bar{p}(1-\bar{p})}.$$

Of course for $\bar{p}$ fixed and when the samples size are small, we can use the binomial distribution (or the Poisson distribution if samples are larger and $\bar{p}$ small) in computing d. Using the same data set as above, the corresponding *np*-chart is given below in Figure 6.9b.

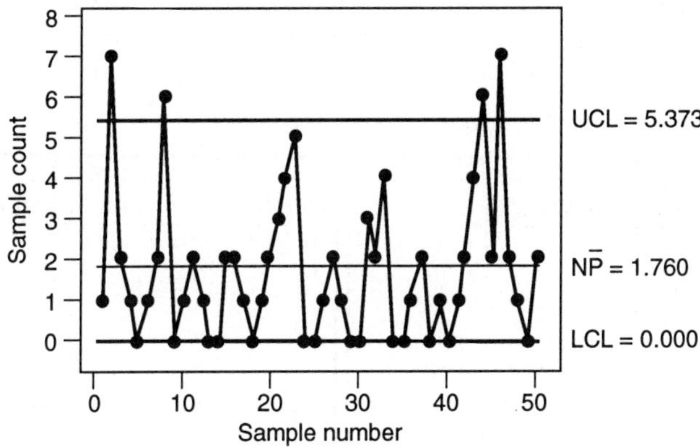

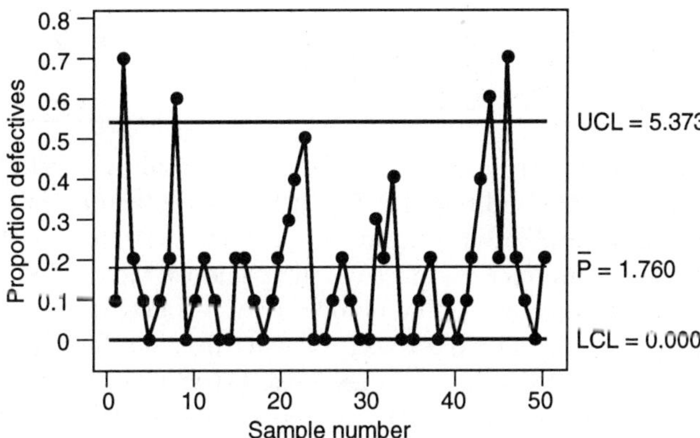

Figure 6.9: The p and np charts.

Problems

1. Compute by hand and by a computer program (MINITAB, SPSS, SAS etc.) the p chart corresponding to the proportion of delivery delays (which would be an important measure of quality) in the Mines Supply Co.

2. A firm produces inexpensive walkie-talkies which are sold worldwide in department stores. The assembly process of these walkie-talkies is labour intensive, and there are some problems with the production. Production has been running at the rate of 1000 units a day. To investigate the problems of quality apparent from consumers' complaints, the production manager decided to sample a lot of size 50 each day for 25 days. The data thus collected pertains to both the sample fraction of nonconforming units and the number of non conformances, and is given in Table 6.3.(a) On the basis of this data, compute the average non-conforming ratio. (b) Compute the UCL and LCL of the attribute proportion defectives charts if 95boundaries. (c) Repeat your calculations by considering the np-chart. (d) Draw the control chart and insert each of the sample results. If there is a day which has been special, in the sense that it is useful for the production manager to look for some assignable causes, then indicate which day (or days) it is.

Table 6.3: The data set.

Day number	number of non conf.	Fraction non conf.	Day number	number of non conf.	Fraction non conf.
1	3	0.07	13	7	0.03
2	2	0.12	14	6	0.09
3	3	0.03	15	5	0.12
4	0	0.00	16	3	0.02
5	9	0.10	17	2	0.03
6	5	0.06	18	5	0.05
7	4	0.10	19	4	0.06
8	12	0.25	20	5	0.09
9	4	0.11	21	8	0.14
10	2	0.03	22	2	0.08
11	5	0.07	23	1	0.04
12	2	0.06	24	0	0.00

3. A shirt manufacturer produces and sells quality shirts to retailers. Each shirt is fully inspected and tested before it leaves the factory for a specialty store. The daily production output is given in Table 6.4 in the second column, while the number of defective shirts sold to 'seconds' retail outlets is given in the third column. The number of non-conformities is also given in the fourth column. The data was collected over 50 days. On the basis of this data, answer the following questions: (a) What is the proportion of defectives each day? (b) What is the average number of defects per defective shirt? (c) What is the number of defects per unit produced? (d) Construct a p-control chart. (e) Construct the np-control chart. (f) If the loss of a

defective shirt equals 20% of its production cost, graph the x-bar chart of shirt cost. (g) Repeat these calculations for the range chart. (h) Construct a confidence interval for the proportion of defectives over a week using the normal approximation (i.e. aggregate your data in weeks of five days). (i) Repeat the previous question using the newly aggregated data. (j) Discuss the effects of aggregation of the data on the construction of control charts. What kind of test would you perform to assure top management that the conclusions one may derive from the aggregated data are essentially the same as those for the detailed (daily) data?

Table 6.4: The data set

Day	Output	# def.	# non conf.	Day	Output	# def.	# non conf.
1	400	10	3	26	500	12	2
2	350	12	5	27	400	8	1
3	660	15	2	28	450	8	4
4	500	25	2	29	400	9	3
5	430	7	5	30	400	5	5
6	250	3	3	31	400	6	4
7	600	2	2	32	600	15	2
8	500	14	4	33	650	9	1
9	400	20	3	34	700	22	1
10	450	15	2	35	690	28	3
11	475	10	2	36	630	14	3
12	380	8	1	37	360	8	2
13	700	7	2	38	700	19	2
14	800	15	1	39	431	7	4
15	450	30	1	40	390	5	1
16	340	10	2	41	580	5	1
17	900	12	5	42	432	8	2
18	120	5	4	43	680	12	4
19	550	10	2	44	457	5	4
20	500	8	4	45	734	11	3
21	400	10	3	46	487	10	3
22	380	4	2	47	700	13	5
23	500	8	2	48	678	8	5
24	540	8	3	49	543	4	3
25	650	7	4	50	400	9	2

The c-chart

The c-chart is a number of defects charts. For example, in any complex transaction there may be a large number of possibilities for non-conforming performance. The number of types of non-conformities is the number of defects to be monitored and controlled. If the type of defects is potentially large and if the probability of each type is extremely large, we can use the Poisson distribution. Namely, let λ be the probability that there is a defect, then the number of defects in a sample of size n is merely λn, or

$$P(c) = \exp(-\lambda n)(\lambda n)^{-c}/c!,$$

which can be used to calculate the upper and lower bounds for the charts (as we shall see below through an example). In particular, the mean and the variance are equal for the Poisson distribution and if λn is the centre line of the chart, then the upper and lower bounds are

$$\text{UCL} \ = \lambda n + d_n\sqrt{\lambda n}; \ \text{LCL} \ = \lambda n - d_n\sqrt{\lambda n},$$

where d_n is a parameter defined according to the risk assumed in constructing the c-chart. Tables for this parameter, based on the Poisson distribution are included in the appendix. When the probability of defect types varies according to the types, we can generalize this probability distribution. If there are K types of defects, each with with probability $\lambda_i, i =, \ldots K$, then the number of defects probability is also Poisson with a mean

$$E(c) = \sum_{i=1}^{K} \lambda_i n.$$

Assuming that these are statistically independent of one another, the variance is equal to the mean, since the sum of Poisson distributed random variables is also Poisson. This can be used to construct intervals and control charts which take account of the defect types and their probability. Generally, if the parameter of the Poisson $\Lambda = \lambda n$ has a Gamma probability distribution, then the probability distribution of c, the number of defects, has a Negative Binomial Distribution (NBD), as we have seen in Chapter 3. This observation can be used again to construct control charts with greater precision. Finally, each of the defect types can be weighted by their severity (namely, their cost). Thus, if w_i is the severity of defect type i, the average adjusted to reflect this weight is given by

$$E(C) = \sum_{i=1}^{K} w_i \lambda_i n,$$

with C being the mean cost of defects rather than the number of types of defects. In this case, the UCL and LCL are given by

$$\text{UCL} \ = \ \sum_{i=1}^{K} w_i \lambda_i n + d_n \sqrt{\sum_{i=1}^{K} [w_i^2 \lambda_i n]^2},$$

$$\text{LCL} \ = \ \sum_{i=1}^{K} w_i \lambda_i n - d_n \sqrt{\sum_{i=1}^{K} [w_i^2 \lambda_i n]^2}.$$

Problems

1. Consider the data set in Table 6.8 expressing the number of defects per sample, and assume that we use a size group of five. Then, construct the c- chart.

2. Consider the walkie-talkie data, and construct a control chart for the number of non-conformities. Then graph each of the sample results and report what conclusions can be reached.

The u-chart

u-charts are used when the sample sizes vary, and we calculate the number of defects per sample, namely, the quantity plotted on the chart is u/k. The chart's central line is thus

$$\bar{u} = \sum c_i / \sum k_i,$$

while the control limits for a sample of size k are given by

$$\text{UCL } = \bar{u} + d_u\sqrt{\bar{u}/k};\ \text{LCL } = \bar{u} - d_u\sqrt{\bar{u}/k},$$

where d_u is a parameter which is equal to 3 for the 95% chance to have all observations fall in the UCL-LCL range.

Problem

Assume the following data set and construct the u-chart (either through hand calculations or using a computer program to do so, such as MINITAB, for example.

1,0,2,1,0,1,2,3,0,1,2,1,0,0,2,2,1,0,1,2,3,0,1,0,0,
1,2,1,0,0,3,2,2,0,0,1,2,0,1,0,1,2,0,1,2,1,2,1,0,2

Individual values charts

Individual values charts do not benefit from the reduction in variability gained when we consider a sample size n. As a result, these measurements involve greater variability (and thus have far more tolerant control lines). Statistically, there is very little that can be inferred from an individual value which is recorded over time. Nevertheless, combining the values observed over an interval of time, there is much that can be said. In Chapter 9, we deal with individual value charts using filtering theory as well as other techniques. Further, we shall consider the control of both the evolution of random walks and their variability, as well as other models which are important in management. For example, problems such as the control of deteriorating systems, processes with drifts and stock price variations are considered. In individual values charts, the standard deviation is estimated from the moving range of pairs of adjacent observations. In this case, if x_i are individual values plotted in the chart, the moving range (of successive values) is

$$r_i = \mid x_{i+1} - x_i \mid .$$

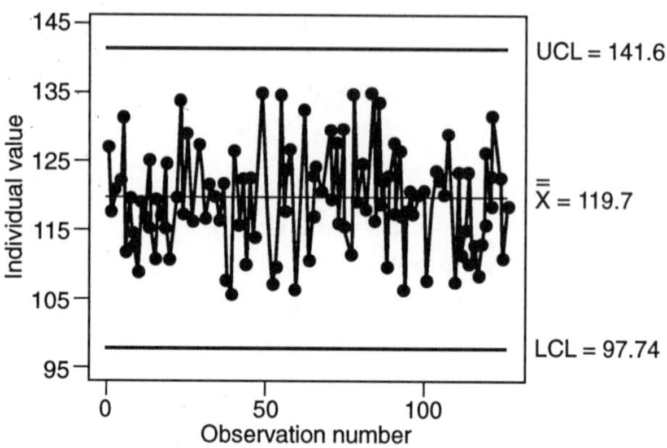

Figure 6.10: Individual values chart.

An estimate for the standard deviation σ is then given by

$$\sigma = \bar{r}/d_2, d_2 = 1.128,$$

where $\bar{r}$ is calculated as the moving range values. The control limits for the chart are the chart's average (or its standard) summed with $\pm 3\bar{r}/d_2 = \pm 2.66$. The theoretical developments underpinning the variability of individual values range charts are lagging. Nevertheless, we shall provide some essential results for such charts in Chapter 9. An individual values chart using our sample data is included in Figure 6.10. Note that the $CL = 119.7$ while the LCL $= 97.74$, UCL $= 141.6$ compared to $119.7, 110.4$ and 128.9 in the x-bar chart. The increased tolerance for variability is due to the fact that no statistical aggregate (samples) are used in computing the statistic drawn.

There are of course other charts such as 'acceptance charts', which are basically asymmetric charts. In these charts, the UCL and LCL are not located at equal distances from the CL. Rather, by specifying both the (α, β) errors, UCL and LCL are constructed at an unequal distance of the CL, reflecting the risks α and β assumed (see Freund, $1957, 1960$). Control charts can be applied and constructed for an extremely large number of industrial and managerial contexts. In fact, any sample statistic can be used to determine the control chart where samples are repeatedly taken and a predictable performance for the statistic is established.

6.4 Pre-control

Bhote (in World Class Quality, 1988) argues that control charts are difficult to explain to operators and to use. Pre-control, which also uses warning limits, provides an alternative which is simpler to construct and use. Pre-control charts are constructed as follows (see also Figure 6.12):

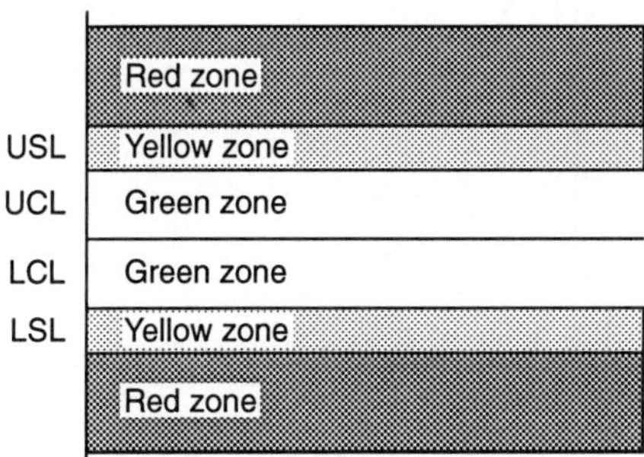

Figure 6.11: Pre-control.

• Divide the specification width by 4. The boundaries of the middle half become the pre-control $P - C$ lines. The area between these lines is called the 'green zone'. The two areas between each $P - C$ line and each specification limit are called the 'yellow zones'. The two areas beyond the specification limits are the 'red zones'.

• Process capability is tested by taking a sample of five consecutive units. If all five fall within the green zone, the process is in control. Full production can now commence. If even one of the units falls outside the green zone, the process is not in control and it is necessary to look for some assignable cause.

• Once production starts, we take two consecutive units from the process periodically. The following possibilities can then occur: (i) If both units fall in the green zone, production is continued; (ii) If one unit is in the green zone, and the other; is in the yellow zone, the process is still in control and we continue production; (iii) If both units fall in the yellow zones (with both in the same yellow zone or one in one yellow zone and the second in the other), then production is stopped and we investigate the cause for such variation; (iv) If even one unit falls in the red zone, there is a known reject and production must be stopped (and the reject's cause is investigated). When the process is stopped (as in cases (iii) and (iv)) and the cause of variation identified and reduced (or eliminated), the second tests (b) – five units in a row in the green zone – must be applied again before production can resume.

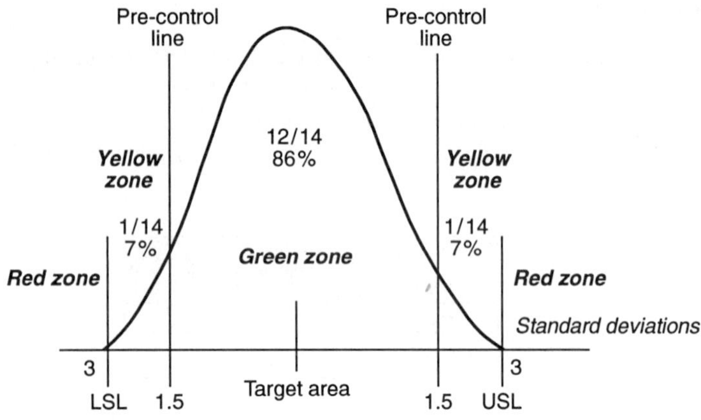

The Pre-control rules:
Draw 2 p-c lines in the middle half of the spec. width

To determine process capability 5 units in a row must be within p-c lines (the green zone). If not, use diagnostic rules to reduce variation

For production, sample 2 units consecutively and periodically

Frequency of sampling: divide the time interval between 2 stoppages by 6

Condition	**Action**
2 units in green zone	*Continue*
1 unit in green and 1 unit in yellow	*Continue*
2 units in yellow	*Stop**
1 unit in red	*Stop**

**To resume 5 units in the green zone*

Figure 6.12: Pre-control (Source Bhote, 1988).

• The sampling frequency of two consecutive units is determined by dividing the time period between two stoppages (i.e. between two pairs of yellows) by six. In other words, if there is a stoppage (two yellows), say, at 9 am and the process is corrected and restarted soon after, followed by another stoppage at 12 noon (two yellows again), the period of three hours between these stoppages is divided by 6, to give a frequency of sampling of every half hour. If, on the other hand, the period between two stoppages is three days, the sampling frequency is every half-day.

This procedure is efficient because of its simplicity and because it satisfies essential risk specifications. Although the α and β errors are difficult to calculate explicitly, this can be done. Bhote points out that if we were to follow such a procedure, then the worst producer α risk (i.e. stopping a process when it should continue) is around 2%, while the worst consumer β risk (to allow the process to continue when it should be stopped) is close to 1.5%. Further, it yields a process capacity close to the zero defects.

6.5 Control charts and the ARL

Run lengths denote the number of samples obtained until a special cause is detected. For example, in Figure 6.13, a run length is represented. Assume that a control chart has been constructed properly; a run length will then be larger if normal operations are maintained (since special causes occur with a smaller probability), while the run length will be smaller (or unduly longer) if the process has changed for some reason (in which case, the probability of special causes has increased). For example, consider an x-bar chart with samples of size n. The distribution of the sample average $\bar{X}$ is thus assumed normal with mean μ and standard deviation $\sigma/\sqrt{n}$.

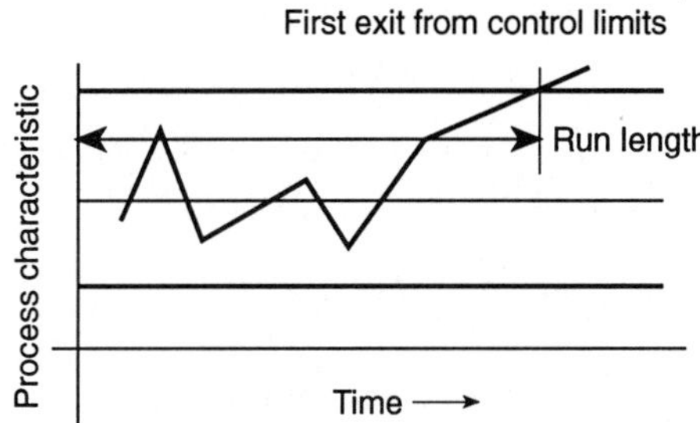

Figure 6.13: Run length.

Thus, if (LCL,UCL) are the lower and upper control limits, the probability of a sample average being outside these bounds is:

$$p = 1 - \text{ Prob } [\text{ LCL } \le \bar{X} \le \text{ UCL}],$$

where both the LCL and UCL are a function of the process parameters (μ, σ) and the sample size n, as we saw earlier. In other words, $p = p(\mu, \sigma, n)$. The probability of a run length, RL, is based on the geometric probability distribution, and therefore

$$f(RL) = p(1-p)^{RL-1}.$$

The average run length ARL and its variance are therefore

$$\text{ARL} = 1/p, \text{ var } (RL) = (1-p)/p^2$$

For example, if $p = 0.01$ then the ARL equals 10. This means that there is a 1% chance of false alarm (i.e. believing that there is cause for concern when this is not the case). Of course, if the process has a mean switch such that $p = 0.1$, then ARL of the switched process is ARL $= 1/0.1 = 10$. This means that on average, once the switch has occurred, it will be detected after 10 samples.

ARLs can be used to design control charts. In fact, in some cases it is simpler to specify the ARLs under null and alternative hypotheses rather than specifying the producer and consumer risks (α, β). Let AQL be the average quality limit a producer is willing to accept and LTFD be the lowest tolerance fraction defectives a consumer is willing to accept. Then, instead of the type I and type II errors (α, β) used earlier, we can specify the producer's risk by the ARL(AQL) that the producer is willing to accept for a false alarm (i.e. incorrectly indicating the process out of control) and the consumer risk by the ARL(LTFD), which indicates the average run length needed to detect a process out of control. Let these ARLs be given by ARL_0 and ARL_1, respectively. Then, risk specifications are given by

$$\text{ARL (AQL)} \geq \text{ARL}_0 \text{ and } \text{ARL(LTFD)} \leq \text{ARL}_1.$$

These risk specifications are then turned into control limits in the control chart as we shall see below through examples.

Problem

1. Consider an x-bar chart with parameters $(\mu, \sigma) = (10, 4)$ and samples size n. Show that the probability p is given by

$$p = \Phi(\frac{\text{LCL} - \mu}{\sigma/\sqrt{n}}) + \Phi\frac{(}{\mu\text{-UCL}}\sigma/\sqrt{n}).$$

2. What is the sample size for detecting a mean shift of 10% in an average run length of 6? What is the ARL if the sample size equals 10?

3. Assume that a process in its normal operating condition has a p equal to 0.005 while in its altered (alternative) state it has a $p = 0.1$. A sample run indicates $RL = 160$. Can you conclude that the process is out of control? If yes or no, then with what (approximate) probabilities? To do so, use the following table (Wetherhill and Brown, 1991, p. 106), where the percentage points denote the cumulative distribution (of the geometric distribution) (Table 6.5).

Table 6.5: The ARL and VRL.

p	ARL	VRL	50%	90%	95%
0.1	10	90	7	22	29
0.05	20	380	14	45	59
0.01	100	9900	69	230	299
0.005	200	39800	139	460	598
0.001	1000	999000	693	2302	2995

6.6 CUSUM Charts

CUSUM charts, just as x-bar charts, assume that the mean process and its variance are known. These charts are extremely important in practice and are used to detect small shifts in the process mean. They will also be a topic of further study in Chapter 9. Assume that the process is stable with a sudden shift at an unknown time (due to some reason and to an out of control state) when the process switches to some other mean. Explicitly, let μ be the process mean, μ_0 the target mean, while μ_1 is the limit tolerable value of the process. This means that values above this mean are considered undesirable, and should therefore be detected as soon as possible. To do so, we take samples of size n and assume (or estimate from the data) the standard deviation, given by σ. Thus, the samples' average and their standard deviation are given by $\bar{x}_i$ and $\sigma(\bar{x}) = \sigma/\sqrt{n}$, respectively. Further, standardized values z_i are

$$z_i = (\bar{x}_i - \mu_0)/\sigma(\bar{x}), \sigma(\bar{x}) = \sigma/\sqrt{n}.$$

Now, assume that we cumulate the sum of deviations from a given target k. Explicitly, we consider the following cumulative processes:

$$\begin{aligned} S_i^+ &= \max[0, S_{i-1}^+ + (z_i - k)], S_0^+ = \text{ initial value,} \\ S_i^- &= \max[0, S_{i-1}^- + (z_i - k)], S_0^- = \text{ initial value.} \end{aligned}$$

Through these processes, S_i^+ can be used to detect a growth in the mean while S_i^- is used to detect a decline in the mean. A chart based on (S_i^+, S_i^-) is called a bi-lateral chart. The parameter k is essentially a coefficient of sensitivity and generally it is suggested to take half the difference of $(\mu_1 - \mu_0)$. That is, k is a function of the mean shift where the process becomes out of control, or

$$k = (\mu_1 - \mu_0)/\sqrt{n}.$$

Note that whenever the sums are negative, the cumulative processes are re- initialized to zero. Further we define an upper control limit h such that when either the sums (S_i^+, S_i^-) are charted and found to be greater than h, this provides a signal that the process may be out of control. The magnitude of h is determined by the risk specifications of the control process. Thus, CUSUM charts have two parameters (k, h). The efficiency of the chart can be calculated in several ways, although it seems that the use of ARLs (measuring the number of samples taken until the upper bound h is reached once the process has switched means and is presumed to be out of control) is simpler to apply in a managerial situation. Tables have been constructed for such a purpose (e.g. see Daudin and Palsky, 1994) and are reproduced below. ARL's are computed in these tables when both the process is in control (i.e. the process mean is μ_0) and when it is out of control (i.e. the process mean is μ_1), so that producer and consumer risks can be accounted for in determining the control parameters. The use of these tables as well as a computer aided example are considered below. In chapter 9 we shall return to a theoretical treatment of this problem, and consider other control charts such as Moving Average (MA), Exponentially Weighted Moving Average (EWMA) charts, and the like.

Example

A level pressure to be maintained in a manufacturing process has a target mean equal to 100mb. The pressure standard deviation is assumed equal to 0.8. A test is to be devised such that a switch can be detected in the means three samples after a switch has occurred (in which case the mean pressure becomes 101). Further, the probability of false alarm (i.e. the producer risk, or type I error) is assumed to occur at most after 500 units have been controlled). In this case, we have, $\text{ARL}_0 = 500$. Using the tables given (Table 6.6, see also Table 6.*E* in the appendix) we then calculate the ARL_1 which corresponds to 3, which turns out to be 3.4. This leads, therefore, to: $\delta\sqrt{n} = 2, h = 2.665, k = 1$. Now, since $\delta = 1/0.8 = 1.25$, we note that $n = (2/1.25)^2 = 2.56$ and therefore the samples size are $n = 3$.

Table 6.6 Average run length for Shewart and CUSUM charts

(AFNOR *X*06*J* - DOC 56).

$\delta\sqrt{n}$	Shewart $L = 3.00$ ARL	$L = 3.00$ ARL(max)	CUSUM $k = 0.5$ $h = 4.774$ ARL	CUSUM $k = 0.5$ $h = 4.774$ ARL(max)	CUSUM $k = 1$ $h = 2.517$ ARL	CUSUM $k = 1$ $h = 2.517$ ARL(max)
0.00	370		370		370	
0.25	281	841	122	369	197	631
0.50	155	464	35	99	69	205
0.75	81	242	16	37	28	76
1.00	44	130	9.9	20	13.6	36
1.50	15.0	44	5.5	10	5.5	13
2.00	6.3	18	3.9	6	3.3	6
2.50	3	9	3.0	4	2.4	4
3.00	2.0	5	2.5	4	1.9	3
4.00	1.2	2	2.0	3	1.3	2
5.00	1.03	1	1.61	2	1.07	2

Example: (Daudin and Palsky, 1994)

A bottling process fills 100 ml bottles with cough syrup. The process control mechanism is expressed in terms of a consumer risk of 0.135% for a volume below the declared level of 99.5 ml. The producer's risk expressed by the upper limit of 100.6 ml is important for two reasons. First, for obvious economic reasons, and second, because users assume that there is only 100 ml, and use this information to regulate their intake of the medicine. When the filling process is in control, the process standard deviation is $\sigma = 0.1$

ml (calculated using 150 samples). Tolerances are set at three standard deviations from the mean such that there will be a 0.0027 probability that the process, while in control, will fill the bottle over or below the acceptable limits, which are given in this case by

$$\mu_1 = 100.6 - 3 * (0.1) = 100.3$$
$$\mu_2 = 99.5 + 3 * (0.1) = 99.8.$$

The tolerance factor δ_1 for the process is thus

$$\delta_1 = \text{Min}\ [(\mu_1 - \mu_0)/\sigma; (\mu_0 - \mu_2)/\sigma] = (100.00 - 99.8)/0.1 = 2.$$

The ARL when the process is in control will be assumed equal to 500, such that $\text{ARL}_0 = 500$ and a process switch ought to be detected following two or three successive samples when the process variation equals $\delta_1 = 2$ (i.e. the $\text{ARL}_1 = 2$ or 3). In this case, our table provides the following results: $\text{ARL}_1 = 2.39, h = 2.105, k = 1.25$ when we assume $\delta_1\sqrt{n} = 2.5$ and $\text{ARL}_0 = 500$. As a result, the sample size is necessarily $n = (2.5/2)^2 = 1.6$ which leads to $n = 2$. Practically, this means that the ARL_1 will be smaller than 2.39 (since $n = 2 > 1.6$)(Table 6.F in the appendix).

The 10 samples in Table 6.7 were collected during such a process. Note that at the 10th sample, S^+ increases over the limit $h = 2.105$. At this time, we can conclude that there is a chance that the process is out of control. Once this is done, the process is restarted with $S^+ = S^- = 0$. This is represented in Figure 6.14, which was computed using MINITAB. This type of chart is called one-sided.

Table 6.7: Sample values.

Sample	Values	Values	Mean	$z_i - k$	$z_i + k$	S^+	S^-
1	99.9	100.25	100.12	0.45	2.95	0.45	2.95
2	100.01	100.13	100.07	-0.26	2.24	0.19	2.24
3	99.96	99.98	99.97	-1.67	0.83	-1.48	0.83
4	99.84	100.06	99.95	-1.96	0.54	-1.96	0.54
5	99.85	99.93	99.89	-2.81	-0.31	-2.80	-0.31
6	99.86	99.94	99.90	-2.66	-0.16	-2.66	-0.47
7	100.05	100.15	100.10	0.16	2.66	0.16	2.66
8	100.00	100.30	100.15	0.87	3.37	1.04	3.37
9	100.07	100.21	100.14	0.73	3.23	1.77	3.23
10	100.10	100.16	100.13	0.59	3.09	2.35	3.09

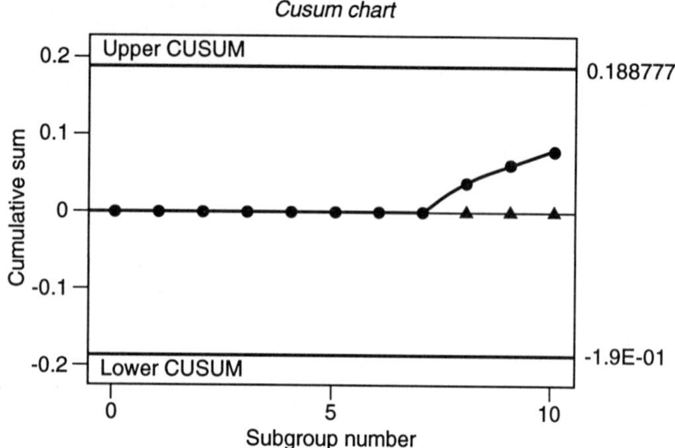

Figure 6.14: One-sided CUSUM charts.

According to these results, we can presume that the process has switched to being out of control between the 6th and 7th samples. The process switch is further calculated by

$$\delta\sqrt{n} = 2.35/(5-1) + 1.25 = 1.84 \text{ or } \delta = 1.84/\sqrt{2} = 1.3,$$

and the out-of-control process mean is estimated as

$$\mu' = 100 + (1.3)(0.1) = 100.13.$$

For comparison, consider the Shewart chart using the same samples of size $n = 2$ and $L = 3$. As a result, the UCL $= 100.21$ and LCL $= 99.79$. It is noteworthy that this chart does not detect the process switch (since the upper control limit is never violated in the 10 samples averages). In fact unless we double the sample size, it would be impossible to detect the switch. This is of course the case only because the process switch was small. If the process switch were to be sudden and significant, then a Shewart chart would be more efficient, indicating the switch before the CUSUM chart.

CUSUM charts can be calculated using real rather than standardized values as shown above. Further, proportions charts, CUSUM u-charts and cusum$-R$ charts may be also used. In the following, we consider CUSUM charts with real values.

Example: CUSUM charts with non-standardized values

Practically, it is often simpler to directly use non-standardized values. In this case we use the following parameters H and (K_+, K_-) instead of h and k

$$H = h\sigma/\sqrt{n}, K_+ = \mu_0 + k\sigma/\sqrt{n}, K_- = \mu_0 - k\sigma/\sqrt{n}.$$

The calculated cumulative sums are then given by the following equations

$$\begin{aligned} S^+ &= \max[0, S^+ + (\bar{x}_i - K_+)], S^+ = \text{ initial value}, \\ S^- &= \max[0, S^- + (\bar{x}_i - K_-)], S^- = \text{ initial value}, \end{aligned}$$

where $\bar{x}_i$ is the ith sample mean. In the case defined earlier, we will have explicitly, $H = 2.105 * (0.1)/\sqrt{2} = 0.149, K_+ = 100 + 1.25 * (0.1)/\sqrt{2} = 100.088, K_- = 100 - 1.25 * (0.1)/\sqrt{2} = 99.9116$.

Problem

Using the data in the previous example, construct a CUSUM chart with the real (non-standardized) values.

There is an alternative approach to studying CUSUM charts based on the V-mask technique. This method is more difficult to apply (for further details see Wetherhill and Brown, 1991 and John, 1990).

6.7 Interpreting charts

There are two essential ways to interpret control charts. First, on the basis of the probability of unlikely events which are observed in the chart; and second, by testing for a pattern of points observed in the chart which departs from a random distribution. Of course, in many cases, 'a look' at the chart can provide an intuitive appreciation of the dynamic evolution of the process. For example, cyclical patterns, stratification of sample results and other non- random patterns of data may suggest behaviours which are not random (and therefore due to some special recurrent causes). To determine whether points are randomly distributed, we can apply a number of tests for randomness (such as run tests) which provides a statistical verification of the process behaviour over time.

In practice, interpretations of control charts are based on the detection of situations which are unlikely in a probabilistic sense. The detection of these situations is a warning that there might be some special causes, or special situations, that warrant further study of their occurrence. When such events recur too often, or there is some pattern exhibited by the data, then there are reasonable grounds to doubt both the processes which generate common causes or the underlying hypotheses in the control chart construction. Criteria should be carefully assessed and selected. Some criteria which are often used in practice include:

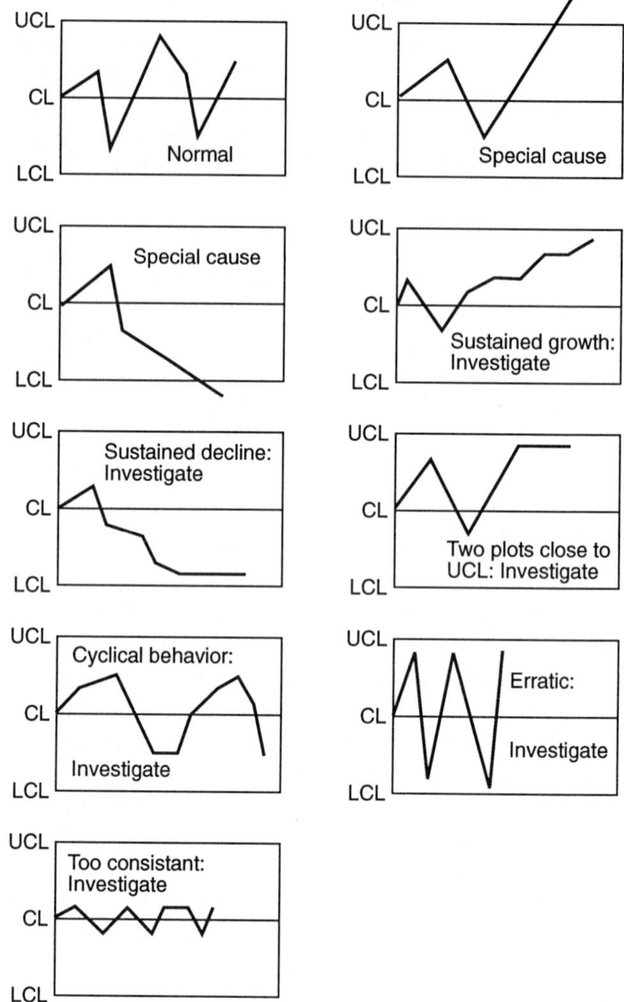

Figure 6.15: Common control charts.

- One or more points outside the control limits UCL, LCL.
- Two or more points near the warning upper and lower limits.
- Periodic patterns which highlight non stationary data behaviour.
- Points that are too close to the centre line, implying that the warning limits were improperly drawn (e.g. due to inappropriate data grouping).
- Run tests, which examine points positioned successively above or below the centre line. For example, a run of 7 points, a run of 10 in a string

of 11 points, a run of 12 in 14 points, a run of 16 in 20 points have such small occurrence probabilities that they may be used to point out potential departures from a stable (controlled) process.

Other run tests, which use the number of points and their distance from the centre lines, include a run of two or three points outside two deviations (σ) limits, or a run of four or five points outside one standard deviation limit. Say that a series of eight consecutive points remain above or below the centre line (CL). The probability of obtaining such an event is $(0.49865)^8 = 0.0039$, where 0.49865 is the probability that a sample average is neither above or below the line, but inside the control limits. Thus, the probability of obtaining such an event is so small that when it occurs, it warrants further attention. It is a simple exercise to calculate the probabilities for each of these criteria. Clearly, they are all small. Various firms, however, use their own criteria. For example, Ford Motor uses the following: (a) a series of eight consecutive points above or below the CL; (b) a series of seven intervals which are consistently positive or negative and; (c) a non-random pattern such as data stratification (or a mixture of populations). In practice, the simultaneous use of too many criteria can be misleading, however, leading to too many false alarms and needless costs. For these reasons, a judicious choice of criteria to use requires a careful managerial judgment based on the risks we are willing to sustain and the costs they imply.

Problem

What is the probability of obtaining six consecutive observations outside two standard deviations from the CL?

6.8 Economic control charts

In recent years, attention has been devoted to the design of control charts based on economic considerations. To do so, it is essential to obtain the COQ and the prior probabilities of assignable cause occurrences. In general, these approaches assume three cost categories for designing the charts:

(a) the costs of sampling and testing

(b) the costs associated with the investigation of an out-of-control signal and correction of any assignable cause found

(c) the costs associated with the production of defective units

We study several cases in Chapter 9 however (since the construction of such charts must consider costs over several periods of time). The economic design of control charts with multiple assignable causes includes two distinctly different modelling approaches. A first approach minimizes cost per unit time. Different assignable costs associated with different assignable causes are then explicitly treated. Moreover, the model allows, while searching for assignable causes, either a continuous operation of the process or stopping production. The model is not always realistic, however, since it only considers single- or double- shift causes. In single-shift causes, once the process shifts to an out-of- control state, no further quality deterioration can occur. In double-shift causes, a second shift can occur due to some assignable cause. However, no matter which two assignable causes have occurred, the joint effect of the two assignable causes will always produce a shift of constant magnitude (Duncan, 1971). The second approach assumes that transitions among assignable causes (i.e. a continuous deterioration of quality beyond the initial shift) are possible. The chart control parameters minimize cost per unit produced, and include stoppage time while out-of-control causes are investigated.

Although most development efforts for the economic design of control charts has concentrated on the x-bar and p charts, there are some extensions to other types of control charts. Taylor (1968), for example, studied the economic design of cumulative-sum control charts. Procedures for the optimal economic design of control charts are well developed and can be applied to a wide variety of business and management problems with slight modification in the cost function.

6.9 The practice of control charts

In practice, control charts are extremely important beyond the mere statistical information they provide. First, they can induce improvements. The ongoing observation of process improvement (or process deterioration) has an immediate and corrective effect. Second, application of control charts require that measures be agreed upon. The ongoing discussion such agreement requires can be beneficial. Third, they can be used as an educational tool, conveying clearly the effects of statistical variation. Of course, control charts are not in themselves sufficient in a quality management program. They are, nevertheless, an essential tool, focusing attention on measurements and control, and thereby building a quality management culture based on something more than rhetoric. Deming (1975) provides a series of cases he has experienced where control charts turned out to be important. Some examples are discussed below.

Example: (Deming, 1975)

Truck drivers pick up shipments and bring them into a terminal for reload and onward movement. Other drivers deliver. A large motor freight company may have anywhere from 10 to 40 terminals in or near large cities. There is a long chain of operations between the request of a shipper to the carrier (usually by telephone) to come and pick up a shipment, and placement of the shipment on the platform of the carrier, ready for reload and line-haul to the terminal that serves the destination of the shipment. Every operation offers a chance for the driver to make a mistake. Table 6.8 shows six types of mistakes, plus all others. Although the frequency of mistakes is small, the total loss is substantial.

Table 6.8: The seven types of mistakes

Type	Description
1	Short on pick up
2	Over on pick
3	Failure to call in on over, short and damaged cartons on delivery
4	Incomplete bill of lading
5	Improperly marked cartons
6	Incomplete signature on delivery-receipt
7	Others

In the first mistake, the driver signs the shipping order for say, 10 cartons, but later on in the chain of operations, someone else that there are only nine cartons; one carton was missing. Where is it? There may have been only nine cartons in the first place, the shipping order was written incorrectly or the driver left one carton on the shipper's premises. The cost of such a mistake includes:

- \$25 to search the platform for the missing carton, or to find the truck (by now out on the road) and search it.
- \$15 on the average to send a driver back to the shipper to pick up the missing carton.
- \$10 to segregate and hold the 9 cartons during the search.
- If the carrier does not find the carton, then the shipper may legitimately put in a claim for it. The carrier is responsible for the 10th carton. Its value may be anywhere from \$10 to \$1000, with the possibility of an amount even greater.

It is obvious that the first mistake may be costly, any one of the seven mistakes will, on average, lead to a loss of \$50. There were a total of 617 mistakes on the record, and they caused a loss of \$31,000 for claims alone. Multiplied by 20, for the 20 terminals, the total loss from the seven mistakes was \$620,000 (this is a minimal amount which does not include the expenses of searching nor administration. Moreover, some mistakes are not included in the total 617, but they cause a loss nevertheless). There were 150 drivers that worked all year long. We postulate the following mechanism, which will distribute errors at random to drivers using a Poisson distribution. The total number of mistakes is 617, and there were 150 drivers. An estimate of the mean number of mistakes per driver would be: $\bar{x} = 617/150 = 4.1$.

The upper and lower 3-sigmas limits for these samples is calculated by the square root transformation (based on the result stated in Chapter 3, that a square root transformation of a Poisson variate can be approximated by a normal probability distribution with the Poisson mean and a variance of 0.5) which yields

$$[\sqrt{4.1} + 1.5]^2 = 12 \text{ upper limit}$$
$$[\sqrt{4.1} - 1.5]^2 = 0 \text{ lower limit.}$$

The upper limit is interpreted to mean that a driver who has made 12 or more mistakes in the year is not part of the system. He contributes more than his share. He is a special cause of loss. Drivers who made $0, 1, 2, 3$ or 4 mistakes, and they too form a separate group. There are then three groups of drivers:

- Drivers that made 12 or more mistakes
- Drivers that made between 5 and 11 mistakes
- The extra careful group, drivers that made 0,1,2,3 or 4 mistakes

What have we learn from this model?

1. The seven drivers with 12 or more mistakes accounted for 112/617, or 18% of the mistakes. They may reduce their rate of mistakes to the average if they knew that they were outliers.

2. Drivers who made 5 to 11 mistakes measure the losses that arise from the system itself. They make the system what it is. They account for (425 – 112)/617 or about 51% of the mistakes. Clearly, about half the losses from the seven types of mistakes arise from the system as it is.

3. The 102 drivers of group C accounted for $192/617 = 31\%$ of mistakes. This group C is worth studying: how do they do it? Did they have easy routes or easy conditions (e.g. daytime pick-ups, inside pick-ups), or do they have a system of their own? If these men have a system of their own, then they should teach the others.

Here we encounter an important lesson in administration. This company had been sending a letter to a driver at every mistake. It made no difference whether this was the one mistake of the year for this driver, or the 15th; the letter was exactly the same! A letter sent to a driver in Groups B or C is demoralizing: the driver's interpretation thereof, which is absolutely correct, is that he is blamed for faults of the system.

The management had failed to see that they face three distinct types of problem. What was needed was a separation of responsibilities for improvement of special causes (to be corrected by the drivers of Group

A), the system itself (to be improved by the management), a study of Group C, and examination of the accuracy of mistake records.

Example

A small manufacturer of shoes was having trouble with his costly rented sewing machines. Operators were spending much time rethreading the machines at a serious loss. The trouble was common to all machines and to all operators. The obvious conclusion was that the trouble, whatever it was, was common, environmental, affecting all machines and all operators. A few tests showed that it was the thread that caused the trouble. The owner of the shop has been purchasing poor thread at bargain prices. The loss of machine time had cost him hundreds of times the difference between good thread and what he had been buying. Bargain prices for thread turned out to be a costly snare.

Better thread eliminated the problem. Only the management could make the change. The operators could not go out and buy better thread, even if they had known where the trouble lay. They work in the system. The thread was part of the system. Prior to the simple investigation that found the cause, the owner had supposed his troubles all came from the inexperience and carelessness of the operators.

Problems

1. Explain why the use of x-bar charts is insufficient by itself.

2. For an x-bar control chart with UCL and LCL at three standard deviations, calculate the α and β risks the chart implies.

3. A process for the manufacture of glass tubes is in control if the mean diameter is 1.0" and its standard deviation is 0.005". Consider a sample size of five and an α value of 0.03. What is the probability of detecting a process switch to a diameter of 1.2" by (a) noting that the next sample follows the same (growth) change as the previous one, and by (b) noting that two successive samples have a mean diameter growth?

4. Twenty samples, each containing 25 product units, are inspected, and the number of defectives is found to equal 12 in total. Construct the p-chart for this problem. Make whatever assumptions you require to obtain this chart.

5. A Just in Time production system delay (the time between an order's production start and its finish) is currently being tested. For 30 samples, each of size 5, the data in Table 6.9 including average production time and average range was assembled. Can we infer on the basis of this data that the JIT production system is in control?

Table 6.9: Data set for problem 5.

Sample	x-bar	Mean Range	Sample Size	x-bar	Mean Range
1	40	15	16	56	25
2	52	24	17	48	16
3	56	76	18	58	17
4	50	11	19	58	24
5	42	3	20	27	22
6	45	25	21	44	22
7	50	36	22	40	14
8	48	14	23	64	7
9	60	40	24	43	11
10	78	13	25	46	28
11	45	22	26	52	12
12	60	25	27	47	6
13	85	18	28	55	13
14	76	10	29	45	97
15	59	20	30	72	21

6. A microwave assembly plant uses both a staff of permanent workers and part- timers. The permanent staff include 70 workers, while the number of part-timers varies from day to day, according to management's forecasts based on future production plans. Following complaints by consumers, a special task force was created to test whether these complaints were indicating an excessive rate of defective units, and whether the use of part-timers had any effect on the reject rate. The data in Table 6.10 was collected over a period of a month. Can you conclude that the process is in control, and whether the part timers have an effect on the proportion of defectives?

Table 6.10: Data set for problem 6.

Day	Part Time	Sample s sizes	No. def.	Day	Part Time	Sample sizes	No. def.
1	40	1240	150	16	20	800	95
2	40	1150	104	17	20	900	70
3	40	1200	190	18	20	900	55
4	10	645	60	19	20	900	105
5	10	670	77	20	10	600	55
6	10	650	80	21	10	600	40
7	15	700	55	22	10	400	30
8	15	700	70	23	10	400	18
9	15	650	80	24	10	400	15
10	10	600	40	25	30	1100	120
11	10	600	30	26	30	1200	110
12	15	750	45	27	30	1000	80
13	10	700	55	28	30	1000	60
14	10	700	88	29	30	1000	95
15	10	700	54	30	30	1000	84

References

Bhote K.R. (1988) *World Class Quality,* American Management Association, New York.

Boulanger Carey, M. (1993) Measurement Assurance: Role of statistics and support from international statistical standards, *International Statistical Review,* **61**, 27-40.

Daudin M.M. and Palsky (1994) AFNOR Document *XO6J*, Cartes de controle, September.

Deming W.E. (1975) On some statistical aids toward economic production, *Interfaces,* **5**, August 1-15.

Duncan A.J. (1971) The economic design of x-bar charts when there is a multiplicity of assignable causes, *J. American Stat. Assoc.,* **66**, 107-121.

Fellner W.H. (1990) Average run length for cumulative sum schemes. Algorithm AS258, *Appl. Statistics,* **39**, 3, 402-412.

Fetter R.B. (1967) *The Quality Control System,* R.D. Irwin Ltd, Homewood ILL.

Freund R.A. (1957) Acceptance control charts, *Industrial Quality Control,* **14**, 13-23.

Freund R.A., (1960) Variables control charts *Industrial Quality Control,* **16**, 35-41.

ISO 9000 (1987) Quality management and quality assurance standards-Guidelines for selection and use.

ISO 10012 (1987) Quality assurance requirements for measuring equipment -Part I: Management of measuring equipment.

ISO/DIS 5725 (1992) Accuracy measurement methods and results, Parts 1,2,3,4,5 and 6.

ISO/CD (1992) Linear calibration using reference materials.

ISO 7870 (1992) Control charts: General guide and introduction.

ISO 7966 (1992) Acceptance control charts.

ISO 8258 (1991) Shewart control charts.

John P. (1990) *Statistical Methods in Engineering and Quality Assurance,* New York, Wiley-Interscience.

Johnson N.L. (1961) A simple theoretical approach to cumulative sum charts, *J. American Statistical Association,* **56**, 835-840.

Neuhardt J.B. (1987) Effect of correlated sub samples in statistical process control, *IIE Transactions,* **19**, 208-214.

Page E.S. (1954) Continuous inspection schemes, *Biometrika,* 41, 100-115.

Shewart W.A. (1931) *The economic Control of Manufactured Product,* Van Nostrand, New York.

Yang K. and W.M. Hancock (1990) Statistical quality control for correlated sample, *Int. J. of Prod. Res.,* **28**, 595-608.

Wetherhill G.B. and D.W. Brown (1991) *Statistical Process Control,* Chapman and Hall, London.

Additional references

Barnard G.A. (1954) Sampling inspection and statistical decisions, *J. Royal Stat. Soc,* **B-16**, 151-174.

Barnard G.A. (1959) Control charts and stochastic processes, *J. Royal Statist. Soc.,* Series B, **21**, 239-271.

Bather J.A. (1963) Control charts and the minimization of costs, *J. Royal Stat. Soc.,* Series B, **25**, 49-80.

Bissel A.F. (1990) How reliable is your capability index, *Appl. Statist.,* **39**, 331-340.

Belanger B. (1984) *Measurement Assurance Programs: Part I: General Introduction,* NBS Special Publ., 676-I.

Bowker A.H. and G.J. Lieberman (1959) *Engineering Statistics,* Prentice Hall, Englewood Cliffs, N.J.

Cowden D.J. (1957) *Statistical Methods in Quality Control*, Prentice Hall, Englewood Cliffs, N.J.

Dodge H.F. and H.G. Romig (1959) *Sampling Inspection Tables: Single and Double Sampling*, New York, Wiley (2nd edition).

Fetter R.B. (1967) *The Quality Control System,* R.D. Irwin Ltd, Homewood ILL.

Kotz S., W.L. Pearn and N.L. Johnson (1993) Some process capability indices are more reliable than one might think, *Appl. Statist.,* 55-62.

Lambert D., B. Peterson and I. Terpenning (1991) Nondetects, detection limits, and the probability of detection, *J. American Statistical Association,* **86**, 266-277.

Lucas J.M. (1982) Combined Shewart-CUSUM quality control schemes, *J. of Quality Technology,* **14**, 1, 51-59.

van Dobben de Bruyn, C.S. (1968) *Cumulative Sum Tests: Theory and Practice*, Griffin, London.

Wald A. (1947) *Sequential Analysis,* Wiley, New York.

Wald A. (1961) *Statistical Decision Functions*, Wiley, New York.

Wetherhill G.B. (1977) *Sampling Inspection and Quality Control,* Chapman and Hall, London.

Appendix 6.A: Control charts tables

Tables 6.A: Mean-range control charts: Case 1 : (μ, σ known) (Revue de Statistique Appliquée, 1988, p.92).

Control limits: $\mu \pm A_1\sigma, \alpha = 0.001$ or $\mu \pm u(.999)\sigma/\sqrt{n}$
Warning limits: $\mu \pm A_2\sigma, \alpha = 0.025$ or $\mu \pm u(.975)\sigma/\sqrt{n}$
Range control limits: $(D_1)\sigma, (D_2)\sigma$
Range upper and lower warning limits: $(W_1)\sigma, (W_2)\sigma$

n	Mean Control A_1	Mean Warning A_2	Range Control D_1	Range Control D_2	Range Warning W_1	Range Warning W_2
2	2.185	1.386	0.00	4.65	0.04	3.17
3	1.784	1.132	0.06	5.06	0.30	3.68
4	1.545	0.980	0.20	5.31	0.59	3.98
5	1.382	0.876	0.37	5.48	0.85	4.20
6	1.262	0.800	0.54	5.62	1.06	4.36
7	1.168	0.741	0.69	5.73	1.25	4.49
8	1.092	0.693	0.83	5.82	1.41	4.61
9	1.030	0.653	0.96	5.90	1.55	4.70
10	0.977	0.620	1.08	5.97	1.67	4.79
11	0.932	0.591	1.20	6.04	1.78	4.86
12	0.892	0.566	1.30	6.09	1.88	4.92

Tables 6.B: Mean-range control charts: Case 2(μ, σ unknown).

Control limits: $\bar{X} \pm (B_1)\bar{R}, \alpha = 0.001$ or $\bar{X} \pm u(.999)/d_n\sqrt{n}, E(\sigma) = \bar{R}/d_n$
Warning limits: $\bar{X} \pm (B_2)\bar{R}, \alpha = 0.025$ or $\bar{X} \pm u(.975)/d_n\sqrt{n}$
Range control limits: $(C_1)\bar{R}, (C_2)\bar{R}$
Range upper and lower warning limits: $(V_1)\bar{R}, (V_2)\bar{R}$.

n	Mean Control B_1	Mean Warning B_2	Range Control C_1	Range Control C_2	Range Warning V_1	Range Warning V_2	d_n
2	1.937	1.229	0.00	4.12	0.04	2.81	1.128
3	1.054	0.668	0.04	2.99	0.18	2.17	1.693
4	0.750	0.476	0.10	2.58	0.29	1.93	2.059
5	0.594	0.377	0.16	2.36	0.37	1.81	2.326
6	0.498	0.316	0.21	2.22	0.42	1.72	2.534
7	0.432	0.274	0.26	2.12	0.46	1.66	2.704
8	0.387	0.244	0.29	2.04	0.50	1.62	2.847
9	0.347	0.220	0.32	1.99	0.52	1.58	2.970
10	0.317	0.202	0.35	1.94	0.54	1.56	3.078
11	0.295	0.186	0.38	1.90	0.56	1.53	3.173
12	0.274	0.174	0.40	1.87	0.58	1.51	3.258

Tables 6.C: Mean–S control charts: Case 1 : (μ, σ known) (Revue de Statistique Appliquée, 1988, p.96).

Control limits: $\mu \pm A_1\sigma, \alpha = 0.001$ or $\mu \pm u(.999)\sigma/\sqrt{n}$

Warning limits: $\mu \pm A_2\sigma, \alpha = 0.025$ or $\mu \pm u(.975)\sigma/\sqrt{n}$

Range control limits: $(F_1)\sigma, (F_2)\sigma$

Range upper and lower warning limits: $(H_1)\sigma, (H_2)\sigma$.

n	Mean Control A_1	Mean Warning A_2	Range Control F_1	Range Control F_2	Range Warning H_1	Range Warning H_2
2	2.185	1.386	0.001	2.327	0.022	1.585
3	1.784	1.132	0.026	2.146	0.130	1.568
4	1.545	0.980	0.078	2.017	0.232	1.529
5	1.382	0.876	0.135	1.922	0.311	1.493
6	1.262	0.800	0.187	1.849	0.372	1.462
7	1.168	0.741	0.233	1.791	0.420	1.437
8	1.092	0.693	0.274	1.744	0.459	1.415
9	1.030	0.653	0.309	1.704	0.492	1.396
10	0.977	0.620	0.339	1.670	0.520	1.379
11	0.932	0.591	0.367	1.640	0.543	1.365
12	0.892	0.566	0.391	1.614	0.564	1.352

Tables 6.D: Mean–S control charts: Case 2(μ, σ unknown).

Control limits: $\bar{X} \pm (B_1)\bar{R}, \alpha = 0.001$ or $\bar{X} \pm u(.999)/d_n\sqrt{n}, E(\sigma) = \bar{R}/d_n$

Warning limits: $\bar{X} \pm (B_2)\bar{R}, \alpha = 0.025$ or $\bar{X} \pm u(.975)/d_n\sqrt{n}$

Range control limits: $(G_1)\bar{R}, (G_2)\bar{R}$

Range upper and lower warning limits: $(K_1)\bar{R}, (K_2)\bar{R}$.

n	Mean Control B_1	Mean Warning B_2	Range Control G_1	Range Control G_2	Range Warning K_1	Range Warning K_2	d_n
2	1.937	1.229	0.002	4.126	0.039	2.810	0.564
3	1.054	0.668	0.036	2.964	0.180	2.166	0.724
4	0.750	0.476	0.098	2.528	0.291	1.916	0.798
5	0.594	0.377	0.161	2.285	0.370	1.775	0.841
6	0.498	0.316	0.215	2.128	0.428	1.682	0.869
7	0.432	0.274	0.262	2.017	0.473	1.618	0.888
8	0.387	0.244	0.303	1.931	0.508	1.567	0.903
9	0.347	0.220	0.338	1.864	0.538	1.527	0.914
10	0.317	0.202	0.337	1.809	0.563	1.494	0.923
11	0.295	0.186	0.395	1.763	0.584	1.468	0.930
12	0.274	0.174	0.418	1.724	0.603	1.444	0.936

Table 6.E: Determination of h and k as a function of the ARL_0(process in control) and ARL_1(process out of control) as well as the deviation $\delta_1\sqrt{n}$ to be detected by the CUSUM chart

(AFNOR $X06J$ -Doc 56).

$\delta_1\sqrt{n}\backslash 0$	100 (ARL_0)	370 (ARL_0)	500 (ARL_0)	1000 (ARL_0)	2000 (ARL_0)	5000 (ARL_0)
0.5	$k = 0.25$ $h = 5.6$ $ARL_1 = 19.3$	$k = 025$ $h = 8.01$ $ARL_1 = 28.8$	$k = 0.25$ $h = 8.585$ $ARL=_1 = 31.1$	$k = 0.25$ $h = 9.93$ $ARL_1 = 36.4$	$k = 0.25$ $h = 11.293$ $ARL_1 = 41.9$	$k = 0.25$ $h = 13.11$ $ARL_1 = 49.1$
0.75	$k = 0.375$ $h = 4.33$ $ARL_1 = 11.2$	$k = 0.375$ $h = 6.00$ $ARL_1 = 15.6$	$k = 0.375$ $h = 6.39$ $ARL_1 = 16.6$	$k = 0.375$ $h = 7.30$ $ARL_1 = 19.1$	$k = 0.375$ $h = 8.22$ $ARL_1 = 21.5$	$k = 0.375$ $h = 9.43$ $ARL_1 = 24.7$
1.00	$k = 0.5$ $h = 3.502$ $ARL_1 = 7.4$	$k = 0.5$ $h = 4.77$ $ARL_1 = 9.9$	$k = 0.5$ $h = 5.07$ $ARL_1 = 10.5$	$k = 0.5$ $h = 5.758$ $ARL_1 = 11.9$	$k = 0.5$ $h = 6.447$ $ARL_1 = 13.3$	$k = 0.5$ $h = 7.361$ $ARL_1 = 15.1$
1.50	$k = 0.75$ $h = 2.48$ $ARL_1 = 4.0$	$k = 0.75$ $h = 3.34$ $ARL_1 = 5.2$	$k = k = 0.75$ $h = 3.54$ $ARL_1 = 5.4$	$k = k = 0.75$ $h = 4.00$ $ARL_1 = 6.1$	$k = k = 0.75$ $h = 4.46$ $ARL_1 = 6.7$	$k = 0.75$ $h = 5.07$ $ARL_1 = 7.5$
2.00	$k = 1$ $h = 1.874$ $ARL_1 = 2.6$	$k = 1$ $h = 2.516$ $ARL_1 = 3.3$	$k = 1$ $h = 2.665$ $ARL_1 = 3.4$	$k = 1$ $h = 3.01$ $ARL_1 = 3.8$	$k = 1$ $h = 3.356$ $ARL_1 = 4.1$	$k = 1$ $h = 3.814$ $ARL_1 = 4.6$
2.50	$k = 1.25$ $h = 1.46$ $ARL_1 = 1.87$	$k = 1.25$ $h = 1.986$ $ARL_1 = 2.29$	$k = 1.25$ $h = 2.105$ $ARL_1 = 2.39$	$k = 1.25$ $h = 2.379$ $ARL_1 = 2.61$	$k = 1.25$ $h = 2.652$ $ARL_1 = 2.84$	$k = 1.25$ $h = 3.016$ $ARL_1 = 3.13$
3.00	$k = 1.5$ $h = 1.132$ $ARL_1 = 1.44$	$k = 1.5$ $h = 1.604$ $ARL_1 = 1.72$	$k = 1.5$ $h = 1.708$ $ARL_1 = 1.79$	$k = 1.5$ $h = 1.943$ $ARL_1 = 1.95$	$k = 1.5$ $h = 2.173$ $ARL_1 = 2.11$	$k = 1.5$ $h = 2.473$ $ARL_1 = 2.32$
4.0	Shewart charts					

CHAPTER 7

Experimental and robust design

7.1 Introduction

The complexity of business problems, organizations, operational and service systems, the number of variables they involve, as well as the often chaotic environment to which they are subjected, make it difficult to use prior knowledge (in the form of mathematical models, for example) to construct and calibrate these systems. In these cases, experimentation is an important approach to generate knowledge which can be used for effective analysis and decision making. When a product is put to use, the number of intervening variables may be too large, some of which may also be uncontrollable. Further, experiments are usually costly; there may be many variables and potentially a great deal of experimental variation and errors, making the experimental results obtained difficult to compare and analyse in a statistically acceptable manner. For such situations, experimental design, when it is properly used, provides a set of consistent procedures and principles for collecting data so that an estimate of relationships between one set of variables, called *explanatory variables*, and another, called *dependent variables*, can be performed (even if there are experimental errors). For example, we might seek to build a relationship between supply delay (the dependent variable) and a number of explanatory variables such as the number of transport trucks (which can be controlled), weather conditions and traffic intensity (which cannot be controlled). When variables can be controlled, this can be used to reduce the amount of experimental variation. In other cases, selection of the levels associated with these variables might be desired and valued in terms of some objective function. The selection of variables' levels is a design problem which we will consider at the end of this chapter. Both the experimental and design problems are extremely important and useful. For example, to test a production process in a factory, it might be possible to limit the number of variables (i.e. maintain them in control) which affect a product's or a process' performance by controlling some of the variables (e.g. the pressure, the temperature used in the process, and so on).

Of course, experimental designs are not an end but a means to generate information, analyse data and make decisions. Even when such decisions are reached, they are based on forecasts, which are in the best of circumstances only forecasts. There may be surprises and deviations from standard operating conditions. These deviations can be controlled through inspection and control charts, as we have seen in Chapters 5 and 6. Alternatively, it might be possible to design products or processes (or both) which would be insensitive to unexpected variations and perform equally well under a broad set of conditions which we might not be able to control. When a product (or process) can perform in such a manner over a large set of variations, it is said to be *robust. Robust design* then consists of selecting controllable parameters which achieve a robust function (at a possibly lower cost). A robust design implies 'fitness to use', even when there can be many unpredictable variations. In this sense, robustness is an essential feature of the design process, product or service, and seeks to 'build quality in the product'. For this reason, robust design is often associated with 'off-line quality control'. This means that control is not performed on-line but off-line.

To use experimental and robust design we require first that:

(a) We define what we mean by quality in precise and operational terms.

(b) We use TQM tools (such as Pareto charts, brainstorming, fishbone or cause-effect diagrams, data analysis techniques and other tools) to select the 'vital few' variables (which we will call *factors*, and that we will use in our experimental and robust design) which are most pertinent to our problem, both from economic and explanatory points of views.

(c) We apply experimental design techniques to gather data which will be meaningful both statistically and economically. This data will be called 'experimental response'.

(d) Estimate a relationship between the response and the experimental factors (the independent variables).

(e) Optimize the controllable parameters (i.e. the design factors) such that the system, the product or the production process being designed conforms to agreed upon desirable operating conditions and over a broad range of environmental and uncontrollable conditions.

(f) Finally, we test, inspect and verify the product or process performance to ensure that it is operating in conformance to the defined standards, and leads to a business process optimization (measured in terms of profits, consumers satisfaction and their variability).

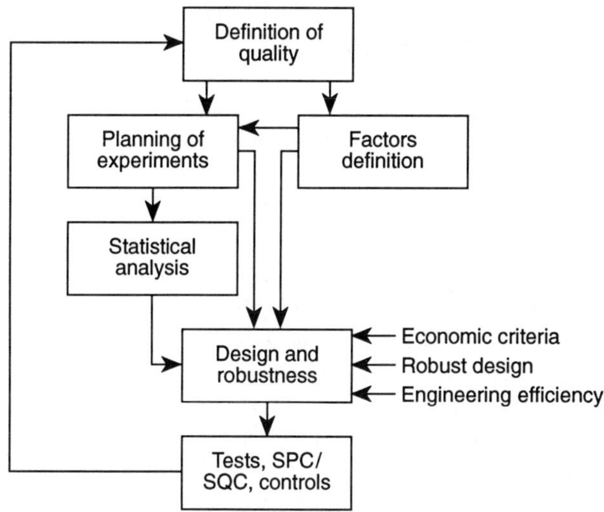

Figure 7.1: The concerns of quality management.

In Figure 7.1 we summarize the concern for quality and the intensive use it makes of TQM tools, experimental design, statistical analysis, applying economic and robust design and, finally, inspecting and testing to verify that the results conform to the design intentions.

To achieve meaningful experimental results, experimental design reduces experimental errors through a choice of experimental plans, the control of factors (by blocking them to specific values) and the application of statistical techniques such as randomization, confounding and replication. In this chapter, we address these problems cursorily. The motivated student should therefore consult the many references for this important and applicable field at the end of this chapter for further study.

7.2 The experimental design approach

Consider a quality performance index y (the response variable in an experiment), and let x and z be two factors which affect y. Assume that x is a factor which can be controlled (such as the temperature of a process, the number of trucks in a fleet and a scheduling technique), i.e. it is the kind of variable that can be fixed to a specified value by the experimenter, used to control experimental variation on the one hand and as a design parameter on the other. The variable z is a noise factor, i.e. factors we cannot control. For example, it might stand for batches, operators, humidity in a lab or the driving speed of a car. This is the kind of 'external' variable that the experimenter cannot keep under control. Therefore, z levels are usually randomly selected or fixed only during the experiments in order to observe the variation in the response y, called Δy, induced by a variation in z, say Δz. Assuming that data regarding (y, x, z) can be gathered, a relationship between y and (x, z) which we do not know *apriori*, and which is written by

$$y = f(x, z),$$

can be estimated. If the function $f(.)$ is known and stable, x, z and y are measured faultlessly, then we will observe a very good fit between the response and the explanatory factor. In practice, this is not the case; measurements are error prone and the relationship which is presumed to exist between (x, z) and y may be intricate. Experimental designs are constructed to allow the estimation of specified forms of relationships. To obtain meaningful data and reduce the experimental variation, some factors (independent variables) may be fixed during the experiment, while others vary without any control and their effects are 'averaged out' in the experiment through randomization of the experimental runs. If some important factors are neglected or others are wrongly included in the experiment, $f(x, z)$ will provide a poor approximation and the response y will probably exhibit large variability. For this reason, when a problem is ill- defined, some experimenters begin by considering a large number of factors and select those factors that lead to an error term that truly (or approximately) has a random behaviour and is preferably small.

Thus, the *purpose of experimental design is to exercise a planned variation in the experimental factors, x, which provide, at least experimental effort, information regarding the response y which will allow a statistically meaningful estimation of the function $f(.)$ and its parameters.* For example, if we can observe faultlessly a value y^* for predetermined values x^* and z^*, then the function $y = f(.,.)$ would at least be known for that point, or $(x^*, z^*) \longrightarrow y^*$. If x and z are fixed and always maintain their level (x^*, z^*), the predicted response y^* might be all we need to reach meaningful conclusions (of course, assuming that there are no measurement errors and that we operate in a stable environment). If this is not the case, we may seek one or more points by changing operating conditions and design parameters and potentially repeat (replicate) such experirements. For example, by considering levels $x^* + \Delta x$ and $z^* + \Delta z$ instead of x^* and y^* we may obtain response $y^* + \Delta y$. The problems we are faced with as experimenters are to specify the factors-levels combination which will be most helpful in revealing the relationship between the response and the experimental factors. Of course, once an experiment type has been selected, there remain a number of problems to be dealt with, including:

- Selection of the factors-levels.
- Determining the number of (experimental) repetitions.

- The restrictions to impose on the experiment.
- Performing the experiment and recording the response.
- Evaluating the results.

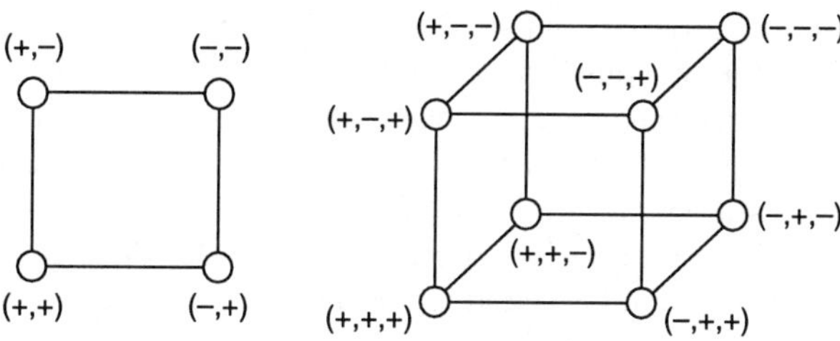

Figure 7.2: The levels of an experiment.

The choice of Δx and Δz define the factors levels. For two levels and two factors experiments, there would be four succinct possibilities, and thus four possible and succinct experiments, yielding four observations of the response y. These are represented in Figure 7.2. To standardize the conduct of experimental design, coding schemes for factors-levels are used. If a factor has two levels, we denote one level by +1 and the other by -1 (or simply + and -). By the same token, for three factors and two levels experiments, we have the three- dimensional graph which is also given in Figure 7.2. The dots in these figures represent the experiment performed with factor levels by + or - for each of the factors. If the factors are denoted by A, B and C, then the dot $(+,+,-)$ means that in such an experiment, the A and B factors are set to their (high) + value, while C is set to its (low) - value. Table 7.1 represents a two factors, two level experiment with four runs and replicated twice. Note that the responses are denoted by y_{ij}, expressing the recorded response at the ith replication of the jth run.

Table 7.1: A two factors, two levels experiment.

Run	A	B	Response Set 1	Response Set 2
1	+	+	y_{11}	y_{21}
2	-	+	y_{12}	y_{22}
3	+	-	y_{13}	y_{23}
4	-	-	y_{14}	y_{24}

Throughout experimental design we often code the factors' levels by setting $x_i = +1$ for the value of one level (typically the higher) and $x_i = -1$ for the value assumed by the other level (typically the lower valued level). Of course, whether we use coded or uncoded variables is equivalent if we note that the relationship between these coded values and their original numerical (or qualitative) values is linear. Explicitly, if a factor

A assumes two levels A_1 and A_2, then by selecting the transformation $x_1 = (+1, -1)$, with $x_1 = +1 = (A_1 - \alpha)/\beta, x_1 = -1 = (A_2 - \alpha)/\beta$, then $\alpha = (A_1 + A_2)/2, \beta = (A_1 - A_2)/2$. We can therefore transform the numerically defined experimental factor levels into ± 1 coded levels. In this sense, an analysis based on the linear (coded) transformation of the levels is equivalent to an analysis based on the uncoded levels, although the former is standardized for two (and as we shall see three) levels experiments.

In a typical experiment we will calculate the average response as well as the response variability through the range, the standard deviation or perform a statistical analysis of the responses and factors-levels. The evaluation of alternative designs, expressed through factor-level combinations, can then be based on either their average response, the response variability or a statistical analysis of the results. For the first run (using the two sets of responses) for example, the average response and its range are

$$\bar{y}_{.1} = \frac{y_{11} + y_{21}}{2}, \bar{R}_{.1} = \max[y_{11}, y_{21}] - \min[y_{11}, y_{21}].$$

Of course, 'the more we replicate the experiments, the better', since each experiment provides only a single sample observation while several sample estimates can reduce the estimates' variance.

Example

Consider a two factors (A and B), two levels (+,-) comparative experiment, given in Table 7.1. The factors assume two values-levels $(40, 20$ for $A)$ and $(1800, 1200$ for $B)$. The average, the range, the standard deviation and standard variables for each factor are then calculated as shown in Table 7.2.

Table 7.2: The experimental setting.

Run	Factor A	Factor B
1	40	1800
2	40	1200
3	20	1800
4	20	1200
Average	30	1500
Range	20	600

A codification of these values, which is agreed on by experimental researchers, can be of the representations shown in Table 7.3.

Table 7.3: Coding schemes.

+1	40	1800	+	40	1800	1	40	1800
-1	20	1200	-	20	1200	2	20	1200
Run	A	B	Run	A	B	Run	A	B
1	+1	+1	1	+	+	1	1	1
2	+1	-1	2	+	-	2	1	2
3	-1	+1	3	-	+	3	2	1
4	-1	-1	4	-	-	4	2	2

Taguchi, for example, uses the coding scheme (1,2) with code '+' denoted by '1' and the code '-' denoted by '2'. We shall use these coding schemes interchangeably. Explicitly, if we write $x_i = \pm 1, i = 1, 2$ and if we estimate a linear relationship through experimental design, it can be written as follows

$$Y = a_0 + a_1 x_1 + a_2 x_2, x_1 = \pm 1, x_2 = \pm 1.$$

Thus, in terms of the uncoded variables, $X_1 = (40, 20)$ and $X_2 = (1800, 1200)$. This corresponds to

$$Y = a_0 + a_1(X_1 - 30)/10 + a_2(X_2 - 1500)/300.$$

Comparative experiments are used to perform experiments under a specified set of factor-level combinations, observe their responses and then compare them. An experimental table such as that given earlier, but based on three factors A, B, and C and setting these factors to their two possible levels, might then look as shown in Table 7.4. In this table, note that $\bar{A}$ and $\underline{A}$ are given by (in case we use only the first experimental set of results)

$$\begin{aligned} \bar{A} &= y_{11} + y_{12} + y_{13} + y_{14}; A = y_{15} + y_{16} + y_{17} + y_{18} \\ \bar{B} &= y_{11} + y_{12} + y_{15} + y_{16}; B = y_{13} + y_{14} + y_{17} + y_{18} \\ \bar{C} &= y_{11} + y_{13} + y_{15} + y_{17}; C = y_{12} + y_{14} + y_{16} + y_{18} \end{aligned}$$

The averages are then calculated simply as indicated in the table. Namely, $A_1 = \bar{A}/4, A_2 = A/4$ and so on for B_1, B_2, C_1 and C_2. The response averages are calculated in a similar manner for each set. Namely, the average over all runs and response sets is given by

$$\bar{Y} = (Y_1 + Y_2 + Y_3)/(3 * 8).$$

A comparative experimental analysis will perform various experiments and compare the results observed. This type of table is often used by experimental researchers. An experiment using an exhaustive set of factor-level combinations is called a 'full factorial', experiment and will be studied later on. In this table the first test (run 1) has factor levels $(+, +, +)$, which stand for factors A, B and C, set at a level coded $(+)$. Similarly, (-,+,-), stands for set B at its level $(+)$ while A and C are set to (-). If just one observation is made at each treatment combination, we then have a total of eight observations. Since the experiments were replicated three times, we have a total of $3\times 8 = 24$ experiments. These results can be used to estimate different effects: main and interaction. Two way interactions are denote by $A \times B, A \times C, B \times C$ while the three- way interaction of this three factors experiment is denoted by $A \times B\times$C. The functional form we can estimate in the two factors experiment which has four distinct runs (experiments) can thus involve four parameters, which we will represent by the following equation, including the linear coefficient and the only two-way interaction $A\times$B. This yields

$$Y = a_0 + a_1x_1 + a_2x_2 + a_{12}x_1x_2, x_1 = \pm 1, x_2 = \pm 1,$$

where a_{12} is the coeffcient of the interaction effect. We shall see in the next section how to compute the parameters of this equation. Similarly, for the three factors, two levels experiment we have the following equation:

$$\begin{aligned} Y &= a_0 + a_1x_1 + a_2x_2 + a_3x_3 \\ &+ a_{12}x_1x_2 + a_{13}x_1x_3 + a_2a_3x_2x_3 + a_{123}x_1x_2x_3 \end{aligned}$$

Table 7.4: A three factors, two levels experiment with three replications.

	Run	A		B		C		Responses #1, #2, #3
	1	+		+		+		y_{11}, y_{21}, y_{31}
	2	+		+			-	y_{12}, y_{22}, y_{32}
	3	+			-	+		y_{13}, y_{23}, y_{33}
	4	+			-		-	y_{14}, y_{24}, y_{34}
	5		-	+		+		y_{15}, y_{25}, y_{35}
	6		-	+			-	y_{16}, y_{26}, y_{36}
	7		-		-	+		y_{17}, y_{27}, y_{37}
	8		-		-		-	y_{18}, y_{28}, y_{38}
Total		$\bar{A}$	$\underline{A}$	$\bar{B}$	$\underline{A}$	$\bar{C}$	$\underline{A}$	Y_1, Y_2, Y_3
No. of Values		4	4	4	4	4	4	8
Average		A_1	A_2	B_1	B_2	C_1	C_2	$\bar{Y}$

Example

In manufacturing food products, there is a wealth of problems which use experimental design. Some of the variables include the shelf life, nutritional values, pH, colour, odor, texture, packaging and additive quantities. These variables (factors) can be measures of performance (or experimental responses), design (controllable) and noise (uncontrollable) factors (variables). Each of these can exhibit erratic behaviour which can be controlled directly and indirectly in planning experiments. There may be other, more or less important factors for the food manufacturer relating to consumers' consumption of food (such as heating intensity, freezing conditions, repeat-freezing, and so on, which determine quality in-use by the consumer). To determine a relationship between these factors, and to use this relationship, experimental design and statistical analysis are used. For example, let the product shelf life be a function of the temperature applied and the quantity of a chemical additive. That is, we seek to estimate the relationship: $y = f(x_1, x_2, z)$ where y = shelf life, the controllable variables are x_1 = additive quantities, x_2 = temperature and z is a set of uncontrollable factors. Of course, $f(.)$ is not known and there can be many other factors affecting food production. Experimental design will establish a procedure which helps in negating these effects (through randomization, as we shall see later on). Assuming that there are no other effects, we can fix the additive quantities and vary the temperature. This is called then a 'one–at–the–time' experiment. Results are given in Table 7.5.

Table 7.5: A one–at–a–time experiment.

Factor I Additive	Factor II Temperature	Response Shelf Life
x_1(Level +)	x_2(Level +)	2.0
x_1(Level +)	x_2(Level -)	3.0

With these results on hand, we can estimate the parameters of a simple mathematical model which keeps x_1 fixed at its + level, and establish a relationship between y–the response and the second factor x_2. Thus,

$$y = a_0 + a_2 x_2, \text{ with } x_1 \text{ set to level} + .$$

In this extremely simple case, the parameters (a_0, a_2) are found by:

$$2.0 = a_0 + a_2(x_2 \text{ at level } +), 3.0 = a_0 + a_2(x_2 \text{ at level}-),$$

which leads to the following values (using the coded variables):

$$2.0 = a_0 + a_2, 3.0 = a_0 - a_2,$$

and therefore to $a_0 = 2.5, a_2 = -0.5$. In other words, the linear relationship estimated would be

$$y = 2.5 - 0.5x_2, x_2 = \pm 1.$$

When the factor x_1 varies as well, such a relationship might no longer be true. Selecting the best response for x_1, set at level +, note that this corresponds to a shelf life of 3.0 and to x_2 set at level -. In a one-at-the-time experiment, we would then repeat the experiment by fixing the level for the other factor (i.e. in our example, x_2 is set at level - and then let x_1 vary to two possible levels x_1(at +) and x_1(at -). In this case, the corresponding mathematical model and the experimental results take the form

$$y = b_0 + b_1 x_1, \text{ with } x_2 \text{ set to level} - .$$

Table 7.6

Factor I Additive	Factor II Temperature	Response Shelf life
x_1(Level +)	x_2(Level -)	3.0
x_1(Level -)	x_2(Level -)	3.8

Superficially, we could presume that the best conditions consist in using the additive and temperatures (x_1 at $-$, x_2 at $-$) (since shelf life is longest and equal 3.8 units of time). Such an approach which uses 'one-at-a-time' measurements can lead to the wrong conclusion by ignoring the interaction effects of the additive and temperature. First, in a one-at-the-time strategy, experiments are to be replicated to ensure that observed differences are not due to chance. As a result, there are at least six experiments to perform. In a full factorial experiment (which consider all factors-levels combinations), four experiments only might be required. Thus, factorial experiments are more efficient than one-at-the-time experiment because they yield more information. If we perform a two levels full factorial experiment, then the experimental results obtained (the response) can be used to estimate the parameters of a linear relationship, inclusive of the interaction effects of x_1 and x_2, as we saw earlier.

Problem

Consider the experimental results given in Table 7.7.

Table 7.7.

Run	A	B	C	Response y
1	+	+	+	y_1
2	-	+	+	y_2
3	+	-	+	y_3
4	+	+	-	y_4

Construct the complete set of linear models that can be estimated using these results. (Hint: Note that the number of possibilities when we consider all factors-levels combinations equals 8 while there are only four independent experimental values.)

The experiments considered so far involve two levels only, making it possible to estimate a system of linear equations (albeit including their interaction effects). There can be experiments with three levels as well, such as Central Composite Designs and Box-Behnken experiments, which we study later on and that provide the means to estimate curvatures (quadratic relationships). For example, a relationship such as

$$y = a_0 + a_1x_1 + a_{11}x_1^2 + a_2x_2 + a_{22}x_2^2 + a_3x_1x_2$$

cannot be estimated through a two-levels experiment, but it can be estimated through a three-levels experiment. Of course, if we do not perform the experiment properly, the relationship we estimate can be misleading. In other words, we can incorrectly interpret the estimated coefficients a_0, a_1, a_2, and so on. To avoid these situations, it is important to appreciate the use of experimental design.

7.3 Experimental design

The organization and realization of an experimental design requires that we define the hypothesis to test. Further, it is essential to maintain a close relationship with a statistician in order to satisfy, on the one hand, the needs of the experimenter, and to ensure the statistical viability of experiments on the other. Coleman and Montgomery (1993) point out that in practice, whenever experimental designs are used, there is usually a gap between engineers or management and the consulting statistician. In practice, it is rare for an experiment to be performed exactly as planned. There are many reasons for this, foremost among them being a knowledge gap between the statistician and experimenter. A statistician may make unwarranted statistical hypotheses regarding a process' stability, may combine control variables in the design and thus miss some important relationships, may violate or not properly exploit known physical laws, may suggest a design that is too large or too small, or may suggest that experiments be performed in an unreasonable order (from a practical point of view). Similarly, the experimenter who is unaware of statistical knowledge may also be the source to numerous errors, such as a poor selection of control variables (e.g. select a range too small or too large to obtain a proper measure of the effects), misunderstand the nature of interaction, will not use randomization appropriately. These lead to measurement errors and to a bias in factors measurements, misinterpretation of results through faulty analysis and incorrect tests of significance. For this reason, getting organized for experimental design is necessary.

Table 7.8: Experimental steps.

Steps in Experimentation	Means
Problem evoked and recognized	Brainstorming, management directives, external effects
Problem definition and objectives of experiments	Ishikawa's diagram, Pareto charts
Select and screen experimenter and statistical support	Allocate responsibility, use proper software support
Select factors, both controllable and non-controllable	Study relevant background, define response, control and nuisance variables
Select an experimental design	Use statistical consulting, define interactions, restrictions and procedures of the experiment
Perform the experiment	Maintain proper experimental conditions
Analyse and present the data	Through software analysis and performance of appropriate tests for results verification
Recommend and implement	Responsibility and coordination

The essential steps to follow are stated in Table 7.8 (adapted and extended from Coleman and Montgomery, 1993). They consist of problem recognition and an application of TQM tools such as brainstorming, Pareto charts and so on. This allows a selection of variables, specifying what is known and not known, stating what can be controlled and what cannot, constructing the experiment, performing it, analysing the data and reaching the appropriate conclusions. Selection of an experimental design procedure is an important and difficult decision, however. A number of approaches can be used. Earlier, we studied the one-at-a- time experiment which failed to recognize interaction effects among factors. We can also perform every possible combination of factor levels, called a 'full factorial experiment'. Other designs include simple comparative experiments, randomized block, Latin squares and incomplete block experiments, fractional factorial, and so on. Each of these has been the topic of intensive research, and is used in certain cases (a function of the experimental costs and our ability to manipulate some of the factors). We outline the factorial experiments below, while in the appendix a number of experimental settings such as randomized block, Latin square, etc. are outlined. Prior to this, we shall elaborate on the basic elements that are needed to comprehend and to construct an experimental design. These are factors and levels, randomization, replication, blocking and finally, balance and orthogonality. It is necessary to understand the meaning of each of these terms in order to appreciate the differences between types of experimental designs.

Factors and levels

Factors of the *quantitative* type have numerical values, while *qualitative* factors have natural categories. Common examples include 'brand', 'product type', 'method' and 'machine type'. The levels to be tested depend on the type of factor considered and the type of relationship which is sought. When multi- factorial experiments are performed, two or three levels are usually selected. The former are selected when the number of factors is large while the latter are selected when it is important to obtain an estimate of a function's quadrature. To compare responses, multiple and paired comparisons of levels can be used. In such experiments, we look for statistically different means, and then select those means that have the better characteristics (tested through subsequent experimentation). For example, for two qualitative factors with an additive response effect, the following statistical model is used

$$Y_{ijk} = \mu + \alpha_i + \beta_j + \epsilon_{ijk} \tag{1}$$

where μ is the global mean expressing the expected response over all level combinations of the factors used in the experiment, α_i refers to the ith level for the first factor A with $i = 1, 2, \ldots, a$, β_j refers to the jth level for factor B, with $j = 1, 2, \ldots, b$, and ϵ_{ijk} is a random term which includes the effects of all other variables. Ideally, these unspecified variables ϵ_{ijk} will be small relative to the factors effects. The index $k = 1, 2, \ldots, n$; is the number of replicates (if applicable) at each combination (i, j) of factors. Replication in experimental design allows an estimate of response variability due to uncontrolled variables in the experiment.

A model such as that above is said to be over-parameterized if there are more unknowns than linear equations. To deal with such problems and still estimate the relationship between the response and the factor-levels, we can impose restrictions to reduce the number of unknowns. Some restrictions include $\sum \alpha_i = 0$ and $\sum \beta_j = 0$. Dummy variables can also be used, as this is often the case in linear regression. Factors with fixed levels are called *fixed factors*. These factors usually correspond to control or adjustment factors which seek to bring the mean to a target value by comparing fixed levels. If qualitative factors are fixed, parameters α_i and β_j are 'fixed' and assume constant and unique values for each level representing the increment or decrement over the global mean (μ). Thus, these levels are fully controlled and the levels' variability does not have an impact on the response variability. A controlled change of fixed levels will affect only the mean response (in which case dispersion about the mean is due to the effects of uncontrollable variables in the environment measured by the experimental error).

A factor is *random* when its levels are selected randomly. Typical examples (which are selected at random while performing the experiment) include batches of raw material, operators, machines, interchangeable tools in a machine or locations. If an experiment uses four batches of raw material and the objective is to measure the response variability due to variability in the batches' characteristics, then batches may be selected randomly. Model (1) can be used to describe an experiment with random factors, but for this case, if A is a random factor, then α_i is not a parameter but a random variable contributing to an increased variability in the response. The observed response variance Y_{ij} is then

$$\text{Var}\ (Y_{ij}) = \sigma_\alpha^2 + \sigma_\epsilon^2$$

which consists of two components: σ_α^2 is the variability in Y due to the variability in the random factor A and σ_ϵ^2 is the additional variability in Y due to 'unexplained' contributions from additional random variables in the environment. If σ_α^2 is larger than σ_ϵ^2, then significant variation reduction can be reached if a control of the dispersion in A levels is possible. If factor B in model (1) is also a random factor, then the variance of Y will also increase and have three components

$$\text{Var}(Y_{ij}) = \sigma_\alpha^2 + \sigma_\beta^2 + \sigma_\epsilon^2$$

Of course,to reduce the variability of Y, the factor (A, B) with the larger variance component will be selected first for control. Statistical models with random factors are also known as 'variance component models'. The null hypothesis tested for such models states that the variance components are null. If the hypothesis is not rejected, then variability for the random factor does not contribute to dispersion in the mean response. Several statistical methods are available for the study of such variation, the easiest one being ANOVA (Analysis of Variance). If fixed and random factors are used in the same experiment, then dispersion and location effects are affected by level selection.

Consider again model (1) with two factors A and B, where A is now a random factor and B is fixed. The model with interaction effects is then

$$Y_{ijk} = \mu + \alpha_i + \beta_j + (\alpha\beta)_{ij} + \epsilon_{ijk} \tag{2}$$

The variance of Y is thus equal to

$$\text{Var}(Y_{ijk}) = \sigma_{\alpha\beta}^2 + \sigma_\alpha^2 + \sigma_\epsilon^2.$$

Here the variance component $\sigma_{\alpha\beta}^2$ describes the interaction effects between factors A and B. If a level j for B can be selected, such that $\sigma_{\alpha\beta}^2$ is minimal, then Y_{ijk} is insensitive to variation in the levels of the random factor A (i.e. it has a low variation with respect to the mean). When factors are random, two approaches to variation reduction can then be used: (1) Reducing the variation of the random factor, i.e. σ_α^2 is minimized and then $\text{Var}(Y_{ijk})$ is reduced, (2) selecting fixed factor levels such that the experimental response will be less sensitive to random factor variation, i.e. $\sigma_{\alpha\beta}^2$ is minimized by a selection of the fixed factor level, instead of by reduction of the random variation. Thus the point of this discussion is to point out that factor and level selection are extremely important, and are necessarily related to the analysis and design of the experiment. Further, the complexity induced by the interaction effects of many factors and their levels selection require a deep understanding of the problem at hand, as well as an appreciation of the statistical implications of such interactions and response variability.

Randomization, replication and blocking

We saw that an experiment consists of a set of 'runs', also called 'experimental units' or 'plots'. Different plot treatments can be applied to each. For example, different teaching methods (the factor) can be applied with treatments including cases and theory (the levels), and so on. Runs (or plots) can be stratified (but not necessarily) into subjects or objects which are then compared through experimentation. Runs assigned to a specific strata then form a block. Stratification is essential for experimental design, for it allows a classification of the units which are compared (such as voting patterns across certain neighbourhoods, products attributes, and so on). Often, such stratification is not possible and thus ways to eliminate the bias introduced by the experiments performed under various and uncontrolled conditions must be found. To do so, we can distinguish three approaches to help us remove the bias and systematic errors arising in the course of an experiment (and thereby reduce the response variability). These are: *randomization, replication* and *blocking.*

Randomization is performed to ensure that repeated experiments are comparable. In any experiment, substantial residual variation can remain so that no test can ever be repeated exactly. Thus, even though experimental conditions might remain the same, the result will not be similar. As a result, it would be doubtful to draw conclusions based on quasi-similar tests. Residual variation may be caused by nuisance factors which can produce trends and signals having little to do with the experimental factors in use. This may also lead to successive experimental results to be correlated, again inducing systematic errors. Randomization (i.e. carrying the experimental runs in a random order) ensures that no treatment is favoured from replication to replication, and thus it removes (or at least in practice it reduces) this kind of error. Thus, randomization can be used to remove experimental bias and reduce the response variance. For example, if several people perform the experimental runs, then the choice of people assigned to runs should be randomized. Similarly, randomization can be applied to take measurements, to select levels, to perform the experiment, and so on. Randomization techniques are simple to apply (any random number table can be used) and, at the same time, they provide experimental data which can be assumed to be statistically independent. Its application, however, increases the cost of experimentation because it increases the number of experiments to perform (because of the number of replicates they require for the procedure to be meaningful).

Replication consists in repeating an experiment a number of times. The underlying theoretical foundation is based on 'the law of large numbers'. When an experiment is repeated, more data is accumulated and thus will allow more reliable estimators to be obtained. Experiments are costly, however, so if there is a way to reduce their required number while providing equivalent information then so much the better. Statistical know-how is thus needed to reduce the need for replication and provide a set of procedures to follow that can guarantee that the data gathered can be compared meaningfully.

Blocking can also reduce experimental variation, and can be applied in many ways. In some replicated experiments, there may be variation within individual replications, that is, some uncontrolled external factor may affect experimental results. In this case, blocking can be used to organize the experiments into groups which are internally homogeneous with respect to the effects of external (noisy) factors. Blocking then provides an estimate of the factors' effects which have a smaller variation. For example, if experiments are performed at different sites, we might consider each site as a block. In a similar manner, if we are testing the quality of manufacture in certain shifts, we might define these shifts as blocks. If the effectiveness of teachers is tested, they might be separated into two groups - male, female - or following any other stratification process.

Balanced and orthogonal experiments

It is sometimes useful to represent variables in a standardized form. To do so, we transform the factors' scores, for example, by

$$\text{STD Variable} = \frac{\text{Response - Average Response}}{\text{Standard Deviation}}.$$

Using these standard variables, experiments can be found which are *balanced* and *orthogonal.* An experimental design is balanced when the factors sum of standardized variables is null. If x_i denotes the value of a standardized variable, the condition for a balanced design is

$$\sum_{i=1}^{m} x_{ij} = 0, \text{ for } j = A, B, C,$$

where m is the number of plots. An experimental design is called *orthogonal* if the scores' cross products is also null (i.e. these factors have no covariation), that is

$$\sum_{k=1}^{m} x_{ik}x_{jk} = 0, \text{ for } i, j = A, B, C, i \neq j.$$

An experimental design can be balanced and not orthogonal, and *vice versa,* or both. These properties are needed to facilitate the analysis and the interpretation of results. When an experimental design is orthogonal, there is no correlation between factors, and the analysis of the results is far more reliable. For this reason, when orthogonal experiments can be designed, they will be preferred over experiments which are not orthogonal.

Problem

Consider the experimental design represented by Table 7.8a. Is this a balanced and/or orthogonal experimental design? What are the factors' averages, their range, standard deviations and their standard deviates? Finally, transform these variables into their coded form and explicitly write the relationship between the numerical and coded values.

Table 7.8a

+1 -1 Run	10 -10 I	20 -20 II	5 -5 III	12 -12 IV
1	+1	-1	-1	-1
2	-1	+1	-1	-1
3	-1	-1	+1	-1
4	-1	-1	-1	+1
5	+1	+1	+1	+1
6	-1	+1	+1	+1
7	+1	-1	+1	+1
8	+1	+1	-1	+1
9	+1	+1	+1	-1
10	-1	-1	-1	-1

7.4 Factorial experiments

Factorial experiments are commonly used in industrial applications which permit the study of several factors with measurements taken at several levels. In such experiments, a specific combination of factor levels is called a treatment or a treatment combination. The objective of factorial experiments is to obtain a general estimate for a response's variable to changes in different factors, or find overall factor-level combinations that give the maximum (or minimum) value to some objective. The multiplicity of factors introduces some complications when comparing experiments, however. When experiments are repeated by changing one factor at the time, the analysis can be misleading, for it might ignore the interaction effects. For this reason, it is appropriate to consider experiments in which variables vary simultaneously, thereby yielding information regarding interaction effects. These experiments, including full and fractional factorial experiments, are considered next.

Full factorial experiments

First, consider experiments with two factors (A and B) only, and two levels (a generalization to an arbitrary number of factors is straightforward). Subsequently, we consider three-level factorial experiments. A full factorial experiment can be used to estimate, as we saw earlier, a relationship given by

$$y = a_0 + a_1 x_1 + a_2 x_2 + a_{12} x_1 x_2.$$

where y represents the experimental response, a_0 is the response at the experiment's centre point, a_1 and a_2 are the effects of factors 1 (say A) and 2 (say B) and, finally, a_{12} stands for the interaction effects of the two factors. Of course, if there are more factors, the underlying mathematical relationship will be more extensive, reflecting all the factors' effects and their interactions. If A is investigated at r levels and B at c levels, we then have then an $r \times c$ complete factorial experiment. If each treatment is replicated n times, we have $r \times c \times n$ tests. Of course, in all cases randomization can be used to reduce the systematic error, either by assigning the experimental units randomly to the treatment combinations or by performing the tests in a random order. Special and often used cases include factorial design in which n factors are investigated, each at just two levels, thus yielding 2^n treatment combinations. This type of design is useful when a large number of factors has to be considered, since it would require too many tests to run each factor at more than two levels. An experiment such as this, which picks out the important factors from a number of possibilities, is often called a 'screening experiment'. Its purpose is to eliminate as many factors as possible from further experimentation. Now, suppose that there are three factors AB and C. The mathematical relationship underlying this model is then

$$\begin{aligned} y &= a_0 + a_1 x_1 + a_2 x_2 + a_3 x_3 \\ &+ a_{12} x_1 x_2 + a_{13} x_1 x_3 + a_{23} x_2 x_3 + a_{123} x_1 x_2 x_3 \end{aligned}$$

Table 7.9.

	Factors Run	A (+)	 (-)	B (+)	 (-)	C (+)	 (-)	Response
	1	y_1		y_1		y_1		y_1
	2	y_2		y_2			y_2	y_2
	3	y_3			y_3	y_3		y_3
	4	y_4			y_4		y_4	y_4
	5		y_5	y_5		y_5		y_5
	6		y_6	y_6			y_6	y_6
	7		y_7		y_7	y_7		y_7
	8		y_8		y_8		y_8	y_8
Total		$\bar{A}$	$\underline{A}$	$\bar{B}$	B	$\bar{C}$	C	Y_1
No. of Values		4	4	4	4	4	4	8
Average		A_1	A_2	B_1	B_2	C_1	C_2	$\bar{Y}$

To estimate the eight parameters of this relationship in a full factorial experiment we require at least $2^3 = 8$ tests (since there are eight parameters in the equation above). Let y be the response for each of these experiments. The data collected can be summarized as shown in Table 7.4. The (+,-) in each of the columns are used to indicate that we introduce at this place the experimental results and calculations are performed by summing the values in each of the columns (and as we shall see below). Assuming no replication, instead of Table 7.4 we obtain Table 7.9 above.

If just one observation is made at each treatment combination, we have then a total of eight observations. These results can be used to estimate different effects: Main Effects, two-way interactions and three-way interaction.

Table 7.10.

Main Effects	2 Way Interaction	3 Way Interaction
A	$A \times B$	$A \times B \times C$
B	$A \times C$	
C	$B \times C$	

Mathematically, assuming that we consider the first set of replicated experiments only, that is responses $y_1, y_2, y_3, y_4, y_5, y_6, y_7$ and y_8, we obtain the following set of equations (once the proper values for x_1, x_2 and x_3 are introduced into the previous equation):

$$\begin{aligned}
y_1 &= a_0 + a_1 + a_2 + a_3 + a_{12} + a_{13} + a_{23} + a_{123} \\
y_2 &= a_0 + a_1 + a_2 - a_3 + a_{12} - a_{13} - a_{23} - a_{123} \\
y_3 &= a_0 + a_1 - a_2 + a_3 - a_{12} + a_{13} - a_{23} - a_{123} \\
y_4 &= a_0 + a_1 - a_2 - a_3 - a_{12} - a_{13} + a_{23} + a_{123}
\end{aligned}$$

$$\begin{aligned} y_5 &= a_0 - a_1 + a_2 + a_3 - a_{12} - a_{13} + a_{23} + a_{123} \\ y_6 &= a_0 - a_1 + a_2 - a_3 - a_{12} + a_{13} - a_{23} + a_{123} \\ y_7 &= a_0 - a_1 - a_2 + a_3 + a_{12} - a_{13} + a_{23} + a_{123} \\ y_8 &= a_0 - a_1 - a_2 - a_3 + a_{12} + a_{13} + a_{23} - a_{123} \end{aligned}$$

In vector notation, we can write:

$$Y = X\bar{a},$$

where X are the factors' values set by the experiment, Y are the responses, and ā is the vector of unknown coefficients (including their products, two and three at a time). Explicitly, the matrix X and vector $\bar{a}$ are given by the following:

$$X = \begin{bmatrix} +1 & +1 & +1 & +1 & +1 & +1 & +1 & +1 \\ +1 & +1 & +1 & -1 & +1 & -1 & -1 & -1 \\ +1 & +1 & -1 & +1 & -1 & +1 & -1 & -1 \\ +1 & +1 & -1 & -1 & -1 & -1 & +1 & +1 \\ +1 & -1 & +1 & +1 & -1 & -1 & +1 & +1 \\ +1 & -1 & +1 & -1 & -1 & +1 & -1 & +1 \\ +1 & -1 & -1 & +1 & +1 & -1 & +1 & +1 \\ +1 & -1 & -1 & -1 & +1 & +1 & +1 & -1 \end{bmatrix}; \bar{a} = \begin{bmatrix} a_0 \\ a_1 \\ a_2 \\ a_3 \\ a_{12} \\ a_{13} \\ a_{23} \\ a_{123} \end{bmatrix}.$$

Often, the data is represented by a table where each run is specified by letters.

If A is set to + and B(or the remaining factors) set to - , the run's name is 'a'. If factor B is set to + and the remaining factors set to -, the run's name is 'b', etc. as represented in Table 7.11. The sign in the columns AC, BC and ABC is determined by multiplying the respective signs in each column A, B and C. For example, in run 1 we have for $AB = (+)(-) = (-)$, for $AC = (+)(-) = (-)$ and for $ABC = (+)(-)(-) = (+)$, and so on for each run. Of course, Table 7.11 also corresponds to the matrix which is represented below, with each row identified by the run number.

Table 7.11.

Run		Av.	A	*B*	AB	*C*	AC	BC	ABC
1	a	+	+	-	-	-	-	+	+
2	*b*	+	-	+	-	-	+	-	+
3	ab	+	+	+	+	-	-	-	-
4	*c*	+	-	-	+	+	-	-	+
5	ac	+	+	-	-	+	+	-	-
6	bc	+	-	+	-	+	-	+	-
7	abc	+	+	+	+	+	+	+	+
8	(1)	+	-	-	+	-	+	+	-
		1/8	1/4	1/4	1/4	1/4	1/4	1/4	1/4

To compute the main and interaction effects we may then proceed by either solving the linear equations or by using the common procedure which uses the table above. In this case, for the 2^3 full factorial experiment, the main effects are calculated by comparing the difference in the response at two levels of each factor, that is

$$\begin{aligned}
\text{Main effects of factor } A &= \frac{\sum(x_1=-1)-\sum(x_1=+1)}{4} = \bar{A}_2-\bar{A}_1 \\
\text{Main effects of factor } B &= \frac{\sum(x_2=-1)-\sum(x_2=+1)}{4} = \bar{B}_2-\bar{B}_1 \\
\text{Main effects of factor } C &= \frac{\sum(x_3=-1)-\sum(x_3=+1)}{4} = \bar{C}_2-\bar{C}_1
\end{aligned}$$

where the sum of $(x_1 = -1)$ is obtained by the experimental results, where the first factor is set to its lower level, and the sum of $(x_1 = +1)$ is obtained by the experimental results where the first factor is set to its higher (+) level. The parameters a_1, a_2 and a_3 of the linear equation for this experiment may be approximately determined by the main effects estimates by dividing these effects by two. We proceed in this way because the main effects measure the response effect when we move from the high (+) to the low (-) level, while the parameter expresses the effect from the centre point, and therefore equals half that effect. To compute the interaction effects we proceed as follows: If there are four observations of the high (+) level of A and four observations at the low (-) level, the average difference between them is an estimate of the main effect of A as we saw above. As a result, if we assume that the results of each of the tests are calculated, we then have the results summarized by the last row of Table 7.11. Using these results,the effects are found by summing the columns results (the + and -) and multiplying by the last row. Explicitly, we have

$$\begin{aligned}
\text{Mean effect} &= \frac{1}{8}[(1)+a+b+c+ab+ac+bc+\text{ abc }] \\
\text{Main effect of } A &= \frac{1}{4}[(a-(1))+(ab-b)+(ac-c)+(\text{ abc-bc })] \\
\text{Main effect of } B &= \frac{1}{4}[(b-(1))+(ab-a)+(bc-c)+(\text{ abc-ac })] \\
\text{Main effect of } C &= \frac{1}{4}[(c-(1))+(ac-a)+(bc-b)+(\text{ abc-ab })]
\end{aligned}$$

Formally, it is written by the following:

$$\begin{aligned}
\text{Mean effect} &= \frac{1}{8}[(a+1)(b+1)(c+1)] \\
\text{Main effect of } A &= \frac{1}{4}[(a-1)(b+1)(c+1)] \\
\text{Main effect of } B &= \frac{1}{4}[(a+1)(b-1)(c+1)]
\end{aligned}$$

$$\text{Main effect of } C = \frac{1}{4}[(a+1)(b+1)(c-1)]$$

The second order interaction effects are also given by the following:

$$\begin{aligned}
\text{AB effect} &= \frac{1}{4}\{[(ab-b)-(a-(1))]+[(\text{ abc } -bc)-(ac-c)]\} \\
&= \frac{(a-1)(b-1)(c+1)}{4} \\
\text{AC effect} &= \frac{1}{4}\{[(ac-c)-(a-(1))]+[(\text{ abc } -bc)-(ab-b)]\} \\
&= \frac{(a-1)(b+1)(c-1)}{4} \\
\text{BC effect} &= \frac{1}{4}\{[(bc-c)-(b-(1))]+[(\text{ abc } -ac)-(ab-b)]\} \\
&= \frac{(a+1)(b-1)(c-1)}{4}
\end{aligned}$$

and finally, the third order interaction ABC is given by

$$\text{ABC effect} = \frac{(a-1)(b-1)(c-1)}{4}$$

We shall consider below some numerical examples which will outline the procedure above.

Problems

1. For a 2 levels, 2 factors A, B and full factorial experiment, demonstrate that the mean effects and the factors' interaction are calculated by

$$\begin{aligned}
\text{Mean effect} &= \frac{(a)+(ab)+(b)+(1)}{4} = \frac{(a+1)(b+1)}{4} \\
\text{Main effect of } A &= \frac{((a)-1)+((ab)-(b))}{2} = \frac{(a-1)(b+1)}{2} \\
\text{Main effect of } B &= \frac{((b)-(1))+((ab)-(a))}{2} = (a+1)(b-1)2 \\
\text{Interaction effect } AB &= \frac{((ab)-(a))-((b)-(1))}{2} = \frac{(a-1)(b-1)}{2}.
\end{aligned}$$

Then, prove these results using the mathematical model corresponding to this experiment.

2. List all the experiments to perform in 2^4 and 2^5 full factorial experiments. Then consider a 3^3, three levels full factorial experiment with three factors.

3. Consider the results in Table 7.12, obtained in eight runs. There are two quantitative factors and a qualitative one taking on values (1) or (0).

Table 7.12.

Run	A Levels	*B* Levels	Qualitative Response
1	250	20	1
2	250	20	0
3	250	30	1
4	250	30	0
5	270	20	1
6	270	20	0
7	270	30	1
8	270	30	0

(a) What are the levels for each factor? (b) What are the standard values for each of the factor results? (c) Write the equation expressing the relationship between the experimental results and the main and interaction effects. Write this relationship in a matrix format, and calculate the parameters of the equation. Finally, draw eight random numbers from a table of random numbers which will determine in what order to perform these experiments. Why can we use such randomization?

Example

A firm is currently assessing its policies regarding its post-sales service (denoted by Factor A) and pricing of its industrial products (denoted by Factor B). It considers two alternatives, for both factors A and B. These levels are:

Factor A-Level 1: Subcontract the post-sales services

Factor A-Level 2: Self-management of the post-sales services

Factor B-Level 1: Warranty not included in sale price

Factor B-Level 2: Warranty included in sale price

A number of objectives-responses were considered, with the firm's market share as being the essential one to maintain. Brainstorming has led to the suggestion that a full factorial experiment will be conducted with each experiment performed in separate markets having currently the same properties and in each of which the firm has the same market share. The experimental results are summarized in Table 7.13.

Table 7.13.

Level +	Sub-Contract	Separate	
Level -	Self	One price	
Factors	*A*	*B*	Response
Run	Service	Pricing	Market Share
1	-	-	0.15
2	+	-	0.20
3	-	+	0.25
4	+	+	0.30

The experimental table is shown in Table 7.14, which can be used to calculate the mean, main and interaction effects as follows:

Table 7.14.

Response		Av.	*A*	*B*	*AB*
0.20	a	+	+	-	-
0.25	*b*	+	-	+	-
0.30	ab	+	+	+	+
0.15	(1)	+	-	-	+
		1/8	1/4	1/4	1/4

$$\begin{aligned}
& \text{Mean effect} \\
= & \frac{(a)+(ab)+(b)+(1)}{4} = \frac{0.20+0.30+0.25+0.15}{4} = 0.225 \\
& \text{Main effect of } A \\
= & \frac{((a)-1)+((ab)-(b))}{2} = \frac{(0.20-0.15)+(0.30-0.25)}{2} = 0.05 \\
& \text{Main effect of } B \\
= & \frac{((b)-(1))+((ab)-(a))}{2} = \frac{(0.25-0.15)+(0.30-0.20)}{2} = 0.10 \\
& \text{Interaction effect } AB \\
= & \frac{((ab)-(a))-((b)-(1))}{2} = \frac{(0.30-0.20)-(0.25-0.15)}{2} = 0.
\end{aligned}$$

In other words, the prediction of market share response can be constructed by writing the following equations:

$$\begin{aligned}
0.20 &= a_0 + a_1 - a_2 - a_{12} \\
0.25 &= a_0 - a_1 + a_2 - a_{12} \\
0.30 &= a_0 + a_1 + a_2 + a_{12} \\
0.15 &= a_0 - a_1 - a_2 + a_{12},
\end{aligned}$$

which leads to the following coefficients: $a_0 = 0.225, a_1 = 0.025, a_2 = 0.05, a_{12} = 0$, representing the linear equation

$$Y = 0.225 + 0.025x_1 + 0.05x_2.$$

An alternative representation of this equation is given as follows

$$Y = \text{Mean} + (\text{Level A-Mean}) + (\text{Level B-Mean})$$

which can be represented graphically as well. In such a graph the vertical axis denotes the response while the horizontal axis denotes the factors. For factor A there are two responses, one at A^+ and another at A^-. The larger response equals 0.25 at A^- and the smaller response equals 0.20 at A^+. Similarly, when B is set to B^+ the response equals 0.25 while the response equals 0.20 at B^-. This is given graphically in Figure 7.3.

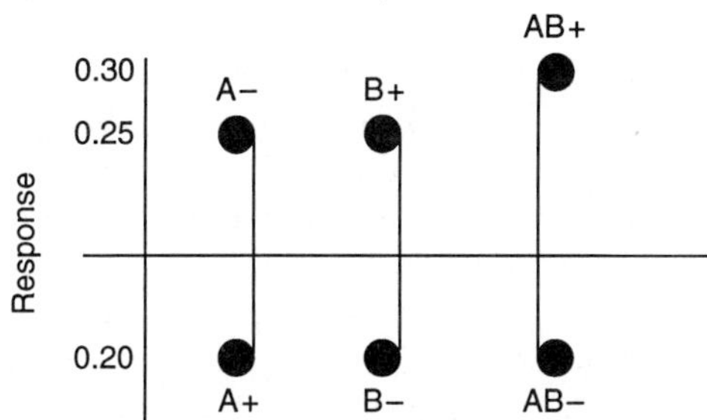

Figure 7.3: The response plot.

We see following this graph that both factors have the same effect on the response (market share). If we combine the levels leading to the largest and lowest responses, we then obtain then the following equations:

$$\begin{aligned}
\text{Response}_{\text{max}} &= \text{Mean} + (A_{\text{max}} - \text{Mean}) + (B_{\text{max}} - \text{Mean}) \text{ or} \\
\text{Response}_{\text{max}} &= 0.2250 + (0.2500 - 0.2250) + (0.275 - 0.2250) = 0.30 \\
\text{Response}_{\text{min}} &= \text{Mean} + (A_{\text{min}} - \text{Mean}) + (B_{\text{min}} - \text{Mean}) \text{ or} \\
\text{Response}_{\text{min}} &= 0.2250 + (0.2000 - 0.2250) + (0.1750 - 0.2250) = 0.15
\end{aligned}$$

as obtained in our example. Practically, the max and min responses are important when we interpret the results since they identify the largest and smallest responses attainable with the selected factor levels. Similarly, the effect of the interaction factor AB can be graphed, which in this case turns out to be 0.30 at $(AB)^+$ and 0.20 at $(AB)^-$.

The theoretical and observed values, as well as the residual values for each of these strategic alternatives, are summarized in Table 7.15.

Table 7.15.

Experiment	Observed Response	Theoretical Response	Residual Error
a	0.20	$0.225 + 0.025 - 0.05 - 0 = 0.20$	$0.20 - 0.20 = 0$
b	0.25	$0.225 - 0.025 + 0.05 - 0 = 0.25$	$0.25 - 0.25 = 0$
ab	0.30	$0.225 + 0.025 + 0.05 + 0 = 0.30$	$0.30 - 0.30 = 0$
(1)	0.15	$0.225 - 0.025 - 0.05 + 0 = 0.15$	$0.15 - 15 = 0$

Note that the residuals are null (since the theoretical and observed responses are identical). This should not be surprising, as we have used four equations (runs) to estimate the four parameters of the model. As a result, there are no degrees of freedom left for the error, and the residuals are necessarily zero.

To interpret the main effects in a linear model such as ours, we can construct main effects and interaction graphs as well as plots on normal probability paper (suggested by Daniel, 1959; 1976), which are used to screen the main effects and select those that are significant. We first consider normal probability plots. To construct these plots the selected least squares estimates calculated above (based on one set or the replicated experiments) are put in increasing order. Then, using normal probability paper, these estimates are plotted against the quantities found. Since all non-significant effects should be approximated on a straight line, such a line is fitted through the plot. Any effect falling away from this line is then considered as significant, while any effect falling on the line is presumed insignificant. Modifications to the basic Daniel plots are the normal-plots and $Q-Q$(Quantile) plots (see also Montgomery, 1991)) which does not require normal probability paper and which are plotted automatically by MINITAB. To understand these plots, consider a sample of size n and let $x_{(1)}, x_{(2)}, \ldots, x_{(n)}$ be the order statistics, assuming that samples have a normal density. Then, the jth order value $x_{(j)}$ corresponds to the $(j-0.5)/n$ quantile of the data, i.e. the probability that a sample value is smaller than this jth value equals $(j-0.5)/n$, or

$$P_j = \Pr(x \leq x_{(j)}) \cong (j-0.5)/n.$$

The normal plot is then given by plotting the estimated effects versus $100(P_j)$. Effects on the line are thus negligible (i.e. they have zero mean), while effects far from the line cannot be assumed to come from a standard normal distribution, and these effects cannot therefore be assumed null. The expected value of the ith order statistic drawn from a standard normal probability distribution in a random sample of size n is approximated by $z(\frac{i-0.375}{n+0.25})$, where $z(s)$ is the $(s)100$ percentile of the standard normal distribution $(N(0,1))$. Then, instead of the special probability paper suggested by Daniel, the $Q-Q$ plot uses standard paper and plot effects versus $z(s)$, which are the plots provided in the MINITAB output.

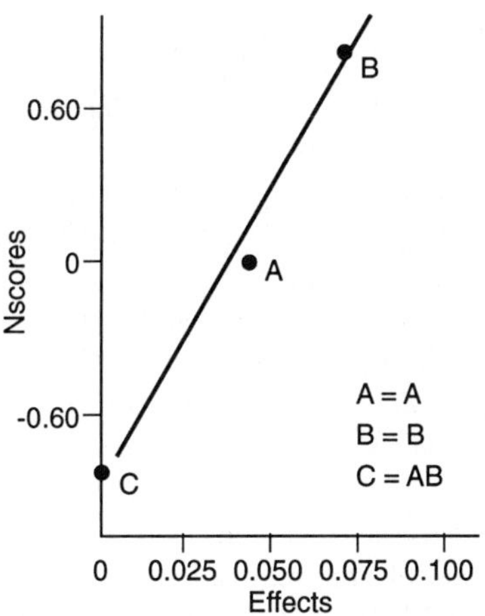

Figure 7.4: The normal plot.

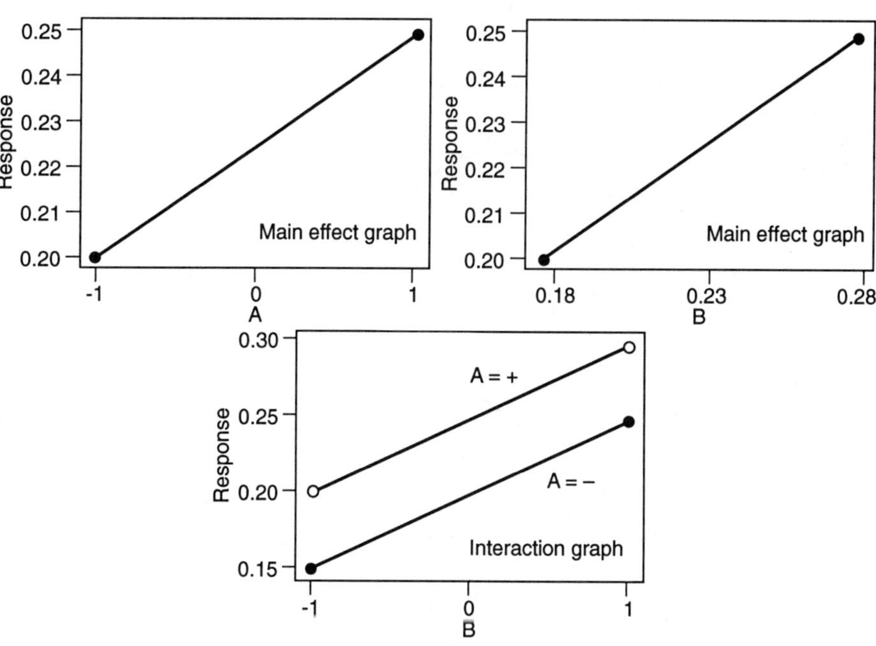

Figure 7.5a: Main and interaction effects graphs.

Main effects graphs for our problem are represented in Figure 7.5a, representing the response on the vertical axis and the levels for each of the factors (first factor A and then factor B). In the interaction graph entries are made for A and B. Note that the lines for A set at + and A set at -, yield parallel lines, which implies that A and B have no interaction effect. This observation regarding the size of interaction effects is extremely important for the design of fractional factorial experiments, as we shall see below. Interaction effects are significant, however, when these lines are not parallel. In fact, consider a hypothetical interaction graph as in Figure 7.5b. We see that interaction effects in case (a) are null, in case (b) they equal a positive number, and in case (c) they indicate a negative interaction. It is possible of course to use computer software that can both generate and analyse the experimental results (such as MINITAB, SPSS, SAS etc.). A computer aided analysis of this example will, of course, reveal the same results as seen in Table 7.16a and its ANOVA table (Table 7.16b).

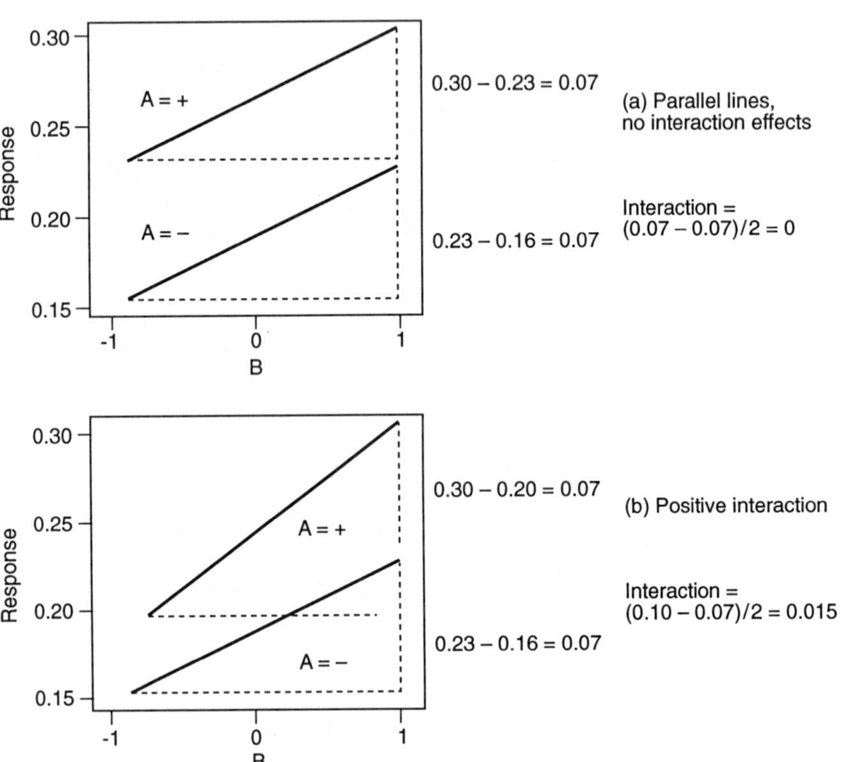

Figure 7.5b: Interaction effects graphs.

Table 7.16a: Estimated effects and coefficients for response.

Term	Effect	Coeff.
Constant		0.2250
A	0.0500	0.0250
B	0.1000	0.0500
AXB	0.0000	0.0000

Table 7.16b: Analysis of Variance (ANOVA) for response.

Source	DF	Seq SS	Adj SS	Adj MS	F	P
Main effects	3	0.01250	0.01250	0.04167	**	
Residual error	0	0.00000	0.00000	0.0000		
Total	3	0.01250				

The response mean values defined for each of the levels of the experiment are also given by the computer as follows:

A	Mean
-1	0.2000
1	0.2500
B	
-1	0.1750
1	0.275

These results can be represented graphically by drawing the response as a function of the factors' values.

When a factorial experiment is not replicated or a fraction is used (as we shall see later), there are no degrees of freedom available to estimate the experimental error. In this case, we can assume that some effects are negligible and use the additional equations to estimate the experimental error variance σ^2. If there are no replications, the 2 factor experiment considered will have the ANOVA Table 7.17.

Table 7.17.

Source of variation	Degrees of freedom (df)	E(Mean Square) MS
A	$a-1$	$\sigma^2 + b\theta^2_{\alpha\beta}$
B	$b-1$	$\sigma^2 + a\theta^2_{\alpha\beta}$
$A \times B$	$(a-1)(b-1)$	$\sigma^2 + \theta^2_{\alpha\beta}$

where $\theta^2_{\alpha\beta}$ is the 'effect' due to the interaction between factors A and B. It would of course, be zero if no such interaction exists. In this latter case, $E\{A \times B\} = \sigma^2$, and an estimate for the error variance is obtained. If this is not the case, we can be misled, since it would subsume that *apriori* what effects are not important in order to estimate σ^2.

Example

The flexibility of a manufacturing process, expressed by the time needed to deliver a customer's order, seems to depend on the following factors: A = Technology type (machine and robot intensive or labour intensive), B = Suppliers (supplier XYZ or supplier pqr), C = Management (centralized or decentralized), and D = Contracting (subcontracting as much as possible or in priority to in- house production). A full factorial experiment was conducted over a period of a year in various parts of the firm located in a number of areas throughout the US. The response time for each experiment is given in Table 7.18a. On the basis of these experiments, a consulting firm was hired to evaluate a relationship between these factors, which will be used subsequently to determine the firm's industrial strategy.

Table 7.18a.

Run	Response	Run	Response
(1)	24	d	21
a	24	ad	22
b	20	bd	20
ab	20.5	abd	27
c	32	cd	31
ac	22	acd	21
bc	21	bcd	21
abc	26	abcd	25

Table 7.18b: Full factorial design

MTB > FFDesign 4 16;
SUBC > XMatrix c2 c3 c4 c5.
Factors: 4; Design:4, 16; Runs: 16; Replicates: 1
Blocks: none; Centre points: 0

Run	Response	A	B	C	D
1	24.0	-1	-1	-1	-1
2	24.0	1	-1	-1	-1
3	20.0	-1	1	-1	-1
4	20.5	1	1	-1	-1
5	32.0	-1	-1	1	-1
6	22.0	1	-1	1	-1
7	21.0	-1	1	1	-1
8	26.0	1	1	1	-1
9	21.0	-1	-1	-1	1
10	22.0	1	-1	-1	1
11	20.0	-1	1	-1	1
12	27.0	1	1	-1	1
13	31.0	-1	-1	1	1
14	21.0	1	-1	1	1
15	21.0	-1	1	1	1
16	25.0	1	1	1	1

The computer generation of the experiments to perform 'in the order' and compatible with the four factors (and 16 runs) full factorial experiment leads to the following results (which are similar to the table above). The corresponding MINITAB computer session which generated the experimental runs above is summarized in Table 7.18b. The response data was stored in column $1(C1)$ while the experimental matrix 4×16 was stored in columns 2, 3, 4 and 5. The FIT-FACTORIAL option in the DOE Macro was then used with a mean effects estimates and plot requests.

Table 7.18c

MTB > FFactorial c1 = c2 c3 c4 c5;
SUBC > EPlot; SUBC > Alias 4;
SUBC > Means c2 c3 c4 c5.
Estimated Effects and Coefficients for $C1$

Term	Effect	Coeff.	Std. Coeff.	t-value	P
Constant		23.594	0.9793	24.09	0.000
$C2$	-0.312	-0.156	0.9793	-0.16	0.876
$C3$	-2.063	-1.031	0.9793	-1.05	0.315
$C4$	2.562	1.281	0.9793	1.31	0.217
$C5$	-0.187	-0.094	0.9793	-0.10	0.925

Analysis of Variance for $C1$

Source	DF	Seq. SS	Adj. SS	Adj. MS	F	P
Main effects	4	43.81	43.81	10.95	0.71	0.600
Resid. error	11	168.80	168.80	15.35		
Total	15	212.61				

In this particular case, the interaction effects are not considered in fitting the equation (since only a linear equation is assumed), and therefore the residual error will necessarily include these effects. Practically, a fit to the main effects only will be meaningful if the residual term is very small (as tested through the ANOVA of the regression above). In our case, it turns out that the residual error is large compared to main effects, and thus this model has a poor fit. Equivalently, we can look at the P column and note that since it is large (60% instead of the 5% required for a reasonable fit), we can conclude that the hypothesis that these effects are null and the null hypothesis cannot be rejected. Of course, we can also seek to fit a higher order polynomial, one which will include interaction effects. In this case, the MINITAB session with interaction factors AB, AC, AD, BC, BD, ABC, ABD, BCD and $ABCD$ can be created, and the request for fitting such terms in the polynomial can indicate the appropriate (interaction factors) columns to select. Alternatively, the model in the Fit Factorial option may be specified as $c1 = c2 \mid c3 \mid c4 \mid c5$. The results obtained are similar in form to those obtained above, although their interpretation is likely to differ. A comparison of such results is left as an exercise, however. Finally, the main effects graph as well as the mean response (delay) expressed as a function of the factor levels settings for this experiment are plotted and given in Figure 7.6. This graph presents the outcomes when testing the hypothesis that the effects are null. In our case, this turns out to be the case in agreement with the numerical analysis where t-values are not significant and the global F value is also insignificant. Of course, since our analysis involved only main effects, this would be acceptable if all interactions were negligible.

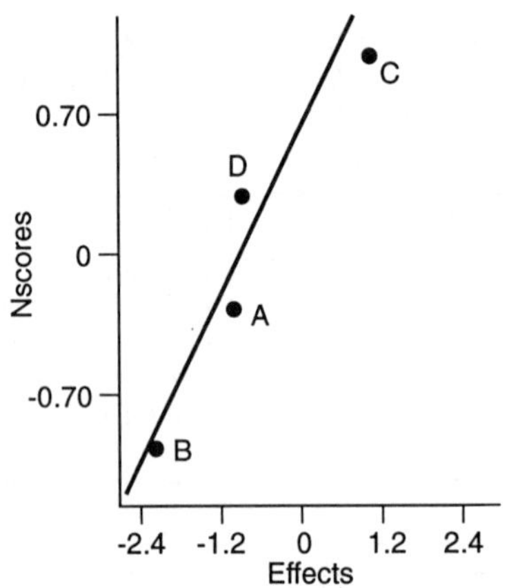

Figure 7.6: Normalized factor scores.

Factor scores at the (+,-) levels can be used to graph the main effects (and interaction effects when these are available). The construction of the main and interaction effects and their discussion in this case is left as an exercise.

Table 7.18d: A=C2, B=C3, C = C4, D = C5; Means for C1

	Mean Response	Std. dev. Response
$C2$		
-1	23.75	1.385
1	23.44	1.385
$C3$		
-1	24.63	1.385
1	22.56	1.385
$C4$		
-1	22.31	1.385
1	24.87	1.385
$C5$		
-1	23.69	1.385
1	23.50	1.385

On the basis of these results we can conclude that all factors (except C) improve the delivery delay, although not equally. The largest effect is due to the second factor (B). Further analysis would take into consideration the interaction effects. An industrial strategy whose objective is to reduce delivery delay will recognize, of course, such a fact.

Problem

Repeat such an analysis by including the interaction factors, and draw the response, main effects and interaction graphs.

Example

In order to determine how to best assemble a product, an experiment with three factors was constructed. The first factor A was used to denote the work group to perform the experiment (there were two such work groups, representing two levels). Factor B was used to denote the type of assembly to use. There were two alternative suppliers whose equipment was also to be tested (the two levels for the B factor). Finally, factor C, denoting the organization of workers, assumes two forms: fully centralized and decentralized (the two levels of factor C). The response variable, which is used to evaluate the factor-level combinations was selected to be the assembly time. Factors and their levels are given in Table 7.19a.

Table 7.19a.

Methods Factors	Work Group 1 Level 1	Work Group 2 Level 2
Workers (A)	Engineers (+)	Technicians (-)
Equipment (B)	Supplier 1 (+)	Supplier 2 (-)
Organization (C)	Centralized (+)	Decentralized (-)

We use the numerical values given by Lochner and Matar (1990) for the 2^3 full factorial experiment (Table 7.19*b*).

Table 7.19b.

Run	*Response*	Av.	*A*	*B*	*C*	*AB*	*AC*	*BC*	*ABC*
1 (a)	160	+	+	-	-	-	-	+	+
2 (b)	187	+	-	+	-	-	+	-	+
3 (ab)	166	+	+	+	-	+	-	-	-
4 (c)	179	+	-	-	+	+	-	-	+
5 (ac)	161	+	+	-	+	-	+	-	-
6 (bc)	184	+	-	+	+	-	-	+	-
7 (abc)	164	+	+	+	+	+	+	+	+
8 (1)	182	+	-	-	-	+	+	+	-
	1/8	1/8	1/4	1/4	1/4	1/4	1/4	1/4	1/4
Aver.(+)			162.8	175.3	172.0				
Aver.(-)			183.0	170.5	173.8				
Main effects			20.2	-4.8	1.8				

A computer aided analysis of the mean effects for this experiment leads to the following estimated effects and coefficients: Constant term 172.88, $A's$ main effect $= -20.25$, $B's$ main effect $= 4.75$ and $C's$ main effect $= -1.75$. These results can be readily obtained when we perform the numerical computations. An analysis of variance is of course performed automatically by the computer as well. To verify these results, note that:

$$\begin{aligned}
\text{Mean effect} &= \frac{1}{8}[(1) + a + b + c + ab + ac + bc + \text{abc}] = \\
&= \frac{1}{8}[160 + 187 + 166 + 179 + 161 + 184 + 164 + 182] \\
&= 172.9 \\
\text{Main Effect} &= \frac{1}{4}[(a - (1)) + (ab - b) + (ac - c) + (\text{abc-bc})] \\
\text{of } A &= \frac{1}{4}[(160 - 182) + (166 - 187) + (161 - 179) + (164 - 184)] \\
&= -20.25 \\
\text{Main effect} &= \frac{1}{4}[(b - (1)) + (ab - a) + (bc - c) + (\text{abc-ac})] \\
\text{of } B &= \frac{1}{4}[(187 - 182)) + (166 - 160) + (184 - 179) + (164 - 161)] \\
&= 4.75 \\
\text{Main effect} &= \frac{1}{4}[(c - (1)) + (ac - a) + (bc - b) + (\text{abc-ab})] \\
\text{of } C &= \frac{1}{4}[(179 - 182) + (161 - 160) + (184 - 187) + (164 - 166)] \\
&= -1.75
\end{aligned}$$

This implies that factors A and B have the greatest effect, while that of C is smallest. This can be used in several ways. First, factor C may be deemed negligible. If this were the case, the maximal and minimal average responses for this experimental setting might be determined on the basis of factor A and $B's$ level settings. That is, the average response is (as calculated above)

$$\bar{Y} = Y/8 = 1383/8 = 172.875 \cong 172.9,$$

while the predicted maximal and minimal responses are

$$\begin{aligned}
\text{Max} &= Y_{\text{max}} = \bar{Y} + (A_2 - \bar{Y}) + (B_1 - \bar{Y}) \\
\text{response} &= 172.9 + (183.0 - 172.9) + (175.3 - 172.9) = 172.9 + 10.1 + 2.4 \\
&= 185.4 \\
\text{Min} &= Y_{\text{min}} = \bar{Y} + (A_1 - \bar{Y}) + (B_2 - \bar{Y}) \\
\text{response} &= 172.9 + (162.8 - 172.9) + (170.5 - 172.9) = 172.9 - 10.1 - 2.4 \\
&= 160.4.
\end{aligned}$$

The interaction effects are then calculated using our previous formula. Explicitly, the AB interaction effect is calculated by:

$$\begin{aligned}\text{AB effect} &= \frac{1}{4}\{[(ab-b)-(a-(1))]+[(\text{ abc}-bc)-(ac-c)]\} \\ &= \frac{(166-187)-(160-182)+(164-184)-(161-179)}{4} \\ &= -0.25.\end{aligned}$$

This means that the increment in the response when moving from $B(-)$ to $B(+)$ is greater when A is set at its lower level $A(-)$ rather than at its $A(+)$ level (of course, provided that the statistical test declares that this difference of -0.25 is statistically meaningful and not only a sampling effect). Numerically, this means that for factor setting $A = +$, we have, $B(-) - B(+) = 160.5 - 165 = -4.5$. Wile for $A(-)$, we have: $B(-) - B(+) = 180.5 - 185.5 = -5.0$. As a result, the interaction factor for AB is given by

$$\frac{-5.0-(-4.5)}{2} = -0.25.$$

which is a negative interaction effect, as we have just seen above. Of course, these results can be graphed as well, identifying graphically the relative effects of factor levels on the response (through the response plot, the main effects and interaction graphs). This is left as an exercise, however. The results obtained through hand calculations can be confirmed by a computer aided analysis. In this case, the session shown in Table 7.19c is performed.

Table 7.19c .

MTB > FFactorial c1 =c2 c3 c4 c5 c6 c7 c8; SUBC > Alias 3.
Estimated effects and coefficients for response.

Term	Effect	Coeff.
Constant		172.88
A	-20.25	-10.12
B	4.75	2.37
C	-1.75	-0.87
AB	-0.25	-0.13
AC	1.25	0.62
BC	-0.75	-0.38
ABC	-0.75	-0.38

Note that MINITAB will perform a full factorial analysis by specifying $c1 = c2 \mid c3 \mid c4$. In this case, MINITAB will create the interaction columns and store them temporarily. An Analysis of Variance for the response is also performed automatically. With these results on hand, we can calculate the average response including the interaction effects. Interaction effects have an extremely important role in both factorial experiments and robust design. They can be used to reduce variability indirectly though proper setting of the factors that have strong positive or negative interaction effects. Their neglect can lead to erroneous presumptions regarding the response. It would be equivalent to assuming that a relationship is linear (additive) when it is not.

Problem

In a hardness process for metallic parts, the effect of the following factors at two levels were studied: A =Temperature (800 and 890^oC), B =Quenching agent (Oil vs polymer P), C = Steel type (Types C_1 and C_2). Factor B is of special interest because a substitution of oil by a polymer means important cost savings. The hardness (in Rockwell grades) for a full factorial experiment are given below. The target value for hardness is 57 units. Conduct an analysis to support the decision about the change of the quenching agent. Note that the experiment was replicated twice.

	A_1					A_1			
	B_1		B_2			B_1		B_2	
C_1	59.5	59.3	59	60.1	C_1	59	59.7	58	57.4
C_2	59.5	58.8	58	59.6	C_2	59	58.8	57	58.2

Fractional factorial experiments

In the initial stages of an investigation, a complete factorial experiment may require too many tests. For example, with seven factors and two levels, the simplest experiment requires $2^7 = 128$ tests. If we are only interested in the main effects and high order interactions are assumed to have a negligible effect (or if we are interested in specific interaction effects), it is possible to estimate these quantities by choosing a suitable fraction of the possible treatment combinations. For example half, of the 2^7 experiments requires $2^{7-1} = 64$ tests. If we were interested in the main effects only, we would then use only seven of the 128 tests. Thus, the remaining 121 tests are basically redundant. If we estimate two-way interactions only, those corresponding to $3, 4, 5, 6$ and 7-way interactions will lead to unneeded experimentation. That is, some of these interactions may not be useful for the experimenter, so we may use this fact to reduce the number of experiments we have to perform. To do so, experiments have to be selected appropriately. Such designs are called 'fractional factorial experiments'. The design and interpretation of fractional factorial experiments is not always obvious, however. Two questions are then raised:

1. What factor-level combinations to include in the experiment?
2. What effects can be estimated from the fractional experiment?

The answer to these questions are given by the procedure used for fractioning the experiment, and by clearly pointing out the alias structure. Fractional experiments incur an information loss which makes it impossible to estimate *all* of the interaction effects, resulting in a confounding of some effects. In other words, the estimation of some effects will be lumped together, and will thus be difficult to distinguish. Of course, a fraction that does not allow estimation of all the main effects cannot be used in a fractional experiment. For example, if there are three factors, for a full factorial experiment we have $2^3 = 8$, tests which cannot be reduced to $2^{3-2} = 2$, a fractional experiment with two tests, because there are only two runs which cannot be used to estimate all three main effects. Thus, a common rule for fractional experiments consists in selecting runs which *will allow an estimation of all a factors' main effects.* Once these effects can be estimated we may turn our attention to fractions that lead to two-way interaction effects. Fractional factorial experiments are extremely important in practice and therefore their study is of special interest. Box, Hunter and Hunter (1978) provide a classification of such experiments as follows.

Resolution III: Here only main effects can be estimated, two-way factor interactions are 'aliased' with main effects, which means that the information regarding main effects is 'confounded' with the information regarding the two- way factor interactions. We must then assume that these interaction effects are negligible, and use the data on hand to estimate the main effects only. To see what this means, we shall consider an example below.

Resolution IV: Main effects and some two-way interactions can be estimated while other two factor interactions are 'aliased' with the two factor interactions.

Resolution V: Here all the main effects and two-way factor interactions can be estimated, and are aliased with high order interactions. Although such fractional factorial designs provide much information, they do not reduce the number of experiments needed by much. For example, if there are five factors, a full factorial experiment which requires 32 tests can be reduced to only $2^{5-1} = 16$ tests.

To appreciate the difficulties in designing and interpreting fractional factorial experiments, we consider a number of examples.

Example: The alias structure

Here we demonstrate how to fractionate a three factor full factorial experiment, and define and develop the alias structure of the fractional experiment. In a three factor two level full factorial experiment, there are of course at least eight runs (if there are no replicates) with levels settings given as shown in Table 7.20a.

Table 7.20a.

Run	A	B	C	AB	AC	BC	ABC
1	+	-	-	-	-	+	+
2	-	+	-	-	+	-	+
3	+	+	-	+	-	-	-
4	-	-	+	+	-	-	+
5	+	-	+	-	+	-	-
6	-	+	+	-	-	+	-
7	+	+	+	+	+	+	+
8	-	-	-	+	+	+	-

Table 7.20b.

Run	A	B	C	AB	AC	BC	ABC
1	+	-	-	-	-	+	+
2	-	+	-	-	+	-	+
4	-	-	+	+	-	-	+
7	+	+	+	+	+	+	+

To obtain a fraction, we must first choose a column (generating the fraction) for which we will no longer be able to estimate its effect through the experiment. Once the column is selected, we keep all the rows with the same sign (+ for example). Explicitly, if we assume that the three-way interaction effect ABC is negligible, then dropping the rows with the - sign in the ABC column we have the results in Table 7.20*b* and thus only four runs, which were numbered $1, 2, 4$ and 7, are kept, which may be used to estimate the three main effects and the mean effect only. Note that columns A and BC, B and AC, as well as C and AB, have the same entries. In other words, the effects A and BC, for example, are confounded (i.e. they are not distinguishable when their effects are calculated). As a result, only the sum effects $(A + BC), (B + AC), (C + AB)$ can be estimated. This important feature of fractional factorial experiments is called the 'alias'. Further, A and BC, B and AC and C and AB are confounded, meaning that only their sum effect is observed. Of course, confounding makes it difficult to interpret the results of the experiment, but knowledge of the alias structure (which is essential) makes it possible to appreciate at least the meaning of the parameters estimated, and thus to make an intelligent evaluation of the experimental results. If interaction effects are known to be very weak such that the effects AB, AC, BC are negligible, then of course the fractional experiment indeed provides an estimate of the main effects. A simple method to construct the alias structure of an experiment proceeds as follows: the alias of A is given by $A(ABC) \bmod (2) = A^2BC \bmod (2) = BC$, while the main effects B and C have $B(AC) \bmod (2) = AB^2C \bmod (2) = AC$ and $C(ABC) \bmod (2) = ABC^2 \bmod (2) = AB$. A summary of the alias is thus as shown in Table 7.21.

Table 7.21.

Effect	Fraction	Alias
I	ABC	ABC
A	ABC	BC
B	ABC	AC
C	ABC	AB
AB	ABC	C
AC	ABC	B
BC	ABC	A

The polynomial estimated through such factorial experiment is no longer given by the eight equations obtained in a full factorial experiment, but by the following four equations only:

$$
\begin{aligned}
y_{11} &= (a_0 + a_{123}) + (a_1 + a_{23}) + (a_2 + a_{13}) + (a_3 + a_{12}),\\
y_{14} &= (a_0 + a_{123}) + (a_1 + a_{23}) - (a_2 + a_{13}) - (a_3 + a_{12}),\\
y_{16} &= (a_0 + a_{123}) - (a_1 + a_{23}) + (a_2 + a_{13}) - (a_3 + a_{12}),\\
y_{17} &= (a_0 + a_{123}) - (a_1 + a_{23}) - (a_2 + a_{13}) + (a_3 + a_{12}),
\end{aligned}
$$

where the four coefficients $b_0 = (a_0 + a_{123}), b_1 = (a_1 + a_{23}), b_2 = (a_2 + a_{13}), b_3 = (a_3 + a_{12})$ are unknown and estimated through the four runs of the fractional factorial experiment. In other words, once we fit the experimental results to estimate the dependent variables' effects, we will observe, for example, $(a_0 + a_{123})$ instead of (a_0), as would be the case for a full factorial experiment.

This example also demonstrates that the application of fractional experiments is not simple.

Example:

Let there be four factors A, B, C and D. If we believe that interaction effects AD, CD are negligible, we can then confound D. To do so, we proceed as follows: If $A = +, B = +$ and $C = +$ then set $D = ABC = (+)(+)(+) = +$. If $A = +, B = +$ and $C =$- then we set $D = ABC = (+)(+)(-) =$-, and so on for each of the parameter settings of the experiment. Demonstrate then that the alias structure used in the fractional experiments is as given in Table 7.22.

Table 7.22.

Main effect	A	B	C	D
Alias	BCD	ACD	ABD	ABC

2-way effect	AB	AC	AD	BC	BD	CD
Alias	CD	BD	BC	AD	AC	AB

3-way effect	ABC	ABD	ACD	BCD	$ABCD$
Alias	D	C	B	A	I

Generally, a full factorial experiment with k factors which requires 2^k runs can be reduced to 2^{k-p} experimental runs by fractioning. k experiments are required to study the main effects, while a combination of $\binom{k}{i}$ experiments is needed to study the interaction effects of i factors (parameters). Further, the weaker the interaction effects, the more we can 'fractionate' an experiment. If factorial experiments are pure, that is of the form 2^k or 3^k, there are well known methods to find the fractions and write down the 'alias' structure. The resulting designs are regular fractional factorial designs which are always orthogonal or completely confounded with a number of runs equalling a power of 2, or $2, 4, 8, 16, 32, 64$, etc.

Problem

The results for a three factors half factorial design are given in Table 7.23.

Table 7.23.

Run	A	B	C	Response
1	-1	-1	1	6
2	1	-1	-1	12
3	-1	1	-1	8
4	1	1	1	10

What is the alias structure of this experiment, and prove that the coefficients for this model are given by: $a_0 = 9, a_1 = 2, a_2 = 0$ and $a_3 = -1$? Once these results have been obtained by hand calculations, perform the appropriate analysis using the computer.

Example: Experimental design in services

Experimental design can be of great use in the design and management of services. In fact, the large number of variables involved in services and the intricate (and interactive) relationships between these variables make it an ideal candidate for experimental design. Here, we shall consider a simple application to demonstrate the usefulness of this approach.

We have seen earlier (Chapter 2) that SERVQUAL suggests that we measure quality along five dimension-factor types: (1) equipment, personnel attributes (look, neatness etc.), the physical environment, etc., (2) reliability, (3) responsiveness, or the propensity to respond to clients requests, (4) 'assurance', or the potential to induce a sense of security for the client, and finally, (5) empathy, or the special attention given to the client. On this basis, a service system was designed using five factors measures each at two levels. To evaluate the response of the service system, a questionnaire was prepared for a number of customers who were asked to express their degree of satisfaction with a specific factors-levels combination. To assess alternative service configurations, a chain of hotels has decided to design experiments which would tell it which factors are most important, and devise the scheme for selecting a 'best' approach to servicing its customers. At first, a full factorial experiment was considered with two levels each. The factors selected, based on brainstorming and SERVQUAL recommendations, are given in Table 7.24. Response was evaluated by a questionnaire that would be prepared, and whose purpose was to evaluate consumer satisfaction on the one hand and the profits realized under each configuration on the other. Each experiment would be run for five months in each hotel location, treating each month as an independent experiment.

Table 7.24

Factor	Level 1 (+)	Level 2 (-)
Equipment Factor *A*	Antique furniture	Modern furniture
Reliability Factor *B*	Non-standardized uniforms in all hotels	Standardized uniforms in all hotels
Responsiveness Factor *C*	Individual service attendance for all customers	Standardized services for all customers
Assurance Factor *D*	Satisfaction guaranteed or money back	No such service guarantees
Empathy Factor *E*	Special training to all employees on manners and human relations	No such training on manners and human relations for employees

Of course, a full factorial design involves $2^5 = 32$ experimental runs (months) replicated five months in each location, which required $5 * 32 = 160$ experiment months. This was deemed too costly, and consulting with a statistician led to the conclusion that a fractional factorial experiment (Taguchi $L8$) would be satisfactory. The possibility of changing one factor at a time seemed too naive and required far too much experimentation. As a result, using a fractional experiment halved twice, or $2^{5-2} = 8$ experimental runs (each run for five months, treated independently) led to the results in Table 7.25, where satisfaction estimates were calculated using a sample of 50 questionnaires while profits were calculated on the basis of monthly income and expenses.

Table 7.25.

Run	A	B	C	D	E	Satisf. Mean	Std. dev.	Profits Mean	Std. dev.
1	+	+	+	+	+	40	6	20	4
2	+	+	+	-	-	35	4	25	6
3	+	-	-	+	+	28	6	20	5
4	+	-	-	-	-	25	7	28	7
5	-	+	-	+	-	32	4	18	4
6	-	+	-	-	+	30	5	17	3
7	-	-	+	+	-	26	3	30	9
8	-	-	+	-	+	33	5	14	6

On the basis of these results, we can analyse the alternative service factors-levels combinations. As we can see, the factor combination in run 1 is highest with a mean score of 40 (out of 50), while the coefficient of variation is $6/40$. If we use the coefficient of variation as an index, then we see that the seventh alternative is preferred ($= 3/26$)! These numbers point out that the choice of service factors-levels combinations are a function of the objective used, and that experimental design does not solve the problem of decision-making but provides estimates on the basis of which the decision-making problem can be handled. But, to do so still requires application of the classical tools of analysis which are applied in business management. We face a similar problem when analysing the profits performance factors-levels combinations. Mean profits are also highest for the seventh experimental run. Note that the standard deviation is also very large, thus a risk averse decision maker will avoid such an alternative. If we maximize the 'signal to noise ratio', the alternative selected will then be the sixth one, providing a score of $17/3 = 5.66$. It is not clear, however, that this is the best decision from a managerial and business point of view. We can thus conclude that the decision making problem, for service factors-levels combinations, is indeed far more difficult that presumed here. Of course, the more robust the service the better, but at what cost? The more consumers who are satisfied and with greater confidence the better, but at what cost? These are questions which are only rendered specific, but not solved through experimental design.

Computer aided example

To generate a full factorial design, we have to specify the number of factors in the design, the number of runs, the number of blocks and the number of centre points (if the design has more than two levels) to be added to the design. If the design is blocked, the centre points are divided equally among the blocks. If the number of centre points specified is not a multiple of the number of blocks, then each of the last few blocks will have one less point than the other blocks. Runs can be randomized or not in the data matrix. If we specify blocks, randomization is done separately within each block and then the blocks are randomized. Fractional factorial design also provides a number of options, including the number of replications for corner points, the fraction to be used for design generation, and the order of interactions to be included. To construct the alias structure, we can choose to display all interactions for designs with 2 to 6 factors, up to three-way interactions for 7 to 10 factors, and up to two-way interactions for 11 to 15 factors. We can also specify the highest order interaction to print in the alias table.

Suppose we have four factors and we seek an eight runs experiment (with no replicates). Further, let's specify that runs are performed in a random manner. The resulting experiment is then a Resolution IV experiment with a fraction 1/2. If we use the design generator $D = ABC$, then the following alias structure and data matrix in Table 7.26 are generated.

Table 7.26: Fractional factorial design.

MTB > FFDesign 4 8; SUBC> Randomize; SUBC> Brief 4.
Factors: 4, Design: 4, 8, Resolution: IV
Runs:8, Replicates: 1, Fraction: 1/2; Blocks: none Center points: 0
Design Generators: $D = ABC$; Defining Relation: $I = ABCD$
Alias Structure: $I+ ABCD$, $A+ BCD$, $B+ ACD$, $C+ ABD$, $D+ ABC$, $AB+CD, AC+BD, AD+BC$

Data Matrix (randomized)

Run	A	B	C	D
1	−	−	−	−
2	−	+	+	+
3	+	+	+	+
4	−	+	−	+
5	+	−	−	+
6	+	−	+	−
7	+	+	−	−
8	−	−	+	−

If eight runs are performed and the results fitted to a polynomial, we will then observe that $A's$ main effect will in fact be the effects of $A+BCD$ (and similarly for the other effects as indicated above).

Example

In the production of adhesives, it is important to evaluate the effects of the polymerization process on the critical properties of the adhesive. Five factors were defined as being most important. These are A = Polymerization time, B = Mixing temperature, C = Initiator-emulsion relation, D = Alcohol and finally, E = Amount of water. A full factorial experiment requires 32 experiments which is deemed too costly. For this reason, a fraction of $2^{5-1} = 16$ runs is being considered. This fraction was selected because it is a resolution V experiment and allows an estimation of both all the main and 2-letter interaction effects (which are deemed sufficient in this case). The relevant response variable of interest is viscosity, for which the results in Table 7.27 were obtained.

Table 7.27

Run	*A*	*B*	*C*	*D*	*E*	*y*	Run	*A*	*B*	*C*	*D*	*E*	*y*
a	+	-	-	-	-	1020	*e*	-	-	-	-	+	1310
b	-	+	-	-	-	1770	abe	+	+	-	-	+	621
c	-	-	+	-	-	1440	ace	+	-	+	-	+	1330
abc	+	+	+	-	-	1250	bce	-	+	+	-	+	1370
d	-	-	-	+	-	1220	ade	+	-	-	+	+	1490
abd	+	+	-	+	-	1550	bde	-	+	-	+	+	1470
acd	+	-	+	+	-	2240	cde	-	-	+	+	+	1500
bcd	-	+	+	+	-	1700	abcde	+	+	+	+	+	1430

A computer aided analysis of these results provides the estimates in Table 7.28.

Table 7.28: Estimated effects and coefficients for response.

Term	Effect	Coeff.
Constant		1419.4
A	-106.1	-53.1
B	-48.6	-24.3
C	226.1	113.1
D	311.1	155.6
E	-208.6	-104.3
AB	-258.6	-129.3
AC	166.1	83.1
AD	311.1	155.6
AE	-88.6	-44.3
BC	-141.4	-70.7
BD	-26.4	-13.2
BE	-136.1	-68.1
CD	58.9	29.4
CE	-41.4	-20.7
DE	3.6	1.8

An analysis of variance would normally be required. A normal plot was generated to screen the effects, as shown in Figure 7.7. Effects far away from the straight line are considered significant.

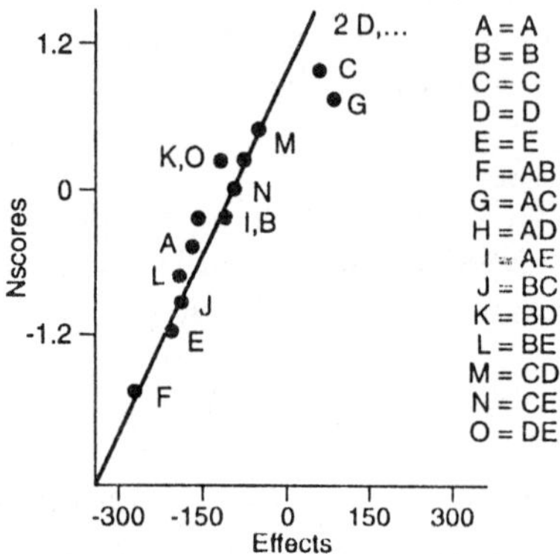

Figure 7.7: Normalized factor scores.

On the basis of this analysis, the more important factors for viscosity are found to be C, D, AC and AD. In other words, assuming that a high viscosity is desired, we should set A, C and D at their high level, while B and E are at their low level. The response equation in this case is given by

$$
\begin{aligned}
Y &= 1419.4 - 53.1x_1 + 24.3x_2 + 113.1x_3 + 155.6x_4 - 104.3x_5 \\
&- 129.3x_1x_2 + 83.1x_1x_3 + 155.6x_1x_4 - 44.3x_1x_5 - 70.7x_2x_3 \\
&- 13.2x_2x_4 - 68.1x_2x_5 + 29.4x_3x_2 - 29.4x_3x_5 + 1.8x_4x_5 \\
&\quad \text{with } x_1, x_2, x_3, x_4, x_5 \in \{0, 1\}.
\end{aligned}
$$

Problem

Interpret the results obtained above using a response plot, as well as main effects and interaction graphs.

Plackett-Burman (PB) designs

Plackett-Burman (1946) designs are another important class of fractional factorial experiments which are orthogonal arrays and (Resolution III) balanced two-level designs as well (see also Goupy, 1990). These designs are used to estimate the main effects only, and are important when it is necessary to perform experiments with a large number of factors while using few runs. The mathematical model implied by PB designs is

$$y = a_0 + a_1x_1 + a_2x_2 + a_3x_3 + a_4x_4 + \ldots . + a_nx_n.$$

Eight runs may be sufficient for seven factors, while 12 runs can be used for 11 factors. PB designs provide the least number of values required to solve the system of linear equations (where levels are set to their appropriate values). Experimental designs corresponding to these situations are given in Table 7.29.

Table 7.29: Plackett-Burman designs

Run	A	B	C	D	E	F	G
1	+	-	-	+	-	+	+
2	+	+	-	-	+	-	+
3	+	+	+	-	-	+	-
4	-	+	+	+	-	-	+
5	+	-	+	+	+	-	-
6	-	+	-	+	+	+	-
7	-	-	+	-	+	+	+
8	-	-	-	-	-	-	-

Run	A	*B*	*C*	*D*	*E*	*F*	*G*	*H*	I	*J*	*K*
1	+	-	+	-	-	-	+	+	+	-	+
2	+	+	-	+	-	-	-	+	+	+	-
3	-	+	+	-	+	-	-	-	+	+	+
4	+	-	+	+	-	+	-	-	-	+	+
5	+	+	-	+	+	-	+	-	-	-	+
6	+	+	+	-	+	+	-	+	-	-	-
7	-	+	+	+	-	+	+	-	+	-	-
8	-	-	+	+	+	-	+	+	-	+	-
9	-	-	-	+	+	+	-	+	+	-	+
10	+	-	-	-	+	+	+	-	+	+	-
11	-	-	-	-	-	+	+	+	-	+	+
12	-	-	-	-	-	-	-	-	-	-	-

Note that the PB design in Table 7.29 with $N = 8$ runs is essentially the fractional factorial experiment $2^{7-4} = 8$.

Computer aided example

PB designs are, as stated earlier, orthogonal designs providing main effects estimates. A list of available Plackett-Burman designs is provided by MINITAB. To obtain a PB design, we first specify the number of factors, then the number of runs (factors must be less than the number of runs, however). The design generated is based on the number of runs, and must be specified as a multiple of 4 ranging from 4 to 48. If the number of runs is not specified, it is set to the smallest possible value for the specified number of factors. A PB design with four factors and 12 runs is given as shown in Table 7.30.

Table 7.30: Data matrix (randomized).

Run	*A*	*B*	*C*	*D*	Run	*A*	*B*	*C*	*D*	Run	*A*	*B*	*C*	*D*
1	+	+	-	+	5	-	-	-	+	9	+	-	+	-
2	-	+	-	-	6	+	-	+	+	10	-	+	+	-
3	-	+	+	+	7	-	-	+	+	11	+	+	+	-
4	-	-	-	-	8	+	-	-	-	12	+	+	-	+

Of course, once the responses to such an experiment are performed, we can fit a linear equation and obtain the main effects estimates.

Problem

Define the 28 runs of a 16 factor PB experiment.

Central composite design (CCD)

Design involving three levels is used often in industry. Its importance arises due to the need to experiment with three levels when we study the factors' curvature. There are both 3^k full factorial designs and incomplete factorial designs. For fractions in the series 3^{k-p}, and when interaction effects are required, the number of runs is very large. An important alternative to this regular fraction is a class of experiments called *Central Composite Designs (CCD).* Such designs require a minimum of 15 runs (however, if only a single centre point is used additional statistical properties can be obtained if several central points are used), so all the main effects and two factor interactions can be estimated. This type of design is formed by augmenting a factorial experiment with axial points of the form $(0, 0, .., \alpha, , \ldots 0)$. By the appropriate selection of α, the design can be made *rotatable.* This means that the response variance will be invariant to the rotation of the coordinate axes in the factors space. Thus, in three factor CCD, the centre point is the centroid of a cube, and runs correspond to a distance α from this centroid located at the cube's sides. Figure 7.8 shows a rotatable design for two and three factors. The usefulness of such a design arises in RSM (as will be seen later), since it allows the estimation of a full second order degree polynomial in k factors when the factorial part is at least a resolution V fraction (Box and Draper, 1977, 1987, 1990). When factor levels in one experiment do not have the same number of levels, we obtain mixed factorial experiments (for example, some factors may have two levels while others have three or more). These experiments are not easy to 'fractionate', however. Typically, for 2^m3^n mixed experiments we could first fractionate each of the 2^m and 3^n factorials, and then combine them.

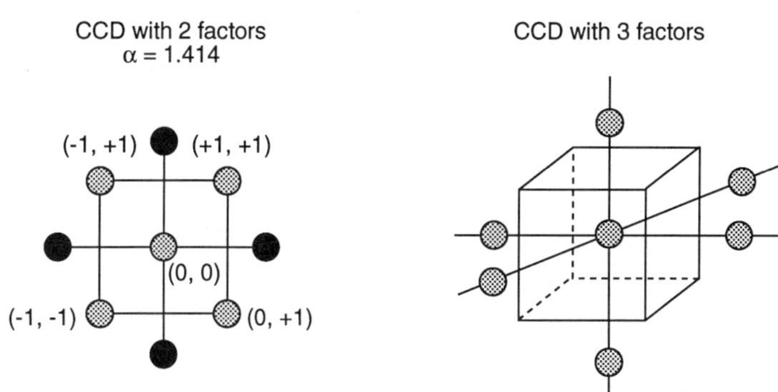

Figure 7.8: Rotatable CCD designs.

Example

Consider a two factors CCD. There are, as seen in Figure 7.8 only nine points, which means that there are nine runs to perform. These are given by Table 7.31.

Table 7.31: The runs of a two-factor CCD.

Run	Factor A	Factor B
1	-1	-1
2	+1	-1
3	-1	+1
4	+1	+1
5	0	0
6	$-\alpha$	0
7	$+\alpha$	0
8	0	$-\alpha$
9	0	$+\alpha$

With such an experiment, and given responses R for each of these runs, it is possible to fit the responses obtained to the quadratic curve

$$y = a_0 + a_1x_1 + a_2x_2 + a_{12}x_1x_2 + a_{11}x_1^2 + a_{22}x_2^2.$$

Table 7.32: Experimental matrix of a two-factor CCD

x_1	x_2	x_1x_2	x_1^2	x_2^2	1
-1	-1	1	1	1	1
+1	-1	-1	1	1	1
-1	+1	-1	1	1	1
+1	+1	+1	1	1	1
0	0	0	0	0	1
$-\alpha$	0	0	α^2	0	1
$+\alpha$	0	0	α^2	0	1
0	$-\alpha$	0	0	α^2	1
0	$+\alpha$	0	0	α^2	1

The experimental matrix X of a two factors CCD is thus as shown in Table 7.32 which is over-specified, since it has six variables unknown. Further, there is no clear way to determine α. The equations, in matrix notation, can be written as follows: $Y = XA$. Now, if we multiply this matrix by its transpose $X^T$and solve for the matrix A which has six parameters, a solution for α can be found (since $X^TY = X^TX\mathcal{A}$, where X^TX is a square 6×6 matrix and therefore invertible). As a result,

$$A = (X^TX)^{-1}X^TY,$$

which provides the equation in α.

Problem
Repeat this analysis for a three factors experiment, and show that the least number of runs needed for such an experiments is 15.

Computer aided example for a CCD design

MINITAB can generate central composite designs for 2 to 6 factors which can then be used to fit the data to quadratic curves (for Response Surface Analysis), and for linear and nonlinear regression. The computer uses as a default the full factorial design in the cube portion of the design, although by proper specification the program can generate fractioned experiments. Runs can be randomized and, if blocks are specified, runs are randomized within blocks. MINITAB allows the addition of centre points by specifying a value for α. When the design is blocked, the centre points are divided equally among the blocks. If the number of centre points specified is not a multiple of the number of blocks, then each of the last few blocks will have one less point than the other blocks. MINITAB's default is to determine the number of centre points and the value of α. Default values of α provide orthogonal blocking and whenever possible, rotatability. If we choose a face-centred design, $\alpha = 1$, a value of less than 1 places the axial points inside the cube; a value greater than 1 places them outside the cube.

Assume four factors and three blocks. The CCD which results from a computer aided session is outlined in Table 7.33. The data matrix is also included.

Table 7.33: Central composite design.

MTB > CCDesign 4; SUBC> Blocks 3; SUBC> Randomize; SUBC> Brief 3.

Factors: 4, Blocks: 3, Center points in cube: 4

Runs: 30, Alpha: 2.000, Center points in star: 2

Data Matrix (randomized).

Run	Block	*A*	*B*	*C*	*D*	Run	Block	*A*	*B*	*C*	*D*
1	1	1	1	-1	-1	9	1	1	1	1	1
2	1	0	0	0	0	10	1	-1	-1	-1	-1
3	1	1	-1	1	-1	11	2	0	0	0	0
4	1	-1	1	-1	1	12	2	1	1	-1	1
5	1	-1	-1	1	1	13	2	-1	-1	-1	1
6	1	0	0	0	0	14	2	-1	-1	-1	-1
7	1	1	-1	-1	1	15	2	-1	1	1	1
8	1	-1	1	1	-1	16	2	0	0	0	0

Run	Block	*A*	*B*	*C*	*D*	Run	Block	*A*	*B*	*C*	*D*
17	2	-1	-1	1	-1	24	3	0	0	0	0
18	2	1	-1	1	1	25	3	0	-2	0	0
19	2	1	-1	-1	-1	26	3	0	2	0	0
20	2	1	1	1	-1	27	3	0	0	0	0
21	3	0	0	-2	0	28	3	-2	0	0	0
22	3	0	0	0	-2	29	3	0	0	2	0
23	3	0	0	0	2	30	3	2	0	0	0

Problem

Generate the data matrix for a CCD with three factors and two blocks. Verify that there are 20 runs and four centre points in a cube, and that $\alpha = 1.682$. To verify these results, use a computer.

Box-Behnken design

Box-Behnken designs are three levels designs. For each design there is at most one way to block. The three factors design cannot be blocked, but four factors can be run in three blocks, and 5, 6 or 7 factors can each be run in two blocks. We can have a number of centre points in such a design. If the design is blocked, the centre points are divided equally among the blocks. If, again, the number of center points is not a multiple of the number of blocks, then each of the last few blocks will have one less point than the other blocks.

Taguchi's orthogonal-outer array designs

One of the more important contributions of Taguchi to experimental design has been the popular introduction of fractional factorial design in industry. In particular, Taguchi devised orthogonal designs with respect to the main effects, and may contain some confounded two-way interactions. The design's orthogonality allows a more precise interpretation of results, and is therefore a useful feature for experimental designs. Both the traditional and Taguchi approaches use brainstorming as the means to select variables. Taguchi's experiments' designation is given in Table 7.34 where the levels notation represents the maximum number of variables assuming no interactions. Note that Taguchi uses both two and three level experiments.

Table 7.34: Some of Taguchi's designs.

Taguchi's Designs	2 Levels	3 Levels
*L*4	3	
*L*8	7	
*L*9		4
*L*12	11	
*L*16	15	
*L*18	1	7
*L*27		13

Some designs may, of course, be generated by the computer. Otherwise, there are publications (such as those of the American Supplier Institute) which have compounded all Taguchi's designs. Some designs are given below.

Table 7.35: Specific Taguchi's designs.

$L_4(2^3)$ Runs	1	2	3
1	1	1	1
2	1	2	2
3	2	1	2
4	2	2	1
	a	*b*	ab

$L_8(2^7)$ Runs	1	2	3	4	5	6	7
1	1	1	1	1	1	1	1
2	1	1	1	2	2	2	2
3	1	2	2	1	1	2	2
4	1	2	2	2	2	1	1
5	2	1	2	1	2	1	2
6	2	1	2	2	1	2	1
7	2	2	1	1	2	2	1
8	2	2	1	2	1	1	2
	a	*b*	ab	*c*	ac	bc	abc

$L_8(3^4)$ Runs	1	2	3	4
1	1	1	1	1
2	1	2	2	2
3	1	3	3	3
4	2	1	2	3
5	2	2	3	1
6	2	3	1	2
7	3	1	3	2
8	3	2	1	3
9	3	3	2	1
	a	*b*	ab	ab^2

7.5 Robust design

Once experiments have been performed and results are, from a statistical point of view, satisfactory, it is possible to decide which design, which process operating condition, which system configuration, etc. to adopt. Of course, if no results are satisfactory, there may be a number of reasons. For example, some important factors may have been neglected (i.e. there was improper factor screening), the experiments were poorly performed so the results are misleading, the levels were badly selected so that even if results are acceptable they are not acceptable from an operational point of view, and so on. Practically, when a result is clearly 'better', there are few problems in selecting the optimal factor-levels setting. Graphical techniques can then be used to highlight the advantage of the desirable result. Problems arise in two circumstances. First, when there are several good solutions and a strategic decision must be made to reach such a solution. (For example, we may have two factor settings leading, on the one hand, to a desirable 'on-target' result, but with a large variability, and on the other, a factor setting which is 'off- target' but with a very small variability.) Concepts such as Taguchi's Signal/Noise (S/N) ratio are considered below and attempt to resolve this dilemma. However, it is important to remember that a design (or parameter) selection is a decision problem under uncertainty which requires that the designer is aware of the risks implied in selecting a particular design. Practically, once experiments are performed, the number of design alternatives is generally reduced to a few, on which we might concentrate our experimental/design effort through replication and the application of appropriate decision criteria. In general, we will state that robustness implies 'choice resistance to design uncertainty', and it will be important for two reasons: first, it assures that a given design will perform as specified over a broad range of (uncontrollable) parameters; and second, it reduces the amount of learning required about a potential design, since in a robust system the value of additional experimentation is smaller. When experimentation is costly, it can be stopped before all the relevant aspects of the response function are known. There are several ways to deal with the design of robust systems that we discuss through problems and examples.

Problems

1. Consider a process which consists of m components, each denoted by $x_i, i = 1, 2, \ldots, m$. Let the system's performance be a function of these components, that is $y = f(x_1, x_2, \ldots, x_m)$. For an operating system, it is necessary that $x_i = x_i^*$, which denotes a standard to be met in order to ensure the system operation. Such a process will be called completely non-robust. Now, say that new components are designed allowing operations to continue in a range of $2e_i$ centred at x_i^*. Thus, operations continue as long as $x_i = x_i^* \mp e_i$. The larger e_i, the costlier is the component to produce. For simplicity, assume an approximate quadratic function for $f(.)$, and state that the variability of a component i is defined by a Weibull probability distribution whose mean is x_i^* and whose standard deviation is σ_i. On the basis of this information, construct an estimate for the mean and the variance of the performance y. How would you use this information to construct a standard specification for the performance y (within 95% confidence interval)? Can you define the optimization problem to design the standard's operating limits e_i?

2. Experimental design in agriculture dates back to R.A. Fisher's work in the 1920*s*(Fisher, 1925). Its application to *robust design* in agricultural research is more recent, however. Design problems arise when it is necessary to develop or select plants that can produce uniform produce in a wide range of conditions (land, weather, etc.). It can also be used to select plants that can be robust to problems of excess irrigation or rain, a lack of water, cold, sun and general weather uncertainty. When plants have to be grown over large areas, this becomes a crucial factor. For an agro-industrial enterprise, it is particularly useful to have produce which is similar even if it has grown in widely differing areas. For example, carrots may have to be small and have a similar taste and composition. Their homogeneity and conformance may define the crop quality (and thus fetch a higher price). Too great a variability can lead to problems in their industrial treatment and to consumers' perceptions that they are of a poor quality. In this sense, robustness is insensitivity to deviation from the assumptions made regarding the variables which cannot be controlled. If we assume that θ is a given characteristic and we let ϵ be a deviation from this standard, and if deviation from the desired uniformity level (of carrots) is given by y, then $y = f(\theta + \epsilon)$ is a simple way to represent such a relationship. Let $Ey = \mu = Ef(\theta + \epsilon) \cong F(\theta, \sigma^2)$ with $\partial\mu/\partial\sigma^2 > 0$. If $\partial\mu/\partial\sigma^2$ is small, it is reasonable to claim that deviations ϵ from the characteristic θ do not affect the performance characteristic y, and thus the process is robust with respect to mean performance. By the same token, if we consider the characteristic variability $\text{var}(y) = \text{var}[f(\theta + \epsilon)] \cong G(\theta, \sigma^2)$, and if $\partial G/\partial\sigma^2$ is small, the process variability is robust with respect to variations in the parameter θ.

Discuss and compare other means to reach robust designs, such as increasing parts reliability, system redundancy, having a greater number of backups to support a system when it breaks down, FMECA, and other means used to manage business and operational risk.

Taguchi's robust inner-outer arrays design

Taguchi's robust or parameter design approach seeks a system's response which is both desired and insensitive to a number of uncontrollable factors representing the 'outer world' (i.e. the consumer and the real environment to which the product, system or design will be subjected). To do so, Taguchi first defines two sets of factors: (1) 'Design factors' assigned to an inner array, which are variables that can be completely controlled; and (2) 'External factors' assigned to outer arrays that will form the cross-product design associated with the Taguchi method. Of course, external factors are variables that cannot be controlled and are therefore the means to introduce noise into the system. For this reason, and to ensure a performance prediction with low variability, Taguchi seeks to determine 'optimal levels' of the design (controllable) factors which are insensitive to the external array (external factors) variations. Variation in the external factors is also introduced through an experimental design such that the response to a given set of parameters (controllable factors setting) will be evaluated along a number of situations prescribed by the experimental framework for the external (uncontrollable factors) array. This procedure is adopted because it will allow selection of the optimal factor setting under external factors variation. Once response data is available, Taguchi recommends the use of a Signal to Noise (S/N) ratio to determine the optimal parameters design.

The implications of Taguchi's S/N ratio index are summarized by three design principles: (1) Produce on Target Mean; (2) Minimize the process variance, and (3) Minimize the sensitivity of the performance when it is put to use (or robustness). These are often summarized by statements such as 'The smaller (variability) the better', 'The larger the better' and 'On target is best'. Technically, Taguchi uses three ratios to quantify these statements. According to Taguchi, robust products are assumed to provide a strong 'signal' (performance) regardless of the 'noise' (the environment's variability). Thus, a signal/noise ratio can be used as a criterion for designing quality in the product. Such an approach resembles the 'Portfolio Approach', well known by business and finance students. Essentially, portfolio problems consist in selecting an allocation strategy among n competing alternatives, each yielding an uncertain payoff. Consider, for example, a set of n attributes for which there is a measure of performance p_i that is assumed to be random. These attributes are correlated, however, and therefore if u is a vector of design variables (i.e. that we can control), we can assume that (using vector notation)

$$E(p) = \mu(u), \ \text{var}\ (p) = \Sigma(u).$$

where Σ is a variance-covariance matrix. Let the standards be p^*, thus deviations from the standard are $p - p^*$. The problem consists in selecting a vector of control variables u which will provide 'the best performance for the product or system'. One approach is to consider the expected minimization of the squared variation such that

$$\min E(p - p^*)^2 = (\mu(u) - p^*)^2 + \Sigma(u) \ \ \text{Subject to } u \in U.$$

There are then three ways to solve this problem: (1) 'Be on target' by setting $\mu(u) = p^*$ and thus $(\mu(u) - p^*)^2 = 0$, (2) Minimizing variability by $\Sigma(u)$ through the selection of u, and finally, (3) through robustness by rendering Σ very small regardless of the controls and environmental operating conditions. Further, use of orthogonal experiments will reduce the effect of factor covariations in estimating the responses. The classical solution of this problem (see the appendix in Chapter 4) by the portfolio approach consists of defining explicitly two alternatives. First, define the useful signal as $E(p)$ and maximize it, or

$$p^* = \max E(p) \text{ Subject to var } (p) = \beta,$$

which provides a set of performances p as a function of the parameter β. This is equivalent to drawing a curve of attributes which will possess a common variability. Inversely, we may seek a design which will minimize the variability while at the same time provide a constraint for the system performance to a given level, say λ. In this case, we have

$$\Sigma^* = \min \text{ var } (p) \text{ Subject to } E(p) = \lambda.$$

This will provide another curve, as shown in Figure 7.9. We note that there is a set of common points which solves both problems. These points are called the 'efficiency set', and therefore provide a range of values which both maximize the signal and minimize the noise (in the sense of variability).

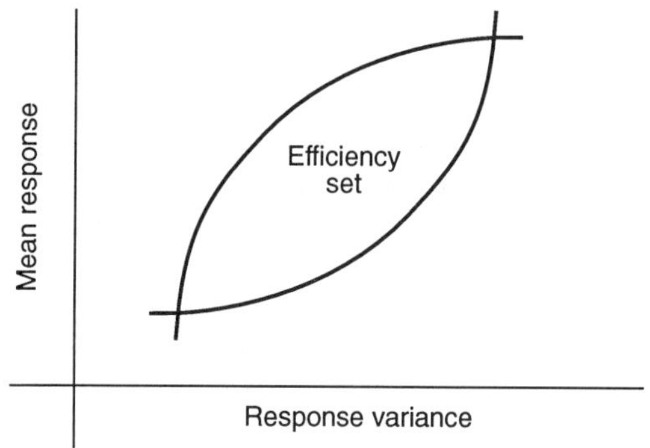

Figure 7.9: The efficiency set.

In designing quality, a similar approach is followed using a different language. Prior to setting manufacturing tolerances, a quality loss function is defined. Suppose that a product has desirable characteristics, which we call 'targets'. Thus, if τ are quantitative measures of targets, and if the true characteristics turn out to be some random values $\tilde{m}$, then the difference $\tilde{m}-\tau$ is a measure of the difference between 'actual' and 'desired' performance. The signal part of the performance is the deterministic part of $\tilde{m}$, say $\bar{m}$, while the noise part is a random variable, say ϵ, whose mean is now assumed to be zero and whose variance is σ^2. In this sense, the difference $\delta = \tilde{m} - \tau$ can be written as $\delta = (m - \tau) + \epsilon$. The squared deviation is assumed to be proportional to the cost. Thus, if c is the cost of counter-measures that might be employed in a factory to control quality, we can define a quadratic loss function $L = c\delta^2 = c[(\bar{m} - \tau) + \epsilon]^2$ whose expectation is $EL = c(\bar{m} - \tau)^2 + c^2\sigma^2$. *If the control of quality consists of the minimization of an expected quality loss function EL*, then this can be achieved in two ways, as seen earlier:

- Set the product parameters on target, or $\bar{m} = \tau$ (maximize the signal).
- Reduce the noise to its least level or $\sigma^2 = 0$ (minimize the noise).

The Taguchi quality imperatives are derived from this function. It becomes a little more complex when we understand that $\bar{m}$ and σ^2 are defined in terms of a number of factors, some of which may be controllable while others may not. If we divide EL by σ^2, we have $EL/\sigma^2 = c(\bar{m}-\tau)^2/\sigma^2 + c^2$, and, therefore, minimization of the quadratic loss function is equivalent to a minimization of the 'signal to noise ratio' $S/N = (\bar{m}-\tau)^2/\sigma^2$. Further, minimizing signal/noise ratio is equivalent to Min MSE $= E(\epsilon^2), \epsilon = (m-\tau)/\sigma$. Equivalently, instead of minimizing the MSE, Taguchi suggests that we maximize the '-log' of MSE, given by Maximizing $-10\log(\text{MSE})$, which is often used by engineers. The corresponding sampling statistic, consisting of observed ϵ_i's, then leads to

$$\text{Maximize } -10\log\sum_{i=1}^{n}(\epsilon_i^2/n).$$

Practically, once experimental responses are available, Taguchi uses a set of three SN ratios and parameter design is performed in two stages: first, minimize the variability; then maximize the 'on-target' objective. The 'on–target' objective is given by the SN_t ratio

$$SN_t = 10\log[\frac{\bar{y}^2}{s^2}] \text{ or 'Nominal the Best'},$$

where SN_t measures the ratio of the mean response squared $\bar{y}^2$ (over the set of experimental variations in the external array) and the response estimated variance s^2. The measurement of variability, however, is given in terms of the following SN_s and SN_l ratios:

$$SN_s = -10\log\sum_{i=1}^{n}(y_i^2/n) \text{or 'The Smaller the Better'}$$

$$SN_l = -10\log\sum_{i=1}^{n}(1/y_i^2 n) \text{ or 'The Larger the Better'}$$

The use of SN ratios is misleading, however (see also Montgomery, 1991, for an extensive discussion), and is subject to a great deal of criticism. For example, maximizing the ratio SN_t is supposed to minimize the variability. This is recommended by Taguchi because he states that the mean and the standard deviation are often related, and thus minimizing the standard deviation directly can lead to a neglecting of the signal. To circumvent these effects, Taguchi recommends a two step procedure. First, finding the parameter setting that maximizes the SN_t, and only then finding the set of factors that has a significant effect on the mean but does not influence the SN_t ratio, and using these factors to bring the mean on-target. It has been shown that, if we were to transform the data and take its logarithm, then analysis of the standard deviation of the transformed data is equivalent to Taguchi's procedure. In other words, a logarithmic transformation of data separates mean and dispersion effects which, in fact, is not the case. To maintain the applicability of this procedure it would then be necessary to select a transformation of data which could establish a separability of the mean and dispersion effects. Such transformations are considered in the appendix. The ratios SN_s and SN_l are even more questionable. First, they will be sensitive to outliers and confound location and dispersion effects (as with the SN_t ratio). The Taguchi approach has been criticized further, as we shall see later on. It is, nevertheless, extremely useful and considered acceptable in many industrial situations. Applications and problems are considered below.

Example:

To design a paper feeder, Taguchi identifies control factors such as the roller material, the roller diameter, the type of springs used, roller contact point and roller tread design. The uncontrollable factors arising from its use might include the paper type, size, warps, surface and alignment. In addition, factors such as humidity, stack height, roller wear and such like are considered as factors which are not controllable. Having defined a quality index of performance such as the uniformity of the service rendered, the design problem consists in selecting the controllable factor combination which ensure that the paper feeder always operates, i.e. under a designed set of uncontrollable conditions. If this can be achieved, then there is no need for inspection and controls. *In this sense, robust design is a preventive approach to the management of quality, since it solves problems before they arise.*

Application of the Taguchi approach

Application of the Taguchi approach is based on the definition of two sets of arrays (factors), an internal-control array and an external-non-controllable array. For each experimental setting based on the external array, an experiment based on the internal array experimental setting is performed. This results in a crossed experimental design. Responses are then evaluated in terms of the mean, the variance (and the Signal to Noise ratios obtained through experimental replication). To demonstrate this procedure, it is best to consider a simple example. Say that we have an experimental setting with three factors in the inner array, A, B and C and three factors in the outer array, A', B' and C'. We shall then use an $L8$

Taguchi experiment for the outer array and an $L4$ Taguchi experiment for the inner array. These experiments are performed on two levels coded by (1,2) as shown in Table 7.36. They represent a half factorial experiment of the inner three factors and a full factorial experiment of the outer array (with eight runs). Results of such an experiment are given in Table 7.37 with the set of eight responses denoted by $R_i, i = 1, 2, \ldots 8$ for each factor-level setting of the outer array. That is, the first response 5.1 is obtained when we set the inner array to levels (1,1,1), while the outer array is also set to levels (1,1,1). The response 8.3 is obtained when the inner array is set to (2,1,2) and the outer array to $(1, 2, 2)$, and so on.

Table 7.36: An inner-outer array full factorial design.

				A'	1	1	1	2	2	2	2	2
				B'	1	1	2	1	1	1	2	2
				C'	1	2	2	1	2	1	1	2
Run	A	B	C		R_1	R_2	R_3	R_4	R_5	R_6	R_7	R_8
1	1	1	1		5.1	3.2	6.4	6.9	6.8	6.8	7.2	6.4
2	1	2	2		5.4	5.9	6.2	7.8	8.3	8.3	9.1	7.4
3	2	1	2		7.2	7.4	8.3	6.9	7.1	7.1	6.5	7.6
4	2	2	1		8.2	7.9	8.5	7.7	7.5	7.5	7.2	8.1

The mean and standard deviation of the responses and for each (inner array) experimental setting were then calculated, and are summarized in the third and fourth columns of Table 7.37, respectively, while the signal to noise ratios (SN_t, SN_l, SN_s) were calculated and inserted in the fifth, sixth and seventh columns.

Table 7.37: Experimental results and signal/noise ratios.

Run	A	B	C	Mean	Std. Dev	SN_t	SN_l	SN_s
1	1	1	1	6.100	1.33202	30.43	33.94	-36.57
2	1	2	2	7.225	1.27588	34.67	38.68	-39.82
3	2	1	2	7.150	0.65247	47.88	39.12	-39.41
4	2	2	1	7.975	0.50356	55.24	41.42	-41.56

Using these results, we can conclude that SN_t assumes its largest value at the 4th run (parameters setting 2,2,1). Similarly, SN_l and SN_s assume their largest and lowest values at that same run. In this case, the optimal design parameters are those selected at the fourth run. A graph of the main effects for each of the factors, as well as the effects of A on the Signal to Noise Index, yields the results shown in Figure 7.10.

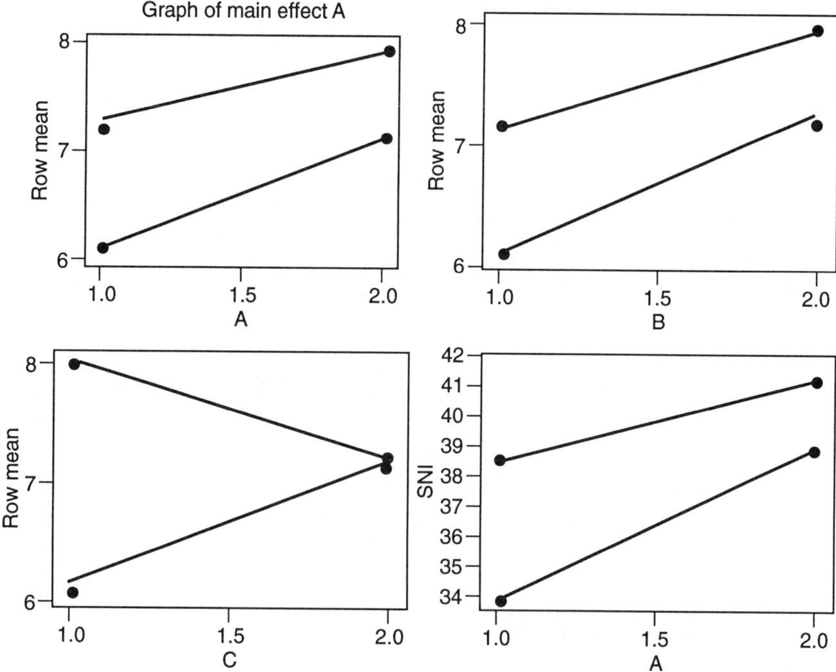

Figure 7.10: The main effects and SNI graphs.

We note that when the graphs are parallel, the interaction effects, of these variables is weak. Of course, if we were to detect a significant interaction, then we would have to run a full factorial experiment for the inner array as well, in order to isolate and determine these interaction effects (and not have them confounded, as is the case in a fractional factorial experiment).

Example: (Maria-Pilar Arroyo)

The objective of the study is to test the substitution of an imported and costly material for another material which is available locally in Mexico in large quantities and at a lower price. The materials' qualities may differ, however. The production process is expressed in terms of factors, some of which can be set (i.e. they can be controlled). Factor-levels combination of the production process is needed to obtain at least as good a product as the imported product, defined in terms of the product life. To do so, brainstorming indicated a response variable $Y (=$ time to breakdown, in days) and six factors, two of which were design factors. These are given below:

Design factors:	*Levels*	
A: Type Casing	A_1	A_2
B: Metal used	B_1	B_2
AXB interaction		
Additives:		
C: Additive #1	C_1	C_2
D: Additive #2	D_1	D_2
E: Additive #3	E_1	E_2
Noise Factors:		
F: Batches of material		
(3 batches were selected)		

Say that we use an Orthogonal Array $(OA)L_8(2^7)$, i.e. seven factors, eight experiments using fractional factorial experiments. Thus, eight runs were performed, with data in Table 7.38 representing the levels of the inner array and three batch values for the outer array. Further, the S/N ratio was also calculated.

Table 7.38: A Taguchi inner outer array design with one external factor at three levels

Run #	A	B	$A \times B$	C	D	E	e	#1 (y)	#2 (y)	#3 (y)	S/N Ratio
1	1	1	1	1	1	1	1	15	14	19	-24.16
2	1	1	1	2	2	2	2	10	14	15	-22.40
3	1	2	2	1	1	2	2	13	15	16	-23.36
4	1	2	2	2	2	1	1	11	8	12	-21.98
5	2	1	2	1	2	1	2	4	7	9	-16.87
6	2	1	2	2	1	2	1	3	4	6	-13.08
7	2	2	1	1	2	2	1	24	22	25	-27.49
8	2	2	1	2	1	1	2	8	13	12	-20.99

Note that each run set $(1), (2)$ and (3) was calculated by varying the batches (the outer array F factor, which meant running the experiment with three batches). These results can now be analy*sed*. First the S/N ratio was calculated pointing to the 6th run with the largest value 13.08. An analysis of variance was performed. The results of such an analysis are summarized in Table 7.39.

Table 7.39: The analysis of variance.

Source of variation	*df*	*SS*	*SS'*	*F*	$\rho(\%)$
A	1	22.68	20.71	11.45	15.07
B	1	37.45	35.48	18.91	25.83
C	1	22.55	20.53	11.4	14.94
D	(1)	(4.08)	-	-	-
E	(1)	(0.68)	-	-	-
$A \times B$	1	48.76	46.79	17.2	34.06
Error (pooled)	3	5.95	13.88		10.10
Total	7	137.39	137.39		100.0

From these results, note that theoretically, the F value is given by, $F(.05;1,3) = 10.128$ and that $s^2 = 1.98$. The optimal combination is thus seen to be $A = 2, B = 1, C = 2$, as pointed out. In this case, the expected response is

$$\eta(\text{Opt}) = -21.29 + (-14.975 + 21.29) + (-19.6125 + 21.29) = -13.2975.$$

Confirming experiments performed at these levels have shown that

$$Y = 5.5\,\text{sec.}, s = 1.732 \text{ and } \eta = -15.12,$$

which turns out to be the optimal design.

Criticism of the Taguchi approach

Ever since the introduction of Taguchi's ideas to design robust systems, a great deal of research has been performed to better understand the approach. Reviews by Tsui (1992) and Nair (1992) provide an overview of current thinking on the Taguchi approach. Criticism is directed to the experimental design, the product array and the analysis. These are discussed next.

The Experimental Design: As seen earlier, Taguchi provides a catalogue of orthogonal arrays and interaction tables in order to assign factors to the inner and outer arrays. An $OA_N(s^m)$ is an $N \times m$ matrix with the property that in every pair of columns each of the possible permutations of elements $(1, 2, \ldots s)$ occur the same number of times. From the 20 arrays in Taguchi's catalogue, two are not orthogonal, $L_9(2^{21})$ and $L_{27}(3^{22})$. These plans correspond to factorial experiments under special combinations of factors (Kackar et al., 1991). Orthogonal arrays are important because their properties enable uncorrelated estimation of each of the factors under study, facilitating the corresponding analysis and interpretation of effects. The arrays have been used extensively and special methods have been given by Taguchi to handle cases of mixed levels or factors with 4, 8 or 9 levels (Taguchi, 1987). For mixed level OA, the methods (combinatorial design) proposed for the construction of arrays have been more sensitive to statistical properties than the cost of experimentation. By contrast,

Taguchi recommends arrays such as $L_{18}(2 \times 3^7)$ and methods which favour economic considerations (i.e. less experimentation). The problem is that some Taguchi plans (such as the idle column method) provide non-orthogonal arrays where the final plan depends upon the coding scheme (Grove and Davis, 1991). Alternative orthogonal main effect plans can be generated by reducing the number of factors or increasing the number of runs. Wang and Wu (1991) developed a general approach for the construction of mixed levels OA. Some of Taguchi's arrays ($L_4(2^3)$ and $L_8(2^7)$) correspond to fractional factorial plans. If all columns are assigned to factors, then this corresponds to Resolution III experiments, as we saw earlier. Taguchi prefers to ignore the interaction effects, although when they are found to be non-negligible, graphs are used to estimate their effect. As a result, some criticism has been that Taguchi does not state explicitly the alias structure, resulting in highly fractioned experiments (which ignore the interaction effects). The $OAL_{12}(2^{11})$, for example, is a Plackett-Burman design and has a complex alias structure which makes it appropriate only to additive models (for further criticism see Wu and Chen, 1992; Fries and Hunter, 1980). The Taguchi approach rarely considers the statistical risks (α, β) for sample design and hypothesis testing using t and $F-$ distributions. Randomization of runs is also rarely used, and the experimental cost is basically neglected. By contrast, these aspects are important in the traditional approach. Nevertheless, Taguchi is credited for the increased attention he brought to applications of experimental design in industry.

The Product Design Array: To compute the S/N ratios, Taguchi uses product arrays, obtained by crossing combinations in inner and outer arrays. The resultant experiment is easy to construct, but it can have several drawbacks (see Shoemaker et al, 1991). Two of the problems are the large number of runs required and the large number of degrees of freedom used to estimate the interactions between the control and noise factors. The interaction of control factors cannot be estimated. Lorenz (1992) suggests that we use the combined arrays of the control and noise factors. The application of combined arrays is difficult, however. Examples for combined (instead of product) arrays are given by Shoemaker et al. (1992) and provide good probabilities of detecting important differences for the main effects and parts of the two-way interaction of control and noise.

Performance measures and the Taguchi methodology: Application of the S/N ratio, implying a quadratic loss function, has been severely criticized. Box (1988) has suggested that transformations of the Box-Cox family (Y^λ) be used. This means seeking a transformation $f(Y)$ such that the transformed data can be modelled with fewer parameters (parsimony) and the location and dispersion effects are well separated. To achieve these objectives, λ must be defined. To do so, Box suggests a graphical method (Lambda plots). The requirements for $f(Y)$ are demanding and cannot be easily satisfied (an extensive discussion of this problem can be found in Pukelsheim, 1991). Instead of modelling the loss function, two alternative approaches have been suggested. Vining and Myers (1990) proposed a 'dual' approach, where RSM (to be studied below) is used to provide separate estimates of the mean and variance. A model, based on control and noise factors, is fitted to the data (where noise factors are treated as fixed effects) and the variance var(Y) is estimated by applying the variance operator on the adjusted model (requiring that the covariances between noise factors be known or could be estimated). To select a robust solution, it is then necessary to set factor levels such that the response sensitivity to the noise factor is close to zero. Another approach, called the 'response model' approach, uses combined arrays. Its basic idea is to model the response (rather than the loss) and then define the factor-level setting to reach a robust solution. The (control) × (noise) interactions are then considered as particularly important because they can be manipulated indirectly (through the controls) to reach a robust factor combination. Because it is important to model the response/factors/noise relationship properly, prior knowledge is important; omission of critical noise factors and a failure to choose the proper response will result in non-robust models.

Although Taguchi's approach can be criticized, it has great merit. First, robust design is an active form of quality improvement, more focused on prevention and on cost savings. Taguchi's parameter design problem expands the methodology of experimental design to include problems of variance reduction and the anticipation of variation by means of design. Taguchi's approach has since improved by developing appropriate statistical methods, some of which were referred to here. More research is required to facilitate the application of these methods to industrial, business and service systems, however.

Response surface methodology (RSM)

RSM is a technique combining experimental design and numerical optimization iterative techniques in search of an optimal response, measured in terms of a given objective. The application of RSM is both an art and a science. It is an art because, initially, experimenters have no knowledge of the shape of the functional form relating the response (objective function) and the experimental factors (both controllables and uncontrollables). Further, they may have no initial clue for selecting factor levels in order to perform experiments. If the underlying relationship is highly complex and non convex, the selection of an initial factor level setting might be crucial for the successful application of the RSM. It is also a science, because considerations of experimental costs, search techniques and design providing the information needed to search for improved factor-level settings (i.e. as needed for application of the iterative technique to improve the design) are also needed, and are based on extensive statistical and optimization know-how. Typically, a functional relationship, usually a linear or a quadratic equation, is evaluated at some point believed to be close to the optimal point. First, experimental design is performed to construct the relationship between the response value and the factor levels setting. Two and three level experiments (full or fractional factorial) are selected according to the fit that can be estimated. Practically, only two levels and linear models are estimated to obtain a 'gross' sense of the relationship relating the response and the factors used in the experiment. Subsequently, when more refined results are needed, higher level experiments are used to estimate non-linear (quadratic and interaction) models. Improvement of the performance measure is obtained by selecting other levels and perform other experiments (and perhaps other experiment types based on the type of relationships we hope to estimate). For example, it is common to use factorial (fractional and full) experiments in the first stage of an experimental investigation with no more than four factors. These experiments are first screening a large number of factors, a subset of which will be maintained. Subsequently, the factorial experiment may be augmented with central points that allow estimation of the response variance. This estimate of the variance is then used to test for the lack of fit of the model. If the model turns out to have a poor fit, other experimental points are then needed (such as the Central Composite Design seen earlier) to provide a second order polynomial estimate of the relationship under study. Of course, replication of the experiment can also be used to improve the estimates and reduce the variance (although this can be costly). After such experiments have been done, probing experiments are made based on directional search (or other) techniques in order to select another factor-level setting for performing the experiments again. For example, a contour map analysis might provide a visual sense for a directional search, a steepest descent algorithm (such as the Newton-Iteration algorithm) can be used to improve outcomes in a subsequent experiment. We could also adopt concepts used in optimization, such as recent genetic algorithms, and mutate the current factor-level setting presumed to be optimal. Thus, there are several issues we must first deal with to apply RSM. These are summarized in Figure 7.11, where both the change of factor-levels setting and the potential choice of a number of experimental types is highlighted. They include

- Selection of the experiments to be performed (fractional, and full factorial design with a centre point for variance estimation).
- Level selection and variable scaling (whether we take two levels for screening or three levels for assessing curvature).
- Test for fit.

  † If the estimated relationship has no fit, then additional

experimentation, emphasizing nonlinear estimates as well, is implemented.

‡ If the estimated relationship, a directional and/or improvement search technique is applied.

- Select a stopping rule to conclude the experiment and reach the appropriate decision.

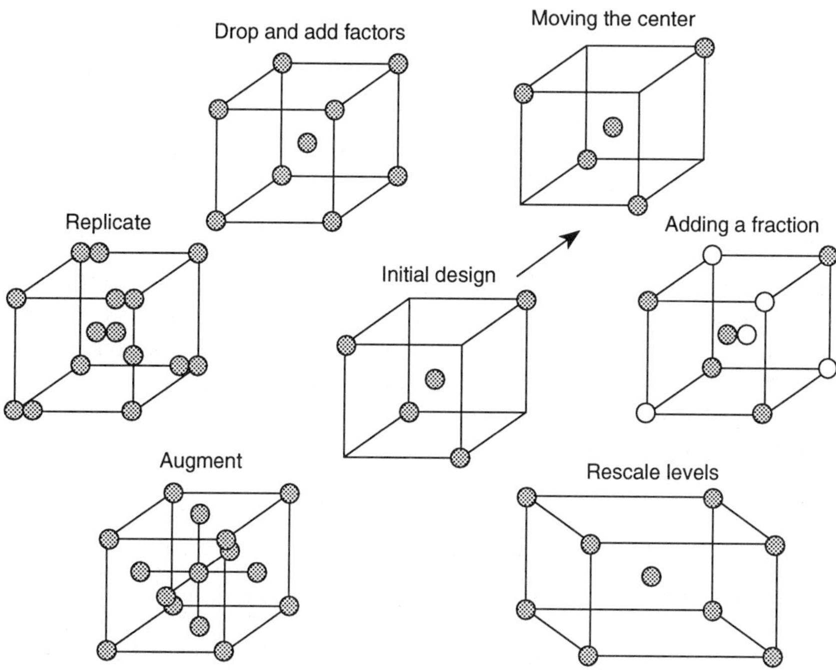

Figure 7.11: RSM iteration procedures (Box, 1993).

RSM, just like experimental design in general, is basically an 'off line' quality control technique because it is usually applied in a controlled environment and level changes are relatively large (something that cannot be implemented in a real life and operating process). Once an optimum (factors- levels) point is selected and applied in practice, there may be some 'fine- tuning' required. At this stage, Box and Draper (1969) have suggested that EVOP be used. This is basically an 'on-line continuous improvement technique' which perturbs marginally the process operating conditions and performs 2^2 and 2^3 factorial experiments with one central point until a significant change in the response is observed. Then, the process conditions are adjusted to the new improved levels. In this sense, EVOP provides some means to learn and continuously improve the process. The need to perturb the process, even with small perturbations, is often difficult for engineers to accept however. A survey of RSM can be found in Myers, Khuri and Carter (1989). Ever since the early 1950*s* when RSM was introduced by Box, Hunter and Wilson (1951), there have been important developments in this approach, emphasizing the determination of robust response in a surface. Namely, finding a set of ranges over a number of factors that can satisfy requirements imposed by customers.

RSM and optimization

To better appreciate the optimization approach used in RSM, consider a function expressing a response y (a performance measure, the dependent variable) to some vector of design factors $x \in R^n$ and a vector of outer factors $z \in R^m$(the independent variables). For the moment, assume that this function is not known and not constrained, and suppose that we nonetheless search for its maximum (or minimum) through RSM:

$$\text{Maximize } y = f(\mathbf{x}, \mathbf{z}).$$

Initially, it can be estimated through experimental design when specific levels for factors ($\mathbf{x}$,$\mathbf{z}$) are selected. Assume that y is believed to have an optimal value and let the unknown function $f(.)$ be differentiable with respect to the $(\mathbf{x}, \mathbf{z})$ factors. A first order condition for such optimality is given by noting that at this point the gradient with respect to design factors equals zero, that is

$$\nabla_x f = 0 \text{ or } \partial f/\partial \mathbf{x} = 0.$$

To find a solution we proceed as follows:

(a) We assume a given solution $\mathbf{x}^k$(levels of the centre point for the design factor) and estimate the response (performance) for a given experiment and a given factors-levels setting. To do so, we can use EVOP, which consists of 2^2 and 2^3 factorial design, as stated above.

(b) We optimize (maximize or minimize) in the direction indicated, and a new point is selected by updating the experimental levels through either a constant step size or through a variable one, depending on the methodology adopted. In this case, the new point is,

$$\mathbf{x}^{k+1} = \mathbf{x}^k + \Delta\mathbf{x}^k.$$

The experimental and optimal design process consists then of the selection of

- One or more experiments with a given factor setting, which acts as a departure factor combination design that is both estimated and tested.
- Select the experimental design that will provide the data to compute performance on the one hand and directional searches on the other.

- Select a methodology, or a mixture of methodologies, to iterate the process of experimentation-optimization such that we can move economically towards the optimal solution. These may consist of (i) Random search, or a search based on brainstorming and prior information available to the design manager. This is equivalent to comparing 'all kind of scenarios' selected randomly and choosing the design with the desirable performance; (ii) Iterative directional searches which can be based on various numerical techniques (such as Newton iteration algorithms, Conjugate Gradient iteration algorithms, with fixed and variables step sizes). Experimental designs may also dictate the search procedure to follow. For example, optimum seeking on a grid, structures of various sorts, etc. will dictate the kind of experiments to perform. In the first case, we can use a full factorial design with three levels in order to calculate both the first and second order derivatives needed for the application of a Newton iteration procedure.
- Select risk (and/or economic) criteria for stopping the search process.

The number of levels used in an experiment is an important consideration to be aware of when we apply RSM. To see why this is the case, we consider the following case, demonstrating the relationship between three level factorial design and application of Newton iteration. Assume that the response function to be optimized is of the form $y = f(\mathbf{x})$, where $\mathbf{x}$ is a vector variable expressing the design experimental factors. Consider a specific point, $\mathbf{x}^k$, then a quadratic approximation (or alternatively a three terms Taylor series expansion) in a neighbourhood $\Delta\mathbf{x}^k$ of this point is given by

$$f(\mathbf{x}) \cong f(\mathbf{x}^k) + (\Delta\mathbf{x}^k)^T \nabla f(\mathbf{x}^k) + \frac{1}{2}(\Delta\mathbf{x}^k)^T \nabla^2 f(\mathbf{x}^k)(\Delta\mathbf{x}^k),$$

with $\Delta\mathbf{x}^k = x - \mathbf{x}^k$. If such an approximation is good, its minimum can be found by taking the first order derivative and equating it to zero. In this case, if $\nabla^2 f(\mathbf{x}^k)$ is positive definite then we can define a point $\mathbf{x} = \mathbf{x}^{k+1}$ such that $f(\mathbf{x})$ is minimized. This point is given by

$$\mathbf{x}^{k+1} = \mathbf{x}^k - [\nabla^2 f(\mathbf{x}^k)]^{-1} \nabla f(\mathbf{x}^k).$$

This equation, called the Newton steepest descent iteration algorithm, provides an iterative formula for improving our guess of the optimal factors-levels setting, but it must be estimated using the experimental design results. The validity of such an iterative improvement algorithm depends upon a number of assumptions which might not be satisfied. First, that $f(.)$ has to be non- singular, and second, that we should be able to estimate the first and second derivatives of $f(.)$ at the point $\mathbf{x}^k$. This may not always be possible, however. If we have a three levels full factorial design, then of course we can try to estimate these derivatives through our experimental results. For example, suppose that the vector x is one-dimensional, and let the levels be $x+\Delta x$, x and $x-\Delta x$. Then the iterative scheme for improving the estimate of the optimal value is given by

$$x^{k+1} = x^k - \frac{[f(x+\Delta x) - f(x-\Delta x)]}{(\Delta x)} \frac{[f(x+\Delta x) - 2f(x) + f(x-\Delta x)]}{(\Delta x)^2}.$$

This will mean that the experimental design will require three levels, denoted $(x+\Delta x), (x)$ and $(x-\Delta x)$ where x is the centre point.

Alternatively, we can search for a direction along which the objective can be improved. The directional derivative is then calculated approximately by

$$\delta f = \frac{f(x+\theta(\Delta x)) - f(x)}{\Delta x}.$$

In such circumstances, whenever the gradient does not vanish we can improve the objective by moving in the best direction (either minimizing or maximizing the objective, depending on the problem). Note that in this case, we can use an experimental design with two levels $(x+\Delta x)$ and (x) but will have to repeat the experiment a number of times (specified by the value we give to θ) until the objective is improved the most. The application of this approach is cumbersome, however, as it requires a new experimental setting at each iteration. Further, we do not take into consideration constraints of various sorts, nor the inherent and uncertain parameters implied in the iteration procedure. Nevertheless, these cases clearly highlight the relationship between the numerical optimization technique used and the type of experimental design we have to perform.

Application of RSM

A firm has two possibilities: either produce a product in-house or buy it through a supplier. The first alternative is deemed preferable only if the delay needed to produce the product can be controlled (and improved). Two factors seem to affect production the most. These are: x_1 = Concentration of the chemical used in the production process; and x_2 = The temperature used in the process. The conditions believed optimal are 70% and 45C. With this information on hand, a decision was made to use RSM in order to minimize the reaction time as well. Initially, a two factors, two levels full factorial experiment with three central points was performed using the factors levels believed to be optimal. The first factor, x_1, was selected with levels at 70 ± 5, while the second factor was selected with levels at 45 ± 5. The actual and coded values of the experiment, as well as the experimental outcomes measuring the reaction time, are given in Table 7.40.

Table 7.40: Application of RSM.

Actual		Coded		Response
x_1	x_2	z_1	z_2	Y, hours
70	45	0	0	82.53
70	45	0	0	79.26
70	45	0	0	84.98
65	40	-1	-1	83.17
75	40	+1	-1	69.98
65	50	-1	+1	80.78
75	50	+1	+1	81.76

Using this data, a first order (linear) model was fitted, leading to

$$Y_i = 82.26 - 3.0525Z_{1i} + 2.3475Z_{2i}.$$

An analysis of the fit as well as an analysis of variance could not reject the hypothesis that there was a lack of fit, and therefore the first order linear model is actually deemed representative of the surface in this region. An improvement was then sought by repeating experiments in the direction indicated by the coefficients of the linear equation. Explicitly, using a 5% increment in x_1, the step size along the gradient, and expressed in terms of the coded variables, equals $(+1, -0.77 = -2.3475/3.052)$. A series of experiments along this direction were performed until no additional improvement in the reaction time was observed. The experimental results are given in Table 7.41.

Table 7.41: Experimental results along the gradient.

Step	Coded	Values	Experimental		Time
	Z_1	Z_2	values		(Hrs.)
0	0	0	70	45	82.26
1	1	-0.77	75	41.15	71.32
2	2	-1.54	80	37.3	67.15
3	3	-2.31	85	33.45	62.38
4	4	-3.08	90	29.6	65.73

A first order experiment with five central points at $(85\%, 35)$ was also performed. The results for such an experiment are given in Table 7.42.

Table 7.42: Experiment for second order model.

Run	Coded Z_1	Values Z_2	Exp.	Values	Time (Hrs.)
0	0	0	85	35	62.63
1	0	0	85	35	64.1
2	0	0	85	35	63.15
3	0	0	85	35	62.43
4	0	0	85	35	63.50
5	-1	-1	80	30	63.50
6	-1	+1	80	40	67.11
7	+1	-1	90	30	66.43
8	+1	+1	90	40	66.21

Using the data at hand, the corresponding first order model was estimated by linear regression:

$$Y_i = 64.21 + 0.508Z_{1i} + 0.847Z_{2i}.$$

This model turns out (following an analysis of variance) to have a lack of fit, implying the need for a second order model. It is in such circumstances that the need for a CCD is expressly felt, so that a higher order model can be estimated. Using $\alpha = 1.414$ with our two factors model, the axial experimental results were found to be as shown in Table 7.43.

Table 7.43.

Run	Coded Z_1	Values Z_2	Exp.	Values	Time (Hrs.)
0	1.414	0	92.07	35	65.92
1	-1.414	0	77.93	35	64.19
2	2	1.414	85	42.07	67.37
3	3	1.414	85	27.93	65.06

A second order model was then estimated leading to the following results:

$$Y_i = 62.928 + 0.56Z_{1i} + 0.832Z_{2i} + 1.108Z_{1i}^2 + 1.688Z_{2i}^2 - 0.958Z_{1i}Z_{2i}.$$

This model, upon further ANOVA, is shown to have no lack of fit, and therefore can be assumed to approximate the response surface around that central point. The ANOVA is reproduced in Table 7.44 for completeness:

Table 7.44: The Analysis of Variance.

Source of variation	df	SS	MS	F
Regression	6	54369.614	9061.602	
Error:				
Lack of fit	3	0.0865	0.0288	0.03, *ns*
Pure error	4	3.9173	0.9793	
Total	13	54373.618		

The stationary point using this quadratic function is of course found by solving

$$\begin{aligned}\partial Y/\partial Z_1 &= 0.56 + 2(1.108)Z_1 - 0.958Z_2 = 0\\ \partial Y/\partial Z_2 &= 0.832Z_2 + 2(1.688)Z_2 - 0.958Z_1 = 0,\end{aligned}$$

which leads to (in terms of the coded variables)

$$(Z_1, Z_2) = (-0.4095, -0.3627).$$

while, in terms of the non-coded variables, we have

$$(X_1, X_2) = (82.9525, 33.1865) \cong (83, 33).$$

The expected reaction time at this point was measured to be 62.6625 hours. This means that the RSM procedure has improved the reaction time from 82.26 hours to 63 hours.

References

American Supplier Institute (1990) *Proceedings of the Symposia on Taguchi Methods,* American Suppliers Institute, Dearborn.

Box G.E.P (1993) Quality Improvement–The New Industrial Revolution, *International Statistical Review,* **61**, 1, 3-19.

Box G.E.P. (1988) Signal to noise ratios, performance criteria and transformation (with discussion), *Technometrics,* **30**, 1-40.

Box G.E.P. and D.R. Cox (1964) An analysis of transformations, *Journal of the Royal Statistical Society, Series* **B 26**, 211-243, discussion 244-252.

Box G.E.P. and N.R. Draper (1969) *Evolutionary Operation: A Statistical Method for Process Improvement,* New York, Wiley.

Box G.E.P. and N.R. Draper (1987) *Empirical Model Building and Response Surfaces,* Wiley, New York.

Box G.E.P., J.S. Hunter and W.G. Hunter (1978) *Statistics for Experiments,* Wiley, New York.

Box G.E.P., S. Bisgaard and C. Fung (1988) An explanation and critique of Taguchi's contribution to quality engineering, *Quality Reliability Engineering,* Wiley, vol. **4**, 123-131.

Box G.E.P., and S.P. Jones (1992) Split-plot design for robust product experimentation, *J. of Applied Statististics,* **19**, 3-25.

Box, G.E.P., and Meyer, R. D. (1986). "Dispersion Effects from Fractional Designs," *Technometrics*, **28**, 19-27.

Cavé R. (1966) Le *controle statistique des fabrications,* 3e ed., Eyrolles, Paris.

Cochran W.G. and G.M. Cox (1957) *Experimental Designs,* New York, Wiley.

Cohen V. (1989) Introduction aux plans d'éxperience, *Rev. Statistique Appliquée,* **37**, 17-46.

Coleman D.E. and D.C. Montgomery (1993) A systematic approach to planning for a designed industrial experiment, *Technometrics,* **35**, 1-12.

Collombier D. (1991) Plans d'expériences et amélioration de la qualité industrielle: Une alternative à la méthode de Taguchi., *Université de Pau, Lab. de Mathématique Appliquée, Rapport* 91/10.

Cornell J.A. (1991) *Experiments for Mixtures,* New York, Wiley.

Cox G.M. (1958) *Planning of Experiments,* New York, Wiley.

Daniel C. (1959) Use of half normal plots in interpreting factorial two levels experiments, *Technometrics,* **1**, 311-341.

Daniel, C. (1976) *Applications of Statistics to Industrial Experimentation,* Wiley, New York.

Duby C. (1989) La méthode Taguchi: Valeurs et limites, *Revue Statistique Appliquée,* **37**, 7-16.

Fedorov V.V. (1972) *Theory of Optimal Experiments,* New York, Academic Press.

Fisher R.A. (1925), *Statistical Methods for research Workers,* Oliver and Boyd, Edinburgh.

Fries A. and W.G. Hunter (1980) Minimum Aberration 2^{k-p} Designs, *Technometrics,* **22**, 601-608.

Goupy J.L. (1990) Etude comparative de divers plans d'éxperiences, *Rev. Statistique Appliquée,* **38**, 5-44.

Grove D.M. and T.P. Davis (1991) Taguchi's Idle Column Method, *Technometrics,* **33**, 349-354.

Hill W.J. and Hunter W.G. (1966) A review of response surface methodology: a literature survey, *Technometrics,* **8**, 571-590.

Kackar R.N. (1985) Off Line Quality Control, Parameter Design and the Taguchi Method, *J. Qual Tech.,* **17**, 4, 176-188.

Kackar R.N. and A.C. Shoemaker (1986) Robust design: a cost-effective method for improving manufacturing processes, *AT & T Technical Journal,* **65**, 39-50.

Khuri A.I. and J.A. Cornell (1987) *Response Surfaces,* New York, Dekker.

Lindley D.V. (1956) On the measure of information provided by an experiment, *The Annals of Mathematical Statistics,* **27**, 986-1005.

Lochner R.H. and J.E. Matar (1990) *Designing for Quality,* London, Chapman and Hall.

Logothetis N (1988) The role of data transformation in Taguchi analysis, *Quality and Reliability Engineering,* **4**, 49-61.

Logothetis N. (1990) Box-Cox transformations and the Taguchi methods, *Applied Statistics,* **39**, 31-48.

Logothetis N. and H.P. Wynn (1989) *Quality through design: Experimental Design, Off-Line Quality Control and Taguchi's Contributions,* Oxford, Oxford University Press.

Lorenz T.J. (1992) Taguchi's parameter design: A panel discussion, *Technometrics,* **34**, 127-161.

Montgomery D.C. (1991) *Design and Analysis Experiments,* Wiley, NY (3rd ed.).

Myers R.H., A.I. Khuri and W.H. Carter Jr. (1989) Response Surface Methodology, *Technometrics,* **31**, 137-157.

Phadke M.S. (1986) *Quality Engineering Using Robust Design,* Englewood Cliffs, N.J., Prentice Hall.

Plackett R.L. and J.P. Burman (1946) The design of optimum multi factorial experiments, *Biometrika,* **33**, 305-325.

Pukelsheim F., Analysis of variability by ANOVA (1991) in *Optimal Design and Analysis of Experiments, Dodge Y., V.V. Fedorov, and H.P. Wynn (Eds.),* North Holland, Amsterdam.

Schoemaker A.C., K.L. Tsui and C.F. J. Wu (1991) Economic experimentation methods for robust design, *Technometrics,* **33**, 415-427.

Stone M. (1959) Application of measures of information to the design and comparison of regression experiments, *The Annals of Mathematical Statistics,* **30**, 55-70.

Taguchi G. (1985) Quality Engineering in Japan, *Comm. Stat-Theory and Methods,* **14**, no.11, 2785-2801.

Taguchi G. and D. Clausing (1990) Robust quality, *Harvard Business Review,* January.

Taguchi G. and Y,. Wu, *Introduction to Off-Line Quality Control,* Central Japan Quality Control Association, Nagoya, Japan, 1979.

Taguchi G., E.A. Elsayed and T. Hsiang (1989) *Quality Engineering in Production Systems,* New York, McGraw Hill.

Tsui K.L. (1992) An overview of Taguchi method and newly developed statistical methods for robust design, *IEE Transactions,* **24**, 44-56.

Verdinelli I. and J.B. Kadane (1992) Bayesian design for maximizing information and outcome, *J. of the American Statistical Association,* **87**, 510-515.

Vigier Michel G. (1988) *Pratique des Plans d'Experiences: Methodes Taguchi,* Les Editions d'Organisations.

Vining, G.G., and Myers, R. H. (1990). "Combining Taguchi and Response Surface Philosophies: A Dual Response Approach". *Journal of Quality Technology,* **22**, 38-45.

Wang, J.C. and Wu, C.F.J. (1991). "An Approach to the Construction of Asymmetrical Orthogonal Arrays", *Journal of the American Statistical Association* **86**, 450-456.

Wu, C.F.J., and Chen, Y. Y. (1992), "A Graph-aided Method for Planning Two- level Experiments When Certain Interactions Are Important," *Technometrics.* **34**, 162-175.

Additional references

Basso L., Winterbottom A. (1986) and H.P. Wynn, A review of the Taguchi methods for off line quality control, *Quality and Reliability Engineering,* **2**, 71-79.

David O.L. (1978) *The Design and Analysis of Industrial Experiments,* Longman Group, New York.

Hahn G. (1977) Some things engineers should know about experimental design, *J. Quality Technology,* **9**, 13-20.

Hahn G.J. (1984) Experimental design in the complex world, *Technometrics,* **26**, 19-23.

Hill W.J. and Hunter W.G. (1966) A review of response surface methodology: a literature survey, *Technometrics,* **8**, 571-590.

Kempthorne, O. (1979) *The Design and Analysis of Experiments.* Robert E. Krieger Publishing Co. Huntington, N.Y.

Kiefer, J. (1959) Optimum Experimental Designs (with discussion), *Journal of the Royal Statistical Society.* Ser B., **21**, 279-319.

Phadke M.S. (1986) Design optimization case studies, *AT & T Tech. Journal,* **65**, 2 March-April, 51-68.

Phadke M.S., R.N. Speeney and M.J. Grieco (1983) Off line quality control in integrated circuit fabrication using experimental design, *Bell Systems Tech. J.*, **62**, 1273-1309.

Ross P.J. (1988) *Taguchi Techniques for Quality Engineering,* New York, McGraw Hill.

Steinberg D.M. and W.G. Hunter (1984) Experimental design: Review and comment (with discussion, *Technometrics,* **26**, 2, 71-130.

Appendix 7.A: Additional experimental design types

Randomized complete block design

When some environmental factor has a substantial effect on experimental results, it is possible to form two (or more) groups, depending on the factor setting. The groups in this case are called blocks. If an equal number of measurements is made for each treatment in each block, and if the order of tests within a block is randomized, then the experiment is called a 'randomized block experiment'. Such a technique is useful because it can increase the precision of experimentation at a lesser cost. When the number of tests forming a homogeneous group is smaller than the number of treatments, we have an '*incomplete block*' design. For example, the following is an incomplete block plan for comparing seven systems (treatments) using three tests:

B	G	A	C	C	A	D
F	F	E	D	G	B	G
E	A	C	F	B	D	E

Such an experiment is randomized when we randomly select which treatment comes first in the block. Incomplete block designs can also be balanced and unbalanced. An incomplete block design is balanced if each pair of treatments occurs together the same number of times. This leads to all treatments being repeated the same number of times in the experiment. It is unbalanced if a treatment occurs say, p, times with one set of treatments and q times ($p \neq q$) with another set of treatments. Therefore, not all treatments are equally observed while performing the whole experiment, some treatments having a larger number of replicates. These designs are also called 'Latin rectangles'.

The objective of block design is not to reduce the response variability. Rather, its intent is to define treatments that provide the 'best' mean response under block variation (using block variables defined using prior knowledge). If not all treatments can be tested in each block, due to time or material restrictions, then we can use incomplete block designs. In this case, the number of treatments (denoted by t) is less than the block size (denoted by k). If each treatment occurs with any of the other treatments the same number of times (denoted by λ) such that the same number of replicates (denoted by r) is performed for each factor level, we then have a Balanced Incomplete Block Design (BIB design) in b blocks. The parameters of the BIB design then satisfy the following conditions:

(i) $bk = rt = N$, the total number of runs

(ii) $\lambda = r(k-1)/(t-1)$ is an integer

(iii) $b \geq t$(also called Fisher's inequality).

To construct BIB designs, a direct method can be used, consisting of taking all combinations of t letters for selecting groups of size k, i.e. $\binom{t}{k} = {}_tC_k$. When the difference between k and t increases ($k << t$), the number of blocks under this method becomes prohibitive. For example, for seven treatments in blocks of size 3, the total number of combinations (blocks) is 30. BIB designs can be obtained using the Fisher and Yates tables, which contain a list of all parameters satisfying the above conditions for $r \leq 10$. Bose, in 1939, had already provided additional cases for up to $r = 12$. It is not possible to find BIB designs with a suitable number of blocks for all parameter values, however. If a treatment occur i times with some treatments and j times with others, such that not all treatments are equally replicated in the experiment, then a Partially Balanced Incomplete Design (PBIB design) results. In incomplete block designs, treatments are not orthogonal to blocks, thus to perform a comparison, an adjustment for blocks is required.

Example

Four cars are compared for gasoline consumption. Tests are performed on four routes. The drivers performing the tests are extraneous. Then by assigning drivers to cars in a random fashion, we obtain a randomized block experiment. Let the cars be: Mazda (A), VW (B), Clio (Renault, denoted by C) and Saturne (GM, denoted by D). Routes are indexed by 1,2, 3 and 4. Thus, a randomized complete block plan whose purpose is to compare the four cars is given by the following (where drivers are assigned to route/car combinations in a random fashion). If drivers are not going to be controlled, then they are assigned at random, and for each route we select a test order for cars.

1	2	3	4
A	C	B	C
C	B	A	B
D	A	D	A
B	D	C	D

Latin square

Latin squares are designs in which each treatment appears exactly once in each row and in each column. For example, the following are 3×3 and 4×4 Latin squares:

$$\begin{matrix} A & B & C \\ B & C & A \\ C & A & B \end{matrix}, \qquad \begin{matrix} A & B & C & D \\ D & A & B & C \\ C & D & A & B \\ B & C & D & A \end{matrix}$$

Latin squares can of course be randomized by randomly ordering the rows and columns. The disadvantage of Latin square designs is that the number of both types of block must equal the number of treatments, which can be restrictive in some cases. Two Latin Squares (LS) are orthogonal if, by using Latin letters for one of them and Greek letters for the other, when they are superimposed, all pairs of letters occur; this implies that one cannot be obtained from the other only by permutation of rows or columns. The next two 3×3 squares, for example, are orthogonal:

$$\begin{matrix} A & B & C \\ B & C & A \\ C & A & B \end{matrix}, \qquad \begin{matrix} \alpha & \beta & \gamma \\ \gamma & \alpha & \beta \\ \beta & \gamma & \alpha \end{matrix}$$

If p, the number of treatments to be tested in aLS, is a prime number or a power of a prime, then there are at most $p-1$ orthogonal squares to choose from. If p is not a prime number, a smaller number of squares is available. To construct a set of orthogonal LS, a method suggested by Bose (1938) can be used. When the number of treatments is too small (for example, 3 or 4), a LS design does not provide enough degrees of freedom to estimate the experimental error. In this case, the basic design is replicated several times. When the number of treatments increases, the LS design becomes too large to be performed. For example for $t = 8$ treatments, the number of experimental runs required is 64. In such cases we use Youden squares. A Youden square is aLS design from which some rows have been eliminated. Essentially, it is a special type of incomplete block design with respect to columns, where the number of blocks (b = number of columns) equals the number of treatments. With respect to rows, the design is a completely randomized block design. For example, the BIB design given before can be written as a Youden square for $t = 7$ treatments, where four rows from the 7×7 Latin square have been removed. The following is then obtained:

$$\begin{matrix} A & B & C & D & E & F & G \\ B & C & D & E & F & G & A \\ C & D & E & F & G & A & B \end{matrix}$$

When the number of factors increases, LS designs are less desirable. For example, for three factors each assuming two levels, there are $2^3 = 8$ combinations, which requires $8 \times 8 = 64$ experiments to be performed. Confounding methods used to generate incomplete block designs can be applied to reduce the number of experiments. Confounding will be discussed later on, but it is roughly equivalent to aggregating several effects into one. Some interesting experiments using confounding in LS designs are given in Kempthorne (1975).

Example

Three cars are compared for gasoline consumption. To do so, three drivers and three routes are selected. The drivers are denoted by the variable x_1, the routes by x_2 and cars by x_3. The LS for such an experiment is given by the following:

	Highway	Village Roads	City
Daniel	Toyota	Renault	GM
Dafna	GM	Toyota	Renault
Oren	Renault	GM	Toyota

The experiments performed are then given by nine combinations. Note that each of the variables is characterized by three levels. Thus, x_1 = (Daniel, Dafna, Oren), x_2 = (Highway, Village roads, City), x_3 = (Toyota, GM, Renault). In this case, 'drivers' are considered an important source of variation. Therefore, instead of assigning drivers randomly to routes (as seen earlier), they are controlled by turning to a more complex design.

Nested or hierarchical experiments

In a complete factorial experiment, a test is made at every possible treatment combination. For this reason, such a design is called a 'crossed design'. It is sometimes impossible to do so, however. Then a nested design may be used. For example, consider a metallic part which requires two holes where the 'roundness' of the hole Y is critical to some measure of a quality characteristic. Then, variability in Y can be due to (1) variability between several machines (denoted by M) in the factory, and (2) variability between the drills, denoted by D within each machine (and therefore denoted by $D(M)$). Thus $Y's$ variability is

$$\sigma_Y^2 = \sigma_M^2 + \sigma_{D(M)}^2$$

To study these two sources of variability on the holes' roundness in a cross-factorial experiment, we require experiments of the same drills on each machine. This might not be feasible because it requires that drills be taken from one machine and be remounted on the other, and then the drilling tests repeated. In practice, each machine has its own set of drills which will not accept other machines' drills. To circumvent these difficulties we use nested experiments, with each drill 'nested' within each machine. In such situations, we compare both the machines and drills, and structure the experiments as follows:

Hierarchical Level 1 Machine $M1$ ■ Hierarchical Level 2 Drills 1,2	Hierarchical Level 1 Machine $M2$ ■ Hierarchical Level 2 Drills $1', 2'$	Hierarchical Level 1 Machine $M3$ ■ Hierarchical Level 2 Drills $1'', 2''$

where the tested drills in each of the machines are different. Nested design, as well as fractional factorial experiments, are commonly used in industry.

Example

Does the quality of teachers or the quality of students determine the quality of grades students receive? To test this age old question, we can test for the hypothesis that grade differences can result either because of teachers' or students' differences. Let Y be the factor denoting students' grades. A first hierarchical level denotes the teachers, while the second denotes the students. If σ_Y^2 is the students' grade variability, σ_P^2 the teachers' variability and $\sigma_{S(P)}^2$ the students' variability within each of the teachers' classes, we have (as above)

$$\sigma_Y^2 = \sigma_P^2 + \sigma_{S(P)}^2.$$

If we have the same students for each class, we can perform a cross-factorial design, but if this is not the case, we cannot. Therefore, we turn to the nested design.

Factors in a nested design can be random or fixed. For example, a metallurgical firm makes aluminum sheets from aluminum residue. The company buys the residue from three different suppliers and then enriches the alloy by adding pure aluminum and other additives. Ingots are prepared and used to make the sheets. The strength of the sheets is one of the critical quality characteristics for the product, and control charts have shown great variability in this characteristic. An experiment would thus be performed to identify causes of strength variation. For this purpose, four batches are selected at random from each of the suppliers and after the enrichment process three ingots are selected from each heat. The strength of two sheets fabricated with each ingot is measured. The appropriate model to describe the experiment is

$$\begin{aligned} Y_{ijkl} &= \mu + S_i + B_{(i)j} + I_{(ij)k} + \epsilon_{(ijkl)} \\ \text{with } i &= 1,2,3; j = 1,..4; k = 1,2,3; l = 1,2. \end{aligned}$$

Here S_i describes the effects of the suppliers and is considered a fixed factor, while the other terms correspond to the random factors: batches within suppliers, ingots within batches and sheets within ingots. The variability in the response Y_{ijkl} is calculated by the following:

$$\text{var } (Y_{ijkl}) = \sigma_e^2 + 3\sigma_i^2 + 4\sigma_b^2,$$

where σ_e^2 measures the sheets' variability contribution, σ_i^2 is the variance associated with the ingots, and σ_b^2 corresponds to batch variability. The strength variability can then be controlled by reducing the variance components' size with efforts directed towards control of the most important source of variation.

Nested designs cannot be analysed as we have done with factorial designs. The hierarchical characteristics of the experiment establishes a statistical dependence of which we must be aware. In some experiments, levels for some of the factors can be crossed, while other factor levels are nested in the combinations. The resulting experiment is then called a 'nested factorial'. The teachers experiment pointed out earlier is such a case.

Split plot, mixture and other experiments

Cox (1958) points out that split plot experimental designs are very useful when one or more factors can be used to provide additional information regarding other factors. In this case, we are less interested in these factors' main effects, and more on their interaction (quadrature) effects. Split plots have a natural usefulness in Taguchi's experimental design, which use two types of factors: design and environmental. In a split plot design, levels for one of the factors are blocks for the levels of other factors. Large differences are expected for the factors that form the blocks.

Levels of the other factors are superimposed on factor A levels by dividing the whole experimental units into several subunits and assigning B levels to the subunits, as in a block design. For this factor, greater precision is reached (smaller differences can be detected) due to the homogeneity conditions used to test all factor levels. We then expect that the subunits' experimental error will be smaller than the whole units' errors. Randomization for this experiment occurs in two stages: first, levels of factor A are randomly assigned to whole units; then levels of factor B are randomized over subunits.

Split-plot designs are useful when large amounts of experimental material are required for one of the factors, and small amounts are required for the other. For example, large batches in a chemical process requiring special preparation at one time can be prepared and then divided, to be processed under different conditions. In other situations, the factor in the whole units is included to increase the scope of the experiment. For example suppose that we compare several anti oxidant coatings. To generalize these results, the tests can be performed under several humidity and temperature conditions that will be assigned to the whole units while the coatings will be in the subunits.

In a split-plot experiment, the statistical model used to analyse the data is given by

$$Y_{ijk} = \mu + \alpha_i + \eta_{ij} + \beta_k + (\alpha\beta)_{ik} + \epsilon_{ijk},$$

with $i = 1, \ldots, a$, the levels of factor $A, j = 1, 2, \ldots, r$, the number of replicates, and $k = 1, 2, \ldots, b$, the levels for the factor in the subunits. For this design, we maintain the same levels of factor B for each level of A, thereby maintaining and considering the interaction terms in the model. The terms η_{ij} and ϵ_{ijk} correspond to the error in the whole units and the subunits. Explicitly, η_{ij} will be estimated only if there are replicates. Differences among A levels are tested via this estimate. Factor B and the interaction terms are tested via an estimate of the subunit error ϵ_{ijk}. If the experiment has a cross-factorial, the two main effects and the interaction would have been tested via a unique experimental error, and equal precision would be applicable to the two factors. In the split-plot design, increased precision is obtained for the subunit comparisons, but at the cost of lower precision for the whole unit comparisons. This characteristic is helpful in deciding which factor should be assigned to the whole units.

As with nested designs, variations to split-plot designs are possible if more factors are included. For example, if subunits are divided to accommodate the levels for a third factor C, then a split-split-plot design is obtained. In other cases, a full factorial experiment can be assigned to the whole units and another to the subunits. Split-plot designs allow for a considerable reduction in the number of experiments, and have been suggested as a good alternative for the product-array used by Taguchi to deal with the problem of robust design. Box and Jones (1992) discuss the advantages for this design and provide an example.

Example

Suppose that ice-cream mixes are prepared using three different stabilizers.

Mixes are frozen under four different conditions, using two temperatures and two storage times (2×2 combinations). An economical experiment can be conducted under a split-block design by preparing three large ice-cream batches, dividing them into four parts, taking a complete set of three mixes and freezing all of them under the same conditions. The experiment requires only three mixes and four conditions in order to have the full factorial experiment.

There are other experimental designs useful for more specific purposes; some of them are special types of the four design classes described earlier. For example, *carry-over designs*, are LS with additional restrictions that allow for correction in the order in which treatments were applied. *Lattice designs* are a special type of BIB (Balanced Incomplete Block) design. *Mixture experiments* are used when the factors are used in proportional form. For example, in some cases wines may involve various mixtures of grapes. In mixing coffee for taste, we could take 20% Colombian coffee, 60% Brazilian coffee, and so on. The experiment is then constrained by stating that the sum of all these proportions is necessarily equal to one. For references regarding these types of experiments, see Cornell (1990).

Optimal Designs

Lindley (1956) and Stone (1959) have suggested that we use the expected gain in entropy ΔH of Shannon to design experiments. The optimal design is then the entropy maximizing design. Of course, this approach ignores altogether the economic issues, and provides only a very partial view of the information. An application can be found in Verdinelli and Kadane (1992). Extensive research is currently being performed on optimal experimental design, based on the optimization of some objective which would provide the experimental design with the greatest amount of information. For example, suppose that experimental data is obtained, and let (y_i, x_i) be the ith run for a response y and design (predictive) factors x. The relationship between these is assumed to be fitted to (see Montgomery, 1992)

$$y_i = f(x_i)'\beta + \epsilon_i.$$

A least squares estimator for β leads to $\beta = (X'X)^{-1}X'y$ where X is an $n * p$ matrix whose ith row is $f(x_i)'$. The covariance matrix of β is $V(\beta) = \sigma^2(X'X)^{-1}$. A design is then said to be D optimal if it minimizes the determinant of $(X'X)^{-1}$. Fedorov (1972) recommends a maximization of $D =| XX'|$ which is a function of the number of runs n. Then for some n, the design will be orthogonal. There are now computer programs which can help generate such designs by specifying what kind of optimality we desire. Practically, the costs and benefits incurred in applying a specific design must be weighed to choose an experimental design. The objectives of experimentation, the statistical precision of the experiment, its informative content and the costs of experimentation are the essential criteria to use.

Appendix 7.B: Data transformation

Box has suggested a monotonic data transformation to separate noise and design factors. The selection of such a transformation is not easy (for further study see Logothethis and Wynn, 1989). A transformation is deemed desirable if it is parsimonious, i.e. it reduces the number of parameters and the cross talk of the data (meaning that it separates location and dispersion effects). There are a number of transformations which were suggested, including power and logarithmic transformations. Suppose that y_{ij} is a data set, then transformations $Y_{ij} = f(y_{ij})$ may be given by:

$$\begin{aligned} Y_{ij} &= f(y_{ij}) = y_{ij}^{\lambda} \\ Y_{ij} &= f(y_{ij}) = \ln(y_{ij}). \end{aligned}$$

When a logarithmic transformation is used, Box and Draper point out that such an analysis is equivalent to that of Taguchi's. To see the effects of such transformations, we consider an example (Collombier, 1991).

Example

Suppose that x is a vector of factors, and let $R(x)$ be the response as a function of the factors' levels. We shall in particular assume two sets of factors, controllable and non-controllable, denoted by x_1 and x_2, respectively. The mean response (of the quality variable of interest) is denoted by $\mu(x_1, x_2)$, and we set R^* as the desired response. The response variability to the parameter setting is $\sigma^2(x)$, which is expressed as some function $f(.)$ of the mean response, or

$$\sigma^2(x) = f(\mu((x_1, x_2))P(x_2).$$

If we first seek a set of levels which minimize the variability while being close to the target, we can then define the following optimization problem:

$$\begin{aligned} \text{Minimize } Y &= \begin{matrix} R(x) \\ x_1 \in \chi \end{matrix} = \sigma^2(x_1, x_2) +^2 [\mu(x_1, x_2) - R^*] \\ \text{Subject to} & \quad \sigma^2(x_1, x_2) = f(\mu(x_1, x_2))P(x_2). \end{aligned}$$

A straightforward minimization with respect to the controllable factors yields a first order condition which can be solved for x_1, namely,

$$\begin{aligned} \frac{\partial R}{\partial x_1} &= \frac{\partial \sigma^2}{\partial x_1} + 2[\mu(x_1, x_2) - R^*]\frac{\partial \mu}{\partial x_1} = 0 \text{ or} \\ \frac{\partial R}{\partial x_1} &= \frac{\partial f}{\partial \mu}\frac{\partial \mu}{\partial x_1} + 2[\mu(x_1, x_2) - R^*]\frac{\partial \mu}{\partial x_1} = 0. \end{aligned}$$

Instead of the response R, minimize some function $G(R)$. The first order condition in the previous case is then equivalent to minimization of the function G if

$$\frac{\partial R}{\partial x_1} = 0 \Leftrightarrow \frac{\partial G}{\partial R}\frac{\partial R}{\partial x_1} = 0$$

and if the second order condition given below is also satisfied

$$\begin{aligned} \frac{\partial^2 R}{\partial x^2} &> 0 \Leftrightarrow \frac{\partial^2 G}{\partial R^2}\frac{\partial R}{\partial x_1} + \frac{\partial^2 R}{\partial x^2}\frac{\partial G}{\partial x_1} \\ &= 0 + \frac{\partial^2 R}{\partial x^2}\frac{\partial G}{\partial R}. \end{aligned}$$

Then the optimization problems are equivalent if the G function is monotonically increasing. That is, the condition $\frac{\partial R}{\partial x_1} > 0$ is equivalent to the transformed problem if $\frac{\partial G}{\partial R} > 0$. For example, set $\frac{\partial G}{\partial R} = \frac{1}{\sqrt{f(R)}}$, since $f > 0, \frac{\partial G}{\partial R} > 0$. In other words, for such a power transformation, minimizing the transformed variable is equivalent to minimizing the original one. Data transformation can have other benefits, such as improving the symmetry, transforming multiplicative into additive models (by taking log transformations, for example), and so on. There is an extensive body of research on this topic (e.g. see Logothetis, 1988, 1989).

CHAPTER 8

Strategic issues, producer-supplier relationships and the economics of quality

8.1 Introduction

The need for a strategy arises because choices are not obvious. Better quality at any price is a naive strategy which recently turned out to be right because the cost of quality has been grossly understated and the benefits of quality entirely unaccounted for. Today it is believed that a comprehensive approach to the design and management of quality is essential to strengthen a firm's competitive position. An investment in quality must be justified by an acceptable rate of return, however. In an article on quality, *Business Week* (August 8, 1994) reports that there is an overwhelming concern that quality must pay. For example, Varian, a Silicon Valley firm, went about reinventing the way it did business with what seemed to be stunning results. A unit that makes vacuum systems for computer clean rooms boosted on-time delivery from 42% to 92%. The radiation-equipment-service department ranked number 1 in its industry for prompt customer visits. But while Varian performed extremely well according to its statistics, it did poorly in the market place. While meeting production schedules, they did not return customers phone calls. Radiation-repair people were so rushed to meet deadlines that they left before explaining their work to customers. The results ended in a lower market share. Over-emphasis on statistical performance and neglect of the firm's 'bottom line' has recurred in many other firms, leading to myopic policies, and subsequently to losses. This has led to reassessment, and a treatment of quality as a means and not an end. A strategic approach to quality must necessarily be sensitive and comprehensive, providing value where it matters and which can be justified.

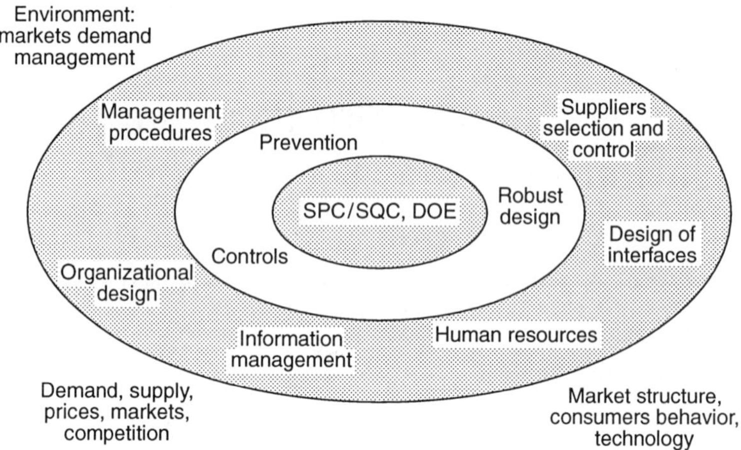

Figure 8.1: The strategic circles of quality

Quality can create value if it:

- Improves products' marketability or the firm's image. It contributes to repeat-purchase, and thereby to long-term profitability.
- Provides a competitive edge. For example, entry to some markets that are well protected can in some cases be reached only through an improvement in quality.
- Meets regulated standards, such as health and security standards.
- Affect the market structure by reducing competition when it is based on differentiation and substitution. Firms with particularly high quality products can, in some market segments, act as if they were a monopoly.
- Improves the social image of a firm because quality can provide greater benefits to society and thus contribute to the firm's long-term profitability.
- Reduces the costs of servicing, of attending to defectives and dealing with customer complaints.

These effects were discussed earlier, but are extremely difficult to evaluate and quantify. To assess their true impact, it is first necessary to conduct a strategic quality audit and to assess its impact in terms of the value quality can add. In Figure 8.1, circles of quality are outlined. Starting from a basic operational concern for the control of quality, emphasizing the control of processes, and expanding outwards to the global concerns of quality, emphasizing profitability and long-term survival. In this chapter, we shall elaborate on aspects of the quality strategy, on producer-supplier relationships, as well as studying the economic approach to quality. In addition, special strategic topics such as technologies and quality software systems are discussed. We shall also briefly review the economic theory approach to quality, which it is important to appreciate in order to formulate a quality strategy.

8.2 Strategic issues and quality management

Strategic alternatives are of course a function of the firm or organization which seeks to devise such a strategy and its definition of quality. A quality strategy can be *explicit,* devised in terms of specific goals which it seeks to attain directly, or be *implicit,* devised in terms of specific actions and organizational change devised to *induce* change, which will improve quality and profitability. If a firm's strategic orientation is upstream, emphasizing product enhancements and costs reduction, then a quality strategy might be defined in terms of technology choices, types of process controls and improvements, quality suppliers and, of course, better management. If the firm does not value improvement in terms of profitability, it risks reducing costs but then also ignoring the customer and the firm's aim to make money. If the firm is market oriented, emphasizing downstream activities, its strategic choices might involve greater attention to market differentiation, post-sales services, market research, advertising, warranty design and so on. This is summarized in Figure 8.2.

In following *a cost reducing strategy,* manufacturing design may have to be re-engineered and simplified to assemble, produce, maintain and service. Cost reduction and product design, appropriately integrated in a manufacturing process, can therefore be a bipolar strategy, improving the strategic advantage through cost reduction and improving quality at the same time. In following a *differentiation strategy,* a firm seeks to answer the following questions. Should it sell excellent products only at high prices or low quality products at low prices? Or perhaps segment its product line by creating a product quality mix? This is a function of competition, manufacturing technology and other variables (such as market penetration). Quality increases consumers' loyalty and, in some cases, the profit margin (if a competitive advantage can be reached through a quality producing technology). Alternatively, differentiation can be reached through the development of new products. In this case, innovation and entering the market at an opportune time can provide a temporary monopoly for the producing firm. Through focusing on quality, a firm can *penetrate* selected market segments while at the same time improve consumers' loyalty. Focusing is both a marketing and a manufacturing strategy which allows the concentration of effort in areas where the firm is expert and has, potentially, a comparative advantage. In this sense, the selection of a quality strategy need not mean a general and uniform movement towards improvement.

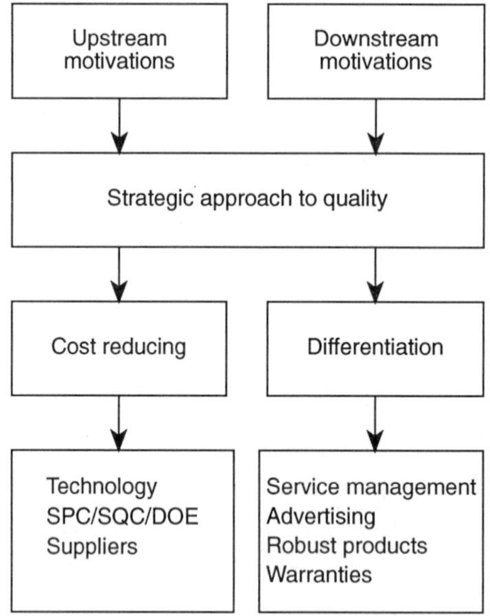

Figure 8.2: The strategic alternatives and tools.

Throughout cost reduction and differentiation strategies, the firm seeks to control variability. To do so, there are three strategic tools:

1. *Improve* the process, its organization, its competence, and so on, and thereby prevent poor quality. In this sense, prevention and improvement have similar effects. This type of control can be construed as 'before the fact' control.

2. Use *controls* such as inspection, control charts and detection schemes, as well as other actions. This type of control can be construed as 'after the fact' control.

3. Construct *robust designs*, which build quality into the system product or service. In this case, the problems of quality production become non-problems. Robust design is, therefore, something more than prevention, since it builds into the product a non-sensitivity to the factors that produce non-quality.

A quality strategy can deal with these three strategic alternatives at the same time. The means applied to these alternatives are not the same however. The foundations of TQM seen in Chapter 2 dealt with the 'hows' of improvement. Chapters 5 and 6 dealt with the 'hows' of control, while Chapter 7 presented experimental and robust design. It is important to appreciate these approaches and their relationship to the firm's strategy as a whole. For example, in Chapter 2 we saw that organizing for Just in Time manufacturing induces a process improvement and the control of quality is primarily achieved through prevention. The relative importance of each of these strategic alternatives is just a matter of degree of shifting over time from much control to no control, from sensitivity to robustness, and to improvement as a perpetual operational goal. These issues have been raised repeatedly and their importance should not be under-estimated.

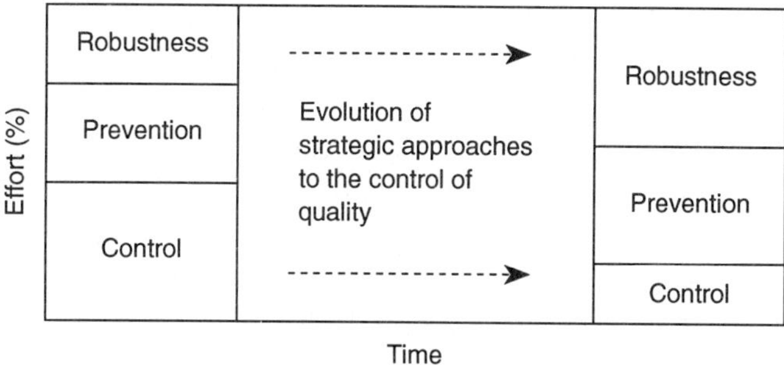

Figure 8.3: The strategic alternatives for control.

The selection of one approach or the other depends upon managerial objectives, the recurrence and the severity of quality problems, evaluated in terms of measurable and financial values. Strategic approaches can vary according to the stage at which a problem of quality occurs. For example, when quality is applied at:

- An intra-process stage, activities based on the reduction of costs of quality, manufacturing costs, the control of variability, distribution costs, and so on, might be dominant.
- A post-process stage, activities such as the development of a marketing strategy emphasizing product differentiation, post-sales services, services contracting, industry agreements that tend to introduce standards acting both as barriers for further competition and seek agreement on the definition of quality (such as food labelling, environmental impact, and so on) might be the more relevant strategic tools.
- A pre-process stage, activities will seek to secure stable sources of quality supplies. Producer-supplier agreements, joint ventures, mutual visits, EDI (Electronic Data Interchange), incentive contracts, and so on, are only some of the means used to ensure the stable inflow of quality products, and thereby allow the firm to focus on what it can competitively do best.

Pre-process activities have been discussed at length in Chapter 2. The growth of purchasing-related functions in industries accounts for this, seeking to assure quality of components, parts, materials and everything the firm uses. Firms are no longer isolated entities striving for competitive advantage. Rather, there are suppliers, joint ventures, know-how sharing agreements, sub- contractors and, in general industrial stake-holders which compete *together* to gain a competitive advantage, as loosely connected entities sharing the spoils of profits on the one hand, and the burdens of failure on the other. Firms such as The Limited, United Technology, Galleries Lafayette, GE, IBM, GM and so on are only name fronts for a multitude of suppliers, vendors and services which often seem to compete explicitly but even more often cooperate implicitly with (and through) their stake-holders.

Strategic alternatives in logistics transportation systems

A transporter can improve the transport process through the extensive training of its drivers and the maintenance of its fleet of trucks and cars. Firms such as United Parcel Service have learned that better training is good business because it results in on-time delivery of cargo as well as reducing the damage done to transported units. It can also control the variability of its service by reducing the probability of equipment failure (through inspection and maintenance). Robust designs are achieved in many ways. For example, in military transports, during critical missions a dispatcher can send a tractor– without trailer ('bobtail') with a loaded tractor-trailer so that in the event that the tractor trailer breaks down, the 'bobtail' can pick up the trailer and continue the mission. In a military convoy, when a vehicle is wrecked, its operator is a trained mechanic who can perform on-the-spot maintenance of a broken down vehicle or tow it. D-Day on the Beaches of Normandy in World War II is also known to owe some of its success to a number of logistic technologies, including a wide variety of personnel and tank support equipment which allowed the clearing of minefields and the removal of damaged equipment. From pre- to post-process, we can see then that such systems emphasize the use of improvement at the pre-process stage, controls at the intra-process stage, and robustness at the post-process stage.

Table 8.1: Strategic Alternatives.

	Controls	Improvement	Robustness
Pre-process		'On target design'	
Intra-process	Reduce variability Zero defects		
Post-process			Flexibility min delays

Of course, firms act in different ways. Hewlett-Packard, when encountering chronic problems with late suppliers' deliveries, realized that communication caused over 60% of all problems, and thus emphasized improved communications with suppliers. This resulted in a significant improvement of on-time delivery, from 21% to 51%, and a saving of $9 million. Federal Express, by introducing computer bar-coding of packages, was able to better control the flow of packages which also allows the more accurate location of packages at all times and an improved customer service. Wal-Mart introduced a computer aided information system in its distribution centers which made information both available and capable of providing answers to logistic transport and stores' supply queries. Of course, these are only some of the many cases where controls, improvement and robust design are implemented in phases of a firm's business. For customer service - an essential function of logistic systems - the many facets and types of controls which can be applied at the pre-process, in-process and post-process levels are summarized in the Table 8.2.

Table 8.2

Function	Pre-Process	In-Process	Post-Process
Customer Service	Establish a climate for good customer service. Provide a written statement of policies in the hands of customers. Design for systems flexibility. Competent technical services	Control deliveries to customers. Control stocks and back orders. System accuracy. Provide emergency support in case of system breakdowns and default	Provide field service support, installation controls, spare parts control, tracking of products, claims, warranty costs and performance of product packaging

Similarly, in transportation, scheduling and packaging we note that the number of tools available to the management of quality are numerous and varied. A few aspects are summarized in Table 8.3.

Table 8.3

Logistic Function	Control of Variability	Process Improvement	Robust Design
Transportation system	Adhere to standard operation procedures	Reduce turnover and personnel development programs	Involve customers in invoicing, increase density of prime mover network, develop emergency support
Transportation rate structure	Calculate rates properly	Implement geographic information system (GIS)	Rate access control
Traffic management	Traffic control points	Implement GIS	Disseminate information over more than one mode

Table 8.3 (continued)

Logistic Function	Control of Variability	Process Improvement	Robust Design
Storage and warehousing	Train cargo handlers and SOP's	Improve layout	Cross-train employees, control spare part invent.
Handling and packaging	Standardize packaging Use bar codes Control routes	Automate, and simplify the packaging process	Package to over-protect, user friendly packages handling
Inventory management	Control levels of inventory, forecast demands	Point of sale scanning and integrate system	Simplify process for BOM updating
Acquisition and production scheduling	Computerize total system	Improve computer model	Allow for sudden changes in markets orders
Order entry and processing	Standardize and simplify forms, and procedures	Set up computer network with major customers for reorders	Render the system foolproof yet allow for changes in cust. orders

Problem: Strategic alternatives in new product development

Quality management may be applied at various phases of the product development cycle. Table 8.4 highlights some of tools which can potentially be used for product control and improvement. A quality strategy consists in the application of limited resources. The table is self-explanatory. Explain how you could devise a global strategic approach, spanning all phases of the product development cycle. Concentrate your analysis on special products such as 'a car', 'a camera', 'a new bicycle', etc.

Table 8.4: Strategic alternatives.

Process	Controls	Improvement	Robustness
Pre-process	Suppliers inspection and controls	Materials sourcing and selection	Product design, robust to materials and uses
Intra-process	Control charts and inspection	Experimentation, training	Production designed for insensitivity to errors
Post-process	Shipments controls, customers follow up	Consumer surveys and product/price redesign	Spare parts design for maintainability

Problem

Explain the importance of and the relationship between a definition of quality, its upstream-downstream emphasis and the strategic tools the firm will use (cost reducing versus market penetration, in applying the alternatives Controls-Prevention-Robustness).

8.3 Audits and why do we have problems?

Understanding why we have problems in producing quality is necessary for the formulation of the quality audit. The management of quality is both active and reactive, on the one hand requiring that actions be taken to improve the 'system' and, on the other, preventing recurrent problems. If problems can be avoided, we may then be able to realize the benefits that tangible investments in quality can bring. We have problems delivering service quality or producing it for a number of reasons:

- Unforeseeable events which can also be uncontrollable. For this reason, both prediction and control can be alternative approaches to dealing with these events. Through prediction we can be prepared to face these events, while through better controls and robust design these unforeseeable events can be managed or rendered irrelevant.

- Adversarial situations which are counter-productive in the production of quality. We shall see that this is the case in producer-supplier relationships. The same situation recurs in interpersonal relationships between workers on the shop floor and management. Adversarial relationships combined with private information lead to situations when one might use information to the detriment of the other, thereby possibly leading to the supply of poor quality to a buyer, which lead to conflicts and the a lack of exchange which is necessary to function properly.
- Moral hazard, which is pervasive and may lead to uncaring employees or partners. Thus, motivation, leadership, information, transparency, combined with tractability, recognition and management, can be elements requiring attention. Moral hazard is discussed extensively in the economic appendix.

There are many other factors which can lead to non-quality and which can be detected through a properly designed and administered audit. Some of these include:

- Over-simplification of the issues involved in producing quality, which is misleading. For example, believing that just training or just new machines are likely to produce quality is naive. Such over-simplification may lead to erroneous assessments. Strategic thinking is needed to integrate the many instruments, organizations, people and controls which are required in managing quality. In this sense, an appreciation of the TQM managerial approach, seeking to coordinate and improve cooperation of a firm's parts, is vital.
- No information is available even though it might be available. This has the effect of inducing uncertainty regarding factors that can be properly managed and, potentially, leading to decisions which turn out to be wrong. Further, no information breeds incompetence and thus produces poor quality.
- Satisfaction which provides an illusion of achievement. In the long-term, this can lead to the entrenchment of ideas, a lack of innovation or a lack of entrepreneurial behaviour, which is required for continuous improvement.
- Poor organization of both the production and control processes. For example, a process which does not search for information does not evaluate outcomes and situations. A process with no certification or controls of any sort, no estimation of severity and consequences, and no long-term evaluation of consequences, but myopicity, can lead to situations where quality will not be produced.
- Non-adaptive procedures (i.e. inflexible) to changing events and circumstances. Decision-makers who are oblivious to their environment,

blindly and stubbornly following their own agenda, is a guarantee for the production of poor quality.

These are also some of the problems to be prevented. Thus, the management of quality must also follow a constructive approach by building the potential to produce quality, not only to control it.

Problem

The following is a partial list of factors that can lead to a loss of customers in a supermarket. Discuss each of these factors in terms of the alternative strategies a supermarket chain manager might follow to reduce them. Each of these alternatives must be characterized by one of the previous three categories: Improvement, Control and Robustness. (1) Long lines at counter. (2) Unfriendly employees. (3) No coordination between stocks availability and advertising campaigns. (4) Difficulty in figuring out where to buy some items. (5) Messy product environment. (6) Unit price information improperly displayed. (7) Employees uninformed regarding prices and location of items. (8) Not enough or too many brand labels displayed.

The Quality audit

Quality audits are used to assemble information regarding the quality attributes and characteristics of a firm, its competition and the environmental states relating to a firm's decisions (their knowledge and technological base, manufacturing process, past performance, market response and loyalties, past records, etc.). The purpose of such audits is to find and identify deviations from agreed upon standards of performance, and to induce (through attention and monitoring) a trend for continuous improvement. Quality audits are usually specific; nevertheless, there are some typical questions a manager may ask whose answers can provide quality diagnostics. Through such audits, it might be possible to assess a firm's strong and weak points relating to quality and with respect to its position in the firm's value chain. An audit can relate to a product, to a customer base, its preferences, its satisfaction, to a service, to suppliers, and so on. Throughout such applications, the audit, its diagnostics and its analysis seek to determine the factors that explain why we have or might have problems producing or providing a quality product or service and, of course, compensating for managing these factors.

The audit questionnaire

The audit questionnaire is determined by the need of the audit. There are essentially three types of audit questionnaire: (1) Internal audit, whose purpose is to improve the intra-processes of the firm and provide assurance to management that the firm's ongoing operations are performing according to standards and to expectations; (2) External audit which is performed to determine whether the audited party is performing properly and thereby providing increased confidence (assurance) that it will supply quality products; (3) External audits performed by a third party, such as the ISO organization, which will certify that the audited firm or organization is performing according to certification standards. These audits are usually performed on an industry scale, and provide an important reference for the selection of suppliers. ISO 10011 – 1, ISO 10011 – 2 and ISO 10011 – 3 provide guidelines for performing such audits. The first set is general guidelines for the quality audit, the second set provides certification criteria for the audited organization while the third set provides guidelines for the management of an audit. Throughout ISO audits, three elements are distinguished: (1) Referential documentation which express the 'things to do' to be a quality performing organization, a quality product or service, or to have an appropriate level of process quality; (2) an appropriate description of operations and processes, which summarizes what is in fact done, and finally, (3) a statement of objectives, which reflects the purposes of the audit. This might include the need for certification, client satisfaction, process improvement, supplier selection, and so on. Deviations from the referential needs induce a managerial concern, which can lead to managerial action, as shown in Figure 8.4.

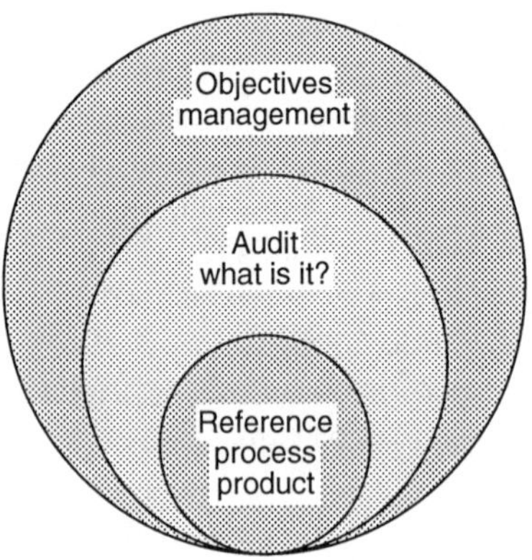

Figure 8.4: The audit process.

The following questions are considerations that can be raised in an audit. They provide a number of potential analyses once the audit objectives and the audit in terms of reference are well stated (Ishikawa, 1987). We shall distinguish below among post-, intra- and pre-process states and their interfaces.

Post-process state:

* What are the market and consumers attributes?

* Are consumers sensitive to quality variations?
* What is the market structure and is there competition?
* Are there quality standards? Whose responsibility are they?
* Is the market open to international competition?
* Are consumers heterogeneous?
* Are markets differentiated in some ways?
* Do certain attributes require 100% conformance?
* Do sales contracts include quality incentive clauses?
* Who performs quality tests (agencies, firms, etc.)?
* What are the penalties for poor quality (liability costs, etc.)?
* What are competition's attributes? Their products, their performance?
* Are products substitutes, differentiated and/or complementary?

it Intra/post process interface state

* What is the process and product positioning?
* What is the product life-cycle?
* Is there a feedback between marketing, production and product design?
* How is post-sales information used in process control?
* Are buyers aware or informed of the products' attributes?
* What are the recall procedures?
* Are there outstanding court litigation cases?
* What is the rate of product return after sales?
* Is there a commercial channel for selling seconds?

Intra-process state

* What is the firm's stand on quality?
* What is the firm's image, and how is the product quality perceived?
* Is there a strategy for product and firm positioning?
* Who defines product attributes in and out of the firm?
* Is the product subject to comparative studies?
* What are the side-effects of a quality assurance program?

Intra-process/technical facets

* Is the firm involved in product design?
* Is the firm involved in manufacturing systems design and its control?
* How is information regarding product spec. changes diffused?
* Are models or sample test products used?
* Are products assured?
* Are control plans fully specified?
* To what extent are self-regulating controls in effect?
* How are controls, production, marketing etc. interfaced?
* How are control results used?

* What is the frequency with which controls are made?
* What are the maintenance programs?
* What are the corrective actions for each default?
* Is there a post-control check?
* Are there mechanisms for learning from errors?

Pre-process state

* How are suppliers selected and monitored?
* Are controls used by suppliers, by whom and how?
* Do we know suppliers' 'specs' and control procedures?
* How are sub-contractors selected, controlled and monitored?
* Is there control of incoming materials and parts?
* How do we deal with non-conforming parts?
* How are procedures for the control of quality applied?
* Who gets reports on complaints, defectives etc.?

Although these questions are far from complete, they provide a guide to some of the concerns of audits. Once a careful audit has been established, strong points and weaknesses are established and a strategy devised for control, improvement and robust design.

Problems

1. Construct a number of questions, say 10, for each of the pre-, intra- post-process states of a logistics firm that specializes in supplying to industrial users items, components or materials just in time.

2. Compare the approaches to the management of quality summarized in Table 8.5 by considering the following applications: (a) Providing bank services at a branch. (b) Controlling on-time delivery of a fleet of trucks. (c) Managing the quality production of a job shop. Further, for one of the cases above, construct a number of questions for which you will require answers, in order to determine how the audited firm is operating.

Table 8.5.

Approach 1	Approach 2
Off-line	On-line
Active	Passive
Data based	Strategy based
Dynamic	Static
Signal/noise	Control variability

8.4 Contract and producer supplier relationships

The supply of quality parts and their control is an important problem for manufacturers. For example, Juran states that 75% of warranty claims can be traced to purchased items. Crosby suggests that 50% of quality problems are due to the quality of purchased items. Traditionally, quality management has emphasized the use of statistical control techniques which seek to detect deviations from agreed upon quality standards. Today, increased attention is given to preventive measures based on special contractual and bilateral relationships between suppliers and manufacturers. This has an effect on both the suppliers' propensity to supply quality products and the control procedures implemented. It is for these reasons that industrial supplies contracts, special relationships and coordination between producers and suppliers are so important. In TQM some attempts are made to integrate suppliers' control procedures into a broad management framework. These attempts, however, are not formalized, and fail to recognize the complex motivations that underlie suppliers' behaviour in a contractual environment. Due to the importance of this problem, guarantees of various sorts are sought in practice to ensure that quality complies with its promise, as specified by the quality supply contract. Of course, such problems are not specific to industrial producers and suppliers but are quite general, spanning the gamut of business transactions where there is an exchange between parties (e.g. buyer-seller of a product or service, franchises, etc.)

We next consider next some of these problems. In particular, we consider supplier-producer relationships, franchises and situations where there may be a conflict between the parties. The problems we consider are relatively simple, and are used to highlight some of the basic considerations we ought to be aware of in such situations. The importance of this topic arises in several circumstances. First, when industrial and business exchanges are defined in terms of contracts. For example, a product which is sold usually has a service contract to go along with it, to assure the buyer that the product's performance will conform to its advertisement. Warranties of various sorts are designed to convey both a signal of quality and to manage the risk of product acquisition. These and other mechanisms are increasingly used by buyers who are demanding risk protection clauses to ensure that they obtain what they expected at the time the transaction was realized. Second, the traditional approach to statistical control (based on Neyman-Pearson theory) has ignored both the element of conflict and measurement costs in the construction of statistical tests (although the Bayesian approach has recognized the importance of costs). In doing so, the traditional approach has underestimated the strategic importance of controls when these are tied to contracts that have retaliatory clauses, and when the agreed upon quality is not supplied. In such cases, threats, the nature of the contract (whether it is a short- or long-term contract) the information available to each of the parties, and so on, have an important effect on the selection of quality control strategies. Although recent research in economic theory has studied such problems, the traditional view of statistical quality control has not explicitly considered these effects. Of course, the TQM approach has increased awareness that industrial cooperation between producers and suppliers is necessary to guarantee better quality, and that through such cooperation it is possible to attain greater productivity and competitiveness. Underlying this belief are the basic facts that conflict is pervasive, and that it can be detrimental to industrial productivity when producers and suppliers are involved. The purpose of this chapter is to elucidate these issues through analysis and a cursory view of industrial practice.

Quality and contracts

A contract is a bilateral binding agreement by which agreed upon exchange terms between two parties are used as substitutes to market mechanisms. This may involve contracts regarding work practices, payments and salary scales and a set of clauses intended to protect each of the parties against possible non- compliance by one of the parties bound by the contract. The essential advantage resulting from a contract is to protect both parties, reduce the uncertainty they may face, and thereby stabilize their respective operating environments. For example, a supplier who enters into a contractual relationship may secure a certain level of sales which brings both profits and stability to its operational plans. A producer could ensure (through inspection sampling) that special care is given by the supplier to materials and parts. Pre-contract negotiations, which vary from situation to situation, provide an opportunity to clarify future terms of exchange, and provide protection for each of the parties once the contract is signed. A poorly designed contract may be disastrous for the supplier and producer alike, since post-contract disagreements can lead to litigations which are usually very costly. For example, if delivery of quality products is not specifically stated in special clauses, suppliers may be tempted to supply sub-standard products. Similarly, in union-management negotiations, overgenerous terms for one of the parties can lead to an environment which will induce poor quality by one of the parties taking advantage of situations as they arise, and potentially cheating or not conforming to the terms of the employment contract. At the beginning of the industrial revolution, overly harsh working conditions induced workers to sabotage their machines by putting their sabot (wooden shoes) into the machines. By the same token, overly protective measures for work, or pay scales based on piece work, only can have detrimental effects on inventory accumulation and on the production of quality (if they are not sensitive to the quality of work as well).

When there is an information asymmetry, i.e. information is not evenly distributed, one of the parties may take advantage of special situations which might not always conform to the terms of the contract (in letter or in spirit). Such behaviour includes cheating, hiding facts, interpreting falsely or to one's own interest certain outcomes and situations. In other words, one of the parties (or both) may resort to opportunistic behaviour (as is pointed out by Williamson, 1985). For example, when the cost of inspecting quality is large and there is an information asymmetry, a supplier can be tempted to supply sub- standard quality (in contrast to the agreed upon and negotiated quality supply contract). To reduce such risk (usually called 'moral hazard'), once a contract has been signed the producer must devise a strategy which will provide an incentive to meet the terms of the contract and sufficient protection in case of supplier default. In these circumstances, inspection helps to detect sub- standard quality. For example, if a part is tested and found defective, a rebate (negotiated at the time the quality contract was signed) can be paid by the supplier which in effect reduces the price of parts to the producer on the one hand, and provides an incentive to the supplier to perform as agreed upon by the terms of the contract. Foreseeing such situations and providing rules for sharing the costs of poor quality are extremely important in determining the actual quality delivered, as well as for instituting controls by both the supplier and producer alike.

Problems

1. Discuss three forms of producer-supplier relationships: (a) conflictual, (b) contractual and (c) partnering. What are the advantages and disadvantages of these organizations?

2. Consider a conflictual relationship between a producer and his supplier. What, in your view, would be the effect of an information asymmetry between the two, and what would be the effect of sharing information? Discuss two imaginary situations involving, in the first case, information regarding product quality and, in the second, information regarding demand requirements for some parts.

3. What are the effects of the dependence of a producer on a unique supplier? Contrast the advantages and disadvantages of a single versus a multiple suppliers outsourcing policy.

4. Define value-based purchasing, and relate it to three organizational variables: (a) Performance and measurement system, (b) functional interaction; and (c) access to external information.

8.5 Quality and contracts: In practice

Quality contracts assume a wide variety of forms in practice, tailored to industrial need and experience. We consider some typical cases below.

The case of Renault and PSA

Renault and PSA (Peugeot) are major car manufacturers that have instituted procedures for the control of parts and materials coming from external suppliers. To do so, they set up a process to evaluate and control suppliers. The Suppliers Quality Assurance Program consists of five steps:

1. Evaluation of a supplier's quality potential.
2. Evaluation of control and design processes.
3. Initial acceptance of first samples.
4. Product quality assurance.
5. Measures of performance.

The first step is realized through an audit questionnaire which seeks to identify the supplier's potential, organization and policies. The essential steps taken at the various stages of a product's life-cycle are assessed. Further, a study of the supplier's flows is used to assess an overall operational conformance to industrial standards (flows in the material handling system, packaging, repairs, stocks etc.).

Table 8.6: Evaluation, control and initial acceptance phases.

Phase	Steps	Responsibility
Control and design of processes	1. Definitions and scope 2. Document for quality assurance 3. Critical appraisal of quality assurance documents	Study group Purchasing department Purchasing management Purchasing management
Reception of preliminary samples	Acceptance of samples and process operations Audit of process and its utilization	Industrial project manager Purchasing management
Product quality acceptance	Notice of product quality acceptance	Purchasing management
Monitoring and measurement of performance	Progress reports	Purchasing management

Steps 2 and 3 have been further broken down, as shown in Table 8.6. We note, in particular, in the right-hand column the organizational responsibility for this function. Finally, when an evaluation has been terminated, the supplier's quality potential is noted by one of the four letters '*A*', '*B*', '*C*' and 'D' (see Table 8.7). The quality policy which Renault and PSA follow is then a function of these notes. A 'D' supplier is not retained, a'C' supplier is used only for very standard pieces, and his products and processes are audited. A 'B' supplier can deal with new parts and new products. Nevertheless, it is believed at this time that Renault and/or PSA should assist the supplier. Finally, an 'A' supplier is a capable supplier whose parts quality and products can be trusted. Such suppliers are usually used when new car models are being developed.

Table 8.7: Suppliers' qualification.

Class	Definition	Qualifications
A	Qualified supplier	Appropriate for new products Little assistance required
B	Qualified supplier but follow through with inspection and improvement program	Appropriate for new products Some assistance required to devise a product acceptance program and procedures
C	Qualifications pending (short-term, 6 to 12 months)	Not appropriate for new products Appropriate for standard components with intensive quality assistance as well as audits
D	Supplier not retained	Supplier not retained

Intra-firm supplier-producer relationships

Increasingly, some firms have reorganized their production and business operations as supplier-producer relationships. It is believed that this allows a decentralization of the firm's operational units and through proper incentives attains optimal performance of the operational (or business) units. Application of TQM tools is then used to highlight the need to cooperate, to coordinate activities and to reach a greater level of performance. In this sense, the TQM approach has been very useful in smoothing the supplier-producer interface and in simplifying the problems of managing units which are independently managed, and in having an inherent joint interest which fosters cooperation (instituted through TQM). In practice, great efforts are invested by top management to demonstrate that the supplier-producer relationship is a win-win relationship, and thereby open an improved communication, coordination and synchronization of operation schedules.

A leading steel manufacturing firm in Europe has followed such a path, and has emphasized management audits of services and operations. In particular, 'inter-unit' contracts and agreements are assessed and evaluated in terms of performance, transparency, opportunistic behaviour (such as cheating and conniving) and the maintenance over time of intra-firm contractual agreements. Through such a system, the firm observed that it was possible to remove from inter-unit exchanges conflicts which are not related to the unit profit and cost objectives (such as jealousy, personal conflicts, self-aggrandizement, etc.), and to possibly construct a system of procedures where responsibility, participation, auto controls and decentralization can be induced.

Marketing channels

Marketing channels of various sorts lead to the creation of supplier-producer relationships involving intermediaries which can be complex to manage. There can, of course, be no intermediaries, in which case a direct relationship between a supplier and producer is established. In both cases, the supply and control of quality are affected by the management of the relationship and by the contracts which are used to regulate it. Problems such as supplier (producer) liability and the responsibility of the intermediary and how it can be managed, audited and controlled are part of an array of business and operational means which can be used to manage quality from its inception to its delivery and consumption by the producer (or the consumer). When there are complex marketing channels consisting of many suppliers, producers, wholesalers, semi-wholesalers, retailers and consumers, the problems of quality management and control become that much greater. This situation leads to problems of intermediaries' management and their control. In practice, we encounter such problems, and thus insights regarding the effects of conflict, channel structure, etc. on the supply and control of quality are clearly needed to improve our potential to manage quality.

Problem

Discuss the effects of having an intermediary in a supply chain. Can it increase or reduce the quality delivered? What are the steps needed to control the intermediary and ensure that he performs according to expectations?

Protocols in supplier-producer relationships

Supplier and producer relationships are in practice formalized by a protocol. Through a clarification of the supplier-producer protocol, the maintenance of a supply contract over time, as well as trust and cooperation, can evolve. Eventually, this leads to the synchronization of operations. For this reason, some firms have invested great effort in *removing the ambiguity regarding the definition of suppliers' quality, and have a glossary added to supply contracts which clearly defines quality.* The following steps might be involved (as encountered in a number of studies):

- Define acceptable and unacceptable quality.
- Classify defects and their importance.

- Establish a procedure for dealing with detected non-quality items.
- Establish communication links between the supplier and producer for testing, communicating and handling poor quality items and related problems.
- Set up an exchange mechanism to communicate needs, changes and improvements in parts, processes and management.
- Set up a timetable for audits, mutual visits and the terms of such visits.
- Clearly point out the qualification procedure for the supplier (whether it be a first, second or third class supplier).
- Exchange quality management and control manuals to create greater awareness of the quality procedures in place.
- Prepare the supply contract.

Of course, these steps are simplified when the firm has an ISO certification which assures that 'proper steps' for the production and management of quality have been set up. Once this is done, tests are, in some cases, conducted by the supplier and the producer (buyer) alike. These tests might be needed for monitoring both contract compliance and to assure the producer (or supplier) that the production process under their control is properly managed.

Quality management and franchises

Franchises involve a mutual relationship between a firm (say, a manufacturer) and one or more firms (say retailers), in which some contractual rules are established for the conduct of business and the sharing of revenues and costs. For example, a franchiser may solely provide the products to be sold by the franchised at an agreed upon price and quality. The franchised, involved directly in the marketing of products, may assume part of the costs as well as (partly or wholly) some of the costs associated with post-sales product failures, repairs and other services.

A franchiser-franchised agreement is usually bound by contractual agreements which are *maintained over time, and which guarantee their mutual incentive to operate and cooperate over time.* The use of quality control can thus provide an added incentive to maintain and sustain the partnership. For a manufacturing franchiser which is extremely sensitive to its national image and quality, the potential to consistently produce goods of an advertised quality is essential to sales and to the franchise growth. In most franchises (such as in the fast food industries, services, etc.), however, the uniformity of the product quality through franchises is an important feature of the franchise business itself, therefore the control of quality and its management are extremely important, and in most cases it is an essential feature of a franchise's operations.

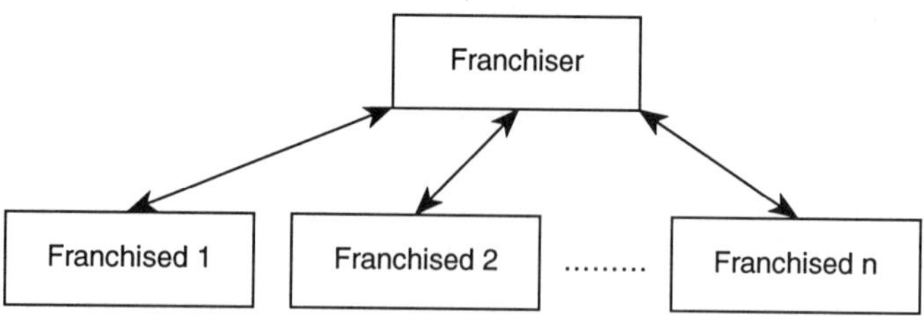

Figure 8.5: Control in franchises.

Some of the questions that recur in franchises, associated with the management of quality, include incentives for the supply of quality by the franchiser and incentives to perform for the franchised. The effect of sharing post-sale costs (such as warranty, post-sales servicing, liability costs, etc.) on the franchiser and franchised provides incentives for quality control. To assess these questions, the development of models and their analysis can be used. In these models, both the franchiser and franchised engage in risk sharing, and privately taken actions by any of the parties affect the outcomes of interest and their probabilities. For example, the franchiser may design an incentive scheme for the purpose of inducing the franchised to act in the franchiser's interest. The franchiser may also agree to contracts that induce the franchised to expend a greater marketing effort (such as maintain a high advertising budget) to stimulate sales (from which the franchised benefits) and to deliver quality products. In this latter case, the franchised and franchiser may reach a price-incentive contract which is sensitive to delivered quality. These contracts will, of course, affect the amount of inspection conducted by both the franchiser and franchised.

Problems

1. Discuss the importance of ISO 9000 qualification for supplier selection. Is such qualification an alternative to audits, a reputation for quality, and so on?

2. A procedure for certification of suppliers is given as follows: (a) Search for potential suppliers, (b) Definition of needs, (c) Test preliminary samples, (d) Qualify suppliers in one of a number of categories, (e) Evaluate proposals by qualified suppliers (e) Implement acceptance sampling plans, (f) Start production and (g) Establish controls and audits of suppliers that were selected. How would you apply this procedure for a new untested product or part against a standard part? What is the importance of price in selecting the supplier in these two cases?

Virtual supplier integration

Robert N Boyce, former CEO of SEMATECH (Austin, Texas), claims that supplier integration is replacing vertical integration. He calls this type of integration 'Virtual Supplier Integration', or as stated by Noyce (Sematch, 1990): *The Japanese have created a competitive edge through vertical integration. We can learn from it by establishing 'virtual vertical integration' through partnering with customers and suppliers. Just like a marriage, we need to give more than we get, and believe that it will all work out better in the end. We should take a long-term view, understanding suppliers' need for profitability and looking beyond this year's buy.* Partnering is referred to as a shift from traditional open-market bargaining to cooperative buyer-vendor relationships. Of course, partnering implies a broad variety of actions taken simultaneously by the buyer and the vendor. It can involve the increased use of long-term contractual agreements, reduction of the number of suppliers, negotiation procedures based on management trade-offs rather than conflict management, strategic coordination and cooperation in product development and market evaluation, integration of computer support systems (such as EDI) and, most of all, developing a relationship based on trust and mutual support.

We next turn to some simple and specific models which elucidate some of the problems encountered in the management of supplier-producer relationships. We use a simple inspection problem involving the Theory of Games (see the appendix), and summarize the basic results. Further study regarding this problem can be found in a number of papers and books we shall refer to. The importance of this example is twofold: first, it clearly demonstrates that there can be a need for inspection and controls independent of the natural uncertainty (randomness) which besiege a firm, but induced by the conflictual environment to which a firm may be subjected. In this sense, inspection and controls are strategic courses of action (in a game theoretic context); second, it provides a conceptual relationship between the terms of quality contracts, the presumed motivations and behaviours of the parties and the type of quality management procedures we might follow. Although a large number of potential situations can be observed in practice, the conceptual framework presented here can be used as a tool for greater comprehension of these situations where conflict and multiple parties are involved in the process of quality production (for additional cases and problems see Reyniers and Tapiero, 1995*a*, 1995*b*; Tapiero 1994, 1995).

Problem

Discuss the differences and similarities between stakeholding, partnering, cooperative behaviour and cooperatives (consult the references at the end of this chapter to answer this question).

Quality supply: inspection and contracts

Assume that a contract for the delivery of materials or parts has been negotiated and signed by a supplier and a producer. Suppose that this contract stipulates explicitly that materials or parts will be of a given quality which can be assured by the producer through inspection. For simplicity, let the supplier and producer be risk neutral and fully informed of each other's objectives and manufacturing potential. Explicitly, assume a supplier of parts whose quality production potential is defined by a number of possibilities, say $2, i = 1, 2$ with $0 \leq p_i \leq 1$, where p_i is the proportion of defective of parts produced if alternative i is used (with $p_1 > p_2$). Thus, if alternative 1 is used, we interpret quality production by the probability p_1 of producing a defective unit. If there are two defective production possibilities, then p_1 corresponds to the production of poor quality and p_2 to the production of high quality. The costs associated with each alternative i include the quality production and control technologies used by the supplier. For alternative i, the unit cost of production borne by the supplier alone is $T_i, \partial T_i / \partial p_i \leq 0$ and the selling price is π. When the producer receives a lot (say of size 1), he may or may not test it. If the lot is tested, a cost is incurred and the outcome observed. If the lot is defective, it is exchanged and the price of the new lot is reduced by $\Delta\pi, \Delta\pi \geq 0$. This rebate can be conceived of as a cost borne by the supplier which is transferred to the producer and provides an incentive for the supplier to deliver good quality products. If the part is not tested by the producer and is defective when sold, then its post–sales failure cost is shared by the supplier and the producer according to some sharing rule which has been agreed upon at the time the contract was signed. We define this sharing rule by a parameter α and let R be the post–sales failure cost, such that $(1 - \alpha)R$ will be borne by the producer and αR by the supplier. Such agreements are usually made in practice at the time the contract is signed in order to avoid expenses associated with court cases and settlements. This situation results in a bimatrix (A, B) of outcome for the supplier and the producer whose entries are $(a_{ij}, b_{ij}), i = 1, 2; j = 1, 2$. Let $j = 1$ denote the producer's decision to test the incoming part and $j = 2$ its alternative not to test the part. In addition, assume that θ is the producer's selling profit (net of manufacturing costs) $\theta > \pi$. For given i and a risk neutral producer, the expected profit will be

$$\begin{aligned} j &= 1 \text{ (Test)}: a_{i1} = \theta - m - [\pi - p_i \Delta\pi], i = 1, 1 \\ j &= 2 \text{ (No Test)}: a_{i2} = \theta - [\pi + (1 - \alpha) p_i R], i = 1, 2 \end{aligned}$$

where m is the cost of testing an incoming part borne by the producer. Similarly, the revenues, net of quality related expenses realized by the supplier, are

$$b_{i1} = [\pi - p_i \Delta\pi - T_i] \text{ and}$$

$$b_{i2} = [\pi - \alpha p_i R - T_i], i = 1, 2.$$

These matrices (A and B) are given explicitly in Table 8.8a.

Table 8.8a: The payoff matrices.

Strategies	Test	No test
p_1	$\theta - m - [\pi - p_1\Delta\pi]$	$\theta - [\pi + (1-\alpha)p_1 R]$
p_2	$\theta - m - [\pi - p_2\Delta\pi]$	$\theta - [\pi + (1-\alpha)p_2 R]$

Strategies	Test	No test
p_1	$[\pi - p_1\Delta\pi - T_1(p_1)]$	$[\pi - \alpha p_1 R - T_1(p_1)]$
p_2	$[\pi - p_2\Delta\pi - T_2(p_2)]$	$[\pi - \alpha p_2 R - T_2(p_2)]$

For example, assume the following parameters: $p_1 = 0.3, p_2 = 0.1, \theta = 10, R = 15, \pi = 7, \Delta\pi = 1, T_1 = 6, T_2 = 8, m = 2.5$ and $\alpha = 0.3$. Then the producer and the supplier payoff matrices are as shown in Table 8.8b.

Table 8.8b: The producer and supplier matrices.

	Test	No Test
p_1	0.8	-0.15
p_2	0.6	1.95

;

	Test	No Test
p_1	0.7	-0.35
p_2	-1.1	-1.45

For the supplier, the strategy consisting of delivering poor quality lots (with a proportion of defectives p_1) dominates the second strategy, to deliver good quality products, as, for both of the supplier's alternatives, $0.7 > -0.35$ and $-1.1 > -1.45$. As a result, the supplier will consistently produce and supply low quality and the producer will fully sample incoming lots. In the language of game theory, we obtain a (Nash equilibrium) solution of pure strategies $x = 1$ for the supplier and $q = 1$ for the producer. The outcomes for each are, for the producer $u_n = 0.8$ and for the supplier $v_n = 0.7$. A general solution for all parameter cases, proven in Reyniers and Tapiero (1995) using game theory, is summarized below.

If we change the parameter set we will obtain other results, compatible with the costs and payoffs of quality implicit in suppliers' and producers' intentionality. Consider the following set of parameters:

$$\Delta\pi = 1, \alpha = .3, R = 1.5, m = 0.25, p_1 = 0.15, p_2 = 0.05,$$
$$T_2 = 1, T_1 = 0.95, \theta = 10, \pi = 7.$$

Therefore, the bi-matrix (A, B) is given by.

$$(A, B) = \begin{bmatrix} (2.9, 5.9) & (2.8425, 5.9824) \\ (2.8, 5.95) & (2.49475, 5.9775) \end{bmatrix},$$

which leads, based on the result below, to the following solution:

$$x^* = 0.963, q^* = 0.091,$$

which means that the suppliers will supply poor quality with probability

0.963 (which can be interpreted as the supplies' unreliability), while the producer will sample only 9.1% of incoming parts. Although this is an unlikely case, it simply points out an extreme condition which can, rationally, occur if the terms of exchange between a supplier and a producer are not appropriately engineered.

Basic result (Reyniers and Tapiero, 1995)

Consider the bimatrix game (A, B), and let q be the probability that the producer tests an incoming unit while the probability of the supplier providing a unit drawn from a poor quality lot with a proportion of defectives p_1 is x. There are then two cases which depend upon the pre- and post-sales rebates $\Delta\pi$ and αR, respectively.

Case A: If $\Delta\pi > \alpha R$, then there is a unique mixed strategy Nash equilibrium which is given by (q^*, x^*)

$$q^* = \frac{(T_2 - T_1) - \alpha R(p_1 - p_2)}{(p_1 - p_2)(\Delta\pi - \alpha R)}$$

$$x^* = \frac{m - p_2(\Delta\pi + (1-\alpha)R)}{(p_1 - p_2)(\Delta\pi + (1-\alpha)R)}.$$

Case B: If $\Delta\pi < \alpha R$, then there are three possible solutions (Nash equilibria): two pure strategies and another mixed strategy.

(i) $(q^*, x^*) = (0, 0)$

(ii) $(q^*, x^*) = (1, 1)$

(iii) (q^*, x^*) an interior solution, which is given above.

These results have several implications. First, the supply of quality and its control in a conflictual environment is a function of the contract's parameters. There may be more than one solution depending on the terms of the contracts agreed upon between the supplier and producer (i.e. on $\Delta\pi$ and αR). In this sense, contract parameters affect post-contract behaviour and can, in some cases, provide an incentive for the supply of high or low quality. The implications of this statement on contract design and management are obvious. The behavioural (pre-posterior) effects of quality contracts cannot be neglected in the design of quality contracts, that is, in the negotiation and selection of rebate parameters $(\Delta\pi, \alpha)$, it should be clear that the subsequent successful implementation of the contract will depend upon the observability, measurability (expressed through quality control) and economic effects of the contract on each of the parties' payoffs. Second, the production costs of the supplier, as well as the selling price by the producer, have an important effect on the type of solutions we can reach. Thirdly, our analysis clearly sets a rationality for the definition of quality density functions (rather than just a proportion of defectives, as used in most quality control studies) based on the processes which underlie the production process. In this case, the quality density function consists of parts drawn from lots with varying proportions of defectives. Further, the probability distribution of the proportion of defectives is given by $0 \leq x_i \leq 1, \sum_{i=1}^{2} x_i = 1, i = 1, 2$. As a result, the mean quality (mean defective supply) and its variance are

$$\bar{p} = \sum_{j=1}^{2} p_j x_j, \ \text{var}\ (p) = \sum_{j=1}^{2} p_j^2 x_j - \bar{p}^2,$$

which were defined previously. Of course, they are a function of the contract's parameters and, generally, a function of the supplier-producer environment.

The problem defined and solved, although simple, sets the quality control problem into an appropriate framework for the control of quality in a conflictual environment. In our sense (and rightly so), quality control sampling is used not only to assure the producer of the incoming product quality, but also as a 'threat' against the supplier if he delivers defective parts. That is, the perceived role and importance of quality control may in fact be far broader than just product assurance, as currently presumed. It may be used to learn more about the production process, as well as to manage the compliance of suppliers to the terms of the contracts.

A sensitivity analysis of the optimal solution (q^*, x^*) also reveals the situations we have defined in our basic result. For example,

$$\partial q^*/\partial(\Delta T) > (<) 0 \text{ in case } A \text{ (in case } B) \text{ where } \Delta T = T_2 - T_1$$

In other words, the greater the cost differential in producing better quality, the more the producer samples if $\Delta\pi > \alpha R$, and *vice versa* if $\Delta\pi < \alpha$R. Similarly,

$$\partial q^*/\partial(\alpha R) < (>) 0 \text{ in case } A \text{ (in case } B)$$

In case A, this implies that if a supplier's share is large or the warranty costs claimed with a defective unit are high, then the producer will be less likely to inspect. For this reason, the size of the parameter α the supplier will be willing to pay for is a signal to the quality potential of the supplier and can thus be used by the producer. Also, $\partial q^*/\partial(\Delta\pi) < (>) 0$ in case A (in case B) which relates the probability of inspection to the rebate cost. In a similar vein, note that $\partial x^*/\partial((1-\alpha)R) < 0, \partial x^*/\partial(\Delta\pi) < 0$, meaning that the larger the producer's cost of defectives, the smaller the propensity to obtain low quality lots. Inversely, $\partial x^*/\partial(m) > 0$, and therefore the larger the inspection costs (or the lower the producer's ability to check the incoming quality), the greater the probability of obtaining defective products.

Finally, a negotiated solution which can improve both the producer and supplier payoff can be reached. In most industrial situations, mutual interests by producers and suppliers lead to cooperation in delivering quality products. But this is not always the case. Given the importance of these questions, it is important to be aware of this and develop an analytic framework for their study. Additional studies and models can be found in Reyniers (1992), Reyniers and Tapiero (1995*a*, 1995*b*), Tapiero (1993, 1995), as well in some of the references at the end of this chapter.

Quality inspection policies are a function of the industrial contract negotiated between a supplier and producer. This provides a wide range of interpretations and potential approaches for selecting a quality management policy. In this chapter we have discussed and shown through a simple example that there is an important relationship between the terms of a contract, the statistical control sampling policy and the supply of quality. In the light of this analysis, there seems to be a strategic value to sampling techniques which should be included in contract negotiations. This is the case, since information asymmetry can lead to opportunistic behaviour while statistical controls can mitigate the adverse effects of such asymmetry. This is coherent with the modern practice of quality management which has gone beyond the mere application of statistical tools, but at the same time has maintained these tools as essential elements needed to produce and manage quality.

8.6 Technology and strategic quality management

Recent decades have witnessed the introduction of integrated automation and computer-based management systems in manufacturing. These developments, heralded by a need to compete and to produce efficiently at greater quality levels (transformed into more stringent standards), are altering the traditional approach to manufacturing, control and management of quality. This transformation is market sensitive, seeking to respond more efficiently to consumer wants and needs through re-engineering of the working place, flexible automation and the design of management concepts which take advantage of computers, information systems and the global growth of business (Tapiero, 1994).

Momentous changes undergone in industry are pointing the way towards more technology, an increased complexity of production tools, and an overwhelming need to integrate the process of production into a broader framework which could encompass the totality of factors directly and indirectly affecting the production process. These changes are inducing qualitative changes in corporate attitudes to production and a greater awareness of the problems of production in meeting performance standards and producing quality. In some respects, quality management is of growing importance because of these industrial and technological trends, and because of the competitive forces they unleash. These changes, however, are imposing new needs and new problems involving the absorption of new technologies, their assessment, and most of all, in managing their incoming complexity. This has an impact on the ability to produce quality and to control it.

Technology has an effect on production which transcends simple productivity benefits. They structurally alter the economies of manufacture, providing significant non-productivity related benefits affecting both the potential to manufacture a broader range of products and the quality of such products. A manufacturing technology has several dimensions spanning some of the following: (a) Information and systems 'intelligence', (b) equipment and capital resources, (c) materials, parts, (d) human resources, both technical and managerial, (e) tooling, accessibility, (f) safety, and (g) reliability and the quality production potential. There may be benefits to introducing technology in each of these strategic elements, but there can also be some drawbacks which will render the production of quality a difficult task. These drawbacks are often forgotten, and for this reason we first highlight some essential ones which are related to management quality.

Sensitivity to system failure: A technology intensive manufacturing system may be very sensitive to a system's failure (due to the intricate linkages to be found in such systems), to external disturbances (such as demands which were not initially scheduled) which necessitate continuous re-scheduling, to unforeseen interventions and to changes in plans. For example, failure of the data collection hardware would cause production stoppage because detailed, real-time data collection is critical for effective operations. In general, such systems are subject to a large variety of errors, albeit occurring with small probabilities. Some of these errors include:

(a) Inaccurate manufacturing databases, which occur for many reasons, including among others: errors in real-time data collection, product coding errors, faulty inventory records, errors in specification of the bill of materials, errors in route sheets, inaccurate estimates of setup, process, transport time, and so on. Since manufacturing databases support many activities, errors in database entries can cause important disruptions.

(b) Deviations in process planning due to uncontrolled delays, poor coordination resulting in bottlenecks, too much scrapping, parts lost and missing tools. These result in improper tooling, larger setup times, and thus poor quality and inefficient manufacturing processes.

(c) Machine blindness. A machine, limited by its design, may not be able to distinguish between various sorts of input materials to the environment within which it is operating (such as temperature, humidity, dust). For example, errors in a manufacturing database (as stated earlier) or in software programming may lead to a machine being fed with the wrong materials and/or cause it to process defectively. Moreover, undesirable changes in a machine's environment can cause manufacturing processes to be out of control, and thereby produce substandard items. To deal with such problems, monitoring and continuous controls may be used. For example, one may integrate CNC, inspection machines and sensors. However, while errors may be reduced to a minimum, a zero- -defects technology may still be elusive, since inspection machines and sensors may not provide information continuously, or may themselves generate measurement errors. Increased complexity arising from system integration may have disastrous effects on the aggregate process performance.

(d) Machine tool deterioration. Machines' wear and tear and misuse can result in defective part manufacturing and (in some cases) to machines breaking. Since tool wear is gradual, one can regularly monitor the wear pattern and determine tool life. However, it is impossible to use a single measurement method based on one type of sensor to determine the tool wear rate and the condition of the tool. Typical methods of sensing tool wear include: changes in tool geometry detected by contact sensors; changes in work piece dimensions sensed by contact or non-contact sensors; increased tool vibration and sound, measured with built-in acoustic-emission sensors; roughness of the work piece surface; changes in tool load; changes in machining temperature; changes in chip deformation.

To detect tool conditions precisely, complex sensory (feedback) systems working in real-time have to be installed. Data on stress and temperature history, machining data and past faults are very useful in the development of such (monitoring) systems.

(e) Inefficient scheduling. In complex manufacturing systems, a part production program determines in real-time all possible routes for a specific part. If the program does not have the required skills, it may lead to blocking or starvation of one or more work stations, resulting in severe under– utilization. Intermittent starvation and bottlenecks may lead to quality problems, since the flow of work will be disrupted.

(f) Tolerance problems in automatic assembly. An item is non-defective if it conforms to some predetermined standards (for example, within some upper and lower tolerance limits). It may happen while assembling two parts that do not fit. In manual assembly, one can notice and reject such pairs. However, in automatic assembly, this may create severe problems. There are three ways to compensate for these problems: first, use tighter tolerances; second imitate human actions (through artificial intelligence support systems); third, use in- -process inspection and process control using probes and laser systems operating on-line.

(g) Unreliability of software operating systems. Software operating systems are the means used to manage complex manufacturing systems. However, mistakes in software programming are common, especially in the early stages of system installation. The consequences of such errors are numerous, and can affect the process. Some of these include routing items to inappropriate machine tools, improper tooling speed resulting in poor system coordination, improper setup, errors in specifying the machine tools or errors in selecting operation processes. All these problems lead to a need for careful inspection, testing and maintenance as well as to quality control. In this sense, advanced manufacturing techniques do not mean that we require less quality management, but perhaps more.

Automation and removal of men from the line: Automation implies the removal of men from the 'production line' and their replacement with machines. Then computer assistance, monitoring and control equipment become necessary. As a result, the manufacturing process becomes much more complex to manage, necessitating both supervisory and inspection tools which previously might not have been required. This can also introduce some non-transparency, which in turn requires greater information and better controls. It can (1) increase the uncertainty that production managers face, (2) increase the 'sensitivity' of the production process to external disturbances and internal mishaps, and (3) reduce the production capacity to adapt. By efficiently using more technology, it is possible to circumvent these difficulties (complexity, sensitivity and uncertainty) and reach greater productivity and better manufactured quality. To do so, it must be recognized that greater sophistication of the production process will imply more 'intelligence', more professionalization and more engineering. Further, data processing and information systems design and management will become dominant. Throughout these problems, quality and the management of quality is an essential dimension.

To solve the problems technology creates, there are numerous approaches we can follow. Of course, there is the Japanese emphasis on 'simplification' as well as a 'counter status quo' that TQM emphasizes, and which was discussed intensely in Chapter 2. But there is also robust design and augmenting flexibility (through highly automated flexible manufacturing systems), and appropriate managerial procedures which increase the firm's potential to adapt. At the same time, however, such systems are far more complex than traditional manufacturing systems, and that too induces and imposes demands for greater control.

The technology feedback loop: Technology sets in motion a positive feedback loop whereby more technology induces a need for more technology, which generates an unstable growth process that must be controlled and managed. For example, the change of one machine to another requires not only a direct investment in the new machine, but also its integration and interface with other machines to realize its full productivity. When the machine is an advanced type, the interfaces will tend to be more complex. If the interface cannot be managed, breakdown occurs. For example, when the ability to control a machine is lost, the process will inevitably end up in breakdown, in a loss of equipment, or at least in a loss of capacity.

This is seen in many firms where advanced equipment is left idle because of a lack of knowledge on how to deal with it. In a systemic sense, a technological process induces a 'complexity' whose control can be achieved if only there is some other technology that can induce a higher level of complexity for controlling the previous one! For these reasons, it is imperative to appreciate the role of learning and the ongoing dynamic processes in introducing new technologies in manufacturing and how they affect the manufacturing process.

Of course, current advances in computer aided quality control systems, robotics, computer vision systems and laser-based quality control devices make it possible to deal with quality in these technology-intensive manufacturing systems. For example, a decline in variable costs of inspection are leading to systems where full control is economical.

8.7 Information technology and quality

Information systems and quality: Systems producing, transporting, managing and interpreting information are needed for two purposes: control and decision making. Both purposes are prevalent in the management of quality, which requires that we appreciate the role and place of information. A data collection system, for example, requires that we choose variables to observe and measure, the statistical procedures to apply (and their justification), data gathering modes (using automatic systems or a set of inspectors and inspection procedures), the frequency of collecting data, etc. Issues of accuracy, aggregation, memory data banks management, and so on, are no less important. Quality information systems are today fully integrated state-of-the-art systems, which use everything software technology can provide and, at the same time, are imbedded in the organizational and management culture of the firm. In its simplest setting, an information system can be viewed as a means to monitor a process and/or organizational changes which are essential for a firm's positioning and decision making.

Quality and software management: Traditionally, computer software in the management of quality was limited to monitoring the performance of systems, as well as helping in the analysis and interpretation of diagnostics. The current and widespread availability of computers and software systems has induced a radical change. Software is designed to enable and stimulate creativity, communication, cooperation, integration, and so on. Table 8.9 highlights some of these purposes.

Table 8.9 Quality information Software.

Purposes	*Applications*
Improve performance, versatility, monitoring and controls	Databases for reporting interfacing and decisions
Improve management by providing data and decision aids for decision makers	Control of plants and processes Materials handling
Coordinate and integrate men, machines, materials and management into one coherent and efficient production system	Design and producibility Communication and integration
Integrate and interface with business functions, such as billing, purchasing, servicing, marketing etc.	

The programming of such software systems involves huge efforts, that also require that quality management tools be applied to ensure their suitability and reliable operation. Defects in a program, usually caused by 'bugs', 'errors' or 'software problems', can be very difficult and costly to detect, inducing malfunction in equipment with catastrophic effects. A radar may direct fire to a wrong target because of a software malfunction, a satellite may enter the wrong orbit, etc. For these reasons, the management of quality in software development and programming has become an important professional activity (see Darrel, 1991; Deutsch and Willis, 1988; Dunn, 1984, as well as the growing number of research papers and books that deal with facets of software and programming quality control and management). We can distinguish between the means and tools and the ends of software management. These are summarized in Table 8.10. The ends, expressing desirable attributes expected from software, include reliability (i.e. a bug-free program), maintainability, usability and 'adaptive reprogramming'. Programs are often subject to modifications in the course of their use. Over time, these modifications can lead to confusion and to program breakdowns. For these reasons, simple and effective documentation allowing proper adjustment and maintenance of the program is an important feature. Usability consists of 'fitness to use' by the client using the program. There can be general purpose and special purpose programs, dealing with specific needs and applications specified by the user. The advantage of special purpose programs is that they can be simpler to use and thus less prone to errors, while general purpose programs, although versatile, can be cumbersome to use and prone to errors. A program can become obsolete very quickly. First, ongoing learning with use as well as new technologies can lead to a program's insufficiency. Further, rapid change in the IT industry, may shorten the life- cycle of a software system drastically. There are then two possibilities: either discard the old program and invest in new IT, or reprogram the program in use. If re-programming is simple (i.e. it is repairable), then for some situations this might be preferable.

Table 8.10.

Means	Tools	Ends
Simplicity	Testing, inspection	Reliability
Modularity	and detection	Maintainability
Robustness	Fault tolerance	Usability
Structured	Adequate documentation	Adaptiveness
Prevention		

The means applied are of two sorts: (a) in programming philosophy and approaches; and (b) in managing the programming process. A simple programming language (implying the use of new generation computer languages), modularity and structured programming are of the former sort. Testing, inspection and detection of bugs by program usage and tests a program can be subjected to, management of programmers and ensuring that programs and programming procedures are transparent are of the latter sort. Of course, just as in the case of industrial and business quality management, software programming can use a control (testing), a prevention and a robust design approach. 'Robust programming' can be 'clients tolerant', i.e. may require the use of fault tolerant codes so that some errors (either in the program or input by the client) can be self-corrected or indicated to the user prior to being run. In can also be program tolerant, designed with a large number of options that will facilitate its future usability, once the client has learned and has begun to appreciate the program's potential.

A software program is considered qualified when it can be shown that it satisfies external specifications, can be maintained, and can be support customer use. Qualification, just as product assurance or process certification addresses a large number of issues and applies various procedures. It is common to apply it to alpha and beta testing. Alpha testing is used in-house by the programmer and the software firm's employees. It consists of repeated tested over a trial period until the software is deemed acceptable by the firm. Problems and questions are then directed to programmers and attended to prior to release of the program. It is practical in testing spreadsheets, DBMSs, accounting systems and measurement tools. Beta testing follows a similar procedure but the program is submitted to clients. An open communication line, self-addressed envelopes with a questionnaire, as well as potential visits to clients may be used to obtain the information required for beta testing. This type of testing has already passed the alpha tests, however. Practically, it would make little sense to let the client discover the program's bugs and errors. Nevertheless, it can be a useful source of information for developing newer versions of the currently commercialized software system.

References

Akerlof G. (1970) The Market for Lemons: Quality Uncertainty and the Market Mechanism, *Quarterly Journal of Economics,* **84**, 488-500.

Carter J.R. and J.G. Miller (1989) The impact of alternative vendor/buyer communication structures on the quality of purchased materials, *Decision Sciences,* Fall, 759-775.

Cox Donald (Editor) (1967) *Risk Taking and Information Handling in Consumer Behavior,* Boston, Harvard University Press.

Darrel I. (1991) *Software Quality and Reliability,* London, Chapman and Hall.

Deutsch M.S. and R.R. Willis (1988) *Software Quality Engineering,* Englewood Cliffs, N.J., Prentice Hall.

Dresher M. (1961) *Games of Strategy: Theory and Applications,* Englewood Cliffs, N.J., Prentice Hall.

Dreze J.H. (1977) Demand Theory under quantity rationing: A note, mimeo., *CORE*

Dunn R. (1984) *Software Defect Removal*, New York, McGraw Hill Inc.

Harris M. and Raviv A. (1979) Optimal incentive contracts with perfect information, *Journal of Economic Theory,* **20**, 231-259.

Holmstrom B. (1979) Moral hazard and observability, *Bell J. of Economics,* **10**, 1, 74-91.

Holmstrom B. (1982) Moral hazard in teams, *Bell J. of Economics,* **13**, 324-340.

Ishikawa K. (1987) The quality control audit, *Quality Progress,* January, 39- 41.

Jacoby Jacob and Leon Kaplan (1972) The Components of Perceived Risk, in M. Venkatesan, (Editor), *Proceedings: Third Annual Conference, Atlanta Association for Consumer Research*, 382-393.

Lancaster, K. (1971) *Consumer Demand, A New Approach,* New York, Columbia University Press.

Luce R.D. and H. Raiffa (1967) *Games and Decisions: Introduction and Critical Survey*, New York, Wiley.

Moulin H. (1981) *Game Theory for the Social Sciences,* New York, New York University Press.

Nash F. (1950) Equilibrium points in N-person games, *Proceedings of the National Academy of Sciences,* 36, 48-49.

Owen, G. (1982) *Game Theory,* Academic Press, New York. Reyniers D.J. (1992) Supplier-Customer interaction in quality control, *Annals of Operations Research.*

Reyniers D.J. and C.S. Tapiero (1995a) Contract design and the control of quality in a conflictual environment, *Euro. J. of Operations Research.*

Reyniers D.J. and C.S. Tapiero (1995b) The Supply and the Control of Quality in supplier-producer Contracts, *Management Science.*

Sematch (1990) *Partnering for Total Quality: Guidebook, Toolkit, Joit assessment guide, Executive implementation and Overview,* Austin, Texas.

Spence A.M. (1977) Consumer misperceptions, product failure and product liability, *Review of Economic Studies,* **44**, 561-572.

Stiglitz J.E. (1987) The causes and consequences of the dependence of quality on price, *Journal of the Economic Literature,* March 5, 1-48.

Tapiero C.S. (1993) The statistical control of quality and random payoff games, *International Conference on Applied Stochastic Models and Data Analysis, Crete, Greece, May* 3-6.

Tapiero C.S. (1994a) Acceptance sampling in a producer-supplier conflicting environment: Risk neutral case, *Applied Stochastic Models and Data Analysis.*

Tapiero C.S. (1994b) Complexity and the New Industrial Management, *OR Insight.*

Tapiero C.S. and L.F. Hsu (1988) Quality Control of an Unreliable Random FMS with Bernoulli and CSP Sampling, *International Journal of Production Research,* **vol. 26**, 1125-1135.

Wallich P. and M. Holloway (1993) Health care without perverse incentives, *Scientific American,* July, 109.

Williamson O. E. (1985) *The Economic Institutions of Capitalism,* New York, Free Press.

Appendix 8.A: Economic theory and quality

Economic theory is concerned with determining the demand, supply and price of quality. Environmental factors affecting and affected by quality choices such as the market structure, uncertainty, information regarding quality and its distribution are important, and have been the subject of considerable study which has an important impact on the management of quality. In particular, producers' decisions regarding the level of product or service quality have been marred by two problems: (1) How much are consumers willing to pay for quality (and thus pricing quality)? (2) How to select a production quality which is both consistent with profit maximization and sensitive to consumers' response (in terms of sales and projected revenues).

Various issues relating to consumers' preferences, market structure and the structural (technological) costs of producing at higher levels of quality enhance the interest in this problem. In a free economy, market forces interact in determining the price and quality which will be supplied and demanded (assuming that the market clears at the proper price for quality). Thus, the market structure, whether it is one of monopoly, duopoly, oligopoly or pure competition, can affect a broad range of quality offerings. These elements, combined with the availability and transparency of information regarding quality will determine the amount of quality it will be economical to demand and supply.

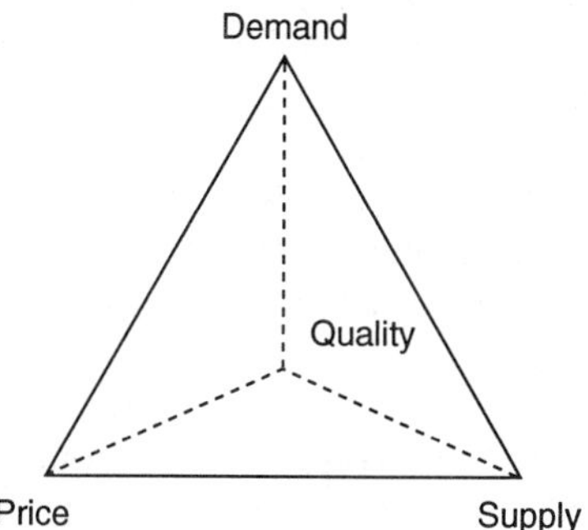

Figure 8.6: The economics and price of quality

Classical economic theory has had some difficulties with integrating quality, however. There are intricate relationships that quality induces which have not yet been understood. This can be attributed to many things, including the intangibility of quality, its multi-dimensional and its relative effects. For these reasons, quality is often defined implicitly in terms of residual values we cannot explain, often called 'externalities'. For example, if a consumer is willing to pay more for a product 'for no apparent reason', we can try to explain such behaviour by quality.

- What are the effects of quality on competition? Does it reduce competition or does it increase it? How is the supply of quality altered when we operate in a monopolistic environment or in pure competition? How is the supply of quality altered when the number of suppliers is reduced?

- What are the effects of quality on consumers' decisions? Is there an intrinsic demand for quality? How much would consumers be willing to pay for quality? What are the effects of uncertainty and information on consumers' decisions?
- What are the effects of quality, its transparency and industrialization on the supply of quality and its price?

These (and other) questions are subject to economic laws regarding demand for quantities and qualities. In this vein, the questions a firm can raise and seek answers to through economic theory include, among others, should the firm produce quality products and sell them dearly or produce lesser quality which will be sold cheaply? Should products be differentiated through information (advertising, for example) or through some other means? Should the firm pretend to sell good quality or not (i.e. when is it economical to conduct false advertising)? What is the optimal level of quality in a monopolistic market? What is the optimal price of quality? Is the demand for a product and the demand for quality the same thing? If not, are they dependent? If so, how much? Assume a blade that yields ten shaves compared to another that yields only one shave; can quality thus defined reduce demand? If yes, then when and if not, why not? If a supplier produces spare parts with a reliability of 0.90 and another supplier proposes the same part with reliability of 0.99, how much would we be willing to pay for the 0.99 parts reliability? We can appreciate that combining the large number of factors which affect quality is indeed a difficult and comprehensive problem.

A firm's environmental setting is equally important, spanning the problems of: (1) government intervention through support, regulation and standards, as well as the management of these standards which are used to limit foreign competition through non-tariff barriers to trade; (2) intermediaries of quality, such as professional groups, trade journals and professionals of some reputation, which would typically expound 'the conventional wisdom' about quality (as is the case in situations such as fashion goods, where fashion leaders are used to formulate the current fashionable style, as well as medical doctors who can claim that a given drug is or is not effective); (3) uncertainty, affecting the process of measurement and decision making; (4) information and the distribution of information regarding quality, which affects economic processes (and is the basic reason requiring controls of various sorts and contracts to assure the delivery of quality); (5) the firm's power and sensitivities to consumers' wants and competition; and finally, (6) the market structure and organization of business activities, including competitive forces that can fashion attitudes and the demand and supply processes. These effects provide broad economic issues of great importance to the management of quality.

Quality, uncertainty and information

Uncertainty regarding a product's attributes and information asymmetry (between consumers and producers) has special importance because of the effects of uncertainty and information on the perception and measurement of quality.

The information conveyed by a product affects its perception. Marketing managers use advertising to convey selective information regarding their products, and thereby enhance the probabilities of purchase. Some of this information may be truthful, but this is not always the case. Truth-in-advertising is an important legislation passed to protect consumers. In most cases, however, it might be difficult to enforce. Courts are filled with litigations on claims and counter-claims, leading to a battle of experts on what and where truth may lie. Similarly, firms are extremely sensitive to negative information regarding their products. Pharmaceutical firms may attain bankruptcy upon adverse publicity whether true or not, regarding one of their products. The Ralph Nader experience against GM, in 'Unsafe at any speed' in the 1960*s* has had tremendous impact upon GM at that time, and the car industry in general. Similarly, and more recently, the Food and Drug Administration warning on the content of benzene in Perrier's sparkling water has more than tainted the company's image, its bottom line profits, and even its future prospects. Of course, the tremendous gamble Perrier has taken to meet these claims, which were not entirely verified, is a sign of the importance Perrier attached to its mark of water quality.

Other means used to manage uncertainty regarding quality include professional organizations (such as the American Medical Association, which will accept only doctors who have been properly trained), the use of the Appellation Controlée by French wine growers, guaranteeing that the wine is of good quality. Consumer reports journals also provide a means to manage uncertainty regarding quality. Information asymmetry and uncertainty can open up the possibility of cheating, however. For example, some 'consumer journals' may receive money in various forms (mostly advertising dollars) not to publish certain articles, and thus will manage uncertainty in a way which is contradictory to its claims. A used car salesman may be tempted to sell a car with defects unknown to the prospective buyer. Given the importance of information, it is essential in the management of quality that information also be managed. In other words, just as the control of variations is an essential feature of quality management, so is the management of information.

Sources of positive information include advertising claims, positive word of mouth, positive product experience, and so on, while sources of negative information may include competing advertising claims, product recalls and claims, negative word of mouth, etc. Although little research is available regarding the effects of information on quality, we may postulate that *negative information has a stronger effect on quality perception than positive information.* As a result, the 'costs' of advertised 'unquality' may be far greater than the benefits of advertised quality. This will, of course, reinforce the need to devise and design products that are of a better quality which satisfy consumers' wants. This asymmetric effect of quality information and its impact on quality, may be due to several factors. For instance, negative information may be more surprising than positive one; negative information is statistically rare, and therefore more significant when it occurs; negative information conveys a clear message, while positive information may be ambiguous; risk aversion may have some effect on consumers' perceptions, who will be more sensitive to brand names and recall negative information; and negative information may suppress positive information.

These observations have an impact on how we may model and explain the effects of information on the management of quality and our strategic approaches to its design and control. Examples were considered earlier. At present, we turn our attention to issues of pricing quality when there is an information asymmetry.

The lemon phenomenon

Akerlof (1970) has pointed out that goods of different qualities may be uniformly priced when buyers cannot realize that there are quality differences. For example, one may buy a used car not knowing its true state, and therefore be willing to pay a price which would not truly reflect the value of the car. In fact, we may pay an agreed upon market price even though this may be a 'lemon'. The used car salesman may have such information but, for some obvious reason, he may not be amenable to revealing the true state of the car. This phenomenon is called *adverse selection.* In such situations, price is not an indicator of quality and informed sellers can resort to opportunistic behaviour (the used car salesman phenomenon stated above). While Akerlof demonstrated that average quality might still be a function of price, individual units may not be priced at that level.

Such situations are truly important. They can largely explain the desire of consumers to buy warranties to protect themselves against post-sales failures, or to favour firms which possess service organizations (in particular when the products are complex or involve some up-to-date technologies). Generally, in transactions between producers and suppliers, the effects of uncertainty lead to the need to construct long-term trustworthy relationships and the need for contractual engagements to ensure that 'the quality contracted is also the quality delivered'. The potential for adverse selection may also be used to protect national markets. Anti-dumping laws, non-tariff trade barriers, national standards and approval of various sorts are some of the means used to manage problems of adverse selection on the one hand, and to manage market entries to maintain a competitive advantage on the other.

The moral hazard problem

Imperfect monitoring of quality can lead to moral hazard. What does it mean? It implies that when quality cannot be observed, there is a possibility that the supplier (or the provider of quality) will use that fact to its advantage and not deliver the right level of quality. Of course, if we contract the delivery of a given level of quality, and if the supplier does not knowingly maintain the terms of the contract, that would be cheating. We can deal with such problems with various sorts of controls combined with incentive contracts which create an incentive not to cheat or lie, because if the supplier were to supply poor quality and if he were detected, he would then be penalized accordingly (according to the agreed terms of the contract). If the supplier unknowingly provides products which are below the agreed contracted standard of quality, this may lead to a similar situation, but would result rather from the uncertainty the supplier has regarding his delivered quality. This would motivate the supplier to reduce the uncertainty regarding quality through various sorts of controls (e.g. through better process controls, outgoing quality assurance, assurances of various sorts and even service agreements). For such cases, it may be possible to share information regarding the quality produced and the nature of the production process (and use this as a signal to the buyer). For example, some restaurants might open their kitchen to their patrons to convey a message of truthfulness in so far as cleanliness is concerned. A supplier would let the buyer visit the manufacturing facilities as well as reveal procedures relating to the control of quality, machining controls and the production process in general.

Examples of moral hazard

1. An over-insured driver may drive recklessly. Thus, while the insured motorist is protected against any accident, this may induce him to behave in an unrational manner and cause accidents, which are costly to society.

2. An over-insured warehouse may be burned by its owner to collect the insurance. Similarly, overinsurance of a transporter may result in careless handling of materials which may have an indirect effect on the quality of products.

3. A transporter may not feel sufficiently responsible for the goods shipped by a company to a demand point. As a result, it is necessary to manage the transporter relationship. Otherwise, this may lead to a greater probability of the transport of low quality.

4. The de-responsabilization of workers in factories also induces a moral hazard. It is for this reason that incentives, performance indexing to quality and responsabilization are so important, and are needed to minimize the

risks of moral hazard (whether these are tangibles or intangibles). For example, decentralization of the work place and getting people involved in their jobs may be a means to make them care a little more about their job and provide quality performance in everything they do.

5. A supplier who has a long-term contract might not care to supply quality parts for the buyer who is locked into such a relationship (contract).

Throughout these examples, there are negative inducements to quality performance. To control or reduce these risks, it is necessary to proceed in a number of ways. Today's concern for firms' organizational design is a reflection of the need to construct relationships which do not induce counter- productive acts.

Some of the steps that can be followed include

- Detecting signals of various forms and origins to reveal agents' behaviours, rationality and performance. A greater understanding of agents' behaviour can lead to a better design of the work place and the information system of the firm and to appropriate inducements of all parties involved in the firm's business.
- Managing and controlling the relationship between business partners, employees and workers. This means that no relationship can be taken for granted. Earlier, for example, we saw that information asymmetry can lead to opportunistic behaviour such as cheating, lying and being counter-productive, just because there may be an advantage to doing so without having to sustain the consequences of such behaviour.
- Developing an environment which is cooperative, honest, open and which leads to a frank exchange of information and optimal performances.

All these actions are important and commonly implemented in a TQM framework. It is therefore not surprising that much of the concern of quality managers and TQM deals with people, communication, simplification and the transparency of everything the firm does.

Information exchange and quality

The demand for quality has induced firms to define various industrial organizational frameworks which are altering the nature of doing business. GM and its suppliers are working closely together. The same applies to almost any major manufacturer. It is increasingly believed that the reduction in the number of suppliers is leading to a sort of semi-integration between the producer and its supplier of parts. Presuming no moral hazard, the uncertainty in quality production induces an information exchange between parties who buy and sell quality products. Such exchanges are bi-directional, relating to

- Information which can prevent faulty operations.

- Information needed for in-process operations.

In addition, it should be noted that such an 'openness' also signals a potentially broader database for learning and improving product quality.

Information asymmetry, health care and quality assurance

We have repeatedly seen that information asymmetry has a perverse effect on business and industrial exchanges as well as in services. This seems to be the case in health care systems, where information asymmetry between the buyers (consumers) and sellers (doctors, HMOs - Health Maintenance Organizations, hospitals, etc.) leads to extremely complex problems. In health care, Wallich and Holloway (1993) claim that customers have relatively little information about the product they are buying and must rely largely on sellers for advice. Doctors (the sellers) are paid according to the number of procedures they perform, regardless of their results (and thus quality). The price paid for this procedure often has no relationship to the cost borne by the buyer, who might be insured directly or indirectly through an employer. This cost is, in any case, paid up front, and thus there is both a double moral hazard on the seller and on the buyer side. It is not surprising, therefore, that the operational solution for health care systems is, to say the least, elusive. There are of course many solutions, each designed to meet political ends and maintain a traditional approach to health care. The English, French and American systems are deeply imbedded in values and rights negotiated over many years. For example, the evolving conventional wisdom in the US seems to be a form of 'Managed Competition', which would stimulate competition between providers of health care maintenance and service, thereby reducing both prices and augmenting the efficiency of service delivery. If a consumer can switch doctors for one reason or another, it might serve some purpose sometime, but the cost of such switches is usually great, and therefore it is not likely to matter. A quality assurance approach, whose purpose will be to *provide information regarding the health care system* and let this information be public (thereby informing the buyers and letting them make their own decisions) is a provocative idea which may moderate the market perversities of information asymmetry in health care. Quality assurance and the diffusion of information it can provide has, in this context, a strategic effect on the system which can reduce, at a small cost, the market inequities. Of course, the question remains of who monitors, audits and provides the information to the public? If firms such as those used in financial markets to evaluate the health of business enterprises can thrive, there may be good reasons to believe that in health care appropriate acceptable health care indices can be devised and diffused on an ongoing basis.

These problems are not unique to health care. To a large measure, TQM, transparency and simplicity in design (and thus control) are 'buzzwords', used to induce and motivate an organization design that can reduce the perversities of information asymmetry, the risks of moral hazard and adverse selection which also exist in an industrial setting.

Appendix 8.B: A review of game theory

Game theory involves decision making between two or more parties competing against one another for the purpose of reaching an objective, each of which may depend upon the other. These problems are, in general, difficult to analyse, as they have to take into account many factors. Game theory is and has been the subject of considerable study. In our case, we considered a special type of game called the *non-zero sum game* and whose solution is defined by the *Nash Equilibrium*. Explicitly, consider a bimatrix game

$$(\mathbf{A}, \mathbf{B}) = (\ a_{ij},\ \ b_{ij}\ ).$$

Let $\mathbf{x}$ and $\mathbf{y}$ be the vector of mixed strategies with elements x_i and y_j, and such that

$$\sum_{i=1}^{n} x_i = 1, 0 \leq x_i \leq 1, \sum_{j=1}^{m} y_j = 1, 0 \leq y_j \leq 1.$$

The value of the game for each of the players is given by

$$V_a = \mathbf{xAy}^T, V_b = \mathbf{xBy}^T.$$

and an equilibrium is defined for each strategy if the following conditions hold

$$\mathbf{Ay} \leq V_a, \mathbf{xB} \leq V_b.$$

For example, consider the 2*2 bimatrix game. We see that

$$\begin{aligned} V_a(x,y) &= (a_{11} - a_{12} - a_{21} + a_{22})xy + (a_{12} - a_{22})x + (a_{21} - a_{22})y + a_{22} \\ V_b(x,y) &= (b_{11} - b_{12} - b_{21} + b_{22})xy + (b_{12} - b_{22})x + (b_{21} - b_{22})y + b_{22}. \end{aligned}$$

Then, for an admissible solution for the first player, we require that

$$V_a(1,y) \leq V_a(x,y); V_a(0,y) \leq V_a(x,y),$$

which is equivalent to

$$A(1-x)y - a(1-x) \leq 0; Axy - ax \geq 0,$$

where

$$A = (a_{11} - a_{12} - a_{21} + a_{22}); a = (a_{22} - a_{12}),$$

that is when,

$$\begin{cases} x = 0, & \text{then} \quad Ay - a \leq 0 \\ x = 1 & \text{then} \quad Ay - a \geq 0 \\ 0 < x < 1 & \text{then} \quad Ay - a = 0 \end{cases}.$$

In this sense there can be three solutions $(0,y), (x,y)$ and $(1,y)$. We can similarly obtain a solution for the second player using parameters B and b. Say that $A \neq 0$ and $B \neq 0$, then a solution for x and y satisfy the following conditions:

$$\begin{aligned} y &\leq a/A \text{ if } A > 0 \\ y &\geq a/A \text{ if } A < 0 \\ x &\leq b/B \text{ if } B > 0 \\ x &\geq b/B \text{ if } B < 0. \end{aligned}$$

As a result, a simultaneous solution leads to the following equations for (x, y), which we have used in the text:

$$\begin{aligned} x^* &= a/A = \frac{a_{22} - a_{12}}{a_{11} - a_{12} - a_{21} + a_{22}} \\ y^* &= b/B = \frac{b_{22} - b_{12}}{b_{11} - b_{12} - b_{21} + b_{22}}. \end{aligned}$$

For further study of games and related problems we refer to Dresher (1961), Luce and Raiffa (1967), Moulin (1981), Nash (1950) and to the extensive literature available on games theory and economics.

CHAPTER 9

The control of quality in a temporal setting

9.1 Introduction

Quality management and improvement involves time in a number of ways. To monitor systems in their inter-temporal perspective, it is necessary to develop models which represent the process of change and which can be used to measure and monitor a process. Measurements (through sampling, control charts and any other method) may then be used to track and detect variations which may be unexpected, and which would require special attention. In Chapter 6, we noted that the approach underlying the application of control charts was the 'search for observations deviating from expectations'. To do so, we presumed that processes were stable and sought to devise 'tests', 'probability assessments', etc. which will reject our presumption that the process or variable being charted were stable. In fact, non-stationarities of various sorts, poor representation of the underlying process, collinearity over time etc. make it necessary to represent the temporal dependence such processes exhibit. Models of various sorts can then be devised to better represent and analyse shifting patterns of data over time, using available statistical means. There are many approaches and methods we can use in such circumstances. To this end, we introduce some basic notions of filtering theory and control charts of processes such as moving average charts, EWMA (exponentially weighted moving average) and ARIMA (Auto regressive and Moving Average Models) and related models. We also introduce notions of integrated control, as well as on-line range control. Some of the results presented here require some careful analysis, which will be relegated to the appendix for simplicity. We first begin by introducing some models such as a Cumulative Sum Process (CSP), MA, EWMA, ARIMA and other models.

9.2 CSP, MA, EWMA, ARIMA and other models

There are numerous models to represent the evolution of processes. Below we consider specific cases, including the MA (arithmetic moving average), EWMA (Exponentially Weighted Moving Average), CSP (Cumulative Sum Processes), and so on.

MA and EWMA

Moving Average (MA) charts are used instead of x-bar charts, for example, when the units produced take a significant amount of time. Let x_i be the sample record over a number of periods $i = 1, 2, \ldots, t$, where t represents the present time, then the average $\bar{x}_t$ at time t, calculated over the last K periods is,

$$\bar{x}_t = \frac{1}{K}\sum_{i=0}^{K} x_{t-i}.$$

There can be a number of such average charts, depending on the length of the series used in computing these averages. The more important the immediate past (and thus the less important the distant past), the smaller the number of points K used in computing this average. We can also consider a weighting of the sample observations giving priority to more recent observations. If w_i is a weight given to an observation i period in the past, then the weighted truncated average is

$$\bar{x}_t = \frac{\sum_{i=0}^{K} w_i x_{t-i}}{\sum_{i=0}^{K} w_i}.$$

It is useful to standardize these weights by letting $\sum_{i=0}^{K} w_i = 1$ and $0 \leq w_i \leq 1$. A special case of particular importance consists in letting w_i be a truncated geometric distribution with

$$w_i = \alpha^i(1-\alpha), i = 0, 1, 2, \ldots.$$

This leads to an exponentially weighted moving average (EWMA) process. Thus,

$$\begin{aligned}\bar{x}_t &= \sum_{i=0}^{\infty} \alpha^i(1-\alpha)x_{t-i} = (1-\alpha)[\sum_{i=1}^{\infty} \alpha^i x_{t-i} + \alpha^0 x_t] \\ &= (1-\alpha)x_t + \alpha[\sum_{j=0}^{\infty} \alpha^j(1-\alpha)x_{t-1-j}] = (1-\alpha)x_t + \alpha\bar{x}_{t-1},\end{aligned}$$

or

$$\bar{x}_t = \alpha\bar{x}_{t-1} + (1-\alpha)x_t, 0 \leq \alpha < 1.$$

The variance for this process is,

$$\text{var }(\bar{x}_t) = \alpha^2 \text{ var }(\bar{x}_{t-1}) + (1-\alpha)^2 \text{ var }(x_t)$$

or, using the notation $\text{var}(\bar{x}_t) = \sigma_t^2$ and $\text{var}(x_t) = \sigma^2$,

$$\sigma_t^2 = \alpha^2\sigma_{t-1}^2 + (1-\alpha)^2\sigma^2,$$

which leads in the long run (when the variances are stable and $\sigma_t^2 \cong \sigma^2$) to

$$\sigma_\infty^2 = \frac{(1-\alpha)}{(1+\alpha)}\sigma^2.$$

If the sample size is n, then σ^2 is the sample variance, which is equal to σ_0^2/n where σ_0^2 is the variance of individual values. Similarly, the long-term average estimate is obviously equal to the mean of the process x_t, equated to μ for clarity, or

$$E(\bar{x}_\infty) = E(x_\infty) = \mu.$$

These results can then be used to test sample MA outcomes, since its mean and variance are determined. In a control chart, the upper and lower limits of control (UCL and LCL) are then defined by

$$\begin{aligned} \text{UCL} &= \mu + k\sigma\sqrt{\frac{(1-\alpha)}{(1+\alpha)}}, \\ \text{LCL} &= \mu - k\sigma\sqrt{\frac{(1-\alpha)}{(1+\alpha)}}, \sigma = \sigma_0\sqrt{\frac{1}{n}}, \end{aligned}$$

where k is taken to be approximately 3 so that the number of false alarms is not too large. These charts, although applied, have received much less attention than CUSUM charts (for additional references see Crowder, 1987, 1989 as well as Robinson and Ho, 1978, AFNOR $X06-031.3, 1993$).

These charts, unlike Shewart charts and much like the CUSUM charts, are efficient for the detection of small shifts in a process. Their advantage is that they can be applied to continuous processes or to processes where past values are important for the determination of the current state. Of course, the smaller α, the smaller the effects of past measurements and the better the detection of small shifts (similar to CUSUM charts). Important shifts are poorly detected by such charts, however. The inverse occurs when α is large. Practically, one takes $\alpha = 0.75$ when we seek to control small shifts and $\alpha = 0.50$ when we seek to control large shifts. Thus, we generally take values for α between 0.50 and 0.75.

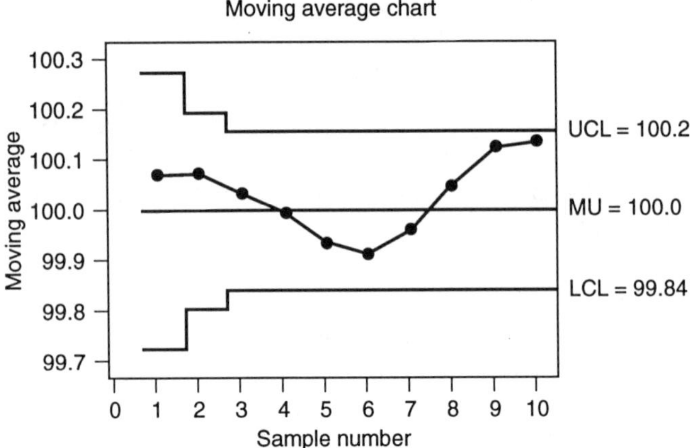

Figure 9.1: MA chart.

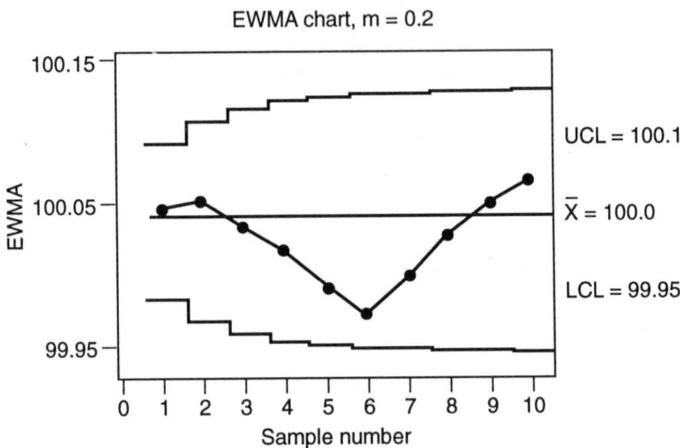

Figure 9.2a: Barrier control.

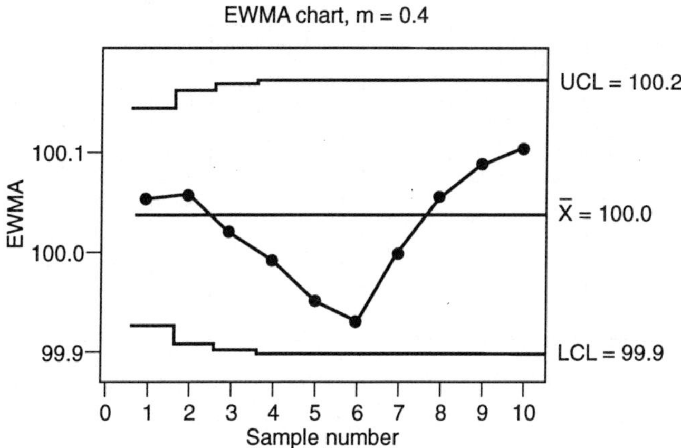

Figure 9.2b: Barrier control.

The ARL of EWMA Charts:

The efficiency of EWMA charts can be measured by their ARL. A table showing the calculation of such ARLs is given in Table 9.1 (AFNOR $X06-031.1, 1993$), where the probability for both the EWMA and Shewart charts of a false alarm is 0.95, and where we use the ARL as a measure of performance. The table is given as a function of the shift $\delta\sqrt{n}$. The first two columns, denoted Shewart, are the results for classical Shewart charts. Note that the table is arranged in pairs of columns. The first denotes the ARL when there is a shift, while the second denotes the ARL_{max}, which is the operational number of runs for such a chart (with a 95% percentile). Further, although we use the parameter α, in many instances a parameter $\lambda = 1 - \alpha$ is used. For example, an EWMA chart with $\alpha = 0.5$ and $n = 1$ will detect in the mean a shift δ of size 1 in 15.2 samples. If we were to use samples of size $4 (n = 4)$, then $\delta\sqrt{4} = 2$, and the shift will be detected in the mean in 3.4 samples. An extensive Table for such calculations can be found in AFNOR documents, as well as in national and ISO standard societies' documents. The parameter k in the table, measuring the number of standard deviations from the mean, were selected throughout the columns to ensure that the ARL under the hypothesis of no shift is correct is equal to 370 (corresponding to three standard deviations from the mean in a Shewart chart).

EWMA charts can be also applied to attributes charts, number of non-conformances per unit charts, etc. The ideas underlying these applications are the same as those above.

Table 9.1: ARL for Shewart and EWMA charts.

$\delta\sqrt{n}$	Shewart $L=$ 3.0		$\alpha = 0.5$ $L=$ 2.978		$\alpha = 0.6$ $L=$ 2.958		$\alpha = 0.65$ $L=$ 2.9445		$\alpha = 0.70$ $L=$ 32.925		$\alpha = 0.75$ $L=$ 2.898	
0.00	370		370		370		370		370		370	
0.25	281	841	196	584	174	515	162	479	149	439	135	397
0.50	155	464	72	210	58	169	52	150	46	132	41	114
0.75	81	242	30	86	24	67	22	60	21	52	18	46
1.00	44	130	15.2	41	12.7	33	11.7	29	10.9	26	10.3	24
1.50	15	44	6.0	14	5.5	12	5.3	11	5.2	11	5.2	10
2.00	6.3	18	3.4	7	3.3	6	3.4	6	3.4	6	3.5	6
2.50	3.2	9	2.4	4	2.4	4	2.5	4	2.9	4	2.6	4
3.00	2.0	5.	1.9	3	1.9	3	2.0	3	2.1	3	2.2	3
4.00	1.2	2	1.3	2	1.39	2	1.46	2	1.55	2	1.7	2
5.00	1.03	1	1.07	1	1.10	1	1.13	2	1.18	2	1.27	2

Computer aided example: *The MA chart*

MINITAB can produce an MA chart based on either subgroup means or individual observations. For our purposes, we used a sample size $n = 2$. The population distribution can also be either specified or estimated from the data set. In our case, it is specified as 100. If we fail to specify it, the computer will of course estimate it using the complete data set. If the standard deviation is not specified, MINITAB also estimates it in several possible ways when the samples sizes are larger than 1. These are based on pooled standard deviation and range estimates based on samples range calculations. The length of the moving average, of course, needs to be specified as well. The resulting MA chart, as well as the data set used for these calculations are, reproduced in Figure 9.1 and Table 9.2.

Table 9.2

Sample	Values	Values	Mean
1	99.9	100.25	100.12
2	100.01	100.13	100.07
3	99.96	99.98	99.97
4	99.84	100.06	99.95
5	99.85	99.93	99.89
6	99.86	99.94	99.90
7	100.05	100.15	100.10
8	100.00	100.30	100.15
9	100.07	100.21	100.14
10	100.10	100.16	100.13

Computer aided example: The EWMA chart

Using the data considered earlier in Chapter 6 and for the MA chart, we produced an EWMA chart using MINITAB. For our purposes, we have used a sample size of 2 and plotted the charts corresponding to the smoothing constants 0.2 and 0.4, respectively. Of course, the larger the smoothing constant, the greater the weight of past data. The computer also allows an estimation of the process variation (i.e. its standard deviation) and the smoothing constants.

CUSUM Charts

Cusum charts were introduced in Chapter 6. These are based on the cumulative sum of samples deviation about their mean. They were found to be useful for the detection of small changes and are defined as follows:

$$Z_t = [Z_{t-1} + (x_t - \mu)]^+, Z_0 = 0,$$

where $y^+ = \max(y, 0)$ and μ is some constant, appropriately selected. Say that when the process is in control, its mean is μ_0 and when it is not its mean is μ_1. A possible choice for μ is then $(\mu_0 + \mu_1)/2$. Then at some time, say i, suppose that we observe a CUSUM Z_i. A decision is then reached based on the following:

$$\begin{cases} \text{If } Z_i > h & \text{process is out of control} \\ \text{If } Z_i > h & \text{process is assumed in control.} \end{cases}$$

The CUSUM approach basically states that an alarm is triggered at some time i if there was at $\tau \geq 1$ periods in the past some switch in the process (from in to out of control). The CUSUM then acts similarly to an SPRT test, in which information is tested sequentially using some threshold limit as we saw in Chapters 5 and 6. If we consider the recurrence relationship above without its truncation at zero, we obtain a CUSUM process, here denoted as CSP. Such processes can be used to represent cumulative damage processes or other situations where a process state is determined by its past history. Its generalization will include the MA and EWMA processes.

Say that a process in control has switched to being out of control $k \geq 1$ periods earlier. At time t, the likelihood of this event is given by (Yaschin, 1993a, 1993b):

$$P_{1k}(y_{t-k-1}, y_{t-k-2}, \ldots, y_t \mid y_{t-k}, \ldots, y_t).$$

The likelihood of such an event not occurring is, however,

$$P_{0k}(y_{t-k-1}, y_{t-k-2}, \ldots, y_t \mid y_{t-k}, \ldots, y_t).$$

A SPRT test for the process switch from the null to alternative state k periods earlier can then be constructed as a ratio of these likelihoods, that is

$$\frac{P_{1k}(y_{t-k-1}, y_{t-k-2}, \ldots, y_t \mid y_{t-k}, \ldots, y_t)}{P_{0k}(y_{t-k-1}, y_{t-k-2}, \ldots, y_t \mid y_{t-k}, \ldots, y_t)} > e^h,$$

where h is the threshold parameter. The log-likelihood of the above function (given individual observations y_t and presuming that there was a switch k

periods earlier) is

$$z_{tk} = Ln \frac{P_{1k}(y_t \mid y_{t-1}, \ldots, y_{t-k})}{P_{0k}(y_t \mid y_{t-1}, \ldots, y_{t-k}))}$$

The likelihood test for $k \geq 1$ is therefore equivalent to

$$\sum_{i=t-k+1}^{t} z_{ik} > h.$$

When the observations are identically and independently distributed, this reduces to the test scheme developed by Page and seen in Chapter 6. As a result by summing the observations over time, we obtain a test which points out whether a change has occurred.

CSP processes

Let x_t be the record of a variable at time t, and let μ be its mean. The difference is $\epsilon_t = x_t - \mu$ which is a random variable with mean 0 and variance σ_t, measuring deviations from this mean. Let z_t be the cumulative sum of deviations $\epsilon_i, i = 1, 2, \ldots .t$. As a result, we have the following linear process which we call the Cumulative Sum Process (CSP):

$$z_t = \sum_{i=1}^{t} (x_i - \mu) = \sum_{i=1}^{t} \epsilon_i,$$

which can be written as follows:

$$z_{t+1} = z_t + \epsilon_t, z_0 = 0, E(\epsilon_t) = 0, \text{ var } (\epsilon_t) = \sigma_t^2, t = 0, 1, 2, \ldots.$$

The record of such a process can be noisy, a function of the sample size which is used to estimate the random variances ϵ. In particular, suppose that the error in measurement is some random variable with mean zero and a variance θ^2/n, where n is the sample size. We denote these errors by η_i and assume that they are independently distributed. Thus, the record y_t of the cumulative sum z_t is given by

$$y_t = \sum_{i=1}^{t} (\epsilon_i + \eta_i) = z_t + \sum_{i=1}^{t} \eta_i, t = 1, 2, .$$

Since the $\eta's$ are statistically independent, their mean is null and their variance is equal to the sum of the individual variances, which is $t\theta^2/n$. The measurement process can thus be defined by a non-stationary measurement process whose mean is zero and whose variance is $t\theta^2/n$. Let ν_t be the error term at time t. Then the CSP can be written as follows:

$$\begin{cases} z_{t+1} = z_t + \epsilon_t, \epsilon_t = N(0, \sigma^2), & z_0 = 0, t = 0, 1, 2, .. \\ y_t = z_t + \nu_t, \nu_t = N(0, t\theta^2/n) & t = 1, 2, 3, \ldots \end{cases}$$

We can study this process using filtering techniques, as we shall see below, which provide conditional estimates of the CSP based on data as it is collected from period to period.

The Random Walk process

When the noise process is not normal, but is given by a Bernoulli random variable, we obtain another CSP process which we call the 'symmetric random walk'. Such a process is often used to model wear and tear processes, the evolution of prices, and so on. This is defined as follows:

$$x_{t+1} = x_t + \epsilon_t, x_0 = 0$$

with

$$\epsilon_t =, \begin{cases} +1 & \text{w.p.} \quad p \\ -1 & \text{w.p.} \quad q \end{cases}$$

where ϵ_t are independent random variables with stationary growth probability $p > 0, p+q = 1$, in the time interval $(t, t+1)$. This process is the well known Gambler ruin problem, and underlies a large number of models. Our purpose in this example is to provide a statistical test for control of the range in such processes using the Average Run Length (ARL).

For this process, we consider the barriers defined by $(-a, b)$ at which we stop the process (see Figure 9.3). Assuming that t is the first time the process reaches this barrier, we have

$$t = \inf \{t \geq 0, x_t = (-a, b)\}.$$

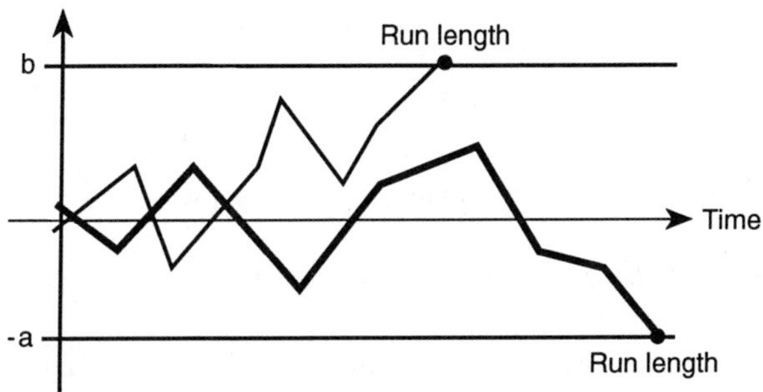

Figure 9.3: Barrier control and ARL charts.

For such a process, it is well known (see Chow, Robbins and Siegmund, 1971, Siegmund, 1985) that the probability of reaching one or the other boundaries is given by

$$P(x_t = -a) \quad = \quad \begin{cases} \frac{1-(p/q)^b}{1-(p/q)^{a+b}} & p \neq q \\ b/(a+b) & p = q \end{cases}$$

$$P(x_t = b) = \begin{cases} \frac{1-(p/q)^b}{1-(p/q)^{a+b}} & p \neq q \\ b/(a+b) & p = q \end{cases} \quad \ldots.$$

Further the Average Run Length (ARL) is then

$$\text{ARL} = E(t) = \begin{cases} \frac{b}{p-q} - \frac{a+b}{p-q}\left[\frac{1-(p/q)^b}{1-(p/q)^{a+b}}\right] & p \neq q \\ ab & \text{if } p = q = 1/2. \end{cases}$$

In other words, let $p = p_0$ denote the process parameters when it is operating according to an appropriate standard (which will mean that it is in control) and let p_1 denotes the process when it is out of control. Then, assuming that $H_i, i = 0, 1$ is a statement of the ith hypothesis,

$$\begin{cases} H_0 : p = p_0 \\ H_1 : p = p_1. \end{cases}$$

We can construct a test based on the specification of the average run lengths under both the null and alternative hypotheses. Suppose that the specified ARL under the null hypothesis is ARL_0, while under the alternative hypothesis it is ARL_1. Then, control parameters a and b can be calculated such that

$$\begin{cases} E(t \mid p_0) \geq \text{ARL}_0 \\ E(t \mid p_1) \leq \text{ARL}_1. \end{cases}$$

A solution of these two equations provides the control parameters $(-a, b)$ for control of the cumulative sum process. A solution of these two inequalities providing parameters (a, b) compatible with the risk specification (ARL_0, ARL_1) can be found numerically.

When a control is imposed only at the upper boundary b then

$$t = \inf \begin{cases} t \geq 0 & x_t \geq b \\ 0 & \text{if no such } t \text{ exists,} \end{cases}$$

and it is well known that the mean and the variance of the run length are

$$\text{ARL} = E(t) = b/(p-q), \ \text{var}\,(RL) = \frac{b[1-(p-q)^2]}{(p-q)^2}.$$

If $p > q$, the standardized random variable $(t\text{-ARL})/\sqrt{\text{var(RL)}}$ converges to a normally distributed standardized random variable, which can be used to construct confidence intervals on the ARL as a function of the hypothesized p and thus allow construction of control schemes for the process parameter p.

Problem

Let $p_0 = 0.05, p_1 = 0.15$, $\text{ARL}_0 = 250$ and $\text{ARL}_1 = 5$. Compute the limits (a, b) which are compatible with these specifications. If there is no such acceptable solution, find the least ARL_1 which can provide an acceptable solution. Once these results have been obtained, repeat your calculations by using the normal approximation and construct the test such that the type I error is $\alpha = 0.05$ while the type II error specified is $\beta = 0.15$.

Auto Regressive Moving Average models (ARMA)

Let w_i be n independently distributed standard normal random variables. Let c_i be n constants and let z_t be given by the weighted average

$$z_t = w_t + c_1 w_{t-1} + c_2 w_{t-2} + \ldots. + c_n w_{t-n}.$$

Such a model is called a Moving Average (moving average process) as we saw previously. We can rewrite this process as a linear system as follows. Let x_t be a vector given by

$$x_t = \begin{bmatrix} w_{t-n} & w_{t-n+1} & \cdots & \cdots & w_{t-1} \end{bmatrix}.$$

By definition, and in vector notation, we have

$$x_{t+1} = Ax_t + Bw_t \text{ where}$$

$$A = \begin{bmatrix} 0 & 1 & 0 & 0 & \ldots.. & 0 & 0 \\ 0 & 0 & 1 & 0 & \ldots.. & 0 & 0 \\ & & & & & & \\ 0 & 0 & 0 & 0 & \ldots.. & 0 & 1 \\ 0 & 0 & 0 & 0 & \ldots.. & 0 & 0 \end{bmatrix}; B = \begin{bmatrix} 0 \\ 0 \\ 0 \\ .. \\ .. \\ 0 \\ 1 \end{bmatrix}.$$

If, in addition, we define the parameters c's by the vector

$$c' = \begin{bmatrix} c_n & c_{n-1} & c_{n-2} & \ldots. & c_1 \end{bmatrix}$$

then

$$z_t = c' x_t + v_t, \text{ where } v_t = w_t.$$

This is called a'vector moving average model'. The EWMA treated earlier is such an example. In a similar manner, consider the following model, called the AR (Auto regressive) process

$$w_t = z_t + a_1 z_{t-1} + a_2 z_{t-2} + \ldots + a_n z_{t-n}$$

where a_i is a set of constants. We can represent this process as a linear system as well. Namely, we can write

$$y_{t+1} = \Lambda y_t + D w_t$$

and

$$z_t = -a' y_t + v_t$$

where the matrix Λ and the vectors D and a are given by

$$\Lambda = \begin{bmatrix} a_1 & a_2 & .. & .. & .. & .. & a_n \\ 1 & 0 & 0 & .. & .. & .. & 0 \\ 0 & 1 & 0 & .. & .. & .. & 0 \\ 0 & 0 & 1 & 0 & .. & .. & 0 \\ .. & .. & .. & .. & .. & .. & .. \\ .. & .. & .. & .. & .. & .. & .. \\ 0 & 0 & 0 & 0 & .. & 1 & 0 \end{bmatrix} ; D = \begin{bmatrix} 1 \\ 0 \\ 0 \\ 0 \\ .. \\ .. \\ 0 \end{bmatrix};$$

$$a' = \begin{bmatrix} a_1 & a_2 & .. & .. & a_n \end{bmatrix}.$$

Of course, we can construct processes which are combinations of AR and MA models. These are called ARMA models, and they have been studied extensively. An ARMA process is defined by a vector difference equation of the form

$$z_t + A_{1t}z_{t-1} + \ldots\ldots + A_{nt}z_{t-n} = B_{0t}v_t + \ldots\ldots + B_{mt}v_{t-m}$$

where the parameters $(A_{1t}, \ldots, A_{nt}, B_{0t}, \ldots, B_{mt})$ are usually independent of the parameter k. The variables $(v_t, \ldots, v_{t-m})$ are zero mean and normally distributed while $(z_t, z_{t-1}, \ldots, z_{t-n})$ is the process output. It is possible to express the set of equations above in a multivariate linear system of difference equations as we have done above. This equation would take the form

$$\mathbf{x}_{t+1} = \mathbf{A}_t\mathbf{x}_t + \mathbf{B}_t\mathbf{v}_t$$

where $(\mathbf{x}_{t+1}, \mathbf{x}_t, \mathbf{v}_t)$ are vectors of appropriate dimensions and $(\mathbf{A}_t, \mathbf{B}_t)$ are matrices which are defined according to the ARMA process used. These models are the subject of much study. The importance of such processes arises when attention must be given to the effect of data correlation in SPC. Additional references include Barnard (1959), Box and Jenkins (1976), Crowder (1987), Hunter (1986) and Alwan and Roberts (1988).

9.3 Filtering and the management of quality

Basic concepts of filtering theory

The filtering problem is defined by Kalman and Bucy (1961) as follows:

> Given the actually observed values of a random process over some interval of time $[t, T]$, find the conditional probabilities of all values at time t of another related measurement random process.

For example, the yield of a process collected over time can be used to estimate the true process yield represented by a model. Once the conditional probabilities relating the model and the measurement processes are found, the estimation problem is resolved. For example, consider the two processes

$$\begin{aligned} \text{Model} : x_{t+1} &= f(x_t, w_t) \\ \text{Measurement} : y_t &= h(x_t) + v_t, \end{aligned}$$

where w_t and v_t are two error terms which are assumed to be zero mean normal uncorrelated random variables with known variances. The function f denotes the model, while h denotes the noisy measurement. Since both processes are subject to random disturbances (w_t, v_t), the evolution $\{x_t, t > 0\}$ and $\{y_t, t > 0\}$ define two stochastic processes. For example, x_t might denote the evolution of a variable such as sales, price, the number of defective units sold, etc., whose dynamic evolution is described by the function $f(.)$, while y_t is the record of this variable which is subject to measurement errors (for example, the number of complaints recorded over time and so on). Let Y^T be the set of all measurements up to and including time, T, that is

$$Y^T = \{y_0, y_1, y_2, \ldots, y_T\}.$$

The conditional probabilities relating the model and the measurement processes are given by

$$P(x_t \mid y_0, y_1, y_2, \ldots, y_T) = P(x_t \mid Y^T)$$

The conditional mean estimate of x_t, which is based on a temporal record up to and including time T, or Y^T, is denoted by

$$E(x_t \mid Y^T) = \hat{x}_{t|T}.$$

Next, let the error estimate be

$$\epsilon_{t|T} = x_t - \hat{x}_{t|T}, \quad \text{with } E\epsilon_{t|T} = E(x_{t|T} - \hat{x}_{t|T}) = 0$$

The conditional error variance is

$$E(\epsilon_{t|T}^2) = V_{t|T}.$$

Filtering theory is concerned with the selection of optimum estimates $(\hat{x}_{t|T}, V_{t|T})$ based on the information collected in the sample Y^T, assuming that the parameters of w_t and v_t, the random error terms, are known. This problems is a fundamental one, underlying prediction (forecasting) and the control of partially observable systems.

If the measurement process Y^T leads (lags) the model process, i.e. $t > T (t < T)$, we obtain forecast (smoothing) estimates. When $t = T$, we call these filter estimates. Namely,

If $t = T$,	Filtering.
If $t > T$,	Forecasting.
If $t < T$,	Smoothing.

As a result, the time phasing of the measurement vector Y^T and the current state at time t of the (quality related) variable measured provide a definition of what kind of problem we have. If we seek to determine a future state based on current state information, it will mean prediction or forecasting. If it seeks to estimate in hindsight a process' parameters (as in capability studies), it will then be called and treated as a smoothing problem. The distinction between these types of problems are important. Further, for some models, in particular linear ones, there are some analytical results which can be used profitably in applications as well as to approximate other more difficult problems. We first consider the simple linear and discrete time filtering problem. This is given by

$$x_{t+1} = a_t x_t + w_t, \text{ where } x_0 \; N(\alpha, \sigma^2),$$

where a_t is a known function of time t, x_t is a variable and w_t is an error term with zero mean and known variance. The time record of x_t is given by a linear measurement process

$$y_t = h_t x_t + v_t,$$

where h_t is given v_t is a measurement error with

$$E(v_t) = E(w_t) = 0, E(v_t w_t) = 0, E(v_t^2) = q_t^2, E(w_t^2) = r_t^2.$$

If $a_t = 1$, this will correspond to a cumulative sum process (CSP). The quality control problem consists, then, in testing the hypothesis that $a_t = 1$ versus the alternative that it is not. Further, given a data set, it might even be possible to estimate a_t or/and the statistical parameters of the model if these are not *apriori* specified. We shall consider an example to this effect later on, however. If we use a Bayesian updating scheme (see Chapter 4), then, if at time $t = 0$ we collect y_0, it can be used to obtain the conditional estimate $p(x_0 \mid y_0)$. Namely

$$p(x_0 \mid y_0) = \frac{p(x_0)p(y_0 \mid x_0)}{\int_{-\infty}^{+\infty} p(x_0)p(y_0 \mid x_0)dx_0},$$

where $p(x_0)$ is the prior probability distribution of x_0, which is assumed to be normal with mean α and variance σ^2. The conditional probability $p(y_0 \mid x_0)$ is the likelihood which has a normal distribution with mean $h_0 x_0 = h_0 \alpha$ and variance $h_0^2 \sigma^2 + q_0^2$. Since all these distributions are normal, they have a reproducing property. That is $p(x_0 \mid y_0)$ has a normal probability distribution where (as we have seen earlier)

$$\hat{x}_{0|0} = \frac{\alpha/\sigma^2 + h_0 v_0/q_0^2}{1/V_{0|0}},$$

$$1/V_{0|0} = \frac{1}{\sigma^2} + \frac{h_0^2}{q_0^2}.$$

At time $t = 1$, we then collect y_1 and obtain the conditional distribution

$p(x_1 \mid y_0, y_1) = p(x_1 \mid Y^1)$, and so on for times $t = 2, 3, 4, \ldots$. At time $t = 0$, we have (by Bayes rule)

$$p(x_1 \mid y_0, y_1) = \frac{\int p(x_0 \mid y_0) p(x_1 \mid x_0) p(y_1 \mid x_1) dx_0}{p(y_1 \mid y_0)}$$

All these distributions are normal with,

$$p(y_1 \mid x_1) = N(h_1 x_1, q_1^2); p(x_1 \mid x_0) = N(a_0 x_0, r_0^2),$$

and after some elementary manipulations, consisting of the application of Bayes' theorem (see Chapter 4), we note that $p(x_1 \mid y_0, y_1)$ has a normal probability distribution with conditional mean $\hat{x}_{1|1}$ and conditional error variance $V_{1|1}$, which are given by

$$\begin{aligned} \hat{x}_{1|1} &= a_0 \hat{x}_{0|0} + K_1 (y_1 - h_1 a_0 \hat{x}_{0|0}), \\ \frac{1}{V_{1|1}} &= \frac{h_1^2}{q_1^2} + \frac{1}{r_0^2 + a_0^2 V_{0|0}}; K_1 = \frac{h_1 (r_0^2 + a_0^2 V_{0|0})}{h_1^2 (r_0^2 + a_0^2 V_{0|0}) + q_1^2}. \end{aligned}$$

Here K_1 is called the *Kalman gain* at time $t = 1$, and it expresses the weight attached to correcting the mean estimate $\hat{x}_{1|1}$ when a time record y_1 is obtained at time $t = 1$. The larger a sample size (i.e. the more precise the observation), the greater the Kalman gain. The term $y_1 - h_1 a_0 \hat{x}_{0|0}$ is also called the 'innovation', and it measures the difference between the expected measurement and the actual measurement. Note that the expectation of the innovation is null while its variance is $K_1^2 \text{var}(y_1) = K_1^2 q_1^2$. In other words, if an innovation is too large, having a probability which is too small, then there will be some basis for believing that the process is not in control. In quality control systems, the behaviour of the innovation is therefore extremely important. If it is very large, it may mean that there is some departure from the expected behaviour of the model and therefore it may require special attention or require further consideration (through additional tests for example). The Kalman gain in our case is inherent to the system and expresses the sensibility of the updating scheme to error correction. If errors are large the gain will be small since the effects of more recent measurements is less sure, while if errors are small, the Kalman gain is large. For example, suppose that there are no measurement error, i.e. $q_1^2 = 0$ and therefore

$$K_1' = 1/h_1.$$

Since

$$K_1' > K_1 = \frac{h_1 (r_0^2 + a_0^2 V_{0|0})}{h_1^2 (r_0^2 + a_0^2 V_{0|0}) + q_1^2}$$

we note that the gain is at most $1/h_1$. When $h_1 = 1$, then $K_1' = 1$, and therefore

$$\hat{x}_{1|1} = a_0 \hat{x}_{0|0} + (y_1 - h_1 a_0 \hat{x}_{0|0}) = y_1,$$

which means that the mean is always taken as the record of the process. The corresponding error variance will naturally turn out to be zero:

$$\frac{1}{V_{1|1}} = \frac{1}{O} + \frac{1}{r_0^2 + a_0^2 V_{0|0}} = \infty \text{ and } V_{1|1} = 0.$$

In general, when Y^t is the available data, Bayes formula is

$$p(x_{t+1} \mid Y^t) = \frac{\int p(x_t \mid Y^t) p(x_{t+1} \mid x_t) p(y_{t+1} \mid x_{t+1}) dx_t}{p(y_{t+1} \mid Y^t)},$$

where

$$p(y_t \mid x_t) = N(h_t \hat{x}_{t|t}, q_t^2); p(x_{t+1} \mid x_t) = N(a_t \hat{x}_{t|t}, r_t^2).$$

The conditional mean estimate and the error variance are then given in recursive form by the following equations:

$$\begin{aligned}
\hat{x}_{t+1|t+1} &= a_t \hat{x}_{t|t} + K_{t+1}(y_{t+1} - h_{t+1} a_t \hat{x}_{t|t}) \\
\frac{1}{V_{t+1|t+1}} &= \frac{h_{t+1}^2}{q_{t+1}^2} + \frac{1}{r_t^2 + a_t^2 V_{t|t}}; \\
K_{t+1} &= \frac{h_{t+1}[r_t^2 + a_t^2 V_{t|t}]}{h_{t+1}^2 (r_t^2 + a_t^2 V_{t|t}) + q_{t+1}^2} = \frac{h_{t+1}^2}{q_{t+1}^2} + \frac{1}{r_t^2 + a_t^2 V_{t|t}}
\end{aligned}$$

An extrapolation to the next period based on the current measurement provides a forecast, which we denote by

$$\hat{x}_{t+1|t} = a_t \hat{x}_{t|t}; \frac{1}{V_{t+1|t}} = \frac{1}{r_t^2 + a_t^2 V_{t|t}},$$

in which case the filter equations can be rewritten as

$$\begin{aligned}
\hat{x}_{t+1|t+1} &= \hat{x}_{t+1|t} + K_{t+1}(y_{t+1} - \hat{x}_{t+1|t}) \\
\frac{1}{V_{t+1|t+1}} &= \frac{h_{t+1}^2}{q_{t+1}^2} + \frac{1}{V_{t+1|t}},
\end{aligned}$$

which describes an estimates' adjustment expressed as a function of the past period's forecasts and the Kalman gain K_{t+1}. Note in this case that x_{t+1} has a normal probability distribution given by $N(\hat{x}_{t+1|t+1}, V_{t+1|t+1})$ which can be used to construct confidence intervals for x_{t+1} reached at time t. Applications are considered below. Extensions to multivariate models, continuous time models as well as various nonlinear processes and measurements have been considered by many authors. There is, in fact, a considerable body of theoretical research and practical applications which make this approach suitable both on theoretical and practical grounds. Some references include Sage and Melsa (1971) and Tapiero (1977, 1988) and Jazwinsky (1970). Conceptually, the filtering approach develops a model representing the evolution over time of a process for which we can exactly or approximately obtain an estimate of the probability distributions of the states when observations are accumulated over time.

The disadvantage (which is also an advantage in some cases) of such an approach is that it forces us to construct a model of the process' evolution. If this model is the true image of 'reality', then the data requirements to estimate, track and control the model (or the situation at hand) are reduced drastically. The greater the number of assumptions made (i.e. the larger the prior knowledge), the lesser are the data requirements. The classical SQC/SPC approach treats such problems as if they occur at one instant, or as belonging to one identical (and not changing) statistical population. As a result, it reduces the amount of data required to evaluate a process by reducing the statistical assumptions made about such a process. Thus, SPC/SQC is in general an aggregative and simplified view of the processes we are supposed to control and manage.

Statistics 'requires and consumes' large quantities of data to be statistically meaningful, while in practice data is costly to obtain, and meaningful data is usually hard to come by. For this reason, it is imperative to construct models and guess what the underlying process is, and only then seek data to confirm (or not) our presumptions regarding the real evolution of states. Control is based on deviations from these presumptions (usually expressed as feedback models) which provide signals that are wrong in such presumptions (and, thereby, control of some sort is necessary), or that data collected simply gave the wrong signal (also called false alarm). The control of quality requires that these particular facets of the problem under study be carefully assessed and valued so that effective quality management and control schemes can be devised in an economic manner.

For quality control purposes, the behaviour of the forecasts' differences can be revealing. If it is large, it may provide a signal that the process ought to be attended to and checked for some special causes (such as breakdown, process change etc.). Explicitly, we have

$$\hat{x}_{t+1|t+1} - \hat{x}_{t+1|t} = K_{t+1}(y_{t+1} - h_{t+1}a_t\hat{x}_{t|t}) = K_{t+1}(y_{t+1} - \hat{y}_{t+1})$$

where

$$\hat{y}_{t+1} = Ey_{t+1} = h_{t+1}Ex_{t+1} = h_{t+1}a_t\hat{x}_{t|t}.$$

Here, $\hat{y}_{t+1}$ is the measurement forecast, y_{t+1} is the actual observation and both are multiplied by the Kalman gain. Practically (in the spirit of acceptance sampling of Chapter 5 and control charts of Chapter 6), we can devise a decision model such that if $| x_{t+1|t+1} - \hat{x}_{t+1|t} | \geq \epsilon$, this can provide a cause for the concern that we may have erred in assuming that the model is behaving as expected.

When the data regarding the process (records) are not perturbed by measurement errors, then the problem is simplified, as we have seen earlier. This is not the case, however, if the model parameters are themselves subject to random variations. In such a case, we can use either a Bayesian approach (as seen in Chapter 4) or a Maximum Likelihood estimation approach. Examples will be considered subsequently however.

The control of a dynamic process: Filtering approach

A dynamic process can, at some unknown time, switch to another trajectory. In this sense, at any particular time a process 'is in control' if the hypothesis that it has not switched to some other process cannot be rejected. Similar to simple processes considered in Chapters 5 and 6, we can consider a process (rather than a parameter) as a null hypothesis. For simplicity, we consider simple binary hypotheses, and summarize some basic results. Let Y^t be a time series representing sample information collected over time, and define two linear dynamic models, each generating a set of theoretical measurements $y_t^i, i = 0, 1$, with known statistical characteristics, where $i = 0$ will be used to denote the null hypothesis process and $i = 1$ denotes the alternative dynamic process. In particular, denote by H_i the hypothesis that the data collected y_t(an element of Y^t) originates from process i, that is

$$H_i : y_t = y_t^i.$$

Let $P(Y^t \mid H_i)$, the likelihood of the time series Y^t given the ith hypothesis, be the conditional probability of the time series given hypothesis i is true. In other words, for $i = 0$, we shall presume that $P(Y^t \mid H_0)$ is the probability distribution of the time series *given that it originates through the process (hypothesis)*$i = 0$. Of course, such a statement can be true or not. For simplicity let c_{ij} be the cost if we assert hypothesis H_i to be true, and then hypothesis H_j turns out to be the true one. If p_j is the prior probability that process j is true, the expected cost of such a decision problem is (as seen in Chapters 4, 5, 6) simply

$$\begin{aligned} R &= p_0 c_{00} P[\text{ accept } H_0 \mid \text{ when } H_0 \text{ is true }] \\ &+ p_0 c_{01} P[\text{ accept } H_0 \mid \text{ when } H_1 \text{ is true }] \\ &+ p_1 c_{10} P[\text{ accept } H_1 \mid \text{ when } H_0 \text{ is true }] \\ &+ p_1 c_{11} P[\text{ accept } H_1 \mid \text{ when } H_1 \text{ is true }]. \end{aligned}$$

We have seen earlier (Chapter 6) that the minimization of this expected cost (risk)R leads to the likelihood ratio test

$$\Lambda(t) = \frac{P[Y^t \mid H_1] \geq p_0(c_{10} - c_{00})}{P[Y^t \mid H_0] \leq p_1(c_{01} - c_{11})} = F.$$

Thus,

$$\begin{aligned} \text{If } \Lambda(t) &\geq F \text{ we accept the alternative hypothesis } H_1 \\ \text{If } \Lambda(t) &\leq F \text{ we accept the null hypothesis } H_0. \end{aligned}$$

where, of course, $P[Y^t \mid H_i]$ is the likelihood of the hypothesis. Because of the monotonicity of this function, it is sometimes convenient to take the log likelihood, in which case

$$\begin{aligned} \text{If } Ln\Lambda(t) &\geq LnF = z, \text{ accept the alternative hypothesis } H_1 \\ \text{If } Ln\Lambda(t) &\leq LnF = z, \text{ accept the null hypothesis} H_0. \end{aligned}$$

A major difficulty remains: how to determine the likelihood probabilities? For the linear dynamic model we have, by the total probability rule,

$$P[Y^t \mid H_i] = P[y_t \mid Y^{t-1}, H_i]P[Y^{t-1} \mid H_i],$$

which defines a recursive equation in the likelihood. Taking the natural log of this expression, we have

$$\text{LnP } [Y^t \mid H_i] = \text{LnP}[y_t \mid Y^{t-1}, H_i] + \text{LnP}[Y^{t-1} \mid H_i],$$

and setting

$$q_t^i = \text{ LnP } [Y^t \mid H_i],$$

then

$$q_t^i = q_{t-1}^i + \text{ LnP } [y_t \mid Y^{t-1}, H_i].$$

But $P[y_t \mid Y^{t-1}, H_i]$ is the probability distribution of the observation at time t based on the filter estimates when we use the ith hypothesis.

Example

Consider, for example, the following dynamic models, each generating a set of theoretical measurements $y_t^i, i = 0, 1$, or

$$\begin{aligned} x_{t+1}^i &= A^i x_t^i + C^i w_t^i, \\ y_t^i &= H^i x_t^i + v_t^i, \end{aligned}$$

with

$$\begin{aligned} E(x_0^i) &= \hat{x}_0^i, \text{ var } (x_0^i) = V_0^i, Ew_t^i = 0, \text{cov } (w_t^i w_{st}^i) = R_t \delta_{ts} \\ Ev_t^i &= 0, \text{ cov } (v_t^i v_{st}^i) = Q_t \delta_{ts}, \text{ cov } (w_t^i v_{st}^i) = \text{ cov } (v_t^i, x_0^i) \\ &\qquad = \text{cov}(w_t^i, x_0^i) = 0 \end{aligned}$$

Thus $P]y_t \mid Y^{t-1}, H_i]$ is necessarily a normal probability distribution with mean

$$E(y_t \mid Y^{t-1}, H_i) = H^i \hat{x}_{t|t-1}^i = H^i A^i \hat{x}_{t-1|t-1}^i,$$

where $\hat{x}_{t|t-1}^i$ is the next period forecast and $\hat{x}_{t-1|t-1}^i$ is the current filter estimate. The variance can be calculated similarly. Therefore, the log likelihood is explicitly calculated by

$$\begin{aligned} &\text{LnP } [y_t \mid Y^{t-1}, H_i] = (-1/2)Ln(\mid H^i V_{t|t-1}^i H^{i'} + Q_t \mid) \\ &- \ (1/2)(y_t - H^i A^i \hat{x}_{t-1|t-1}^i)'(H^i V_{t|t-1}^i H^{i'})^{-1}(y_t - H^i A^i \hat{x}_{t-1|t-1}^i), \end{aligned}$$

where $V_{t|t-1}$ (and the conditional mean estimates) is the variance evolution given by

$$\hat{x}_{t|t}^i = A^i \hat{x}_{t-1|t-1}^i + K_t^i]y_t^i - H^i A^i \hat{x}_{t-1|t-1}^i], \hat{x}_{0|0} = \hat{x}_0$$

$$\begin{aligned} \hat{x}^i_{t|t-1} &= A^i \hat{x}^i_{t-1|t-1} \\ V^i_{t|t-1} &= A^i V^i_{t-1|t-1} A^{i'} + C^i R^i_{t-1} C^{i'} \\ V^i_{t|t} &=]I - K^i_t H^i] V^i_{t|t-1}, V^i_{0|0} = V^i_0 \end{aligned}$$

and the Kalman gain is

$$K^i_t = V^i_{t|t-1} H^{i'}] H^i V^i_{t|t-1} H^{i'} + Q^i]^{-1}.$$

As a result, the decision to accept one dynamic process compared to another is given by comparing the log likelihood ratio to some threshold, or

$$z(t) = q^1_t - q^0_t + \text{ LnP } [y_t \mid Y^{t-1}, H_1] - \text{ LnP } [y_t \mid Y^{t-1}, H_0]$$

and

$$\text{If } z(t) \geq \eta \text{ then accept } H_1$$

where $\text{LnP}[y_t \mid Y^{t-1}, H_1]$ is given above and η is expressed in terms of the costs c_{ij} we have defined earlier. Applications, approximations as well as special cases are treated next.

9.4 Applications

Statistical control of a temporal process

Say that x_t represents a quality variable which is being improved through investments in total quality management, denoted by u_t at time t. Measurements are given by observation of a firm's performance (e.g. the number of complaints, the firm's sales, the number of services performed, etc.). Assuming that the process is operating in a normal state, hypothesize a 'null' evolution and measurement processes which are represented by the following:

$$\begin{aligned} H_0 : &\quad \text{The null operating process} \\ x_{t+1} = &\quad f(x_t, u_t, w_t); y_t = h(x_t) + v_t, \end{aligned}$$

where w_t and v_t are error terms, normally distributed for convenience. Derive (through linear approximations) recursive equations for the conditional estimates $\hat{x}_{t|t}$ and $V_{t|t}$. If $E(y_t) = Eh(x_t) = H(\hat{x}_{t|t}, V_{t|t})$ and $\text{var}(y_t) = Ev^2_t + \text{var}(h(x_t)) = Ev^2_t + G(\hat{x}_{t|t}, V_{t|t})$, construct a control scheme using the confidence interval for $E(y_t) = H(\hat{x}_{t|t}, V_{t|t})$. Explicitly, let α be the (producer) risk, and say that PA denotes a tolerance performance differential. Then,

$$P[\mid y_t - H(\hat{x}_{t|t}, V_{t|t}) \mid \leq PA] \geq 1 - \alpha.$$

By the same token, we can construct the alternative hypothesis

$$\begin{aligned} H_1 : &\quad \text{The alternative operating process} \\ x_{t+1} = &\quad f'(x_t, u_t, w'_t); y_t = h'(x_t) + v'_t, \end{aligned}$$

with

$$\begin{aligned} E(y_t) &= \text{Eh}'\ (x_t) = H'(\hat{x}_{t|t}, V_{t|t}) \text{ and} \\ \text{var}\ (y_t) &= E(v'^2_t) + \text{ var}\ (h'(x_t)) = \text{Ev}'^2_t + G'(\hat{x}_{t|t}, V_{t|t}). \end{aligned}$$

Given a probability β(the type II error, or consumer risk), then

$$P[|\ y_t - H'(\hat{x}_{t|t}, V_{t|t})\ | \geq PB] \leq \beta,$$

where PB is a tolerance performance differential. On the basis of the type I and II errors thus defined, we construct appropriate ranges, say F_t, such that as long as $y_t \in F_t$, the process is in control (and we accept the null operating model). Otherwise, we cannot accept this model.

Consider the special case:

$$H_0 : x_{t+1} = ax_t + w_t, y_t = x_t + v_t, w_t \cong N(0, \epsilon^2), v_t \cong N(0, \theta^2),$$

where 'a' is a known constant. The conditional estimates $\hat{x}_{t|t}$ and $V_{t|t}$ associated to this null operating process are

$$\begin{aligned} \hat{x}_{t+1|t+1} &= a\hat{x}_{t|t} + K_{t+1}(y_{t+1} - a\hat{x}_{t|t}), \\ \frac{1}{V_{t+1|t+1}} &= \frac{1}{\theta^2} + \frac{1}{\epsilon^2 + a^2 V_{t|t}} \\ K_{t+1} &= \frac{\theta^2 + a^2 V_{t|t}}{(\epsilon^2 + a^2 V_{t|t}) + \theta^2} \\ E(y_t) &= E(x_t) = \hat{x}_{t|t} \text{ and } \text{ var } (y_t) = V_{t|t} + \theta^2. \end{aligned}$$

For the alternative model we assume

$$H_1 : x_{t+1} = \delta x_t + w_t, y_t = x_t + v_t, w_t \cong N(0, \epsilon^2), v_t \cong N(0, \theta^2).$$

For this alternative process, the conditional estimates are $\hat{x}'_{t|t}$ and $V'_{t|t}$ with

$$\begin{aligned} \hat{x}'_{t+1|t+1} &= \delta\hat{x}'_{t|t} + K'_{t+1}(y_{t+1} - \delta\hat{x}'_{t|t}), \\ \frac{1}{V'_{t+1|t+1}} &= \frac{1}{\theta^2} + \frac{1}{\epsilon^2 + \delta^2 V'_{t|t}}; \\ K'_{t+1} &= \frac{\theta^2 + \delta^2 V'_{t|t}}{(\epsilon^2 + \delta^2 V'_{t|t}) + \theta^2}, \end{aligned}$$

and finally

$$E(y'_t) = E(x_t) = \hat{x}'_{t|t} \text{ and var } (y'_t) = V'_{t|t} + \theta^2_t,$$

and thus, the 'producer' and the 'consumer's' risk for this type of problems are defined by

$$\text{Prob}\ [-PA \ \leq \ \frac{(y_t - E(y_t))}{\sqrt{\text{var}(y_t)}} \leq PA] \geq 1 - \alpha$$

$$\text{Prob}\left[-PB \leq \frac{(y'_t - E(y'_t))}{\sqrt{\text{var}(y_t)}} \leq PB\right] \leq \beta,$$

where PA and PB are the parameters to be selected appropriately as a function of the risks α and β.

Problems

1. Assume that measurements are not perturbed by errors, but consider δ as a random variable. In this case, proceed as above and obtain the interval estimates for a producer and a consumer risk.

2. Consider the univariate exponential smoothing model,

$$\begin{aligned}
\mu_t &= \mu_{t-1} + \eta_t, t = 1, 2, \ldots T \\
y_t &= \mu_t + \epsilon_t,
\end{aligned}$$

where ϵ_t and η_t are serially independent normally distributed random variables with means zero and variances σ^2 and σ_0^2, respectively. Using this model, demonstrate that the Kalman Filter for the conditional estimates of the time series μ_t, is given by

$$\begin{aligned}
\hat{\mu}_{t+1|t} &= \hat{\mu}_{t|t-1} + K_t(y_{t+1} - \hat{\mu}_{t|t-1}), t = 1, 2, \ldots T \\
p_{t+1|t} &= p_{t|t-1} - \frac{p^2}{1 + p_{t|t-1}} + (\sigma_0^2/\sigma^2), \\
K_t &= \frac{p_{t|t-1}}{1 + p_{t|t-1}}.
\end{aligned}$$

Then demonstrate in steady state that K_t is time invariant and equal to

$$K = \frac{-(\sigma_0^2/\sigma^2) + \sqrt{(\sigma_0^2/\sigma^2)^2 + 4(\sigma_0^2/\sigma^2)}}{2},$$

and therefore the filter reduces to the exponential smoothing model

$$\hat{\mu}_{t+1|t} = (1 - K)\hat{\mu}_{t|t-1} + K y_t.$$

Example: Perfect measurement and random parameters

Consider the case $a_t = \tilde{a}$, which is a random variable with unknown mean and unknown variance, a and σ^2, respectively, or

$$x_t = \tilde{a}x_{t-1} + \epsilon_t, x_0 = N(\hat{x}_0, \sigma^2(x_0)),$$

where ϵ_t is a random variable which has a zero mean and a variance σ^2. We assume that at any time t, the record of this process is perfectly recorded, namely

$$y_t = x_t.$$

Furthermore, we let x_0 be distributed as a normal probability distribution with a known mean $\hat{x}_0$ and known variance $\sigma^2(x_0)$ as seen in Chapter 3. Say that at time n we have the data set $x_i, i = 0, 1, 2, 3, \ldots n$. If we apply the log likelihood estimation technique (as in Chapter 3), then estimates for the parameters of the probability distribution of $\tilde{a}$, are given by

$$\hat{a}_n = \sum_{i=1}^{n} \frac{x_i x_{i-1}}{x_{i-1}^2}; E(\sigma_n^2) =) \sum_{i=1}^{n} [x_i - \hat{a}x_{i-1}]^2 / n.$$

Therefore, assuming that the parameter has a normal probability distribution, we can test on the basis of the cumulative sums x_t the null hypothesis that the estimate at time t is $\hat{a}_t = 1$, against the alternative that it is not. If, in addition, we assume that records are perturbed by measurement errors, the calculations are slightly more complex.

Problem

Show that given the perfect records of the process the mean and variance estimate of ã are given by

$$\begin{aligned} \hat{a}_n &= \hat{a}_{n-1} + \frac{x_n x_{n-1}}{x_{n-1}^2} \\ E(\sigma_n^2) &= [(\sigma_{n-1}^2) - \bar{x}_{n-1} \frac{x_n x_{n-1}}{x_{n-1}^2}] \frac{(n-1)}{n} + \frac{x_n - \hat{a}_n x_{n-1}}{n} \end{aligned}$$

where $\bar{x}_n$ is the average of past records, or

$$\bar{x}_{n-1} = \frac{1}{n-1} \sum_{i=1}^{n-1} x_{i-1}$$

9.5 Control of the Range Process

The control of quality requires that we predict and control a process variability. Prior analysis has emphasized the control of the means only. At present we generalize such studies to the control of the range of a Cumulative Sum Process (CSP). This is an important problem which has been unsolved in the past. The results presented here are based on Vallois (1993) and Vallois and Tapiero (1995a, 1995b). For simplicity, we provide only the basic results since proofs are lengthy and difficult.

Consider the range of an ongoing process. Rather than controlling the average through a combined x-bar and range charts (to control the within sample variation, see Chapter 6), we seek to control the range itself (and thus detect outliers or points which exhibit unexpected variability). Let $x_i, i = 1, 2, \ldots$ be the record of this process. Namely, at any time $t + 1$, the process can either increase or decrease by a unit with the same probability, or

$$x_{t+1} = x_t + \epsilon_t, x_0 = 0$$

with

$$\epsilon_t = \begin{cases} +1 & \text{w.p.} \quad 1/2 \\ -1 & \text{w.p.} \quad 1/2 \end{cases}$$

where ϵ_t are independent random variables as defined above. Consider now the range of an ongoing process and let the range at time t be

$$R_t = \max[x_1, x_2, x_3, \ldots, x_t] - \min[x_1, x_2, x_3, \ldots, x_t].$$

A controlled process will have a predictable range process, while an uncontrolled process points out to some unlikely process variation. Practically, range control can help locate and control outliers (which it is often very important to do). The range process was first introduced by Feller (1951), who remarked that it is, in general, difficult to compute the R_t distributions for a fixed t. Since R_t is a growing process, we can equivalently study its inverse process. Namely, that this is the first time that the process has a range which is greater than n, or

$$\theta(n) = \inf(t \geq 0; R_t > n).$$

Clearly, $\{R_n < a\}$ is equal to $\{\theta(a) > n\}$, and therefore the law of R_t can be studied equivalently through the probability law of $\theta(a)$. Such a result is given by Vallois (1993) (see also Vallois and Tapiero, 1995a). Then the mean of $\theta(a)$ and its variance are given by

$$E(\theta(a)) = \frac{a(a+1)}{2}; \text{ Var } (\theta(a)) = \frac{(a-1)a(a+1)(a+2)}{12}.$$

Of course, if we divide the random variable $\theta(a)$ by its mean, we obtain a standardized random variable with mean 1 and variance

$$\frac{\text{Var}(\theta(a))}{[E(\theta(a))]^2} = \frac{(a-1)(a+2)}{3a(a+1)}.$$

When the amplitude a increases, this variance tends to $1/3$. For example, for an amplitude of 9, this variance already equals $(1/3)(88/90)$, while for an amplitude of $a = 2$ it equals $(1/3)(2/3)$. This standardization can, of course, be used to construct tables and approximations using other distributions. If the unit for the amplitude is very small, we approximately obtain

$$\text{Var } (\theta(a)) = \frac{a^4}{12}, E(\theta(a)) = \frac{a^2}{2} \text{ and } \frac{\text{Var}(\theta(a))}{[E(\theta(a))]^2} = \frac{1}{3},$$

which happens to be the mean and the variance for such a process when the underlying stochastic process is a Wiener process (see Vallois, 1993 and Imhof, 1992). When the process is asymmetric, the ARL of the range process is more difficult to calculate. We summarize for this purpose two basic results of Vallois and Tapiero (1995b). For a birth-death random walk which is defined by:

amplitude's ARL is given by the following:

$$x_{t+1} = x_t + \epsilon_t, x_0 = 0$$

$$\epsilon_t = \begin{cases} +1 & \text{w.p.} \quad p \\ 0 & \text{w.p.} \quad r \\ -1 & \text{w.p.} \quad q \end{cases}$$

where $p+q+r=1$ and $\lambda = q/\text{p}$. Then, the ARL of an amplitude a is given by:

$$E(\theta(a)) = \frac{1}{p(\lambda-1)}\left(\frac{(a+1)^2}{\lambda^{a+1}-1} - \frac{a^2}{\lambda^a - 1} - \frac{1}{\lambda-1} + a\right)$$

Of course, when $r = 0$, this corresponds to an asymmetric random walk. When $q = p$, we have also shown that

$$\text{ARL } = E(\theta(a)) = \frac{a(a+1)}{4p}$$

which corresponds to the symmetric random walk when $p = 1/2/$. These results also allow the testing of asymmetric random walks based on ARL's, thereby complementing the process tests considered earlier. Let ARL_0 and ARL_1 be the specified average run lengths under the hypotheses when the process is in control and when it is out of control. In this case, the ARLs risk specifications imply that

$$\begin{cases} E(\theta(a \mid r_0)) \geq \text{ARL}_0 \\ E(\theta(a \mid r_1)) \leq \text{ARL}_1. \end{cases}$$

Applications as well as a comparison with other tests are considered in Vallois and Tapiero (1995b) to problems of detection, estimation and the control of variability. Of course, these tests will be a function of the specified ARLs as well as the amplitude at which the tests are performed.

9.6 Design of control schemes and economic charts

In many instances, it is necessary to determine the parameters of charts based on economic criteria. When a chart process can be defined in terms of cycles, each cycle being identically and independently distributed, we can then apply renewal theory arguments and calculate the long-term average cost by the average cycle cost. Thus, if renewal cycles can be defined, T is the cycle time and $C(T)$ the expected cycle cost with the following

$$\bar{C} = \lim_{T\to\infty} \frac{1}{T}\int_0^T c(\tau)d\tau = \frac{E\int_0^T c(\tau)d\tau}{E(T)} = \frac{C(T)}{E(T)},$$

where $c(.)$ are the instantaneous costs incurred at some time $\tau \in (0,T)$ within a cycle. There are a considerable number of applications using this approach and most charts have been studied using this approach. We consider only a simple example to demonstrate the applicability of this renewal reward approach.

Application: Monitoring Over Time

The monitoring problem over time consists in selecting the frequency, method and quantity of data to be recorded. Typically, processes are operating in real-time, and thereby continuously generate information regarding their operational state. Continuous time sampling may be too costly. Collecting samples at infrequent intervals of time may lead to some important events passing by undetected. Methods of sampling are, of course, important and fundamental issues in statistics (which is a crucial consideration for the data to be meaningful). In a temporal setting, there are other (but clearly related) problems, such as should data be collected at regular or irregular intervals of time, should spot checks (i.e. randomized in time) be used to control the process at hand, etc.? When we augment the frequency of sampling intervals, we obtain a more reliable record of the process at hand. But if we only take single measurements, we may lose something of the estimates' precision (which can lead to important mistakes). Both our uncertainty regarding the process and measurement costs are the basic elements to use in determining a monitoring policy over time. When a process is unstable, varying from instant to instant, it would be better to sample frequently, while when a process is stable, the sampling frequency can be reduced. In practice, management's quest for data and an increased concern for monitoring performance has led to the development of vision and automatic systems which can provide, once a fixed investment cost has been incurred, the potential to sample frequently at low cost. In this sense, automation for process monitoring is extremely important. Thus, frequency of sampling, timeliness, data reliability, accuracy and relevance to decision making and simplicity are important elements we must necessarily evaluate and be aware of in the management of quality in its temporal setting. The problems we consider here are obviously based on simplifications. Below we consider as an example the problem of monitoring a CSP process.

A process produces defectives units following some random process. Suppose that each time a measurement is recorded, it provides a perfect estimate of the state of the system. We also define C_i as the cost of a unit measurement and let the cost of quality be a function which is proportional to the process variance (i.e. lack of control). For simplicity, we shall also assume that when no measurements are taken the estimate of the process variance increases linearly over time. Say that we do not take any measurements for ΔT periods of time. Then, the process variance increases linearly and equals $(t)\theta^2, 0 \leq t \leq \Delta \mathrm{T}$. Approximately, over two successive measurements, the average cost is

$$\min_{\Delta T} AC = \{C_i/\Delta T + (1/\Delta T)\int_0^{\Delta T} Ct\theta^2 dt\}$$
$$= C_i/(\Delta T) + C\theta^2(\Delta T)/2.$$

where AC is the average cost and C is a proportionality constant for the cost of quality. Thus, a first order condition for interval sampling is

$$0 = -C_i/(\Delta T)^2 + C\theta^2/2$$

and the optimal frequency at which data is to be collected is

$$\Delta T^* = \sqrt{2C_i/C\theta^2}.$$

The larger the cost of quality parameter C and the larger the uncertainty (due to the variance parameter θ^2), the more frequent the measurements. Further, the greater the inspection cost, the less frequent the inspections. This simple model highlights some essential ingredients which underlie the selection of fixed interval sampling. When measurements are error prone, this analysis has to consider filtering techniques as well (for an early study and applications in inventory control, see Tapiero, 1977a).

Now assume that we collect measurements at random times in order to deal with the question of whether costs increased or decreased through spot (random) measurements. For this case, the average cost is given by

$$AC = \frac{C_i + E\int_0^{\Delta T} Ct\theta^2 dt}{E(\Delta T)} = \frac{C_i + E(\Delta T^2)C\theta^2}{E(\Delta T)}$$
$$= \frac{C_i + [E(\Delta T)^2 + \text{var}(\Delta T)]C\theta^2/2}{E(\Delta T)}$$

From this expression, we can already see that if we keep mean intervals constant, then measurement variability augments the average cost compared to systematic measurements by an amount which is proportional to the variance of the measurement intervals, or $[\text{var}(\Delta T)/2E(\Delta T)]C\theta^2$. In this restricted sense, it is best to collect data systematically.

9.7 Other problems

The valuation of controls and the design of plans must be assessed in the light of the basic motivations which induce sales, service, manufacturing costs and profit making. For this reason, it is important to integrate quality management and its control in a broader framework, closer to the primary purposes and functions of the firm. Our premise is that quality control plans can be devised better if we were to consider the spillover effects of quality, including

- The effects of servicing costs on quality control, and *vice versa.*
- The effects of the sales and repeat purchase process.
- The relationship between quality control, liability, warranty costs and, in particular, on the manufacturing quality intent of a firm.
- The effects of quality control on learning, manufacturing, productivity improvement and cost reduction.
- The integration of quality control information and its management on maintenance programs, and in managing the risks inherent in manufacturing.

In chapter 8 we considered in great detail the integration of quality control in producer-supplier relationship, the effects of information asymmetry and the prevalent effect of conflict relationships on the control of quality. It is customary to view the control of quality and the manufacturing of quality as a function that stands on its own. Japanese management techniques, attempting to primarily reduce the complexity of manufacturing processes and produce at high levels of quality, have recognized that such an approach, isolating the control of quality from other manufacturing functions, is mistaken. As a result, this has led to both a redefining of the control of quality as part of the 'process' and to a strategic view of the control of quality. Some of the elements which have changed the quality management process include: (1) Repositioning the functions of quality control efforts as being much more than quality management; (2) emphasizing the quality improvement process; (3) emphasize the mutual relationships and endogenize the process of managing quality and its control as part of the process of manufacturing management which has been primarily concerned with the production of quantities.

Thus, the management of quality seeks to integrate quality with business functions, closer to consumers and to suppliers, and closer to the process of production and its technology. To see how the study of such topics might be achieved, we consider specific models which are analysed and used to obtain some strategic insights regarding the positioning of quality control in manufacturing and its economic rationality.

Integration of quality control and reputation

A product quality reputation, expressing the effects of past faulty products or past poorly delivered services, affects current demands. In particular, let $\tilde{N}_t$ be the size of lots produced and sold at a given time (there are therefore no inventories, and production is made to order). For our purposes, we assume that $\tilde{N}_t$ is a function of prices p_t and the product quality reputation $\tilde{x}_t$ where '$\sim$' over a variable specifies that it is a random variable. Thus,

$$\tilde{N}_t = N(p_t, \tilde{x}_t).$$

Prices are not a function of quality, while product reputation is. Explicitly, we assume that reputation is defined by a moving average of a proportion of products sold and found defective. Thus, if at $t, \tilde{N}_t$ were sold, part of which Z_t were faulty, then we assume

$$\tilde{x}_{t+1} = \alpha x_t + (1-\alpha)\tilde{Z}_t/\tilde{N}_t,$$

x_0 given, $\alpha \in [0,1]$, and therefore $x_t \in [0,1]$ with α a smoothing constant. The number of post-sales failures is, of course, a function of the product design quality and the control efforts and procedures instituted in the manufacturing process. It will be convenient for this example to write the product quality as a reliability R, where

$$\tilde{R} = \begin{cases} r & \text{with probability } \theta(u) \\ 0 & \text{with probability } 1-\theta(u). \end{cases}$$

Here, θ is the probability that either the unit has been properly manufactured or it was poorly manufactured and detected by some control $u.A$ unit which is poorly manufactured and not detected is therefore $1-\theta(u)$. A unit, properly manufactured, can still fail, however, since standard specifications will allow such an event. This design reliability is denoted by r. For this reason, we obtain the random reliability R above. As a result, if at time t the quantities produced and sold are N_t, then the number of units which are defective are a random variable which has the mixture binomial distribution

$$\tilde{Z}_t =, \begin{cases} B(N-n, 1-\tilde{R}) & \text{with probability} \quad [\theta(u)]^n \\ B(N, 1-r) & \text{with probability} \quad 1-[\theta(u)]^n \end{cases}$$

where $B(N-n, 1-\tilde{R})$ denotes the binomial distribution with parameters N and $1-\tilde{R}$. The quantities inspected are given by n or N, each with its own probability of lot acceptance or rejection, or

$$\tilde{I}_t = \begin{cases} n & \text{with probability} \quad [\theta(u)]^n \\ N & \text{with probability} \quad 1-[\theta(u)]^n, n = 1, 2, \ldots \end{cases}$$

If the unit production costs is denoted by $c(r,\theta)$, we can then define a profit which is given by

$$\tilde{\pi}_t = [p_t - c(r,\theta)]N_t(p_t, x_t) - c_i\tilde{I}_t - c_f\tilde{Z}_t.$$

The expected profit per unit at time t is thus

$$\begin{aligned}\pi_t &= [p_t - c(r,\theta)]N_t(p_t,x_t) - c_i n_t[\theta(u_t)]^n - c_i N_t(p_t,x_t)(1-[\theta(u_t)]^n) \\ &- c_f(N_t(p_t,x_t) - n_t)(1-R)[\theta(u_t)]^n - c_f N_t(p_t,x_t)(1-r)(1-[\theta(u_t)]^n).\end{aligned}$$

The integration quality and reputation can now be analysed by considering an appropriate time horizon over which the inspection and control efforts u are optimized. The problem solution is given in Tapiero, Ritchken and

Reisman (1987) and provides a motivation for further study. Alternatively, we can consider the profits as a random variable, written as follows:

$$\tilde{\pi}_t = [p_t - c(r, \theta)]\tilde{N}_t(p_t, \tilde{x}_t) - c_i \tilde{I}_t - c_f \tilde{Z}_t,$$

and therefore, an appropriate control by the producer might be the specification of the risk α, such that

$$\text{Prob } (\tilde{\pi}_t \geq 0) \geq 1 - \alpha, \text{ or}$$
$$\text{Prob } ([p_t - c(r, \theta)]\tilde{N}_t(p_t, \tilde{x}_t) \geq c_i \tilde{I}_t + c_f \tilde{Z}_t) \geq 1 - \alpha,$$

which provides a condition on the amount of sampling n. Of course, such a distribution is difficult to calculate analytically, but approximations are possible. Numerical analyses as well as extensions of this problem are left as exercises.

Integrated Learning

Production experience or learning is one of the essential factors affecting the cost of production. Studies by economists, management scientists and industrial engineers have emphasized the cost/volume effects of manufacturing techniques (to prevent defective units and smooth the production learning process). In these approaches, quality was not considered 'part of the learning process'. This is in contrast to current conventional wisdom, where learning and the control of quality are integrated.

A potential approach to integrate learning and quality consists of the following. Say that x_{t+1} is a variable which expresses the amount of knowledge, experience, etc., a function of which defines the production cost per unit, and let N_t is the production volume at that time. Then, we can use the following relationship:

$$x_{t+1} = x_t + N_t.$$

A general model was developed in Tapiero (1987) where the amount of learning through quality control is introduced. In particular, let $\tilde{I}_t(\phi)$ be the amount of quality control performed at time t, which is a function of the procedure ϕ used. If, in addition, we let recent experience be more important, then we can write

$$x_{t+1} = \alpha x_t + \beta e_t N_t + \gamma \tilde{I}_t(\phi).$$

As a result, the variable x_t is stochastic. Of course, the greater the amount of control, the greater the growth of x_t and therefore the greater the learning. On the basis of such an approach, it is possible to assess the effect of quality control on the production experience curve.

References

AFNOR X08-031.3 (1993) Carte de Controle des Sommes Cumulées (Doc. written by MM. Daudin and Palsky), September.

Alwan L.C. and H.V. Roberts (1988) Time series modeling for statistical process control, *Journal of Business and Economic Statistics,* **6**, 87-95.

Antelman G.R., and I.R. Savage (1965) Surveillance problems: Wiener processes, *Naval Research Log. Quarterly,* **12**, 1, 35-55.

Barnard G.A. (1959) Control charts and stochastic processes, *Journal of the Royal Statistical Society, Series* **B, 21**, 239-271.

Basseville M. (1988) Detecting changes in signals and systems-A survey, *Automatica,* vol **24**, no. 3, 309-326.

Basseville M. and A. Benveniste (eds) (1986) *Detection of Abrupt Changes in Signals and Dynamic Systems,* Lecture Notes in Control and Information Sciences, vol **77**, Berlin, Springer Verlag.

Bather J.A. (1963) Control charts and the minimization of costs, *J. of Royal Stat. Society,* **B, 25, 1**, 49-70.

Bather .A. (1971) Free boundary problems in the design of control charts, *Transactions of the 6th Prague Conference on Information Theory, Statistical Decision Functions and Random processes*, 89-106.

Benveniste A., M. Basseville and G. Moustakides (1987) The asymptotic local approach to change detection and model validation, *IEEE Trans. on Automatic Control*, AC-32, no. **7**, 583-592, July.

Box G.E.P. and G.M. Jenkins (1976) *Time Series Analysis, Forecasting and Control,* Second edition, Holden Day, San Francisco.

British Standards Institution (1981) *Guide to Data Analysis and Control Using Cusum Techniques,* BS5703.

Chow, Y.S., H. Robbins and D. Siegmund (1971) *The Theory of Optimal Stopping,* Dover Publications, New York.

Crowder S.V. (1987) A simple method for studying run length distributions of exponentially weighted moving average charts, *Technometrics,* **29**, 401-407.

Crowder S.V. (989) Design of exponentially weighted moving average schemes, *Journal of Quality Technology,* **21**, 3, 155-162.

Feller W. (1951) The asymptotic distribution of the range of sums of independent random variables, *Ann. Math. Stat.,* **22**, 427-432.

Hunter J.S. (1986) The exponentially weighted moving average, *Journal of Quality Technology,* **18**, 19-25.

Imhof J.P. (1992) A construction of the brownian path and its inverse process, *Annals of Probability,* **13**, 1011-1017.

Jazwinsky .H. (1970) *Stochastic Processes and Filtering Theory,* Academic Press, New York.

Kalman R.E. and R. Bucy (1961) New results in linear filtering and prediction theory, *Trans ASME, J. Basic Engineering,* vol **83D**, 95-108, March.

Moustakides G.V. (1986) Optimal stopping times for detecting changes in distributions, *Ann. Stat.* **13**, 1379-1387.

Page E.S. (1954) Continuous inspection schemes, *Biometrika,* **41**, 100-114.

Patton R.J., P.M. Frank and R.N. Clark (Eds.) (1989) *Fault Diagnosis in Dynamic Systems: Theory and Applications,* Prentice Hall International, UK.

Pollak M. (1987) Average run lengths of an optimal method of detecting a change in distribution, *Ann. Stat.,* **15**, 2, 749-779.

Robinson, B.P. and T.Y. Ho (1978) Average run lengths of geometric moving average charts, *Technometrics,* **20**, 85-93.

Sage A.P. and J.L. Melsa (1971) *Estimation Theory: with Applications to Communications and Control,* New York, McGraw Hill Book Co.

Siegmund D. (1985) *Sequential Analysis, Tests and Confidence Intervals,* Springer. Verlag, Berlin

Tapiero C.S. (1977) *Managerial Planning: An Optimum and Stochastic Control Approach,* Gordon Breach, New York (2 volumes).

Tapiero C.S. (1977a) Optimization of information measurement with inventory applications, *Infor,* **15**, 50-61.

Tapiero C.S. (1987) Production learning and quality control, *IIE Transactions,* 19, no. **4**, 362-370.

Tapiero C.S. (1988) *Applied Stochastic Models and Control in Management,* Amsterdam, North-Holland, Publ. Co.

Tapiero C.S., A. Reisman and P. Ritchken (1987) Product Failures, Manufacturing Reliability and Quality Control: A Dynamic Framework, *INFOR* (Canadian Journal of Operations Research).

Vallois P., On the range process of a bernoulli random walk, *Proceedings of the Sixth International Symposium on Applied Stochastic Models and Data Analysis,* vol. II, Editors, J. Janssen and C.H. Skiadas, World Scientific, 1020-1031.

Vallois P. and C.S. Tapiero (1995a) Moments of an amplitude process in a random walk and approximations: Computations and applications, *RAIRO,* 1-6.

Vallois P. and C.S. Tapiero (1995b) The range process in random walks: Theoretical results and applications, *Working Paper,* ESSEC, Cergy Pontoise, France.

Willsky Alan S. (1976) A survey of design methods for failure detection in dynamic systems, *Automatica,* **12**, 601-611.

Willsky A.S. (1986) Detection of abrupt changes in dynamic systems, in *detection of Abrupt Changes in Signals and Dynamical Systems,* M. Basseville and A. Benveniste (Eds.), Lecture Notes in Control and Information Sciences, LNCIS 77, Springer Verlag, 27-49.

——— and H.L Jones (1976) A generalized likelihood ratio approach to the detection and estimation in linear systems of jumps in linear systems, *IEEE Trans. on Automatic Control,* **21**, 108-112.

Yaschin E. (1993) Performance of CUSUM control schemes for serially correlated observations, *Technometrics,* **35**, 37-52.

Yaschin E. (1993) Statistical control schemes: Methods, applications and generalizations, *International Statistical Review,* **61**, 41-66.

Zehnwirth B. (1985) Linear filtering theory and recursive credibility estimation, *Astin Bull.,* 19-36.

Zhang Q., M. Basseville and A. Benveniste (1992) Early warning of slight changes in systems and plants with application to condition based maintenance, *IRISA, Working Paper no. 671,* July.

Index